Life in Ancient Egypt

Life of the
ANCIENT EGYPTIANS

by Eugen Strouhal

with photographs by
Werner Forman

Foreword by Geoffrey T. Martin

UNIVERSITY OF OKLAHOMA PRESS

Norman

Published by the University of Oklahoma Press, Norman,
Publishing Division of the University, by special arrangement
with OPUS Publishing Limited, London, England.

Translated by Deryck Viney

First printing.

ISBN 0-8061-2475-x hardback

Library of Congress Catalog Number: 92-54140

This book was designed and produced by
OPUS PUBLISHING LTD,
36 Camden Square, London NW1 9XA

The following excerpts from Miriam Lichtheim's *Ancient Egyptian Literature
Three volumes*, © 1973–1980 Regents of the University of California are included
by kind permission of the University of California Press: Vol.I: pp.62–3, 196–7;
Vol.II: pp.63, 64; Vol.III: p.199.

The following illustrations were reproduced from photographs taken by the
author: 25, 44, 47, 71, 78, 97, 106, 128, 129, 134, 143, 160, 198, 219, 222,
223, 229, 252, 266–270, 279, 280, 283, 285, 286.
Other illustration sources: Bildarchiv Foto Marburg 87; IGDA Milan 37, 85;
Kodansha Ltd 101, 164, 251; Milan Zemina 11, 30, 39, 111, 123, 158, 224.

Half-title page 1   Hand reaching for figs on a table. Detail of a wall painting from Sheikh
Abd el-Qurna, West Thebes. 18th dynasty, Amarna period.

Frontispiece 2   Woman bearing offerings. Fragment of a limestone relief from Saqqara.
18th dynasty. *Cairo, Egyptian Museum*

Opposite 3   Birds and a butterfly in a papyrus thicket. Detail of a wall painting from a tomb
in Sheikh Abd el-Qurna, West Thebes. 18th dynasty

Filmset in Photina by Southern Positives and Negatives (SPAN), Lingfield, Surrey
Illustration films originated by La Cromolito 20098 S. Giuliano Milanese, Italy
Printed by Vincenzo Bona, 10156 Torino, Italy

Contents

Foreword

THE PIONEER EGYPTOLOGISTS of the early nineteenth century were much interested in the daily activities of the inhabitants of the Nile Valley, at the same time being intrigued, at a period when they were struggling to decipher the texts and papyri, by their religious and funerary beliefs. Sir John Gardner Wilkinson (1797–1875) was the first Egyptologist to write a comprehensive account of everyday life, largely based on the material he had seen and recorded in the Theban necropolis. His *Manners and Customs of the Ancient Egyptians, including their private life, government, laws, arts, manufactures, religion, agriculture, and early history, derived from a comparison of the painting, sculptures, and monuments still existing, with the accounts of ancient authors*, was first published in 1837. It went into several editions, the last and best, edited by Samuel Birch, appearing in 1878. The extended title of the book gives an idea of the wide-ranging nature of Wilkinson's mind, at a time when Egyptology was still in its infancy. *Manners and Customs* was an extraordinary achievement, and even today, a century and a half after its original publication, can still be consulted with profit.

Most of the artifacts that throw light on daily life that have come down to us derive not from settlement sites where the people lived, but from tombs. From the earliest times, royalty and the élite classes had sufficient wealth and influence to fill their funerary monuments with everything that was needful of a congenial existence in the Underworld. Prudent persons of standing would no doubt commission and pay for choice equipment during their lifetime. Lesser folk would be content to select the necessary items from the stockrooms of funerary workshops. Well-to-do royal craftsmen, such as those who lived at Deir el-Medina in the New Kingdom, would be in the happy position of being able to make their own funerary furnishings. Not all the material placed in tomb-chambers was made especially for the Afterlife. Some of it was certainly used during the tomb-owners' lifetime, and later was incorporated in the collection of items carried to the tomb in the funeral procession. Who knows, such a doleful event might have given the excuse, on the part of surviving relations, to get rid of pieces of furniture or other bric-à-brac that was outmoded or giving offence to the eye, or might have been cluttering up the house. We should always remember that the ancient Egyptians were real human beings, susceptible to all of the emotions, as we know from many written and pictorial sources, that are the common lot of mankind.

But tomb equipment is only one of the rich sources of information about the daily life of the Egyptians. A great deal of evidence survives in the ruins of town-sites, some of which, like Memphis and El-Amarna, are now being exploited to the full by archaeologists. With modern scientific techniques and a better understanding of what settlements can be made to reveal, a mass of documentation is now at our

4   Young princess picking grapes.
Ivory panel. 18th dynasty,
Amarna Period.
Private collection

disposal for analysis, interpretation and assimilation. Here one need only mention plant and food remains, drainage and sanitation, installations for the manufacture of pottery and the baking of bread, as well as the organization and distribution of water resources. When towns are allowed to fall into decay or are completely abandoned by their inhabitants in favour of another site, not unnaturally most of their belongings are taken with them. The bits and pieces they leave behind for the archaeologist to excavate augment the knowledge gained from better-preserved artifacts found in tombs. The story is different when a town or village is abandoned precipitately and the residents have no chance of returning to retrieve all their possessions. (There is some evidence to suggest that this is what happened in the last occupation phase at Deir el-Medina.) Rich pickings await the fortunate excavator of such a site, and the evidence obtained can revolutionise our understanding of many aspects of Egyptian civilisation, not least when documentary and inscribed material is also present. Here again the 'classic' site is Deir el-Medina. From the labours of a number of famous philologists, particularly Professor Jaroslav Černý, a Czech scholar like the author of the present monograph, we are brought face to face with the actual inhabitants of one Egyptian village in the second millennium BC – admittedly, not a typical one because of the specialised nature of their work of hewing and decorating the royal tombs in the Valley of the Kings and the Valley of the Queens in Western Thebes. We see them, for example, marrying, squabbling, bargaining, bartering, stealing and taking one another to court. The inscribed potsherds and flakes of stone (ostraca), as well as papyri, illuminate these and other aspects of their daily lives, bringing into closer focus the material that was brought to light from the excavation of their houses, shrines and tomb-chapels.

Egyptian tombs as well as town-sites are replete with information about mundane affairs. The bulk of the information, not unnaturally, concerns the lives of kings, courtiers and administrators, but very often quite humble Egyptians are depicted and named on tomb walls. A wide range of activities is represented in the reliefs and wall-paintings, from military campaigns, temple worship, agriculture, domestic concerns, manufacturing and craftsmanship, to the manifold aspects of survival in the Netherworld.

All these sources, and others, are utilised by Dr Eugen Strouhal in his vivid and beautifully illustrated book on life in ancient Egypt. Previous studies on a similar theme include the classic work of Adolf Erman, *Ägypten und ägyptisches Leben im Altertum* (1885, and later editions), which was a wide-ranging and seminal work but is now largely outdated. The work of Pierre Montet, *La Vie quotidienne en Égypte au temps des Ramsès* (1946), was somewhat circumscribed, and was not as thorough. Eugen Strouhal has an excellent grasp of the material, and has a distinct advantage over his illustrious predecessors in that he is a physical anthropologist of international standing as well as an archaeologist. His discussions of the anatomical material and his familiarity with the medical texts are not the least valuable aspect of his book. We learn much about life expectancy, hygiene, diseases and traumas. For many years, Dr Strouhal has been involved with field expeditions in Egypt and the Sudan, sponsored not only by his native country Czechoslovakia, but also by other European nations, including Great Britain. He is currently examining an enormous accumulation of skeletal material found by the joint expedition of the Egypt Exploration Society and the Leiden Museum at Saqqara. He is part of a distinguished tradition of Czech involvement in Egyptology: František Lexa, Zbyněk Žába, Jaroslav Černý. His new book is warmly welcomed and recommended.

Geoffrey T. Martin
Edwards Professor of Egyptology,
University College London

Preface

Every visitor to the land on the banks of the Nile, or reader of books on the art and civilisation of the ancient Egyptians, is surely awestruck by the monumental architecture and colossal statues. And that visitor or reader, too, is surely enchanted by the charm of small works of art as well as by the glitter of the gold, silver, glass and semi-precious stones used to embellish exquisite objects.

Remarkable as this artistic and cultural legacy of ancient Egypt is, no less remarkable is the seemingly spontaneous appearance of such material and intellectual wealth. It appears to have emerged 5000 years ago from the abyss of prehistory – quite suddenly and out of nothing. Leaving aside Mesopotamia to the east, the ancient Egyptians were surrounded by a barbarian world when they crossed the threshold of civilisation in such spectacular style.

Superficially, the achievements of ancient Egypt are the achievements of a long line of illustrious kings and their supporting class of nobles. Little thought is spared, as a rule, for the unknown creators whose effort and patient skill lies behind the marvellous works that we admire. Those kings and their nobles would have been long forgotten had not the hands of workers and artists built pyramids or elaborate tombs for their coffins. And yet, while there is an abundance of books about the art, the gods, the kings and the nobility of ancient Egypt, there is a paucity of literature about the life of ordinary people. And what little there is is not readily accessible to the general reader.

To write about the life of the ancient Egyptians is more difficult than to describe their works. The most important direct source of knowledge – the archaeological research of their homes – is not extensive, because so far the research activities in Egypt have been concentrated in the realm of the dead. That is where we find at least a reflection of ancient life, captured in the reliefs and paintings on the walls of the tombs of the nobles. These were not pictures as decoration but scenes of offerings including the making of objects and products without which eternal life of the deceased was thought not possible.

Written sources containing references to everyday life include literary, instructional and medical texts, documents and contracts. They are supplemented in important detail by the reports of those Greek and Roman authors who gained first-hand knowledge of Egypt.

In this book use is made of another, less common source – the mummies and skeletons of the ancient Egyptians, which can tell us a great deal thanks to continuous advances in biological and medical research methods. They provide direct evidence of physical characteristics, diseases and life span which would be hard to ascertain by other means.

This book is an attempt to recreate a picture of the life of the ancient Egyptians from conception and birth to death and burial. The text about the working life has been divided into several parts, starting with the producers – the farmers and the stockbreeders, the artisans and the artists and the builders of the great construction projects. The organisers are also here – the scribes and the priests, the budding scientists, the physicians and the mummificators. However, the ruling establishment – the king, members of his family and the nobles – have been brought into the narrative only in the absence of other appropriate sources to illustrate a particular fact or by way of contrast with the life of ordinary people. The institutions, the laws, the economy, religion, mythology, literature, art and other aspects of ancient Egyptian civilisation have been dealt with in other works.

This book is primarily concerned with the ancient Egyptian as a physical and social being. It is concerned with the everyday drudgery of the farmers, with the working methods of the craftsmen, the amount of effort involved and the effect on the health of the producers. A look at the back-breaking work in the quarries and on the construction sites leads to a scrutiny of the conditions in which the great building projects came to be realised, including the many hazards involved.

At home, the woman was exposed to the risks connected with pregnancy, childbirth and the post-natal period. Life in the ancient world was by no means

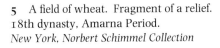

5 A field of wheat. Fragment of a relief. 18th dynasty, Amarna Period.
New York, Norbert Schimmel Collection

idyllic. Fatal accidents, endemic (especially parasitary) diseases, occasional outbreaks of epidemics, but mainly high infant mortality reduced drastically the average life expectancy. And the burgeoning civilisation had no means of dealing with the growing problems of hygiene and sanitation.

Presenting the narrative in thematic chapters as opposed to the usual chronological treatment is not without disadvantages. While this approach allows a more coherent discussion of individual aspects of life, the limited extent of the book does not permit the mention of any but the most significant changes that occurred during the 3000-year evolution of ancient Egyptian society. This book does not and cannot attempt a full coverage of everything that comes under the broad heading of 'life'. Instead, it offers the reader an insight into the most interesting and most characteristic aspects of the life of those ordinary people who contributed so much to ancient Egypt – and in some measure to the birth of our own civilisation.

Eugen Strouhal

CHAPTER ONE

The Start of Life

AWARENESS OF THE function of the male semen and the sex act may be as old as the human race itself. Certainly from the 5th millennium before Christ, with the spread of cattle-breeding in the farming cultures of neolithic Egypt, humans must have acquired a wealth of practical knowledge by observing these processes among domestic animals. The ancient Egyptians would express themselves in simple, uninhibited language. 'The man lay with his wife one night and she became pregnant.' These are the kind of words we find in religious legends attributing the origin of pharaohs to the union of a queen with one of the gods, whereby the ruler publicly proclaimed his divine descent. The most familiar example is the story of the origin of Queen Hatshepsut as inscribed on the walls of her temple at Deir el-Bahari. 10

The tale begins when the mightiest of the New Kingdom gods, Amun of Thebes, is advised about the Queen-mother designate by the wise god Thoth. 'The girl you spoke of is called Ahmose. She is fairer than any woman in this land. She is the wife of the ruler Ankhkheperkare, King of Upper and Lower Egypt (Tuthmosis I), who is endowed with life everlasting . . .'

Amun, who had meanwhile disguised himself as King Tuthmosis, was now brought by Thoth into the Queen's presence. 'The sublime Amun, lord of the throne of both the Kingdoms, had transformed himself into His Majesty her husband, King of Upper and Lower Egypt. He found her asleep amid the luxury of her palace. Awakened by the divine fragrance, she smiled upon His Majesty. He thereupon approached her ardently and showed himself in his godlike form. She rejoiced at the sight of his beauty. His love suffused her whole body and the palace was filled with the divine sweetness of all the perfumes of the Land of Punt.'

The next scene shows the couple conversing: 'After he had done with her all that he would, Ahmose the Royal Consort and Mother said to His Majesty, the sublime God Amun: "How mighty is your strength, my lord! Your countenance, how magnificent! You have united my majesty with your own glory. My whole body is imbued with you."

'Then Amun, lord of the throne of both Kingdoms, said to her: "Khenemetamun Hatshepsut is the name of your son, whom I have placed within your body . . ."'

The legend incidentally demonstrates what store was set by conjugal fidelity. The god had to disguise himself as the Queen's husband before he could make advances to her. It is worth noting, too, that the future Queen Hatshepsut is described in the legend as a 'son', so as to assert the legitimacy of her accession.

Familiarity with the idea of insemination is apparent in other legends, not to mention portrayals of the god Min with sperm ejaculating from his erect penis. Several texts use the old Egyptian terms for the sexual organ, *henen* (always shown hieroglyphically as tumescent), and for the glans penis, *beh*, from which the sperm, *mu*, is ejaculated. The Egyptians distinguished the whole scrotum with its contents, *herwy*, from the actual testicles, *inesewy*. The Ebers medical papyrus describes two vessels leading into each testicle as conducting sperm from its supposed source – the bones. The Egyptians evidently knew that the sperm was somehow connected with the testicles but had no idea that it actually arose there. The notion that it originated in the bones related to the belief that a child acquires all its hard tissues from its father and its soft ones from its mother.

The anatomy and physiology of the female sex-parts, by contrast, were only broadly understood. Documents speak of the uterus (*shed*) and of the labia majora (*septy shed*) as its 'lips'. The vagina, described in the Pyramid Texts as the counterpart of the penis, is vividly termed *kat*, the 'mortar'. The name *mut remets*, 'mother of man', is applied to the womb proper (or to the placenta, according to some scholars) as the site of the embryo's development. For the embryo in general, human or animal, the word was *suhet*, 'little egg'; *wenu* was applied to the human embryo exclusively.

The ovaries and Fallopian tubes had no special names. The latter were thought of as part of the womb, while the ovaries possibly went unnoticed. The hieroglyph for *idet*, another term for the uterus, represents not a human uterus but the 'two-horned uterus' of cows and other animals. This is one reason for thinking that the Egyptians'

Previous page **6** The hippopotamus goddess Taweret protected women in childbirth. Hathor, shown here as a cow, was a nursing mother-goddess. That was not her only role: she is wearing the crown of the goddess of love – the sun disc with horns and the feathers from the crown of Osiris, the god of death. Hathor is seen emerging from the hills of West Thebes, the site of the necropolis, because she was goddess of death as well. Book of the Dead of Userhetmos. 19th dynasty. *Cairo, Egyptian Museum*

7 King Sesostris I paying homage to Min, the god of fertility, shown with erect phallus as usual. Limestone relief from the King's sacred barque shrine. Great temple of Amun at Karnak. 12th dynasty

knowledge of anatomy was derived from the slaughterhouse, not from human autopsies or the quite different field of embalming. They viewed the womb as an organ floating free in the belly but liable to cause trouble if it were in the wrong place.

The ever-observant Egyptians had noticed that both 'horns' of the uterus open out into the abdominal cavity. Less correctly, they believed that the sections of the alimentary canal coming from the mouth and from the anus ended likewise. This imaginary connection had its cosmological parallel in the story of the sky-goddess Nut swallowing the sun each evening and giving birth to it again the following morning; likewise she ate up the stars at daybreak and released them from her womb at dusk.

That not uncommon idea may have been inspired by rare cases of extra-uterine pregnancy, when the embryo emerges from the throat or rectum. It also gave rise to the notion that non-genital, especially oral, intercourse could lead to conception. There is a hint of this in The Tale of the Two Brothers, where a princess swallows a splinter from the tree into which her husband has been transformed, and immediately becomes pregnant. The idea recurs also in the legend of the air-god Shu and the goddess of moisture, Tefnut, begotten by one of the ancestral deities, Atum, who had swallowed his seed.

The concept of uterus, abdominal cavity and alimentary tract all intercommunicating afforded the Egyptians a logical explanation for sterility. If a woman could not conceive, then these connections must have been blocked. Hence one of the practical tests for fertility, consisting in placing such substances as onion or garlic in the vagina and noting whether the smell could be detected in the woman's breath the following day. Other tests involved administering orally or *per vaginam* herbal preparations made with the milk of a woman who had borne a male child, or date flour dissolved in beer: if the patient vomited she was not sterile. Further tests required only external observation. If a woman, say, had one eye of an Asian and the other of an African, she was judged incapable of conception. The complexion, the pattern of the mammary veins and the state of the breasts were also thought to provide clues: full, firm breasts meant that pregnancy was possible, flabby ones showed it would be difficult or impossible.

Egyptian women dreaded sterility as a curse and a disgrace, and sought to remedy it by inserting dates and other specifics into the vagina or by massaging the thighs and belly with menstrual blood. They thought that menstruation ceased during pregnancy simply because the blood was being diverted to create and sustain the embryo. Women would also plead for help from the gods or from the spirits of the dead, as we see from votive figurines of women lying naked on a couch beside a child.

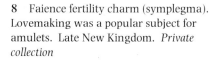

8 Faience fertility charm (symplegma). Lovemaking was a popular subject for amulets. Late New Kingdom. *Private collection*

9   The colonnade of the birth house (mammisi) of Harsomtus, born from the mystic union of Hathor and Horus. Built by Ptolemy VIII Euergetes II, the birth house is situated south of the temple of Horus at Edfu

10   To enhance the legitimacy of her reign, Queen Hatshepsut had herself portrayed as Sphinx, with the usual ceremonial beard, attribute of a male king. From the Queen's temple at Deir el-Bahari, West Thebes. Painted limestone. 18th dynasty. *Cairo, Egyptian Museum*

Experience provided a fairly accurate notion of the normal length of gestation. Ancient Egyptian estimates varied from 271 to 294 days, compared with the modern figure of 282 days from the onset of the last menstruation, and were somewhat longer than the 269 days now calculated from the date of conception. The Egyptian reckoning can be deduced from marriage contracts. A sherd in the Strasbourg city museum speaks of a trial period of 275 days required to show the bride's honesty in swearing at her marriage that she was not pregnant. On a sarcophagus in the Berlin Egyptian Museum we read: 'Your mother carried you until the first day of the 10th month,' that is for 271 days (there were 30 days to every Egyptian month).

Egyptian doctors were equipped with pregnancy tests that carried legal weight when, for example, a widow remarried or a dispute arose over inheritance. These were based not on clinical practice but on theories of analogy. Thus, if a live being were growing in a woman's body her urine must needs contain creative matter that could equally well stimulate the growth of corn or plant foliage. (Modern research incidentally confirms the presence in such urine of hormones which, like plant-growth auxins, can induce earlier flowering.)

Other early indications of pregnancy were held to include a greenish skin-hue, a hot neck and cold back, and changes in eye-colour, muscle tone and circulation. One test prescribed in the Berlin papyrus (No 3038) was to give the subject milk from a woman who had had a male child, mixed with melon puree. If it made her sick, she was pregnant.

Beliefs about the urine of pregnant women also gave rise to tests for determining the sex of an unborn child. Urine from a woman carrying a male foetus was supposed to promote the growth of wheat plants, evidently because 'wheat' was a masculine noun, while that from a woman with a female embryo would make barley sprout quicker, 'barley' being grammatically feminine. (The method was tested in the early 1960s by Professor Ghalioungui of the Ein Shams University in Cairo and found, not surprisingly, to be completely ineffective.)

About the course of pregnancy and its complications we have less to go on. More depictions of pregnant women have survived from prehistoric than from later periods. They include the neolithic figure recently unearthed by a French expedition at Kader, near Khartoum in Sudan; several other smaller and cruder figurines are known from the Predynastic Period. Reliefs of dynastic times rarely display pregnancy, though one in the 6th-dynasty Ankhmahor mastaba in Saqqara shows a pregnant woman standing, and those in the 18th-dynasty temple of Hatshepsut at Deir el-Bahari and in the temple at Luxor from the time of Amenophis III, depicting the legend of the divine parentage of the king and queen, display their pregnant mother. Alabaster vases in the shape of naked pregnant women have also survived from those times, along with jugs in the form of mothers-to-be kneeling with their arms across their laps like the hieroglyph signifying 'to conceive, or be with child'. We also find clay models of women lying naked in bed. All these figures served the magical purpose of warding off complications during pregnancy and, above all, averting still births.

Women pursued their normal and often strenuous way of life up till the last moment of pregnancy. Cruel evidence of a casual attitude to pregnancy comes from the grisly skeletal remains of a pregnant 16-year-old Nubian girl who had been brutally beaten – perhaps punished for her condition. Both her arms and legs had been broken and she had finally succumbed to a blow that pierced her skull.

Ancient Egypt was on the other hand familiar with methods of preventing conception or inducing abortion, referred to simply as 'departure from the pregnant'. These included sundry douches, such as hot oil. Artificial abortion was a ground for prosecution, though sometimes legally condoned when circumstances justified it.

A variety of remedies were recommended for averting an unwanted abortion. A mixture of onions and wine, or of the leaves and fruit of different herbs along with oils and honey might be applied to the genitals to stop bleeding. Vaginal medicaments derived from various plants were held to induce 'contraction of the womb'. To prevent stretch-marks remaining after childbirth women would apply various

unguents to the belly, aristocratic ladies favouring the mild *behen* oil (*baq*) obtained from the fruit of *Moringa aptera*, the horseradish tree.

We now come to the actual delivery, and here the medical papyri are almost totally silent. Evidently this matter was left to the midwife, being regarded as a normal event outside the purview of medical science, possible complications apart.

Not even in ancient Egypt, however, could childbirth proceed without pain. 'One day Ruddjedet felt sick and suffered severe birth-pangs', we read in the early New Kingdom Westcar Papyrus, telling the story of the wife of a priest of Re. And a prayer to the god Amun includes the plea: '. . . Hasten hither like the north wind, for she has come to full term. She is racked with pain; her time is due.'

It was taken for granted that other women should be present at the delivery. In the story just mentioned the god Re, who was the real father, sent four goddesses to help, and midwives figure in the childbirth scenes depicted in *mammisi*, the temples commemorating royal births. A relief in the Ankhmahor mastaba, again, shows a seated woman supported by two midwives, presumably at the onset of labour, and the role of divine obstetricians is described in the Westcar Papyrus: 'Isis stood in front of her, Nephthys behind her, while Heket hastened the delivery. The child emerged into her hands and was one cubit in length; its bones were strong, its limbs were covered in gold and its head-covering was of true lapis lazuli. After cutting the cord, they washed the baby and laid it to rest on a cushion.'

Before the delivery the mother would usually move into a 'childbed arbour', a light structure of poles and greenery set up in the corner of the garden or courtyard, or on the roof of her house. Here she would remain until the period of purification was over.

Most of our information about childbirth procedures is gleaned from illustrations, notably reliefs in the *mammisi* erected in the vicinity of major temples and consecrated to the mystery of the union of queen and god from which the king in question had issued. One lost relief from Armant, known from drawings made by early excavators, showed the naked Cleopatra kneeling in childbirth – a posture adopted by Egyptian country women to this day. The three women standing behind her are clearly tutelary goddesses, with Neith to the fore; the third goddess is holding the life-symbol *ankh*. Three more women kneel in front of her, the first, who holds the baby, being evidently the midwife, the second apparently a wet-nurse and the third yet another assistant. The hieroglyph *mesi*, 'giving birth', itself represents a woman kneeling for the event.

13 An alternative posture for childbirth, less frequent according to some investigators, was to squat over two large bricks with a gap between them. A relief in Cairo Museum shows a woman sitting inside a brick structure with her hands on her knees and her

11 A pregnant mourner fainting at a funeral. Relief in the mastaba of Ankhmahor, Saqqara. 6th dynasty

Below 12 Part of an inscription from a temple wall or a trial piece showing a woman giving birth while kneeling on two bricks. This stylised representation forms the hieroglyph denoting child-bearing. Graeco-Roman Period. *London, British Museum*

Right 13 A squatting woman giving birth, assisted by two goddesses Hathor who, with Taweret, was invoked during childbearing. Relief from the temple of Hathor at Dendera. Ptolemaic. *Cairo, Egyptian Museum*

elbows and forearms resting on the edge. This simple birth-stool is mentioned in texts and the position also appears as one of the hieroglyphic symbols for 'birth'.   12

Deliveries are usually portrayed in the normal advanced stage where the head and arms have emerged first. According to the Westcar Papyrus the umbilical cord was not cut till the baby had been cleansed and bathed and the afterbirth placenta called *kh*, had appeared. There are no references to the navel being bandaged. Separation was evidently carried out only when the umbilical circulation had ceased. Cord and afterbirth both had magical associations and were thought to be invested by a spiritual *alter ego* or double of the child. They were sometimes dried and preserved to accompany the individual even to the grave.

Few midwives received special training such as was given in the celebrated House of Life at Sais in the Delta. The literature accords them the epithet 'sweet'. The infant is described as slipping smoothly into the hands of one such, while another supports the mother from behind. Not every midwife had the skill or knowledge needed for her task and obstetric ignorance or carelessness must have cost many a mother her health or even her life. The vocation was considered 'unclean' and held in low esteem.

Doctors seem never to have specialised in obstetrics or gynaecology and were only called in when complications had arisen. To bring on labour it was recommended in the Ebers medical papyrus that the mother should sit naked on a *niaia* plant and await

results. A compress round the lower half of the abdomen, with a layer of straw and reeds beneath it, was thought to speed up a sluggish delivery by 'freeing the child from the womb'. Discharge of the caul and placenta was supposedly facilitated by a douche of warm oil containing crushed chips of a freshly made vase. Doctors sought to assuage labour pains, often described as very intense, by giving the patient intoxicating drinks, mostly beer.

Three types of birth were distinguished: normal or 'satisfactory' (*hotep*), complicated or 'difficult' (*bened*), and protracted (*wedef*). Attempts were made to speed up a dilatory birth by burning terebinth resin near the woman's abdomen, or by massaging it with saffron powder in beer, or marble dust dissolved in vinegar, which was thought to ease the pain.

There are references in the literature to multiple as well as single births. On one stele (equivalent to a modern gravestone) belonging to the brothers Horus and Suty and now preserved in the British Museum we read: 'I rejoice in my brother, who is of the same kind as myself, having issued from our mother's body on the same day.' The English expert on ancient embalming methods Dawson found a pair of strikingly similar, probably identical, twins among mummies of the Roman Period. The story of Ruddjedet in the Westcar Papyrus speaks of her giving birth to triplets. And the legend according to which the gods Osiris, Horus, Seth, Isis and Nephthys, progeny of the ancestral earth-god Geb and sky-goddess Nut, were born on five consecutive days has been held to reflect experience of an actual case of quintuplets.

If a sickly baby was thought likely to die, its chances were assessed by the strength of its cries and its facial expression. Where there was still doubt, the infant was for three days put on a diet of milk containing a ground fragment of its placenta. If it vomited, the end was near; if not, it would survive.

The mother's well-being, too, was often in jeopardy during pregnancy and childbirth. There are references to complications in the medical texts, but direct evidence can be gathered from mummies and other remains, notably of women with a narrow or deformed pelvis. The skeleton of a negroid woman of the Byzantine era in Nubia shows that she died giving birth to a child whose head was wedged in her pelvic entrance. In the tomb of King Horemheb in Saqqara we discovered, among the fragmented remains of his queen Mutnodjmet, the tiny bones of a fully developed foetus. In all probability she died in childbirth. Her pubic bones bore signs of previous difficult deliveries which had no doubt undermined her health, but she had persevered in the hope of prolonging the 18th dynasty by presenting her husband with an heir until the last attempt, when she was between 40 and 45, cost her her life. In the 11th dynasty, again, Princess Hehenhet is known to have undergone a

Above left **14** Bes, protector of women in child-birth, dancing with a tambourine to amuse other gods or to ward off evil spirits. Wood with a layer of gesso. 19th dynasty. *London, British Museum*

Left **15** A magical wooden amulet in the form of a mother and baby lying on bed. Its purpose was to ensure a safe and easy birth. 19th dynasty. *London, British Museum*

Above **16** A clay fertility figure of a woman. The face and body are crudely executed. Fibres with small mud 'pearls' stuck on were once threaded through the little holes in the hair. The elaborate head-dress, prominent bust and pudenda highlight the erotic nature of the figure. Middle Kingdom. *Berlin, Ägyptisches Museum*

troublesome delivery that resulted in a fistula connecting her vagina and bladder.

Lengthy deliveries could also lead to a prolapsed uterus and vagina such as we find in the naturally-dried remains of a woman at Gebelein from the Predynastic Period, and similar cases were discovered by Sir Grafton Elliot Smith and J. Wood Jones during the earliest Nubian expeditions at the beginning of the 20th century. The Ebers Papyrus gives an accurate account of a prolapsed womb and recommends treatment by 'means calculated to restore the uterus to its place', such as fumigation coupled with application of turpentine oil, dried excrement or wax models of the ibis, symbolising Thoth, the god of wisdom. Elsewhere this source prescribes infusions of herb extracts or beer, or again plugging with a pessary. It is hard to believe that any of these procedures could have been helpful, except the last.

There is no direct evidence of deaths from puerperal fever but it must have occurred, if only as a result of infection from the vaginal infusions. Fatalities could also have ensued from excessive loss of blood, uterine collapse, retention of the placenta, or eclampsia.

The special risks of childbirth were reflected in the shorter average life expectancy of Egyptian women compared with men, in contrast to the reverse situation in developed countries today. The pattern shows up in demographic analysis of ancient Egyptian cemeteries and is confirmed by mummy collections in museums. Thus the average age of adult men from the Late Period burials in the above-mentioned tomb of Horemheb at Saqqara was 33, while that of women was four years less. Examination of mummies in Czechoslovak collections by the author produced an average age of 43.7 years for the adult males and 41.3 for the adult females.

Given the limitations of contemporary treatment and the absence of any preventive care, it is not surprising that Egyptian women frequently resorted to the irrational. The chief tutelary deity of women in pregnancy, childbirth and breast-feeding was the goddess Ipet-Taweret, depicted as a pregnant hippopotamus standing 6 on its hind feet and carrying in its front paws a magic knife or the wondrous knot of Isis, the *tyet*. This last symbolised the tampon tied in the depths of Isis' womb by the god Atum to protect the unborn Horus from the destructive wiles of Seth. A similar role was played by the goddess Neith, who was particularly popular from the Ethiopian Period onwards. Thoth, the god of wisdom symbolised by the ibis or the baboon, was also called upon to help. The goddess Hathor, guardian of womenfolk 13 and domestic bliss in general, was believed by Egyptians to be present at every birth so as to ensure its happy outcome. The same function was served by the goddess Isis, her sister Nephthys and the amiable Heket with her frog head. Severe labour pains, again, were thought to be eased by the breath of the god Amun, coming in the guise of a cool northerly breeze. The grotesque dwarf-god Bes was supposed to vanquish any 14 demons assailing the mother and baby. Midwives would place on the mother's belly a magic ivory knife shaped in a crescent and decorated with carvings of tutelary deities along with snakes, lions, crocodiles, fabulous beasts and devils.

The Westcar Papyrus tells us that the wife of the priest of Re underwent a post-natal cleansing period of only 14 days. This was in fact the period that women spent in the 'childbed arbour' depicted on several New Kingdom sherds. The mother is shown dressed in an elaborately fringed, diaphanous garment, sitting on a bed whose legs are carved to represent the god Bes with a baby in her arms or lying beside her. A woman is offering the mother dishes of milk or suchlike; behind her is a monkey on its hindlegs, holding a roll of cloth, while a girl stands fanning the mother. For the mother's cosmetic needs there is a vessel containing a cone of ointment, and a mirror. The picture is usually outlined with trailing leaves and flowers, suggesting the arbour where the whole event took place.

In view of the dangers threatening both mother and baby, notably puerperal fever and intestinal infections, only a proportion of the infants born had a fair chance of survival. The population nevertheless increased steadily. So we must assume that Egyptian women gave birth frequently, even though the physiological effect of prolonged nursing – usually for three years – would have been to delay the onset of the next pregnancy.

CHAPTER TWO

Carefree Childhood

17 The ancient Egyptians' tenderness towards children is illustrated by the statue of Akhenaten kissing one of his daughters (probably Meritaten). Only in the Amarna period did Egyptian art allow such glimpses of intimacy. Unfinished limestone statue from the workshop of Thutmose the Sculptor at Tell el-Amarna. 18th dynasty. *Cairo, Egyptian Museum*

18 Mother's milk, believed to be a potent remedy, was kept in jars in the form of the goddess Isis suckling Horus. From Saqqara or Abusir. *St Petersburg, Pushkin Museum*

EVEN IF SAFELY delivered, the newborn Egyptian's future was far from secure. Infant mortality was high, but with every successive day the chances of survival improved. The death-rate was highest of all in the first few days, rather less when averaged over a month and still lower for the first year. Natural selection played its part by eliminating the weak and sickly or those with congenital defects and deformities. Many succumbed to disease, especially to infections that were so prevalent where hygiene was poor. The Egyptians, of course, laid the responsibility on Seshat, goddess of writing and arithmetic, who settled the length of each life at the moment of birth. They thought also that the Fates, the 'seven Hathors', influenced the infant's destiny.

The graves of children examined by archaeologists do not provide a sufficient basis for estimating infant mortality. It seems that many children, especially the newborn, were not interred in their own graves in the official cemeteries. If an infant died during or soon after delivery together with its mother, it was normally laid to rest in her grave. Sometimes such bodies were placed in clay vessels and buried near the home, or directly beneath the floor. And there are grounds for supposing that dead children to whom the family had had no time to form an attachment were often exposed at the edge of the desert to be scavenged by wild animals and birds of prey, or cast into the Nile, or a canal, where crocodiles disposed of them.

The number of children's graves in the burial sites is accordingly smaller than would correspond to estimates of mortality based on parallels from less developed countries. In the 1st/2nd dynasty cemetery at Abydos, for example, infants account for only one grave in seven, whereas at the Wadi Qitna burial site in Nubia (3rd to 5th centuries AD) 43 per cent of all mounds were found to cover the remains of infants and young children, while at the secondary cemetery of Abusir (Late to Ptolemaic Periods) the proportion is 50 per cent.

Children's graves often exhibit signs of parental piety and indeed affection. No efforts were spared to preserve the body of a child as carefully as an adult's, so as to ensure it a long existence in the hereafter. Rich families had their little ones embalmed, placed in their own separate coffins and sometimes wrapped in linen, covered with a layer of plaster and decorated with polychrome motifs. Bodies of poor children were protected only by linen wrappings or palm-frond mats.

Lucky charms and personal adornments – pearl, coral or shell necklaces, rings, bracelets, ankle-bands and the like – would be laid over the bodies. Even if the funeral equipment of the young was relatively modest, it included vessels of various sorts and, above all, toys.

High though infant mortality was in ancient Egypt, families were usually large. There are no direct statistics, but if in theory a woman gave birth on average at three-year intervals she could bear eight offspring between her 15th and 40th years. And even if every second or third child died in infancy or later childhood, an average of four to six per family would have survived.

Turning now to the happier aspects of family life, we note that parents in ancient Egypt were as much exercised as their modern counterparts with choosing the right names for their young, regarding these as an inseparable part of the child's personality. Sometimes a name was conferred during the birth itself, based on words uttered by the mother or by one of the real or imaginary beings assisting at the delivery. They were often lyrical and expressed delight at the new arrival: 'Welcome to you', 'This boy I wanted' or 'The pretty girl has joined us'. Other names extolled some deity: 'Thoth is powerful', 'Re is loving', 'May Amun protect him', 'Mut guard him'. Or they might express devotion to the reigning monarch: 'Sneferu is good', 'Long live Khephren' and so on. The choice was usually made by the mother, less often by the father or by both together. Alongside the given or 'maternal' name it was customary, especially in the Old and Middle Kingdoms and again in the Late Period, to add a second, usually a nickname.

The most essential need for the child's early development was of course nutrition, and the only way to ensure this in those days was the natural one of breastfeeding. Mothers were concerned that there should be an adequate supply of milk and doctors, according to the Ebers Papyrus, used to test its quality by smelling it. To increase the flow they recommended rubbing the nursing mother's back with oil in which the dorsal fin of a Nile perch had been stewed.

Children were suckled openly without embarrassment, the mother squatting or kneeling on the ground with her child on her lap as shown in a number of reliefs, such as the one depicting the 12th-dynasty Princess Sebeknakht nursing her baby. A unique Amarna relief even portrays Queen Nefertiti feeding one of her six daughters. The popular figurines of Isis giving suck to her son Horus sometimes featured in household altars, or were worn in miniature by women as amulets.

If a mother was short of milk she resorted, as so often in Egypt, to magical remedies. They might be incantations, such as 'O thou who livest on the water, hasten to the Judge in his divine abode, to Sekhmet who walks behind him, and to Isis, ruler of Dep, saying: "Bring her this milk!"' There must have been a magic purpose, again, in the popular ceramic jugs that depicted a nursing mother squeezing her breast, indeed they may have been used to hold surplus milk. Hollow female figures into which milk could be poured that then ran out through holes bored in the nipples were an example of sympathetic magic.

Milk from mothers who had borne male children was regarded as a potent

19   Mother with a baby straddling her left side. Ebony. Predynastic. *Berlin, Ägyptisches Museum*

Top right **20**   The baby's position can be seen more clearly in the rear view of the same statuette. *Berlin, Ägyptisches Museum*

Left **21**   Woman reaching for a sycamore fig, supporting with her left hand a child held in a broad band of cloth. The child bears the 'side-lock of youth'. Unusually, the woman's legs are crossed. This 25th-dynasty relief from the tomb of Montemhet in Luxor is based on a painting in the 18th-dynasty tomb of Menna. *New York, Brooklyn Museum*

Right **22**   A young woman, apparently black, nurses a nude baby. Her hair is cut in Nubian style in five small clumps. On each of her shoulders sits a small monkey, and another is on the ground. Faience. Late Dynastic – Ptolemaic Periods. *New York, Norbert Schimmel Collection*

medicine, stored in little jugs shaped like a kneeling Isis holding her ailing child Horus to her bosom, and used to treat intestinal complaints, babies' colds and even adult eye infections. The treatment could be reinforced by reciting such spells as 'Flow out, Daughter of all Colds, who breakest bones, gripst the skull and dost painfully molest the seven openings of the head! O companion of Re, give honour to Thoth! Behold, I bring thee thy medicine, thine own saving potion, the milk of a woman who gave birth to a he-child . . .' Crushed papyrus stems and certain seeds were sometimes added to this milk, which was then supposed to send a child to sleep for a day and a night. Specialists have suggested that the seeds were those either of the opium poppy or of henbane.

The Egyptians seem to have suspected that a child's health could be affected by 'medicine' administered to its nursing mother. One highly favoured 'cure' for a sick child was for its mother to consume a mouse. To make doubly sure, no doubt, the same mouse's bones would then be placed in a little canvas bag tied with seven knots and hung around the child's neck as a talisman.

An infant was fed on demand by its mother who carried it with her. Breastfeeding went on for much longer than was the custom elsewhere – normally it continued for three years. In Ani's Instruction a son is enjoined to be good to his mother because she has endured so much for his sake:

> When your time was due and you were born,
> she accepted the burden
> of having her breast in your mouth for three years.

When a Czechoslovak team looked at the figures for infant mortality in the cemetery around the mastaba of Ptahshepses in Abusir (Late to Ptolemaic Periods), it discovered that three- to four-year-old children died more frequently than younger ones, who would still have been breast fed. The switch to solid foods evidently brought about an increase in intestinal infections, contributing to a higher death-rate.

If a mother did not have enough milk of her own or belonged to the upper classes and could not, or would not, nurse her baby, she entrusted it to a wet-nurse. It was mostly women from the poorer families who supplemented their incomes by wet-nursing. If such a woman was asked to feed a child of similar background she would take it into her own home and bring it to its parents at stipulated intervals so that they could see how it was faring. In the case of wealthy clients, however, the wet-nurse would move into the house of the child's father.

The legal relations between parents and wet-nurse were sometimes regulated by written contracts, some of which have survived from the later periods of Egyptian history. Before an agreement was finalised the nurse would have a trial run. The contract stated for how long she was being hired; she was under obligation to provide milk of proper quality, not to nurse any other child except her own, and to eschew pregnancy and any sexual activity. If her charge fell ill, it was her duty to tend it. Her employer, on the other hand, undertook not to remove the child before the agreed time, to provide clothing and oil for massaging the child, and to pay the nurse at prescribed intervals both for the milk she was to give and for the cost of her own food.

Aristocratic ladies, especially queens, almost always used a wet-nurse even if they were fit enough to breastfeed themselves. Their children were also attended to by whole groups of nurses and tutors. There were special officials, the so-called 'royal male-nurses', who were personally responsible for the standard of care devoted to the king's offspring and are depicted carrying princes and princesses in their arms.

It was taken for granted that, because of the physical contact, a special relationship would develop between child and wet-nurse. The nurse's name or portrait sometimes features in the mural decor of her formal charge's tomb alongside those of parents, wives and offspring. Royal wet-nurses came to enjoy considerable status and influence at court; some were accorded near-divine honours when they died.

Children who had shared the same wet-nurse, moreover, developed a close personal rapport which might last all their lives. We know for example that the mother of Qenamun, who became chief seal-bearer and land-steward to Amenophis I, was also wet-nurse to the infant prince. This may have had a great bearing on Qenamun's successful career. King Tuthmosis III, again, is known to have chosen his nurse's daughter to be his chief wife.

Pharaohs depicted in *mammisi* and in funerary temples are often shown ostentatiously sucking, as befitted their divine origin, at the breast of this or that goddess, most commonly Hathor, but sometimes Semataweret, Sehathor or Heset, and frequently, from the time of Sethos I, Isis. Along with the goddess' milk they would be imbibing divine life and the insuperable power needed for the rigours of monarchy. At a mortal level, we find analogous scenes where a calf and a boy are drinking together from a cow's udder. The oldest example of this comes from Beni Hasan (12th dynasty).

A folk version of the theme of the divine wet-nurse occurs in the popular type of ceramic in the shape of a goddess with a hole in the nipple through which milk flowed when it was poured into the vessel. In excavating the Late Period necropolis of sacred animals at Saqqara, members of the Egypt Exploration Society recently came across a faience statue of the goddess Taweret from whose right breast milk emerged when poured in through the mouth. A similar vessel was found early in the 20th century by Ludwig Borchardt in the funerary temple of the 5th-dynasty king Sahure at Abusir. Such figures may have been used as breast-substitutes in weaning children.

A more common device for this purpose, however, was a small hemispherical dish with a spout that was either a closed cylinder or beak-shaped and open along the upper edge. The oldest example known comes from the Middle Kingdom tombs at Lisht. Such artefacts were long thought to be lamps, but in the excavation of Nubian cemeteries of the 3rd to 5th centuries at Wadi Qitna and Kalabsha South we found them almost exclusively in graves of children under six, which suggests that they have been used for drinking milk and other liquids.

The same function may have attached to certain peculiar hollow horn objects tipped with a carved spoon or head of Hathor which feature in several statues of women with babies. Christine Desroches-Noblecourt conjectured their use for vaginal douches or enemas, but Paul Ghalioungui saw them as vessels for sucking milk, or oil.

Inexperienced mothers must have gained most of their knowledge of infant-care from talking to older friends, but there were collections of written precepts available. The Spells for Mother and Child have survived as papyrus No 3027 in the Berlin collection. Though these include much that is superstitious or misleading, the admirable intention of helping mothers and children reflects the yearning of every Egyptian woman for the god-given boon of offspring.

The chief concern in these *Spells* is to safeguard nurslings and toddlers against the ills that afflicted a large proportion of them, especially in the poorer classes. Evidence of this comes from the high incidence of 'Harris lines' in X-rays of the hand and foot bones – lines of dense bone tissue occurring when growth was slow. They indicate periods of serious illness or starvation, and the age when these befell the child can be estimated from the exact position of the lines.

The most common infant malady was infection of the alimentary canal. The spells designed to ward off infection or to expel the pathological agent can be highly emotive:

> Come on out, visitor from the darkness, who crawls along with
> your nose and face on the back of your head, not knowing
> why you are here!
> Have you come to kiss this child? I forbid you to do so!
> Have you come to cosset this child? I forbid you to!
> Have you come to do it harm? I forbid this!
> Have you come to take it away from me? I forbid you to!
> I have made ready for its protection a potion from the
> poisonous *afat* herb, from garlic which is bad for you,

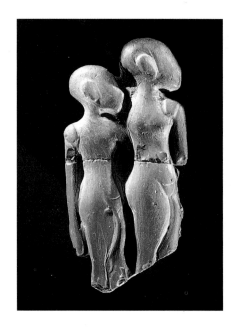

23 Amarna princesses as children with arms around each other's shoulders. Red glass inlay. 18th dynasty. *University College London, Petrie Museum*

24 Two children of the dwarf Seneb sucking their fingers. Detail of the family group (see ill. 263). Painted limestone. Giza. 4th or early 5th dynasty. *Cairo, Egyptian Museum*

25 Father and his naked children with partly shaved heads and the side-lock of youth. Painting in the tomb of Inherkha, Deir el-Medina, West Thebes. 18th dynasty

26 Hathor in the form of a cow suckles a royal infant. Painted sandstone statue from the chapel of Tuthmosis III in Deir el-Bahari, West Thebes. 18th dynasty. *Cairo, Egyptian Museum*

from honey which is sweet for the living but bitter for the dead,
from the droppings and entrails of fish and beast
and from the spine of the perch.

Skin troubles like *neshu* (eczema madidans, perhaps) were also frequent, as well as various infections described in the Ebers medical papyrus such as those of the tonsils and lymphatic glands, which were treated mostly with poultices. There were tropical diseases, too, that affected the young. On many infant remains we find patches of spongy or trabecular bone structure on the roof of the eye-sockets or the outer or inner surfaces of the skull vault, associated with severe forms of anaemia. Rickets, on the other hand, so familiar in northern climes, was almost unknown among Egyptian children. Prescriptions in the medical papyri show that doctors were able to cope with urinary failure and incontinence, bronchial and tracheal infections and other ailments.

Prophylaxis was served not by hygiene or inoculation but by frequent repetition of spells and the wearing of charms. The various parts of a child's body were protected, for example, by being identified with those of gods. 'The crown of your head is the crown of Re, oh my sturdy child, the back of your neck is that of Osiris, your forehead is the forehead of Satis, ruler of Elephantine, your hair is the hair of Neith, your eyebrows are those of the Mistress of the East, your eyes are the eyes of the Lord of the Universe, your nose is the nose of the Teacher of the Gods, your ears are the ears of the Two Cobras, your forearms are those of the Falcon, one of your shoulders is the shoulder of Horus and the other belongs to Seth ...' This had to be recited each morning when the child's amulet was being tied to its arm.

Amulets were manifold. Some had the form of symbols ensuring health, long life, 15 happiness, constancy, contentment and other desirable attributes; some depicted gods. The magic number 7 often recurs; one charm, for instance, consists of seven agate and seven gold beads strung on seven flaxen threads woven by two mothers who were sisters. Another one, found in a child's grave, is a hollow clay ball with scraps of paper, rags and a child's curls inside it.

After their period of purification, women carried on their daily activities again with no restriction. When they left the house they took even the smallest child with them in a sling worn in front, or in a fold of their clothes over the shoulder or left hip. With 21 both hands free, mother could work unencumbered.

Among the toys described by Sir Flinders Petrie were dolls representing mothers with children sitting on their backs with legs apart, or on the mother's shoulder or hip. Modern practice incidentally recommends the legs-apart position for cases of imminent congenital dislocation of the hips.

As children grew and started to walk they became less of a burden; feeding and clothing were no longer such a problem. In the 1st century BC the Greek historian Diodorus Siculus records that 'they cook the best simple food available, namely the lower parts of papyrus stems if there is a fire to toast them over ... So up to the time when it is fully grown the child costs its parents little more than twenty drachmas or so.' The child would also get its share of gruel and normal adult food, chiefly unleavened bread – with no doubt the odd sip of beer.

In the warm Egyptian climate children could rove around naked even out of doors, as many mural reliefs and figures show. Nudity seems to have been stressed as the outward token of childhood, so that we sometimes see an otherwise quite naked child wearing a thin girdle, necklace, bracelet or other trinket. Only in later times was nudity thought unsuitable for older girls, who then started to wear the long tunic of adult women.

A further badge of childhood was the long tress of hair left hanging down over the 25 right ear while the rest was cropped short. Sometimes it was braided into a straight or curved queue. These tresses were worn up to the age of ten or beyond. They are recorded frequently as far back as the Old Kingdom. In the New Kingdom they were also the mark of a prince or of a *sem*, the priest who acted the part of the heir to the throne at royal funerals. The young god Horus, whose sobriquet Harpikhrod – 'Horus

the child' – appears later in Graeco-Roman guise as Harpocrates, also sported the child's coiffure. A schematised, S-shaped side-lock also served as a hieroglyphic symbol for 'child' or 'youth' in general.

24 Another motif commonly used to symbolise tender age is one copied from daily life, namely the right index finger stuck into the mouth by way of dummy as in modern times. We find this in depictions of young gods as well as of mortal children.

In the Old Kingdom young girls usually wore their hair short, or sometimes had a ponytail falling down the centre of the back. It either curled up naturally at the end, or was weighted with a spherical or disc-shaped ornament. From the Middle Kingdom onwards this fashion was affected by young dancing-girls and acrobats.

The habit of close-shaving the whole head except for a few tufts of curled or frizzy hair at the top came evidently from the south. We see it chiefly among Nubians – who still do it – and, in the New Kingdom and later, among young black Africans.

Children had their games and toys in Egypt, of course, as everywhere. In that inviting climate they normally played out of doors, using any objects that came their way – pebbles, pieces of wood or cloth, handfuls of sand, flowers . . . Birds, household pets and monkeys were popular playthings too.

However, youngsters were capable of making their own tops, rattles, simple blowpipes and, above all, a wide assortment of dolls from mere pegs swathed in cloth, through figures sketchily carved out of a flat piece of wood and painted, up to dolls made out of glazed clay, stone, or rags and thread. Even miniature beds have been found, and other items of furniture for dolls or puppets to use.

Some children, or their parents, used wood or other material to make carvings or models of crocodiles or leopards that could open their jaws and wag their tails. Elephants or human dummies with movable limbs, and a cat with glass eyes and a mouth that opened have also turned up.

In the 12th-dynasty remains of the workers' town of Illahun Sir Flinders Petrie discovered a number of toys that children had fashioned out of mud. In addition to crude human figures there were many stylised animals – little pigs, sheep, dogs (or jackals), water-birds, tortoises, lizards and crocodiles – as well as bricks, boats, balls, dot-patterned hoops and even miniature mummies in their sarcophagi.

There was a wide gamut of games to play, too. Children could amuse themselves by walking along planks, racing, wrestling, running and jumping. On the upper register of one relief in the 6th-dynasty mastaba of Mereruka we see a boy balancing on the outstretched arms of a friend, which are resting on the shoulders of two other lads. Two groups of boys have locked elbows for a tug-of-war, and a little further on three youngsters are running a race.

27 Girls forming a 'living roundabout', a game described in the inscription as 'pressing the grapes'. (See ill. III.) Others, holding mirrors and hand-shaped rattles, enjoy 'Hathor's dancing game'. Tomb of Mereruka. Saqqara. Early 6th dynasty

28 A girl pulling a thorn from her friend's sole at harvest time. Tomb of Menna, West Thebes. 18th dynasty

In the middle register there is a group having a war-game. Three boys, holding ostrich feathers in their right hands sloping back over the shoulders, are marching around a 'prisoner' whose arms are folded; three others face the prisoner, holding 'insignia of rank' in their left hands – wooden poles ending in a model hand, scourge and sceptre. Nearby squats a boy with arms stretched out to defend himself while his playmates strike out with their fists; evidently he has to guess which one hit him.

The lowest register illustrates girls at play. On the left four of them have linked up in a ring, the hieroglyphic inscription explaining that this was a game called 'pressing the grapes'. Beside them a band of five girls are doing the Hathor dance, holding hand-shaped wooden rattles in their left hands and mirrors in their right.

Evidence of the fondness of the very young for dancing comes from the masterly engraving on the bottom of an oblong wooden box of unknown function, attributed on stylistic grounds to the late 18th dynasty. This shows a group of people under a doum palm (*Hyphaena taurica*, a tree still common in Nubia). To one side a young man plays a long flute to the barking of a dog; on the other two little children are dancing in time, their heads cleanshaven except for the characteristic Nubian-type tufts. A monkey climbs up the palm and wild ducks scud across the sky to complete the bucolic scene.

Egyptian familiarity with ball games is apparent from excavated balls made of papyrus, cloth or leather, stuffed with straw, thread or horsehair. Several Middle Kingdom tomb murals at Beni Hasan depict groups of girls throwing a ball from one to the other, while others juggle with up to three balls or play a kind of equestrian game where the losers apparently had to carry the winners around on their backs. Other children's sports were fishing, target-shooting, donkey-riding and swimming in the canals that criss-crossed the whole country. Royal offspring enjoyed the use of artificial pools.

Tomb murals often display scenes from young life where the children's bodies are quite dwarfed by the legs of the grown-ups. The 18th-dynasty harvest scene in the tomb of Menna at Sheikh Abd el-Qurna, for instance, has two little girls tugging each other's hair over a neat pile of cornstalks; below a young lass is pulling a thorn out of her friend's sole. Some unusual episodes appear such as a boy throwing stones at a date palm to knock down the fruit.

Affection for children radiates from many a family scene. One of the oldest and most remarkable finds of its kind comes from the mastaba of the vizier Ptahshepses at Abusir near Cairo. This fragment of a relief originally adorning the wall of the tomb shows part of a man seated with a little boy on his lap. His left arm encircles the boy's waist, while the boy rests his own right arm on his father's shoulder. The youngster is

29 In another detail of a busy harvest scene two young girls tussle over the wheat they have gathered. Tomb of Menna, West Thebes. 18th dynasty

30 A boy under attack from four others to shouts of 'Watch it! You're kicking me', 'Ouch! my ribs' and 'Get a taste of that!' Relief in the tomb of Ptahhotep, Saqqara. 5th dynasty

naked except for the typical child's ringlets hanging down the side of his head; he wears a small pectoral on his chest, and an amulet on a chain. The scene probably represents Ptahshepses himself with his young son.

From about the age of five children's pastimes began to prepare them for the labours of adult life, as we see in some of the 18th-dynasty tomb murals of Sheikh Abd el-Qurna. In the tomb of Khaemhet, for example, a boy is shown walking alongside the ploughman, scattering seed; in that of Menna young girls, unclothed, are helping with the harvest, while in Userhet's we see children gathering ears of corn in sacks. Elsewhere we see youngsters bringing corn to the granaries or fetching food for the harvesters out in the fields. An ostracon found at Deir el-Medina shows them putting a smooth finish on earthenware vessels.

The years of carefree childhood seem to have ended with the ceremony of circumcision, *sebi*, performed in ancient Egypt only on boys as far as we know. There is no exact information on the age at which it was done, most writers referring it broadly to the second decade of life. There is no question of it having been carried out shortly after birth, as happened among the Jews. The mummy of a 10-year-old prince mentioned in Smith and Dawson's monograph still had the childish hairstyle and was uncircumcised. Surviving depictions of circumcision all show boys without the long tress. The 12th-dynasty provincial princeling Khnumhotep found it worth mentioning that his reign had begun 'before he was circumcised'.

To settle the question of the age of circumcision it is important to be sure of its purpose. Even if its hygienic advantage in the Egyptian heat is clear to modern minds (since the removal of the foreskin prevents the accumulation of bacteria and smegma, recently shown to be carcinogenic) the ancients were unaware of this. Although it was a surgical operation it was carried out not by doctors but by priests, and circumcision is not mentioned in the medical papyri. It seems, then, that it was a specifically religious ritual. This also accords with the fact that the instrument used remained always a hooked flint knife, even when sharper metal knives had become available. The same type of knife, significantly, was used to make the ritual incision in eviscerating mummies.

There is a rare portrayal of a circumcision in the 6th-dynasty mastaba of
31 Ankhmahor at Saqqara, where a boy stands naked, firmly gripped by an assistant. His left arm rests on the head of the seated priest, who holds the boy's penis with his left hand while he cuts off the foreskin with his right. In the episode shown alongside stands another man, holding the boy's penis and applying some ointment to it. Some investigators have seen this as a preliminary stage in which lime is being applied to reduce sensitivity by the formation of carbonic acid. Others interpret it as post-

operative treatment of the wound. The operation must have been a painful one and was performed in septic conditions with no disinfectant, so that suppuration and other complications must have occurred sometimes.

That the custom was a very ancient one can be inferred not only from the use of an outmoded instrument but from the fact that the old Egyptian word for the penis, *henen*, signifies the organ minus the foreskin (*tem*). The term for the uncircumcised member, *kerenet*, is documented only from the time of the New Kingdom, when large numbers of uncircumcised foreigners came into the country. Circumcision was found already in naturally-dried mummies of the Predynastic Period in Nubia.

The ritual character of the operation also emerges from the fact that large groups of boys were circumcised together. A stele of the First Intermediate Period records the circumcision of 120 boys at one time. The ceremony was clearly related to the initiation rites common elsewhere in Africa at the time of puberty, where young men being inducted into adult male society proved their manliness by submitting to various tests, including the ability to withstand pain. Edward Wente recently researched the probable age of ancient Egyptian boys and girls at the climax of puberty and came up with 14 for the boys and 12–13 for the girls. It would follow that boys usually underwent circumcision around their 14th year.

Occasional portrayals of unclothed labourers and craftsmen in mastaba murals show that circumcision was common, though not mandatory, among the lower classes in the Old Kingdom. Only in the Late Period do we find that it had become compulsory for the priesthood, where it was associated with the notion of ritual purity. It is known that King Piankhi in the 25th dynasty eschewed contact with the uncircumcised Libyans. In keeping tally of the numbers of enemy slain in battle distinction was made between the circumcised (such as the 'Sea Peoples') where only the hands were cut off, and the uncircumcised, such as the Libyans, whose sexual organs were also removed. Circumcision among the Egyptians is mentioned by Strabo in Roman times and it has remained a regular custom among Copts as well as Moslems to this day. Even though the operation is now performed in infancy, it is still a ceremonial affair.

Circumcision of girls (clitoridectomy), not uncommon in Egypt today, is carried out exclusively by women in strict secrecy. This is probably why we have no information about its practice in ancient Egypt; if it did occur, it was probably even then the concern of a narrow circle of female relatives. No evidence from mummies has been published, but possibly they have not been examined carefully enough. Textual references to 'uncircumcised virgins' suggest, however, that female circumcision was known. For girls, as for boys, it may have been the stepping-stone into adult life.

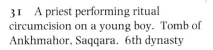

31   A priest performing ritual circumcision on a young boy. Tomb of Ankhmahor, Saqqara. 6th dynasty

CHAPTER THREE

Education and Learning

32 The invention of writing was attributed to Thoth, god of learning and wisdom and patron of scribes, seen here in his baboon aspect. A scribe with an open papyrus roll on his lap is in attendance. Serpentine. 18th dynasty. *Berlin, Ägyptisches Museum*

IN ANCIENT EGYPT the child's world was not as clearly separated from the adult's as it tends to be in modern Western society. As the years went by childish pastimes would give way to imitations of grown-up behaviour. Children would more and more frequently be found lending a hand with the less onerous tasks and gradually acquiring practical skills and knowledge from their elders. By precept and example, parents would instil into them various educational principles, moral attitudes and views of life. Thus from a tender age they would receive their basic education in the bosom of the family. For girls, this was usually all the schooling they would get, but for boys it would be supplemented by proper training in whatever line they chose, or was chosen for them.

Education, of course, covers both the general upbringing of a child and its training for a particular vocation. The upbringing of boys was left largely in the hands of their fathers, that of girls was entrusted to their mothers. Parents familiarised their children with their ideas about the world, with their religious outlook, with their ethical principles, with correct behaviour toward others and toward the supernatural beings in whom everyone believed. They taught them about folk rituals and so forth.

Educational principles are summarised in a number of ancient Egyptian treatises now commonly called the Books of Instruction. The advice given in them was designed to ensure personal success consonant with the needs of the state and the moral norms of the day. Truth-telling and fair dealing were enjoined not on any absolute grounds, but as socially desirable and at the same time more advantageous to the individual than lying and injustice, whose consequences would rebound against their perpetrator. The Books of Instruction contain rules for the well-ordered life and elements of morality that include justice, wisdom, obedience, humanity and restraint. They mostly took the form of verses addressed by a father to his son as he stepped into his shoes or started to help his ageing parent. Similar admonitions were delivered by a king to his heir. Most of these books were compiled by senior officials; humbler scribes, like Ani, only played a part in later times.

Many copies were made of these Books of Instruction, since they also served as teaching texts in the schools for scribes. Seven complete and five partial texts have survived, while the existence of others is known from fragments. The one which appears to be the oldest is by the celebrated Imhotep, vizier, architect and physician to 261 the 3rd-dynasty pharaoh Djoser. This text has not survived, but is mentioned in the Harper's Song in the tomb of King Inyotef. Another is the Instruction Compiled by the Noble and Royal Prince Hordjedef for His Son. The two authors of these very ancient books were held in such esteem as to be deified. Of other educational treatises perhaps

33 Author of the famous Instruction, vizier Ptahhotep, being carried in a palanquin. Painted limestone relief. Tomb of Ptahhotep, Saqqara. 5th dynasty

Right **34** A seated scribe at work, perhaps taking dictation. Section of a relief from the tomb of Yenuia. Saqqara. Late 18th–early 19th dynasty

33 the most important is the Instruction of Ptahhotep, City Administrator and First Minister during the reign of His Majesty Djedkare Isesi, Ruler of Upper and Lower Egypt during the 5th dynasty. The following passages deal with the art of 'elegant and effective speech'.

> . . . You should only talk when you are sure you know your subject.
> He who would speak in council must be a word-smith.
> Speaking is harder than any other task
> and only does credit to the man with perfect mastery . . .
>
> (366–369)

> Be prudent whenever you open your mouth.
> Your every utterance should be outstanding,
> so that the mighty men who listen to you will say:
> 'How beautiful are the words that fly from his lips!'
>
> (624–627)

Nevertheless Ptahhotep rates fair dealing higher than learning:

> You may tell a wise man from the extent of his knowledge,
> a noble man by his good deeds. (526–527)

32

In contrast to the hierarchic structure of Egyptian society in those days, this injunction to respect the opinions and knowledge of simple folk has quite a democratic ring:

> Do not boast of your knowledge,
> but seek the advice of the untutored
> as much as the well-educated. (52–53)

> Wise words are rarer than precious stones
> and may come even from slave-girls grinding the corn.
> (58–59)

Ptahhotep urges his readers to exercise justice and warns against intriguing for self-aggrandisement, bribery, extortion of debts from those unable to pay and insatiable accumulation of property. His manual abounds in concrete advice on how to behave in various situations – at banquets, in the exercise of high office, towards friends, wives, petitioners, paupers and so on.

The spiritual high-point in this genre is reached in the Instruction of Amenemope at the end of the 2nd millennium BC, some of which is closely comparable with passages in the Old Testament Book of Proverbs. It includes, for example, this call for justice and forbearance toward the poor and widows:

> Do not move the boundary-stone in the field
> nor shift the surveyor's rope;
> do not covet a cubit of your neighbour's land
> nor tamper with the widow's land-bounds. (Ch. VI)

> Covet not the poor farmer's property
> nor hunger after his bread;
> the peasant's morsel will surely gag in the throat
> and revolt the gullet (Ch. XI)

> If the poor man is found to owe you a great debt,
>   divide it three ways;
> remit two parts and let the third stand.
> That, you will see, is the best way in this life;
> thereafter you will sleep sound and in the morning
>   it will seem like good tidings;
> for it is better to be praised for neighbourly love
> than to have riches in your storeroom;
> better to enjoy your bread with a good conscience
> than to have wealth weighed down by reproaches.
> (Ch. XIII)

> Never let a powerful man bribe you
> to oppress a weak one for his own benefit. (Ch. XX)

There is a similar foretaste of Christian morality where Amenemope urges consideration toward the afflicted:

> Mock not the blind nor deride the dwarf,
> nor block the cripple's path;
> don't tease a man made ill by a god
> nor make an outcry when he blunders. (Ch. XXVI)

In the surprisingly developed moral code revealed by these excerpts, virtue will be rewarded for reasons that can be summarised as follows: behave justly toward your god, your king, your superiors and your inferiors too; in return you will enjoy health, long life and respect. When judging the dead, god will deal with you in accordance with your past conduct. Those you leave behind, too, will be glad to acknowledge your good deeds by reciting life-giving words and by bringing gifts to ensure you life eternal ... The supreme aim of the Egyptian moral system was to help maintain harmony and order in the world created by god and maintained by the king.

Alongside the inculcation of general rules of morality there was, of course, formal vocational training. Young men did not usually choose their own careers. Herodotus (II, 164) and Diodorus (I, 74) refer explicitly to hereditary callings in ancient Egypt. This was not in fact a system of rigid inheritance but an endeavour, as one Middle Kingdom stele puts it, to pass on a father's function to his children. Several other sources confirm that this happened with the consent of the king or his plenipotentiaries. Thus we find throughout Egyptian history a tendency for even the highest offices to remain in the same families. Towards the end of the Middle Kingdom, for example, there was a virtually dynastic line of viziers, and in the Ramessid period the offices of the supreme priests of Amun were passed on from father to son. The supreme priest Remi (Rai) relates in fact that Amun has permitted him to appoint two sons and two grandsons to high priestly posts within his jurisdiction, and expresses the hope that after his death his own office will go to members of his family from generation to generation in perpetuity.

It was in any case common practice for an official to take on his son as an assistant, so that the succession became more or less automatic. This was also the implication of joint rule at the royal level. A son was commonly referred to as 'the staff of his father's old age', designed to assist him in the performance of his duties and finally to succeed him. Even if the Instructions of Ani declare that 'offices have no offspring', the families of officials certainly tried to keep their jobs for their heirs. At the end of the New Kingdom, when the power of the monarch was weakening, officials began openly claiming the right to take over their fathers' jobs and this led to what had been previously forbidden – the sale of offices.

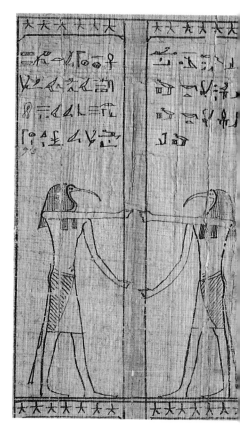

Above **35** The text on the right is written in hieratic script, a cursive development of hieroglyphic script which simplified the original signs and aided speed in writing. The left-hand side, above the figures of Thoth in his Ibis-headed aspect, is written in hieroglyphs. Part of the papyrus Book of the Dead of Kahapa. Late Period. *Private collection*

36 Hieroglyphs in their most decorative form appear on the interior coffin of Petosiris, relating Chapter 42 of the Book of the Dead. Multi-coloured glass paste on wood. Early Ptolemaic Period. *Cairo, Egyptian Museum*

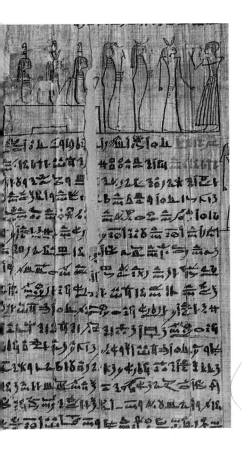

There were of course exceptions, such as where no male progeny were at hand. But since succession by the son was the most common situation, even a young assistant from another family came to be called the incumbent's 'son' or 'child'. There were also cases where a youngster of lowly origin was able by his own skill and industry, or through personal patronage, to reach high office up to the very summit, as did Ptahshepses in the 5th dynasty and Amenhotep, son of Hapu, in the 18th dynasty.

Fathers, then, were their sons' most frequent tutors, especially during the years when those sons were 'assisting' them or acting as their 'staffs of old age'. If the paternal office could only accommodate one person, normally the eldest son, any further sons would queue up behind other men who had no sons of their own, or whose positions allowed the adoption of more than one successor as apprentices.

An exception to the above was the pharaoh, who did not attend to his children's upbringing himself and left this to special tutors. Recent excavations at Abusir, for example, have acquainted us with one Idu, tutor to the royal children. At the king's palace the princes and princesses learnt the elements of writing, grammar, style, literature and mathematics. We know that the princesses joined in because one of them is portrayed with a writing tablet in her hand, and we know also that Senenmut, the vizier and royal architect, taught Hatshepsut's daughter Nefrure. Children of the highest-ranking courtiers were allowed to join the classes too, so that embryo 'schools' came into being where a whole group of children was instructed by one teacher.

Girls from ordinary families only received minimal education. They clung to their mothers, who taught them how to manage a household and instilled in them the basics of right living. In the higher strata girls also learned to sing, dance and play musical instruments. Few of them learned to write, as the rarity of their signatures on documents of the later periods reveal.

Farmers' children too only received scant instruction. From an early age they would be going out to the fields, boys and girls alike, to lend a hand in simple tasks like gathering and winnowing the corn, tending poultry and in time cattle, and so forth. 29 Fishermen, boatmen and others would also take their young folk along with them for 39 practical experience.

Pictures of craftsmen at work, on the other hand, rarely show children present. There is one of a boy handing a leg of meat to a butcher; other examples show a lad helping an older man to smooth down a ceramic vessel, and a boy playing in a row of musicians. In the army youngsters were used as grooms and batmen.

Writings of the Roman Period contain some interesting data about the training of weavers and spinning-girls. It started at the age of 12 to 14 and lasted from one to three, or exceptionally five, years. For the first two and a half years the apprentice worked for nothing; later he or she was paid a small wage, spending all day in the teacher's workshop and only returning at night if home was nearby. A test was probably given at the end of the apprenticeship. At this time weavers usually sent their children to be taught by colleagues in the same trade. The master undertook, if he failed to get his pupil through the whole course, to return whatever payment the father had advanced for the apprenticeship.

There is documentary evidence about the schooling of sculptors and painters in the inscription of Irtisen who, at the king's urging, initiated his eldest son into the secrets of his art. An artist had to be familiar with conventional symbols and ornamental motifs, with traditional postures and the laws of proportion in both human and animal figures. Sherds have survived on which various motifs have been chiselled out or painted with a brush. On one of those from Deir el-Medina a learner has tried to carve a human head, face, eye and ear, a headless god striding with the *was* sceptre in 38 his hand, and Osiris and Isis sitting opposite one another in a tabernacle. Patterns for relief-carving have survived from as far back as the 3rd dynasty; sculptors' models only from the Late Period. Those studying the arts were taught by full-blown artists, and had to present a qualifying piece at the end as proof of competence and completion of the course.

The apprenticeships we know most about are those of the scribes. In the Old

Kingdom each scribe taught his successor – usually his son – individually. From the First Intermediate Period onwards there is evidence of whole classes run for trainees in this field. In the New Kingdom they existed in the capital city of Thebes (there was one in the Ramesseum, for example, and a second purportedly at Deir el-Medina) and in later times such institutions were run at other centres too. These were not of course true schools in the sense of independent bodies with full-time teachers. All major offices such as the royal chancelleries, military headquarters and the administrative bodies of the temples with their associated Houses of Life took care of the training of as many scribes as they would need for themselves, the teaching being done by their own staff. For this they were able to use the oldest known textbook, the *Kemyt*. Pupils, mostly the sons of scribes, were taken on at the age of between five and ten.

35   The scholars had first of all to master reading and writing, both in the hieratic script for daily use and in the formal hieroglyphic. In place of exercise books they usually had recourse to the cheapest and ever-available material – pottery sherds or limestone fragments, the so-called *ostraca*. Less frequently they would write on papyrus, as a rule on sheets written on before (*palimpsests*), having wiped off or coated the original text, unless it had sufficiently faded. They also had a kind of practice tablet, a wooden board treated with a smooth white plaster that could be washed down and if necessary covered with a fresh layer. In the Graeco-Roman Period it

37   Children help harvesters, filling baskets with grain to be taken away. The man on the left is pouring grain into a *heqat* container which held about one bushel. Fragment of a tomb painting from West Thebes. New Kingdom. *Turin, Museo Egizio*

38   This limestone fragment was used for practice by an apprentice who covered it on all sides with unrelated reliefs and engravings. There is a falcon's head, an ear and a face. Date and origin unknown. *Prague, Náprstek Museum*

became common for students to use waxed boards for engraving with a metal stylus.

Lists have survived of hieroglyphs, or whole words, written out for practice. Sometimes students had to transcribe hieroglyphic characters into hieratic, which were more difficult because their shape was much less suggestive of the objects originally depicted. More advanced pupils could try copying out entire texts like the *Kemyt*, eulogies of the king, accounts of the beauty of the royal palaces, old official documents, model letters and reports etc. Attention was paid to grammar (hence dictation exercises) and to stylistic practice.

A 19th-dynasty textbook, now called Papyrus Anastasi I, was used for teaching the geography of Asia and arithmetic sums in military context in humorous form. Foreign languages were not a regular subject. Even in the New Kingdom knowledge of languages was rather exceptional; the Amarna correspondence in the cuneiform script could have been undertaken by resident foreigners. Nor did religious texts and rituals feature in the curriculum of the standard schools for scribes, though they were an important subject in the academies attached to the Houses of Life.

Along with writing, stress was laid on reading, usually in unison by a whole class. Pupils had to show that they understood the text, could analyse the meaning and remember the exact words, so they had to learn by heart whole passages, particularly literary ones. Great store was set on ability to memorize, far more than on originality, logic or critical thought, just as in the Quranic schools of the Muslim world today.

There was relatively little interest in mathematics. Its teaching was limited to the simple arithmetic and algebra which scribes needed as administrators responsible for registering landholdings, calculating harvests, making inventories of cattle and other property, etc. There were textbooks of arithmetic, but these only offered examples with no general rules.

Students were exhorted to show enthusiasm and affection for their subjects. The 12th-dynasty scribe Khety, for example, advises his son who is about to go off to a palace school for scribes: 'Learn to write, for this will bring you more benefit than all the other skills I have enumerated. Each single day of schooling will do you good and your schoolwork will last you for ever, like the very mountains.'

Since not every pupil, however, showed the requisite zeal, the schoolmaster's aids

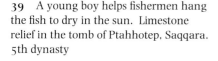

39 A young boy helps fishermen hang the fish to dry in the sun. Limestone relief in the tomb of Ptahhotep, Saqqara. 5th dynasty

in those days included the stick. 'A boy's ears are on his back: he hears, when he is beaten', runs an old Egyptian proverb. Boys of the more rebellious sort might have their legs tied together in case they thought of running away.

Length of schooling differed widely. The high priest Bekenkhonsu recalls that he started school at five and attended for 11 years, during the last few of which he was already 'in charge of King Sethos I's breeding stable'.

At 16 he was appointed junior priest or *wab*. We read on the other hand of one assistant (hence not fully trained) scribe who was already 30. But this must have been exceptional.

Teachers were drawn from the ranks of experienced, or pedagogically gifted, scribes who as part of their duties had to ensure the supply of future adepts either by classroom teaching, or by initiating students into their own work while they continued in office. Education had not in those days yet established itself as a separate discipline.

The ancient Egyptians nevertheless held education in high regard and saw it as a privilege. A few talented individuals without formal schooling still managed to acquire sufficient knowledge to shine in their own field. And there were of course plenty who tried, as everywhere, to compensate for their lack of education by intriguing or currying favour in high places – sometimes as high as royalty.

CHAPTER FOUR

Courtship and Entertainment

Left 40 Two ladies chat at a banquet. One is proffering to the other a lotus flower to smell. Each has on her wig a solid perfumed grease cone which in the warm room gradually melted, releasing a cooling fragrant substance. Painting on limestone from the tomb of Nebamun. Dra Abu el-Naga, West Thebes, 18th dynasty. *London, British Museum*

Above 41 Women are often represented in paintings making music, in this instance playing the lyre. Painting on limestone. Tomb of Djoserkareseneb, West Thebes. 18th dynasty

As YOUNG EGYPTIANS of both sexes crossed the threshold of maturity the unfamiliar world of romance and love would open up before them. Around them stretched an idyllic countryside where breezes rustled the crowns of the palm trees, spreading sycomore figs afforded grateful shade on hot days, herds of cattle grazed in lush green meadows and the still waters in the elbows of river-creeks were dotted with white lotus blossom or packed with papyrus thickets where birds twittered. Young lovers above all would relish the delights of nature and feel inspired to yet more eloquent praise of one another's beauty.

The astonishingly fresh quality of old Egyptian love poetry, with its fullest flowering in the time of the Ramessid kings, affords an insight into the world of those lovers of long ago.

The lips of the beloved are compared to a lotus bud, her arms to the curving boughs of young trees, her hair to the fowler's net. A favourite source of lyric metaphor was the pomegranate:

> What says the pomegranate tree?
> My pips are like her teeth,
> my fruit like her breasts.

This poetry abounds with happy phrases for the tender feelings of lovers, who from the 18th dynasty onwards were accustomed to call one another 'brother' and 'sister'. We are given glimpses of the private games they played, as when a girl speaks of her delight in bathing together in the river, so that she can allow her lover to see her beauty. Or again we read of a boy who would lure his girl to a secret spot among the reeds – but she proposes a different hiding-place, under a sturdy pomegranate tree. Those in love sought discreet trysting places everywhere, in garden summer-houses, in tents, in papyrus stands or even in lonely cemeteries. The adoring male seeks to overcome every obstacle that separates him from his beloved; he wishes that the bolted wooden door of her bedroom were only made of straw, or that he could cross the broad Nile to join her:

> The love of my desiring
> lies across the river.
> Wild waters separate us,
> a crocodile lurks in the shallows.
>
> I leap into the river and start to wade across.
> I have no fear of the depths,
> no fear even of the crocodile.
> The river is like dry land to me.

Love gives me strength,
love is my magic spell.
I gaze on my heart's longing;
she stands before me.

In Egyptian poetry equal justice is done to the girl's feelings. When she thinks of her beloved her heart pounds; if he is far off she is sick with yearning. (Ancient Egyptians, interestingly enough, regarded the heart – just as we do – as the seat of the affections, as well as of the soul and the reasoning faculty.)

Erotic desire is expressed in chaste and delicate terms. Thus a girl is pictured as artfully laying snares for her lover, seducing him with her glances, binding him with the beauty of her hair, chaining him with her necklace and branding him with her signet ring. She displays her full charms to him as she sheds her clothes beneath the sycomore fig.

How delightful, my beloved,
to go down with you to the river.
I look forward to the moment
when you will ask me to bathe before your eyes.

I shall sink into the water
and come up again holding a red fish.
It will be happy in my fingers.
I shall lay it between my breasts.

Come and watch, beloved!

In this literature the consummation of desire is expressed with the frankness of people close to the rhythms of nature; there is no whiff of vulgarity. If the young man catches his beloved alone in her house he will lose no time, intoxicated with her fragrance, in fulfilling his wishes on the bed where she lies. He hugs her and takes off her clothes, strokes her thighs and breasts till her heart is bursting; she clings to him, senses his passion and welcomes his whole body. Thrilled by the wonder of this moment, she wishes it could last forever ... We know from other passages that intercourse was commonly described as 'building tents'. As long as the partners had no other ties, nothing stood in their way.

Affection was customarily expressed, in the African manner, by rubbing noses. This involved a symbolic 'exchange of breath'. Breath was in turn seen as the prime token of life, whence arose no doubt the concept of the spirit as the underlying substance of life. But erotic tales, which abounded above all in the Late Period, show that mouth-to-mouth kissing was also practised; there are examples of this in the art of Amarna too. Deep affection radiates from a letter written by one girl to her lover: 'Esenofre, the singing-girl of Amun, says: "How is it with you? How I long to catch sight of you. My eyes are as big as Memphis, I so hunger to see you. Here I am, calling to Thoth and to all the gods of his house, 'Good health to you! May you live and be praised for what you do!'"

The patron goddess of lovers was Hathor, lady of love, joy and beauty, styled 'the Golden' in erotic poetry. A girl would beg the goddess to appoint her as her lover's bride; a boy would beseech her to grant him the girl of his choice.

Egyptian literature makes clear that youth and entertainment belong together. The young have the time and energy for pleasure, they make merry more spontaneously and enjoy movement, sport, dance, music and song. If their days are taken up with work or study they can still expect to be free at sunset, when nature brings a cool breeze after the boiling sun. General jollity now sets in and the sounds of music-making and dancing feet continue long into the night. The ancient rhythm of work and play prevails on the banks of the Nile to this day.

And on days off, and general holidays, there could be no stopping the crowds. We know from accounts of the life of the royal craftsmen at Deir el-Medina that they had one day off in ten. Then there were the official holidays, with which the Egyptian calendar abounded. Some were tied to events recurring on fixed dates. New Year was

42   A tambourine-playing dancer wearing ear-rings, necklace and bracelet as well as a revealing pleated garment and a narrow waistband of pearls. Part of an incense spoon. They were a favourite New Year present, accompanied by wishes of long earthly life and revival after death. Wood. 18th dynasty. *Berlin, Ägyptisches Museum*

43   Two pairs of singers and musicians at a banquet. They are playing the flute and the double clarinet; one is beating the time by slapping his knee and snapping his fingers as is the singer who also cups his ear. Painted limestone relief from the tomb of Nenkhefetka. Saqqara. 5th dynasty. *Cairo, Egyptian Museum*

44 Harp, lute and tambourine woman
players. Painted limestone relief.
Tomb of Rekhmire, Sheikh Abd el-Qurna,
West Thebes. 18th dynasty

of course celebrated. The harvest festival lasted several days, nor was any work done during the five 'extra' days after the nominal end of the 360-day year. (There were 12 calendar months of 30 days each.) Special holidays were assigned for each divinity popular in this place or that. The public took part with gusto in royal festivities for the king's accession or coronation; in the foundation rituals – 'rope-stretching' ceremonies – of the most important building projects; in the *sed* held in the 30th year of every reign and every third succeeding year; in the solemn erection of the *djed* or pillar symbolising the continuance of the reign. And finally in the king's funeral. There were cemetery holidays, too, when sacrifices were made in the presence of the bereaved. And the cardinal family events – births, marriages, deaths – were all occasions for private ceremony.

Egyptians never stinted their gratitude for the blessing of life, and made good use of it in the spirit enjoined by the Harper's Song inscribed in the tomb of King Inyotef:

> Enjoy yourself while you live,
> put on fine linen,
> anoint yourself with wonderful ointments,
> multiply all your fine possessions on earth,
> follow your heart's command on earth,
> be joyful and make merry . . .

The same philosophy is echoed in the Instruction of Ptahhotep:

> Be merry all your life;
> Toil no more than is required
> nor cut short the time allotted for pleasure;
> it offends the spirit to be robbed of its time.
> So waste not an hour more than you must
> taking care of your household;
> wealth will come even if you indulge your own wishes,
> it will be useless
> if you thwart them.

Dancing is perhaps the most straightforward expression of joy, transmuted into harmonious movement. On the walls of the Egyptians' tombs we find countless pictures of the dancing that accompanied celebrations, feasts, religious services and funeral rites, but it was equally a part of their everyday enjoyment. As soon as anyone started, the rest quickly joined in. So we rarely find solo dancing portrayed.

Irena Lexová distinguished between dancing as exercise in 'active relaxation' after

work, and gymnastic dancing that shades into acrobatics and involves the harder movements and figures requiring great flexibility and long training. Dances imitating animal movements are less commonly recorded in Egypt. Pair-dancing in the modern manner, with man leading woman, was unknown, and in the Egyptian context the term refers to a group of girls dancing round in pairs, holding hands. In group dancing each participant executed his or her own turns without regard to what the rest were doing. There were also specialised dances of a military, dramatic, lyrical or grotesque character, and those designed for funeral or religious purposes.

Significantly, members of both sexes are never portrayed dancing in the same episode, but always men and women separately and the latter more frequently. There is no clear borderline between dancing and acrobatic or gymnastic performances. Scenes that have survived show, for example, groups of girls spinning round, performing a back bend (the finest of these appears on an ostracon in Turin's Egyptian Museum); a group of girls leaning back with one leg on the ground and the other in a high-kick; girls lifting or throwing one another or performing somersaults and the like. In other depictions there is true dancing with elegant leg-movements and charming gestures, with torsos bending and heads inclined as rhythm required.

That dancing has a very long history in Egypt is clear from predynastic clay figures whose hands are raised above their heads and in scenes with women in this posture accompanied by men shaking rattles on predynastic vessels. In the Old Kingdom jumping, stamping and sporting elements come into the repertoire, while by the time of the New Kingdom conventions had been relaxed and the dance had blossomed out into manifold forms with livelier, smoother and more graceful movements. The national dances of neighbouring peoples – Nubian, Lybian and Syrian – also made their appearance. In the Late Period most recorded dancing was in the context of public feasts or religious rites.

Several scenes have survived that show women clapping their hands to keep the dancers in time. The dancing-girls usually wore brief open-fronted, or fringed, skirts or on other occasions loose tunics (diaphanous in the New Kingdom) with shoulder-straps, or were simply draped in long shawls. Sometimes they danced naked except for a narrow ribbon across the belly.

45 Part of a banquet scene with two young dancers entertaining the guests to the accompaniment of a double flute and handclapping. Contrary to the convention of representing figures in profile, we are shown two of the women full-face and, judging from their wigs, they must be shaking their heads to the music. The sense of movement in this superb painting places it among the best examples of Egyptian art. Painting on limestone from the tomb of Nebamun. Dra Abu el-Naga, West Thebes. 18th dynasty. *London, British Museum*

46 An acrobatic female dancer performs a graceful back bend. Her long wavy hair and scant dress enhance the picture's erotic quality. Fragment of a painting on limestone. Deir el-Medina, West Thebes. 18th dynasty. *Turin, Museo Egizio*

From the muscular thighs of some dancers it has been inferred that they were professionals. Such girls are indeed mentioned in the records under the name of *khebeyet*, particularly in the royal harems; they are described as 'well-nourished and friendly', which might have meant much more.

Dancing went along with music and song, especially singing to a musical accompaniment. Specialists say that instrumental music on its own did not exist in ancient Egypt and that the unaccompanied voice was rare. In the Old Kingdom the accompaniment was provided by a single instrument, seldom by more than one. In the New Kingdom the singer either accompanied him or herself – we often see a harpist singing – or was supported by a larger or smaller mixed ensemble. In later times the number of instruments gradually declined again.

Of the wind instruments, one of the oldest was the flute, made of reed or wood, or later even of metal. It is illustrated on a predynastic sherd as well as on a slate palette from Hierakonpolis, so it may have originated in Egypt. An Old Kingdom relief shows a yard-long flute, held on the slant; the older short kind, held horizontally, was also still in use. The number of finger-holes varied from three to five. It was originally blown – in prehistoric times we are told with the nose, but with the mouth in the dynastic periods – through an opening at one end. But in the course of the New Kingdom the end was closed off and the opening shifted to the side. Around this time the flute began to give way to other instruments. However, it never disappeared altogether and it has survived to this day under the Arabic names of *nay* and *uffafa*. Judging by the pictures, the tunes of the songs were played only by male flute players, accompanied sometimes by a clarinet.

Another instrument documented from predynastic times in Egypt was the spiral pipe which also served for communication at a distance, as in the hunt. Clarinets are known from the 4th dynasty and indeed are still in use under the name of *zummara*. Though the trumpet first appears in illustrations of the early New Kingdom, it probably existed in the Old Kingdom too. The finest example of gold and silver trumpets is the pair found in the tomb of Tutankhamun. Trumpets were also used for signalling and became standard military equipment. The long oboe, played with a double reed, spread to Egypt from Asia Minor in the course of the New Kingdom; it is usually shown played in pairs by women. Instruments made from animal horns do not appear in any reliefs, but do in terracotta models of the New Kingdom. During the Ptolemaic Period other instruments of Greek origin arrived, including the double flute *aulos* and the pan-pipes. In the 3rd century BC an Alexandrian Greek, Ktesibios, invented the water-organ by combining the pan-pipes with a keyboard. Being driven by air from a bellows regulated by water-pressure, the new instrument was dubbed

47 Nefertari playing *senet*. *Senet*, which means 'passing', was universally popular from the earliest times, and came to double as a religious ritual. On tomb walls and in Books of the Dead, the deceased is portrayed seated at the *senet* board before an invisible adversary, striving to 'pass' to the next world without mishap. Painted relief in the tomb of Queen Nefertari, Valley of the Queens. West Thebes. 19th dynasty

48 Gaming disc with a scene of two dogs chasing gazelles. Mastaba of Hemaka, an official of King Den. Black steatite inlaid with alabaster. Saqqara. 1st dynasty. *Cairo, Egyptian Museum*

49 An unusual archaic tower-shaped ivory piece for a board game from a 1st-dynasty burial. Umm el-Qa'ab, Abydos. *Berlin, Ägyptisches Museum*

hydraulos. Hellenistic instruments became so popular in the Roman Period that they almost drove out the native ones.

Of the string instruments, the harp was known as early as the Old Kingdom in a form almost identical to that of the Sumerians; specialists are not yet agreed whether it originated in Mesopotamia or on the Nile. In view of its size it was placed on the ground, the player supporting it with one hand and plucking the strings – from 11 to 13 in number – in a kneeling or standing position.

From the New Kingdom on, three more stringed instruments were added to the Egyptian range. One was a small, vertical, sharply bent harp from Babylonia, of which one magnificent example is the pride of the Louvre. Another was a long-necked lute or mandolin with a long oval resonating body out of wood covered partly in leather, partly by a thin sheet of wood with an opening to release the sound. Finally there was the lyre, which unlike its Greek counterpart had seven strings.

An essential part of the orchestra were the percussion instruments that kept the dancers in time. The simplest of these were bone or ivory clappers carved in the shape of curved arms and either struck against the musician's body or held in each hand and knocked against each other. One typically Egyptian instrument was the *sistrum*, a hand-rattle with free-moving metal strips strung on a series of horizontal wires. The metal handle was sometimes decorated with a head of the goddess Hathor. It is of interest that similar rattles are used ritually today by priests of the Ethiopian church, which adopted them under Coptic influence. The sound produced by another type of rattle, the *menat*, came from several rows of beads joined by two chains, with a long metal handle. In the Late Period Egyptians became acquainted with cymbals, pairs of concave discs about 15cm across attached to the players' hands with leather straps. Finally, there were bells, large and small.

Instruments using a membrane included the cylindrical drum, about a metre high with a laced-on leather skin at each end, that was found in a Middle Kingdom tomb at Beni Hasan. Both military and civilian scenes depicted in New Kingdom sites feature drums of various sizes, often slung over players' necks with leather belts. They were struck not with sticks but with the fingers or open palms. Tambourines also occurred.

Musical performances often involved 'cheironomy' conducting using signs and

gestures by which a dancer, singer or orchestral or choral leader (conductor) could 43
determine and modify melody, rhythm and dynamics.

Though we can conjecture the sound of ancient Egyptian music from the range of instruments mentioned, the art of musical notation was never developed, so the melodies will probably remain unknown forever. In the New Kingdom they almost certainly employed a heptatonic scale under Near Eastern influence, and indeed they may have done so from the start. Their idioms no doubt lay somewhere between those of modern Arab music and those of Black Africa. Some scholars have sought their traces in the upper reaches of the Nile or in the oases of the Western Desert, for example at Siwa.

Like us, the ancient Egyptians tried to improve their leisure hours with social entertainments, including games. The careful visitor to Egyptian sites will sometimes have noticed checkered rectangles marked out on the pavements, where some ancestor of modern draughts was evidently played. The most common such game was the *senet*, for which the field was divided into three rows of 10 squares. The 47 playing board was either of wood, stone, clay, bone or faience if it was not cut straight into the pavement. Pieces of the opposing sides were distinguished by their size or their shape. A number of game-board engravings have survived in the mastaba of Ptahshepses at Abusir and recent Czechoslovak digs at the temple of King Raneferef and Queen Khentkaus have uncovered quantities of playing pieces.

In the game of *taw* which the Hyksos invaders popularised throughout the country, there were 20 squares in three rows of 4, 12 and 4. Other games of the sort are recorded with different numbers of squares. They were all position games, usually played by two people sitting facing each other. Unfortunately we do not know the rules of any of them.

The 'snake game', *mehen*, could be played by up to six people. It used a long field scratched out on the floor and stone pieces in the shape of dogs, lions and balls that were moved along it. In another, portable, game played in the Middle Kingdom sets of pegs ending in little heads of dogs, jackals and other beasts were stuck into a row of 30 or 60 holes drilled in a board. Here again we can only guess what the rules might have been.

Amusements for young men, particularly nobles and princes, included sports and drill, and in the barracks army recruits practised these by way of physical training. But there is no evidence of girls taking part in any exercise apart from the sport and acrobatic elements in dancing.

The favourite male sports were confrontational – wrestling, boxing and fencing 50 with sticks. Of these the most frequently documented from earliest times, particularly 51 in the Middle Kingdom tombs of Beni Hasan and on New Kingdom sherds, is wrestling. We see for example one wrestler at the start of a contest, holding his opponent's arm in his right hand and trying to grasp the back of his neck with the other. Later we see him holding the other man's calf in his right hand and trying to throw him down with his left hand, which is pressed against his neck. At another point one contestant, with legs astride, has managed to toss the other over his back. The holds used have reminded some experts of free-style Graeco-Roman wrestling, while others detect elements also present in Japanese wrestling. The earliest international stick-fencing championship was held at the court of Ramesses II, when young soldiers of the pharaoh vied with units of Egypt's foreign allies. The competitors had leather helmets tied under the chin and carried heavy sticks. The high-born spectators probably counted the number of blows scored by each side in the duels. Alas, we are not told which side won.

Running featured in the royal *sed* ceremonies in which the pharaoh, on the 30th anniversary of his reign and every third year thereafter, would show his continued physical prowess in a long-distance solo run. The recently discovered stele of King Taharqa (25th dynasty) shows that real long-distance races were also organised. Among other track-and-field events we have two portrayals of high- and long-jumping, and one of weight-lifting.

Dating from the 18th dynasty kings and princes, in particular, enjoyed shooting

with the bow at targets while riding two-wheeled chariots. The crown in this field goes to Amenophis II. He had his skill recorded for posterity on the so-called Archery Stele, the inscriptions on which are an unrivalled source of information about the history of sport in ancient Egypt. It was from this period on that kings, princes, top-ranking potentates and the military cream of the mobile units practised racing in two-wheeled chariots, or less commonly on horseback. There were popular ball-games, too, of whose rules we are ignorant, and sundry gymnastic exercises, especially balancing.

Of water sports, swimming was not unnaturally a popular pastime from the earliest days in a country which not only had the Nile but the many canals and side-streams that joined it. There are early dynastic seals showing swimmers in action. The biography of Khety in the First Intermediate Period mentions the sport, along with running and archery, as part of the education of young royalty and nobility. Some New Kingdom ointment spoons have handles finely carved in the shape of swimming girls, who also feature in love poetry.

Boat-racing is recorded too, with the oarsmen standing and sitting by turns. And also angling and hunting, in which princes and young aristocrats delighted in proving their skill.

Sports could be pursued in the open everywhere, though the stele of Amenophis II found beneath the Sphinx at Giza speaks of some special archery site in the north. From textual references and portrayals of spectators we can gather that organised sporting events took place, especially when the king was the leading figure. During certain periods of Egyptian history in particular royal prowess took on a mainly symbolic or religious significance.

The focus for informal entertainments was provided by the inns or beer houses. Here, as in other climes and times, singing, gaming, dancing and perhaps recitation went on, but in contrast to the banquets of the rich, boys and girls now sat next to each other. Merrymaking proceeded without constraint while people drank and the beer went to their head. Whereas elsewhere citizens went sensibly to bed soon after nightfall, lamps stayed lit in the beerhalls far into the night and no one had heard of closing-time. A teacher at one school for scribes had to admonish a pupil for unseemly behaviour in his cups. 'I hear you are neglecting your papyri and abandoning yourself to dancing. You haunt one tavern after another, driven by your thirst for beer. People avoid you as you stagger along the street. You should try and cut out drinking and realise that drunkness robs you of your dignity. You are being false to your own spirit.' The streets of the main cities in particular were no doubt thronged at night with tipsy young men, soldiers and foreigners. It was in the beer

50 Two youths in kilts boxing with unprotected fists. Relief in the tomb of Ptahhotep. Saqqara. Late 5th dynasty

51 Boys fencing with papyrus stalks. Relief in the tomb of Ptahhotep. Saqqara. Late 5th dynasty

53 A swimming girl carved in wood as a handle of a cosmetic dish whose container is in the form of a duck. 19th dynasty. *London, British Museum*

52 Women wearing wigs performing a ritual dance as part of the *sed* festival, celebrating 36 years of the reign of King Amenhotep III. Limestone relief from the tomb of Kheruef. West Thebes, 18th dynasty. *Cairo, Egyptian Museum*

houses, too, that women of easy virtue angled for custom. Ani warns the reader against them in his Instruction:

> Beware of the strange woman
> unknown to people in her town.
> Do not ogle her as she goes by
> or try to know her intimately.

However, the best-meant advice was useless. The libidos of young men (who married much later in life than the girls) were too strong to be suppressed. They would go off in high spirits with ladies of pleasure to their houses which sometimes – as Mariette showed in the case of Abydos – formed an enclave.

We would never have known in any detail what went on in those houses but for the long-concealed and only recently published testimony of Papyrus 55001 in the Egyptian Museum of Turin, a large pictorial manuscript of the early 20th dynasty. The right-hand side of this is devoted to satirical scenes of animal life, such as we find in other papyri, sherds and bestiaries. But on the left side we are presented in the frankest and typically Egyptian manner with intimate glimpses of sexual behaviour. The museum acquired this document around 1820 and it was perused by a whole series of Egyptologists, starting with the famous Champollion. But no one dared to publish it in full. Not till 1973 was it finally published by Joseph Omlin.

There are 12 episodes, like the picture-stories in tomb murals or modern comic 54

strips. We are given a running guide to the erotic adventures of a middle-aged man with a young girl, brief captions reproducing their conversation in direct speech.

We cannot be sure of the identity of the hero, a rather seedy man with a bald pate, a few tangled wisps of curls on his neck and an unshaven face. From the fact that he is circumcised Omlin deduces that he is supposed to be a priest, but this is not convincing. As previously stated, any man might be circumcised, and it will be shown in a later chapter that from about the 19th or 20th dynasty priests did not allow a single hair to grow on their head, face or anywhere else. The man is not wearing the usual kilt, knotted in front, but only a triangular loin-cloth with a long tail. His racial type is not clearly enough drawn for us to concur with Omlin that he was more probably Syrian than Egyptian.

The female character in the story is unquestionably a prostitute. Her figure accords with the Egyptian ideal of the body beautiful – firm breasts, pronounced buttocks and conspicuously long legs. She is dressed only in a bordered belt slung between waist and pubis. On her head she has a wig (in some episodes it appears decorated with a lotus blossom), around her neck a double necklace, a few bangles above and below the elbow and round rings in her ears. One caption gives her profession as that of *heset*, i.e. a singing-girl in the service of Hathor, goddess of love.

Successive episodes depict varieties of intercourse known to the ancient Egyptians, with an interval after each act for the girl to tidy herself up. Then comes a scene where the girl is enticing the man onto the bed with her, and another where she and two other women are carrying him, either asleep or the worse for drink. In the next she is bending over him as he lies, stroking his head and chin to reawaken his interest.

The captions, not all of which have survived, quote the woman stimulating her partner with cries of 'Let me make it nice for you', 'Don't be afraid', 'You're with me, look!' and 'O you wicked man!' In conjunction with the pictures, these snatches of small-talk afford unique insight into the most private details of ancient Egyptian life.

In his analysis of these scenes Omlin finds various parallels with religious ritual in the postures of the two characters and suggests that some details are deliberately exaggerated in character with the other, satirical part of the papyrus. The satire is directed, he believes, at the class of dignitaries and the priesthood. From references to warfare on the label of the papyrus he deduces that it had circulated among military people. Whatever the motive behind the document it cannot be denied that, like every other illustrated artefact in ancient Egypt, it had its roots in observation of real life.

It is important to realise that representation of the sex act was never itself taboo in Egyptian art. Concern for sexual vigour reflected not merely erotic interest but, above all, the general anxiety to secure male heirs. It was symbolised *par excellence* by Min,

54 A prostitute adorned with nothing but a lotus flower, necklace, bracelets and a waistband is making up her face with a brush. She holds a mirror in her left hand. Next she is shown during intercourse with an unshaven bald-headed man endowed with an enormous phallus. Turin papyrus No. 55001. 19th dynasty. *Turin, Museo Egizio*

55 In this scene the prostitute is enticing the man onto the bed with her. Turin papyrus No. 55001. 19th dynasty. *Turin, Museo Egizio*

patron deity of the cities of Koptos and Akhmim, who is depicted with erect phallus on temple walls. Min and other gods received from men anxious to cure their impotence or enhance their libido sacrifices in the form of votive figurines that showed a man sitting or kneeling with a grossly exaggerated penis. Other such objects show a man kneeling in front of a standing woman, or over a woman lying on her back with her legs drawn up or kneeling forward. In the New Kingdom such scenes appear on sherds as well, and we find amulets in the form of the male or female genitals, or of 149 men with erect organs and of couples copulating.

Various aphrodisiac drugs were used to increase potency. One was a plant of uncertain identity, *menhep*, whose determinative was the male member and a plant that was under the protection of the goat of Mendes (another virility symbol). Other favourites were the long-leafed cos lettuce, with its thick milky juice (in maturity) suggestive of semen, the mandrake, silphium and many more medicinal herbs. In the demotic Tale of Setna a woman who comes to the temple for advice about her apparent sterility is told to pick colocasi, boil it, add some of the concoction to her husband's drink and then lie with him in the certainty of conceiving. There was but a thin line between medicine and magic, witness the highly dubious use for the same purposes of the sperm of another man or of an animal, or its blood, put into a drink or smeared on the penis. For good measure there were also methods, exclusively magical, for attaining the contrary end of suppressing passion in a female rival, or in a mistress' husband, by covert administration.

It must be noted that portrayals of naked breasts, or of the genitals of naked men at 102 work, normally had no erotic significance for the practical minded Egyptians, living as close to nature as they did. Details of the sex-lives of the gods, again, crop up continually in Egyptian religious mythology. Consider the case of Isis, the wife of Osiris, who after long searching finds all the scattered parts of her husband's body – he had been murdered by Seth – except for his penis. This had been swallowed by an oxyrhynchus fish, which resembles a male organ with an extended foreskin. Isis then puts the body together again with an artificial replacement for the missing part. Temple reliefs at Abydos, Dendera and on the island of Philae, show Osiris lying with erect penis and Isis as a bird above him. A further example is provided by the cult of Hathor, patron of bodily love and Egyptian counterpart to Venus. She was supposed to come periodically from her seat at Dendera to visit her husband Horus at Edfu 271 (Behdet). There are stories again of a king in the guise of a crocodile who steals men's wives to violate them, and of the divine conception of Queen Hatshepsut and others, with vivid details of intercourse such as were quoted at the beginning of Chapter I.

Erotic candour became fully public in the 18th dynasty, when the expansion of the Egyptian empire into Asia brought many alien influences into the country, such as homage to the love-goddesses Qadesh and Astarte, the romantic poetry that went with it and the cult of youthful female beauty. Not only did bodily charms cease to be 178 hidden; the diaphanous material worn by young ladies artfully emphasised them. 60 Dancers and servant-girls walked around quite naked except for a narrow girdle 45 draped from the hips above the *mons veneris*.

In the course of the 19th dynasty, interestingly enough, scenes of loose behaviour suddenly disappear. Siegfried Schott found a picture of naked serving-women in an 18th-dynasty tomb which had been used again in the following dynasty, the figures being then painted over to appear clothed in contemporary style.

As for deviant behaviour, there are records of homosexual practices in ancient Egypt, disapproved of at Memphis but tolerated elsewhere. King Pepy II, for example, was reproached for having carnal relations with his general Sisene in a tale dating to a much later period. Again, a dead man is described as saying in self-defence, when he came to judgement: 'I committed no sexual misdeeds. I had no boy-lover.' There are depictions of sodomy in Egyptian art. Herodotus implies that embalmers sometimes indulged in necrophilia, and so says that it was allegedly the custom in the Late Period of entrusting female corpses to them only on the third day. Pederasty was disapproved of, and in Ptahhotep's Instruction we are told: 'Do not sleep with a woman who is still a child...'

CHAPTER FIVE

Marriage and the Standing of Women

56 Queen Ankhesenamun affectionately anointing her husband Tutankhamun's collar with perfumed unguent from the jar she holds in her hand. Detail of the back of the King's throne. Tomb of Tutankhamun, Valley of the Kings West Thebes. 18th dynasty. *Cairo, Egyptian Museum*

THE WEDDED STATE was to ancient Egyptian minds the ideal part of the divine order. Monogamy is documented even from predynastic times. A young man who had hitherto led a bachelor life and sometimes had a high time of it, but had now attained a certain social standing, would go to the house of his chosen's father to ask for her hand.

Entering into a marriage was described as 'making a wife' or 'taking a wife', but in accordance with the prevailing patriarchal system it seems that the girl's father had the main say. Nor were the views of her mother to be ignored, as an eager girl's words reveal in a love-song: 'Little does he know how I long to embrace him, and for him to send word to my mother.' If the girl had no father, an uncle would step in.

The ratio of love-matches to arranged marriages is not clear from the evidence. We have a biographical inscription of the Ptolemaic Period where a woman says: 'My father gave me in marriage' to so-and-so.

In the absence of any pre-existing agreement it seems that the girl's consent to a marriage was unimportant until the 26th dynasty, when brides also began to have a say. It is then that we find marriage contracts using not only the formula 'I have made you into a wife', but also, putting the woman's side, 'You have made me into a wife.' Whether there was a period of engagement before marriage we cannot tell.

At what age did young people marry in those days? Age is not usually mentioned in the contracts. References to child-marriage or early maturity among Egyptian girls repeated in some popular accounts have no basis in fact. We have already seen that the average age of puberty was 12 to 13 among girls and around 14 for boys. The Instruction of Ani exhorted boys to

> Take a wife while you are still young,
> so that she can bear you a son.

It would follow that attainment of sexual maturity was a precondition of marriage. One Ptolemaic document gives the lowest age for a bridegroom as 15, which agrees exactly with this reasoning. At an even later time the Instruction of Ankhshoshenq advised boys precisely: 'Marry at 20, so that you can have a son while you are still young.'

Probably, then, a man could marry as soon as he was physically mature and had reached a point in his chosen career that ensured his ability to provide for his wife and for the children they could expect. Ptahhotep, whom we have so often quoted, writes: 'If you have already made yourself a name, then start a family . . .'

We know of cases on the other hand where very 'mature' men took wives many years younger. The scribe Qenherkhepeshef of Deir el-Medina, for example, married the 12-year-old girl Nanakht when he was 54. Again, having established the age of Queen Mutnodjmet when she died we can deduce that she was between 25 and 30 when the 50-year-old General Horemheb chose to marry her. This was of course a classic marriage of convenience, enabling Horemheb to join the ruling family of the 18th dynasty and secure the throne.

It was a different matter for brides, who did not need to wait till they attained social status and could not afford to see their youthful attractions waning. The earliest known ages for brides are quoted by Pestman from Roman Period documents that speak of marriage at 8, 9 and 10. And the label of one late mummy states, in a demotic hand, that the body was of a married girl who had died at the age of 11. Others have argued that such cases were either exceptional or were scribes' errors. Erich Lüddeckens, an outstanding student of Egyptian marriage contracts, found from analysis of Ptolemaic contracts that most of the brides were aged 12 or 13. Reconstruction of the biographies of the Amarna princesses has produced the same figure, and the Ptolemaic Period woman mentioned above as having been 'given in marriage' by her father was 14 when this occurred.

It seems reasonable to conclude, then, that in contrast to men, some girls married as early as, or soon after, puberty, that is between 12 and 14. Pre-pubertal marriages, however, were quite customary in the royal families, where for dynastic reasons they were often early unions of brother and sister. A well-known example is the marriage of Tutankhamun and Ankhesenamun. Since he died aged about 18 after a nine-year reign, he must have been nine when he married, although she may well have been older.

Marriages between kin were familiar among the common folk. Step-brothers and sisters married, as did uncles and nieces quite frequently, and cousins still more so. Marriages between cousins are indeed a regular occurrence in Egypt, and particularly in Nubia, to this day. Between very close blood-relations, however, it was wholly exceptional among ordinary people. Jaroslav Černý investigated 490 marriages from the First Intermediate Period up to the 18th dynasty and found only two cases where the partners were brother and sister. After the time of Tuthmosis III it is hard to prove the occurrence of close-kin marriages since it was now becoming normal to call a wife or girlfriend 'sister'. One sibling marriage is attested by the stele of Ptah, the 22nd-dynasty high priest of Memphis. Here both parents had the same family lineage. But the father was a commander of Libyan mercenaries and may have been deliberately adopting the customs of the Egyptian court.

In the royal family it had been almost mandatory since time immemorial for marriages to be solemnised between the closest kin, the notional prototype evidently being the mythological sibling-spouses Osiris and Isis, who had come into this world to raise humans from savagery, teach them the elements of civilisation and proclaim the wisdom and omnipotence of the gods. As the king saw himself as a god-incarnate he hoped to pass on his exclusive divine status to his successor. Accordingly he had no hesitation in taking as wife his sister or step-sister (as did Seqenenre Tao II, Ahmose I, Amenophis I, Tuthmosis I, Tuthmosis IV, Ramesses II, Merenptah and Siptah), his daughter (Amenophis II, Akhenaten and Ramesses II who went so far as to marry three of his daughters) or even his aunt (Sethos II). Ptolemy II and his successors all married one of their sisters. These last were kings of Greek blood, but they took care to adhere strictly to old Egyptian practice in their marriage policy as in everything else. Interestingly enough, investigation of the many kin-marriages in the 18th, 19th and Ptolemaic dynasties by Marc Armand Ruffer has revealed no evidence of degeneration resulting from persistent inbreeding.

Examination of 161 marriages among commoners in the Ptolemaic Period, 24 per cent of which were between siblings, shows the power of example even in those days. It was evidently hellenistic influence that weakened the barrier between exclusively royal practice and that of the people. During the reign of the Roman emperor Commodus it was reported that as many as two-thirds of marriages in the city of Arsinoe (formerly Crocodilopolis, capital of the Faiyum) were between very close kin.

Another feature of ancient Egyptian marriage custom is that the partners usually

Below 57 Nefertiti, the beautiful wife of King Akhenaten and mother of the six princesses of Amarna. This unfinished head was to be one of the elements of a composite statue. That artist captured the sensibility, grace and beauty of a woman of great spirit and importance. This is arguably the most beautiful of all the known portraits of Nefertiti. Brown quartzite. The studio of Thutmosis at Tell el-Amarna. 18th dynasty. *Cairo, Egyptian Museum*

Right 58 Nofret and Rahotep, two courtiers whose portrayal reflects the great importance of their positions. Nofret was designated as 'one known to the king'. Her husband Prince Rahotep was probably the son of King Snofru. He held the titles of High Priest of Re at Heliopolis, Director of Expeditions and Chief of Construction. The coloured diadem worn by Nofret over her wig represents a silver band with ornamental inlays. Her collar was made of semi-precious stone beads and pendants. According to artistic convention the man's complexion is much darker than his wife's. This is one of the masterpieces of Egyptian art. See also ill. 80. Painted limestone. From the mastaba of Rahotep and Nofret, Meidum. Early 4th dynasty. *Cairo, Egyptian Museum*

came from the same social stratum. There were however exceptions, such as Naunakhte in the 20th dynasty who married first a scribe and then an artisan, or King Amenophis II who fell for the commoner Teye and made her his principal wife.

No obstacles seem to have been put in the way of marriage between people of different racial background. An Egyptian could marry a Syrian or Nubian girl, and an Egyptian woman could become a foreigner's wife. The kings themselves might take princesses from abroad as secondary wives. Ramesses II, for example, wed the Hittite princess Maathornefrerure and granted her the same title of 'Great King's Wife' as he did to his principal wife Nefertari. From the Late Period on, Egyptians were regularly intermarrying with Greek colonists in some of the Delta towns, just as in the Roman Period they did with Latins, especially in the Faiyum.

Marriage of a free man to a slave, by contrast, was regarded as mere concubinage and enjoyed no legal protection; any ensuing children remained slaves. To contract a proper marriage, a slave-woman had first to buy her freedom or to be adopted. A man was free to adopt any children he had by a slave.

This raises the question of how many wives an Egyptian was allowed to have. In theory there was no limit, but in practice it would have depended on the man's means. Most Egyptians were content to have only one wife. Marriage was an expensive matter for the man, and the whole contract system provided such far-reaching safeguards for the material rights of wives and children that most men could only afford one wife at a time.

In the Old Kingdom only royalty and the highest officials of noble blood could think of having secondary wives. Naguib Kanawati found only 16 possible cases of polygamy among dignitaries of this period, although others were recently discovered by Břetislav Vachala at the Giza cemetery. During the First Intermediate Period the custom spread to governors in charge of the various regions and other senior scribe-officers. In the Late Period, Herodotus (III, 92) tells us that monogamy was then as much the rule in Egypt as in Greece. But there may have been another upsurge of polygamy in the Graeco-Roman Period, for Diodorus (I, 80, 3) quotes it as common among laymen, whereas the priesthood were restricted to one wife.

The royal palaces tell us something about life in the harems. In the tombs of Ay and Tutu at Amarna there are pictures of harems surrounded by high walls with guards posted at every entrance. The occupants were formally termed 'confined women' and we see each of them, with her children, installed in one of the many chambers. They came together, however, for communal work, entertainments, feasts and celebrations, and there are reliefs that show them dancing and singing to instrumental accompaniment. The harems were elaborately organised with a staff of servants, scribes, guards and overseers whose official titles, such as 'watchman of the royal concubines', were quite explicit.

The New Kingdom site of Medinet el-Gurob has recently been shown by Barry Kemp to include a complete harem-palace, rivalling in size the nearby, but separate, royal palace. In addition to the king's principal and a number of secondary wives it housed female servants, women engaged in domestic crafts like weaving, and nurses to look after the royal children.

60 The ladies of the harem might number anything up to several hundred. The Mitannian princess Tadukhepa, a secondary wife of Amenophis III, brought with her 317 servants chosen for their beauty. Considering the number of wives and other females in his harem, the attribution of 200 children, 111 of them sons, to Ramesses II may be no overstatement.

Harem life must certainly have been a delight for the pharaoh as he dropped in on his favourites or amused himself in the presence of many ladies together. One of the reliefs in the temple at Medinet Habu shows a nude Ramesses III playing draughts with a group of equally unencumbered girls, wearing only wigs, sandals and necklaces. Relations between the various members of the harem, however, cannot always have been amicable. The favour that one of them enjoyed with the king at a particular time often aroused the others' envy. In their efforts to secure the succession for their own first-born, women were ready to intrigue even against the king himself.

59 Amun placing the crown on the head of Hatshepsut, one of the few reigning queens, who kneels before him dressed as a pharaoh. Relief on the top of a fallen obelisk erected by the Queen in the temple of Karnak. 18th dynasty

60 A concubine from the harem of King Amenhotep III, representing the ideal of a New Kingdom consort. Ivory. 18th dynasty. *New York, Brooklyn Museum*

It was probably a plot hatched by Teye, one of his secondary wives, that cost Ramesses III his life. Ammenemes I was murdered in similar circumstances.

What are we to make of the guards, serving-men and other male harem staff? There is nothing in the Amarna reliefs to suggest that they were eunuchs. We know that the Egyptians castrated animals but of human castration, even of slaves, there is no evidence anywhere. The definitely eunuchoid features that gradually appeared in King Akhenaten were most likely due to disease of the hypophysis or mesencephalon. The absence of sexual organs in some mummies, such as those of Tuthmosis III and Merenptah, where they are replaced by cloth-and-resin artefacts, arose from embalming difficulties; any putrefying or otherwise damaged part had to be restored so that the mummy was complete.

To return to the common folk as they finished their preparations for a wedding: the long-awaited day arrived; an excuse for great celebration and feasting. Not only the happy couple and their families, but all their relatives and hosts of acquaintances took part. Unlike our weddings, these events were neither specifically religious ceremonies nor legal acts involving the state. They were simply social occasions on which a man and a woman committed themselves to a common existence whose special purpose was to produce and bring up children, and so ensure the family's lasting prosperity and the parents' continued life in the world to come. The wedding probably comprised a motley series of traditional activities, with feasting, story-telling, song, music and dance. No detailed accounts survive, so we have only fictional passages to go by. The Tale of Prince Setna, for example, mentions a royal sibling-marriage. The royal father arranges for the bride and her rich dowry to be brought to the bridegroom's house by night, after a splendid banquet. The jollity of these occasion comes out also in the account of Ramesses II s wedding with his Hittite princess.

The kinship terms in old Egyptian themselves show that the basic unit of society was the nuclear family. They only define relationships of the closest sort – father, mother, brother, sister, son and daughter. There were no names for more distant relationships and these had to be paraphrased.

The merrymaking over, the bride would move to her husband's house – hence the description of a wedding as 'entering the spouse's house' or 'founding a house'. Only in rare cases did the man transfer to the home of his new wife, which she would normally be sharing with her parents, and the sources imply that such 'matrilocal' marriages did not always work out well. One New Kingdom ostracon sherd has a man complaining about his wife and her family, who had twice shut him out of the house. A New Kingdom papyrus tells of a man obliged to share a home with his father-in-law. One way or another, however, the wife once married became 'mistress of the house' and so achieved her supreme and specific role of decision-making on domestic issues and on the children's upbringing.

It is in the Third Intermediate Period that we meet the earliest examples of a special class of written marriage contract recording the material rights of wife and children. Such documents could be effected either on the wedding day or at any time later, even after the children had been born; some contracts in fact give the children's names. Originally such contracts were between husband and father-in-law, the latter acting as a kind of proxy for his daughter. Only later do we find contracts drawn up between the partners themselves. There seems to be reference to one 'maintenance document' already in a text of the 6th dynasty. True contracts are first mentioned in the New Kingdom; actual texts, written in hieratic or demotic cursive script, have survived from the 22nd dynasty up into the Graeco-Roman Period. Erich Lüddeckens examined about a hundred of them, all relating to the middle classes. They usually start with the date and the names of the man and woman and go on to state the parents' names, the man's profession and, if he is not a native, his ethnic origin – Nubian, Libyan, Greek, Blemmyan or whatever. The following sections record the fact of marriage and confirm that the man has given his partner the so-called 'wife-gift'. This could have developed from the original purchase price of a wife. It consisted of a small collection of articles – jewelry, money or corn – valued in fractions of a silver *deben* corresponding altogether to about the cost of a slave. In the course of time the gift in kind fell into abeyance, remaining as a paper credit payable to the wife in the event of divorce.

A later form of contract, known from about 517 BC, records that the woman brought her dowry to the man when she married him, a 'payment in consideration of becoming his wife', of which the husband had usufruct while the marriage existed. This was a sum either in cash or payment in kind amounting to three silver *deben*. It is not quite certain whether the wife actually paid it out.

Some contracts contained a 'dotation' or alimony clause stating the sum to be provided by the wife (or by her father) to compensate the man for his future outlay, and specifying her annual food and clothing. This obligation continued to rest on the husband even during the wife's temporary absence, or after a divorce where she was not demonstrably at fault. The man also had to commit all his past and future earnings to the support of his wife, and in case of divorce he had to pay her a share of them, usually one-third.

A contract of this type goes on to list the beneficiaries of the man's estate, who might be the children, or the eldest son, or the children indirectly through their mother in the case of her being sole legatee. Otherwise the widow was normally entitled to one-third of the estate and the children or other relatives in childless marriages, to the remaining two-thirds. The widow could inherit everything if her husband adopted her as his daughter.

There were normally provisions covering property that the wife herself had brought into the marriage, usually domestic equipment and sometimes a donkey, the chief means of transport in those days. These items, the value of which was quoted individually and *in toto*, remained in the wife's possession for ever. The same applied to the husband's exclusive property.

Such a contract concluded with an oath by which the man confirmed his obligations towards his wife, and his signature was sometimes appended here. The name of the scribe attesting the contract is given, and on the back are the names of the witnesses – anything from three to 36 in number – who also sometimes added their signatures. Significantly, no woman's signature ever appears among them. The contract was usually lodged with a third party (often the woman's father) or in a neighbouring temple.

Marriages, even those secured by contract, were not always idyllic and breaches of the marriage-bonds are frequently recorded. Yet on the whole Egyptian husbands treated their wives decently. They were told to do so in the Instruction of Ptahhotep:

> Love your wife ardently,
> feed her and clothe her,
> fragrant unguents are good for her body.
> Make her happy all her days;
> for she is like the field that brings benefit
> to its owner.

In the Instruction of Ani, again, we read how important it is to trust one's wife:

> Do not check on your wife in her house
> when you know that she is competent.
> Do not say 'Where is this thing? Fetch it!'
> when she has already put it in the right place.

Portrayals of married couples in statuary, paintings and reliefs in the tombs of highly-placed men and royal craftsmen alike radiate unmistakably the tender relations between partners united in the expectation of earthly bliss. They are usually shown standing or sitting side by side, holding hands. Often the wife has an arm thrown round the neck or shoulder of her husband, less frequently vice versa. Sometimes the wife stands meekly behind her husband or is drawn on a smaller scale, the artist intending to show not the woman's innate inferiority but the particular importance of her husband; in other cases they are of equal stature.

In the New Kingdom even the loving relationships of kings and queens, hitherto concealed behind the walls of the royal harem, are publicly advertised in word and picture. Amenophis III, for example, had memorial scarabs made to record for posterity his marriage to Teye. Since she was not of royal blood it must indeed have been a love-match, and the relationship remained firm despite the King's having a particularly large harem and choosing his own daughters as his concubines. This is borne out by the fact that when the King died, Queen Teye had a wooden tablet made showing the couple locked in embrace and inscribed with a dedication to her 'beloved

61 An intimate scene from the life of King Akhenaten's family, showing the three youngest children with their parents. On the Queen's lap sits the youngest daughter Ankhsenpaaten; her older sister, standing on her mother's knees, is trying to attract her attention by touching her chin. The children's excessively long heads have been shaved. The oldest daughter Beketaten, with the side-lock of youth, is being given an ear-ring by her father. This sunk relief, representing the royal family as 'Holy Family', was found in a private chapel of a house in Amarna. Painted limestone. 18th dynasty.
Cairo, Egyptian Museum

brother'. There are many fine Amarna reliefs, too, that depict the tender feelings
between Akhenaten and Nefertiti, with the King holding his wife on his lap or
publicly kissing her as they drive past in a two-wheeled chariot. Mutual affection
56 radiates again from the depictions of Tutankhamun with Ankhesenamun.

There is another touching tribute to a happy marriage in the Leiden Papyrus
No 371. A letter addressed by a widower to the spirit of his late wife contains the
words: 'I did not sin against you or give your heart cause for anger . . . I did not allow
that you should suffer through anything I did as your husband. You never found me
betraying you like some peasant when I entered another house . . .'

Pictures of parents surrounded by the tiny figures of their children make an even
more delightful impression. There is for example a stele showing Ankherkau with his
wife Wabet and their sons and daughters in their tomb at Qurnet Murai, the girls
holding quails and one of them having a lock of hair straightened by her father. Or
61 there is the famous Amarna relief showing the royal pair sitting facing one another:
Akhenaten is lifting up one of their little daughters to give her a kiss; another is on
Nefertiti's lap, pointing at her father, while the third, held on her mother's arm, plays
with the tail of a cobra-shaped *uraeus* in the royal crown.

All in all, the Egyptian women could not complain of their lot in comparison with
the lives of women in other countries, or indeed those of women in many an Eastern
country now. In day-to-day matters she was in numerous respects an equal partner,
subject of course to her social background. We have plenty of evidence of this from
prehistoric times onwards. The wife was always entitled to her own grave and
funerary gifts, statues, steles, false-doors, etc. Even in the range of offerings laid in her
grave a woman's burial was no different from a man's of the same background.
However, it was quite common for the more affluent women to be buried with their
husbands. Certain names were given to women and men alike.

Written records of the Late and Ptolemaic Periods testify that a woman also

Above **62** A man and his wife share the
tasks of ploughing the field, sowing the
seed and harvesting the crop. From the
Book of the Dead of Lady Cheritwebeshet.
Painting on papyrus. 21st dynasty.
Cairo, Egyptian Museum

63 Many women – especially girls – had
to work as humble servants. This one is
carrying on her head a basket of loaves
and pieces of meat. Painted wood.
Middle Kingdom. *London, British Museum*

enjoyed her own legal personality. She could dispose freely of her own property, which even after marriage remained separate both from the husband's and from their joint possessions. One odd case is known where a wife lent her husband a sum of money (at an extortionate 30 per cent interest) for three years, and he had to secure the loan with his entire estate.

A woman could freely enter into all kinds of contracts, not only with her husband but with wet-nurses, gardeners, merchants and so on; she could even contract herself into slavery to a creditor or a temple authority. In this case the purchaser incurred the duty to protect the slave and ensure her well-being, nourishment and all daily needs. On the other hand a woman, like a man, was entitled to liberate any of her slaves and often did this by adopting them.

A woman could also take a case to court. One example is summarised on a limestone ostracon from Deir el-Medina: Today's date. Citizen Eset sues the workers Khaemipet, Khaemwaset and Amennakhte, claiming: 'I am entitled to the work-rooms of my husband Panakht.' After consultation the judge gave his verdict: 'The woman is in the right. Let her husband's workrooms be given to her.'

Steffen Wenig, author of a major study of women in ancient Egypt, even concluded that women enjoyed equal pay for equal work, and Shafiq Allam has argued that they had complete freedom of movement. An inscription in the temple of Ramesses III at Medinet Habu declares that a woman could go 'wherever she wishes, unhindered, with her clothes piled on her head'. There was of course a propaganda point here – to argue that the King's peace policy had achieved safety of movement for all citizens.

The household was the woman's domain and her chief mission was, as has been said, to bring up children. At home she ground corn, baked bread, brewed beer, cooked food, spun flax and wove cloth from it. Farmers' wives also helped them in the field, as we see for example on wall paintings in the tomb of Sennedjem at Deir el-Medina, or winnowed and sieved corn at harvest-time as shown in the vault of Nakht at Sheikh Abd el-Qurna. Women were employed in the workshops of dignitaries or in temples as weavers, washerwomen, bakers or millers. Some became professional singers, musicians, dancers or beauticians; some used to tie bouquets and wreaths; many poor women and slaves served in wealthy households. And there were of course prostitutes.

Women were almost never admitted to public office, though documents do mention women as overseers of an eating-place, a wigmaker's shop, a studio selling ointments and cosmetics, a centre for singers, a spinning workshop, a royal harem and so on. We hear of women doctors and of their female overseer. In later periods the wives of senior dignitaries and noblemen liked to append strings of official functions to their names, but these were often only honorary titles.

Queens, of course, as 'wives of god', that is of the pharaoh whom they accompanied in public, occupied a special position. In reality, however, even they carried out no official duties. Only in rare cases does it appear that an ailing or ageing king appointed his queen co-regent and entrusted certain governmental tasks to her. This may have been the case with Nefertiti, perhaps also with Teye; both conducted their own correspondence with foreign rulers.

Throughout the long history of Egypt we know of several reigning queens with the full authority of a 'living god'. The best known was Hatshepsut in the 18th dynasty, who originally ruled as regent on behalf of the young Tuthmosis III but after two years seized the throne and ruled on her own for another 20. Another was Twosre, wife of Sethos II, who ruled for two years alone after the death of her little son. The third was the famous last Ptolemaic monarch, Cleopatra VII. The situation was thought so unusual in the 18th dynasty that Hapshepsut called herself a king and had herself portrayed with that typical male royal attribute, a stylised beard under 10 the chin.

From the New Kingdom onwards, or perhaps earlier, women found employment in the temples either as junior (rarely senior) permanent priests or, probably more often, as honorary temple servants for a limited period. This was most common in the shrines of goddesses such as Hathor, Isis, Neith, Satis, Sakhmet and Bastet, or in

funerary temples where they prepared sacrifices for the dead. Contrary to what is sometimes imagined they were neither virgins living in chastity like nuns, nor temple prostitutes nominally serving some male deity, but married women of all classes with wives of dignitaries, officials and priests predominating. They received payment in kind for their services.

Even more women, perhaps, served in the temples as singers, musicians and dancers. From the most gifted of these were selected the professional simulators of the goddesses Isis and Nephthys in the oldest mystery plays celebrating the death and resurrection of Osiris.

Among the senior temple offices, women could become overseers of the chorus, orchestra or dancers, or of the temple treasures. From the New Kingdom onwards a woman could hold the important post in the temple of Amun at Karnak of 'wife of god', usually filled by the queen or one of the princesses. Amun's earthly harem was made up of ladies from the aristocracy.

All married women in Egypt had of course one role *par excellence* – to provide their husbands with a male heir.

The birth of a son was an occasion for wild excitement, for this meant, above all, the arrival of someone who in due course would be the chief actor in the funeral ceremonies and so secure immortality for his own father and mother. Women who failed to provide a son were in an unenviable situation. The most common remedy was to procure a concubine for their husband, usually a slave-girl, and to adopt the son (or all the children) that she bore.

Adoption is first documented from the reign of Tuthmose III (18th dynasty), but was probably an ancient custom. The earliest known case is recorded on an ostracon bearing a letter that recommends a certain childless man to adopt an orphan. One record of an adoption tells us that the woman Nanefer, together with her husband, brought a slave who bore him a son and two daughters. After her husband died Nanefer took charge of the children, adopted them and brought them up. Her own young brother actually married the elder girl, and Nanefer also adopted this brother so that he could inherit an equal share in her own and her husband's estate.

Finally to the question of conjugal fidelity. Every wife owed exclusive loyalty to her husband; she had to obey his every wish and command. The husband, however, either to secure an heir or just because he so fancied, was entitled to take a secondary wife. Being head of a patriarchal family he also made demands on the female servants – usually slaves – in the household, who had to render him services of any kind. (It was possible, but not mandatory, to adopt any ensuing offspring.) A man who did not take advantage of this opportunity could proudly declare at the Judgement of the Dead: 'I did not covet my servant-girl.'

In contrast to these male prerogatives there were strict customs that protected the family from outside interference. The most serious offence was deemed to be adultery, whether by the man taking a fancy to his neighbour's wife, or by the woman who was seduced, regardless of whether the man was married or not. Culprits were publicly flogged, or branded forever by having their ears or nose cut off. Banishment to Nubia or to the stone quarries was a more merciful alternative to the expected death penalty.

According to the Middle Kingdom Westcar Papyrus a priest and magician whose wife had been unfaithful arranged for the seducer to be caught by a crocodile and brought before the king, who ordered the seducer to be thrown to the said crocodile, and for the woman to be burnt and her ashes scattered into the Nile.

The story of the brothers Anubis and Bata, preserved in the New Kingdom d'Orbiney Papyrus, echoes that of the biblical wife of Potiphar seducing young Joseph. The wife of Anubis had designs on her brother-in-law Bata. When Anubis finally learned that it was she who had instigated the treachery, he stopped pursuing his brother, but had his own wife slain and her body thrown to the dogs.

It is not surprising then that the various Instructions, such as those of Ankhshoshenq, warn sternly against infidelity. But references in non-literary sources as well as on papyri and sherds show that it nevertheless occurred. On the

other hand we have records of oaths sworn in temples by wives whose honour had been impugned, protesting that they had never committed adultery since the day they married. Men were not measured by the same yardstick; not a single such affidavit by a husband has ever turned up.

Infidelity of the wife (never of the husband) was also one of the most frequent grounds for divorce. Other possible grounds were the wife's barrenness, any defect in either partner causing repugnance in the other, or the decision of either to marry a third party. Divorce, like marriage, was not a legal act involving the secular or the religious authorities. It was a private transaction by which one partner released the other from the marriage bonds. In most cases it was the man who released the woman; not till the period of Persian rule do we find women separating from their husbands at their own wish, though it had been possible even in earlier times for a wife's father or brother to take her away from a husband found guilty of a heinous crime such as tomb-robbing.

A divorced wife had to vacate the conjugal home, though sometimes the man might let her stay on for a limited time. A woman then often became an unwelcome burden for her own parents. After divorce, both partners were free to remarry.

Starting in the 6th century BC we find divorce agreements drawn up by the ex-husband and providing for a financial settlement. If divorce had taken place at the husband's wish, the wife was entitled to take away everything she had contributed to the household. The man for his part had now to pay the stipulated wife-gift, to return the sum she had produced for 'becoming his wife', and to hand over one third of their jointly acquired possessions as well as anything that had originally been earmarked as inheritance for the children and was therefore legally theirs. He had also to pay a 'divorce forfeit' sometimes amounting to one third of his own property, automatically doubled if he intended to remarry. For a man, then, divorce involved a substantial loss of resources, which must have dissuaded many from a rash decision. But a woman divorced without fault on her side was fully safeguarded in material terms.

However, if a woman was unfaithful her husband could dismiss her with no financial compensation. A woman divorced at her own request received back only her own private belongings and her share of the joint property, but no divorce forfeit in this case. Another consequence was that her name and portrait were deleted from the tomb which the couple had been preparing throughout their life together. One unpleasant aspect for the man was the court's fondness for interrogating a rejected wife, whose testimony was unlikely to redound to the husband's credit. So there were many disincentives to casual divorce that must often have rescued marriages going through bad patches.

CHAPTER SIX

Homes and Communities

67 The house of an important scribe, built on a platform for protection against damp and above the level of inundation. From the Book of the Dead of Nakhte. Painted papyrus. Late 18th dynasty. *London, British Museum*

THE WEDDING gaiety has now subsided; the new couple have entered the house which the bridegroom will normally have built beforehand with the help of his relatives and friends. From now on, this is where their life together will unfold. The standard they achieve will depend on the husband's job and his standing in the highly stratified society of ancient Egypt. So will the size of the house, the number of its rooms and their contents. What can archaeology tell us about all this?

We know in fact much less about the Egyptians' homes in this world than about their 'eternal homes' – the tombs which were part of the extensive cities of the dead on the desert fringes. Constructed as these were of long-lasting material in accordance with the Egyptians' belief that they constituted everlasting residences, the tombs are mostly well-preserved and accessible to modern archaeologists. Lying outside the areas now settled or cultivated, concealed under a layer of desert sand, many of them have proved despite the forays of recent or earlier tomb-thieves to contain objects so precious that they are the pride of the world's great museums.

How different is the case with the remains of ancient Egyptian towns and villages! These lie in the alluvial basin of the Nile, often built over in modern times and always covered by deep layers of sediment. Having wrestled with the difficulties of buying a plot and the immense labour of removing the topsoil, the archaeologist digs his way down only to discover that the ancient buildings he is seeking were made of sun-dried bricks, wood and pressed clay, and that most of their contents were of organic material. The high humidity of the soil will have destroyed many of these, leaving only fragments of trivial articles of daily use that will hardly find a place of honour in any museum show-case.

It is no surprise, then, that few expeditions have investigated residential settlements, and when they did these were largely outside the Nile Valley or present areas of population. Petrie examined the 12th-dynasty colony of Sesostris I's pyramid-builders at Illahun in the Faiyum in 1890–91, and dug up the nearby New Kingdom town of Merwer (now Medinet el-Gurob) in 1888–90 and 1903–04. Hearst's American expedition excavated the little 18th-dynasty township near Deir el-Ballas in 1900. The new town of Akhetaten, built by the 18th-dynasty reformer-king Akhenaten on the right bank of the Nile near modern Amarna was partially explored by Borchardt before the First World War and by the Egypt Exploration Society between 1921 and 1937, and again since 1977; a Michigan University team looked at the Roman Period town of Karanis in the desert above the northern rim of the Faiyum Oasis in 1923–31; during the 1920s and 1930s the French Institute of Oriental Archaeology in Cairo sent Bernard Bruyère to examine the village and cemetery of the royal tomb-builders at Deir el-Medina (18th to 20th dynasties);

between 1971 and 1975 an Austrian team explored the remains of an early dynastic settlement near the Giza pyramids. Anything else we know has resulted from chance findings or brief probes.

The present state of knowledge allows us to distinguish three basic types of development in ancient Egyptian settlements: planned, unplanned (but nuclear and on a restricted, perhaps walled, site), and unrestricted, non-nuclear, where there were no limits to building.

The second and most common kind arose over long periods in random fashion according to the immediate needs of the inhabitants. They expanded in the course of generations and were many times rebuilt, so that the ground-plan becomes more and more confused with a labyrinth of narrow, oddly twisting alleys, passages, squares and courts, with little open space remaining and only occasional trees. At the densest population points, squeezed inside the walls, space soon ran out and houses grew upwards to two or, less commonly, three storeys. Only temples and palaces, surrounded by high ramparts, presented oases of tranquillity with their ample grounds and regular architectural design.

Excavations have not yet given us a reliable picture of how the Old Kingdom capital of Memphis was laid out. It is thought to have been a conglomeration of residential areas, mostly walled to protect them from attack, of temple areas likewise encircled,

and of royal fortress-like palaces covering a total area of 13 by 6.5km. There were gardens and fields in among the populated quarters and the town probably never developed into a close-knit entity.

All we know about Itjtawy, the Middle Kingdom capital, comes from textual indications that it lay somewhere near the edge of the Faiyum Oasis; the exact site has never been identified.

A reconstruction of Thebes, capital of the New Kingdom, has been attempted by the Egyptian scholar A. Badawy. All he had to go on, however, was a few pictures of houses on the tomb walls of dignitaries of West Thebes, together with his own knowledge of town and village planning in modern Egypt. He envisages Thebes as a compact, walled township, its streets lined with close-packed houses often several storeys high.

Clay models of the Middle Kingdom 'soul houses' and pictures in Theban burial chambers, particularly that of Djehutinefer (18th dynasty), give us a rough idea of the residences of magnates in the major cities. The ground floor, and basement where it existed, would contain craftsmen's workshops, places for food production (bakeries, maltings and kitchens), cattle stalls and storerooms. On the first floor the owner would have a number of rooms for receiving guests and conducting official business. Not till we reached the second floor would we find his private apartments – dining room, bedroom, perhaps a bathroom and the separate women's quarters, the harem. The floors were connected by a stairway extending up to the flat roof. Here there was space for granaries, fuel stores and even a light shelter where it would be pleasant to sit or sleep in the cool northerly breeze. Sometimes there was modest accommodation for servants here as well.

In the planned type of settlement such as we find in Illahun, Akhetaten or Deir el-Medina, not only is the pattern more regular, often gridiron-style, but the social affiliation of the residents is often more obvious. Class contrasts are most conspicuous at Illahun (the ancient Hetepsenusret), set up at the edge of the Faiyum Oasis by Sesostris II. It forms a rectangle of 400 by 350m, marked off by a brick wall and subdivided by a further wall into a smaller western portion 150m wide, and a larger one to the east, 250m wide. Over 200 dwellings were crammed into the western part, few of them with a floorspace of more than 100m². They consisted of three to seven rooms, plus terraces. The largest room was for receiving guests, a few more were for the family to live in, and the remainder served for storage. These were houses used by the labourers and craftsmen engaged in building the nearby pyramids.

The eastern section of Illahun contained only a dozen or so houses, each covering an area of some 1000m², in the largest case 2400m². The nucleus of each one was a big square court with shady porticos leading to one or more reception rooms whose ceilings were supported by two to four wooden pillars on stone pedestals. Other exits led to a kitchen, a row of storerooms and the women's and servants' quarters. At the end of a long corridor one came to the owner's private rooms and those reserved for his guests. There might be 60 or 70 rooms in all. The structures adjoining the bedrooms were presumably bathrooms and lavatories. These houses were designed for senior officials and courtiers.

The city of Akhetaten stretched for almost 9km along the Nile. Its central part had a geometrical ground plan and was divided lengthwise by three broad highways, with a series of narrower roads at right angles to them. Here, too, there was a certain number of great mansions and a far larger number of little houses, reflecting the social differences among the inhabitants. They were not strictly segregated, however.

Facing each other in the middle of the town were King Akhenaten's residence and the government palace, joined by a bridge spanning the busiest street. The great temple of Aten had two-thirds the area of the largest temple in Egypt, that of Amun at Karnak which covered 31 hectares. Another, smaller temple of Aten stood to the south of the residence. And the King had yet another huge, high-walled private palace on the Nile bank near the northern rim of the city, where he spent his leisure time with his family.

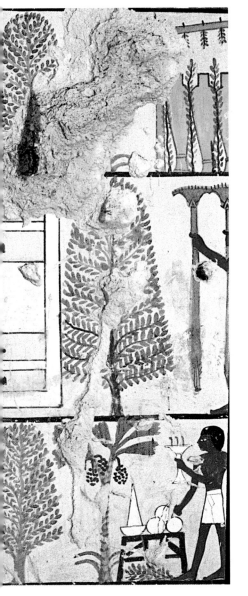

68 A Theban villa shown in ground-plan. In the garden there are different kinds of trees and a pool. Painting on limestone, tomb of Minnakht. Sheikh Abd el-Qurna, West Thebes. 18th dynasty

70

Next in size after these buildings came the 'Amarna villa' type, a model of which, reconstructed by the American Egyptologist Seton Lloyd in 1933 on the basis of archaeological findings, has often been reproduced in popular works as a 'typical' Egyptian house. It was in fact an exclusive type of residence for dignitaries of the highest rank.

The visitor came through an entrance in the massive peripheral wall into an extensive garden shaded by date and doum palms, pomegranate trees, sycomore figs, acacias and other trees and shrubs concealing pergolas with vines trained over them. Near the centre was a rectangular pool full of fish, its surface blossoming with lotus and other water plants. (Judging from tomb paintings the houses of Theban dignitaries may have boasted similar delights.) Round the edge of the garden were service buildings containing kitchens, artisans' workshops, food processing areas, stables, cattlesheds, barns and granaries. Every such lordly mansion was a self-sufficient economic unit.

At the far end of the garden, raised on a plinth, stood the residence proper, entered up a flight of steps and faced with a commanding colonnade. One passed through a vestibule into the reception hall, a large north-facing area covered with a flat roof on four to 12 wooden pillars over three metres high. The walls were clad in white stucco with animal, floral and geometric decorations. Small windows placed high in the

69 Foundations of houses in the village of Deir el-Medina, established during the 18th dynasty for the community of workers who excavated and decorated the tombs in the Valley of the Kings and the Valley of the Queens.
18th–20th dynasties

walls allowed air to circulate but let in no direct rays from the scorching sun. There was a sunken fireplace in the middle of the stone-tiled floor and guests could sit on earthenware benches or on floor mats.

The inner areas of the building, where the owner actually lived, ran round a taller square hall whose roof was commonly held up by four 4-metre columns, so that light and air came in from above. Against the far wall stood a seat for the master and mistress of the house; near it was a water-tank for washing, and the family altar. Here too the walls were decorated with frescos. This room in turn gave on to a number of smaller ones, the most distinct of which was the bedroom, with a recess for the bed in the thicker wall on the south side which insulated the sleeper from all outside noise and protected him or her from the summer heat, while in winter the heat was conserved. Adjoining the bedroom were a cloakroom, bathroom and lavatory. One particular room, previously thought to be a 'woman's room', has more recently been explained by P. T. Crocker as an office for the master of the house. Stairs led up to a flat roof, on which was a loggia for sitting or sleeping in during the hottest part of the year. Each of these 'Amarna villas' comprised between 20 and 28 rooms.

Houses of all sizes and designs can be found at Amarna, however. A computer analysis of the dimensions and features of 500 Amarna houses, seen as a reflection of the country's social structure, was done by Christian Tietze not long ago. He found that between 7 and 9 per cent of the population belonged to the élite – the highest-ranking officials, high priests and generals who worked closely with the pharaoh and controlled the political, religious and military affairs of state; these owned the largest luxury villas with numerous rooms.

Middle-ranking administrators, priests, master craftsmen and officers, who played a part in organising society and made up about a third of the citizenry, enjoyed housing standards up to, or rather better than, their modern counterparts in terms of floor space, density of occupation and furnishing. The rest of the people – physical labourers and artisans constituting over half the population – lived in the smallest and worst-built houses, sparsely furnished and situated in the most crowded sites.

More light on the housing conditions of the poor has recently been shed by Barry Kemp's further investigation of the walled village south of Akhetaten, constructed inside a 65 metre square. Five narrow streets running north-south gave access to six rows of dried brick houses of almost identical size, most of them packed close together in twelves; 38 of these have been examined. Detailed investigation of 'Gate Street No. 8' shows it to comprise four ground-floor rooms with an entrance in the western wall. The front room was divided by a low wall into two parts, the larger part to the north serving as a hall while the smaller section against the south wall was a working

70 Clay model of a house with an arched doorway and a staircase leading to the roof, which has a water outlet and a vent to catch a cool breeze. In hot weather the inhabitants spent most of their time on the roof. Funerary models like these were called 'soul houses'. Middle Kingdom. *London, British Museum*

area with an emplacement to support a stone quern. In the central room, the living area proper, there was a clay dais running round two sides which bore the marks of the matting that originally covered it. A level structure projecting inwards from the dais still contained the bottoms of two pottery hearths with the remains of ashes in them. Heating was indeed essential during winter nights with the temperature hovering around freezing point. Circular depressions in the mud floor were used for storage vessels. From this area there were two separate entrances to the two interconnecting rear rooms, of which the smaller (on the south side) had a low clay dais along one wall that probably used to have a bed on it. The larger rear room to the north was mainly taken up by a brick staircase wedged between the internal wall and a pillar, both of clay. The upper flight of the stairs turned east and at this point was supported by a layer of closely spaced wooden poles, leaving a kind of cupboard below.

The rubble found in the central and rear rooms contained remains of building material from which the nature of the original roof could be reconstructed. It was made of untrimmed acacia-wood beams laid across the building at 70cm intervals, with poles (apparently of tamarisk) placed over them close together, longitudinally. These in turn supported a layer of clay, reeds and loose grass. The debris in the central room also included two limestone slabs and an almost completely preserved wooden window frame and shutter that had probably been built into the upper part of the eastern wall of this room. The ceiling was some 1.8 to 2 metres from the ground, but was omitted from both halves of the front area intended for animals and as the master's working area. The stairway, lightly roofed over its southern part, led to a small area over the bedroom; this was left open and, judging from fragments of a standard cylindrical bread-oven, ashes and blackened sherds, must have been the kitchen. It led in turn to a room over the central ground-floor area, covered with a light roof of grey mud, remains of which bear the impressions of roofing-reeds. This furthest room offered the greatest privacy and was very likely reserved for women.

The poor people in Amarna were worse off than the inhabitants of the village at Deir el-Medina where the builders and decorators of the royal tombs lived. It is of interest that though this village survived for four-and-a-half centuries the ground level never rose as a result of demolition and levelling. Whenever an area was rebuilt, the original floors and foundations were used again, suggesting that housing regulations were in force. Another distinctive feature here is that some of the houses were grouped in clusters round a common courtyard. Barry Kemp suggested that these were used by second generation couples living apart from the founding couple

71 A team of workmen making mud bricks. Two men fetch water from the pool in big jars; one man is standing in a mixture of mud and chaff while another is filling a wooden frame with it, adding to the rows of drying bricks. Painting on limestone in the tomb of Rekhmire. Sheikh Abd el-Qurna, West Thebes. 18th dynasty

72 Stone-masons at work and a cross-section of a house. Relief fragment. Tell el-Amarna. 18th dynasty. *El-Minya Museum*

but constituting a single extended family. Such islands constituted five blocks with narrow streets running parallel between them.

The houses in this village each covered an area of 5 to 6m by 16m, with a short side facing the street. The walls were of sun-dried bricks, sometimes with a footing of quarried stone. The flat palm-stem roof was convenient for storage and for sleeping in the hot summers. One entered through a stone-framed wooden door opening inwards. In the first room, where guests were received, there was a little sanctuary in the corner with steps up to it. The second, and largest, room had a ceiling supported by one or two wooden pillars and a built-in bench of dried brick. Of the two remaining rooms one was plainly the kitchen, with its clay oven, water-vessel, corn-mill, mortar and array of pots and baskets. The other was for sleeping, either on a wooden bed or on a clay bunk covered with matting. Underground cellars provided storage room, and there were sunken water-containers near the entrance.

The third kind of development, that of a scattered village community of houses in random groups, can be seen at Deir el-Ballas, where it stretched for nearly two kilometres between the fertile Nile valley and the desert. No doubt there were others.

Egyptian housebuilding techniques developed over a period of several millennia. As early as neolithic times people had been making huts out of wooden poles and rush mats daubed with mud. Sun-dried bricks have been found in predynastic remains and their use was greatly extended in the 1st and 2nd dynasties for building large tombs, temples, royal palaces and other major structures. Stone came gradually into use, but at first only rarely, for such features as floors, doorsills, lintels and wall-facings. To increase the cohesion of a long run of wall, builders adopted projecting pillars alternating with concave recesses on the Mesopotamian model. The corners of buildings would be protected against damage and flaking with a cladding of timber, matting and other material. Door-frames and roof-beams were also made of wood, or there might be a barrel-vault roof constructed with dried bricks, known since the Old Kingdom.

A revolution in building techniques was sparked in the 3rd dynasty by Djoser's brilliant architect Imhotep when he used the most durable material of all, stone, for 261 the whole complex of the royal pyramid at Saqqara. From this time on architecture evolved along two main lines. One was the monumental building in stone, largely at royal behest, of palaces, temples and the pharaohs' mausolea, at first pyramids and later rock-tombs. Stone became the symbol of perpetuity and guaranteed the tomb owner his 'everlasting home'. Where clay bricks were used in any of these buildings it was probably for reasons of economy. Quarried stone bonded with a loamy clay was also used in areas outside the Nile Valley where there was a shortage of brick-clay.

Alongside this activity, the traditional technique based on sun-dried clay bricks survived in the construction of homes. There was always enough high-quality clay in the muddy flood-plains of the Nile.

71   The manufacture of dried bricks is vividly depicted in paintings in the 18th-dynasty tomb of Rekhmire. Men in short aprons are shown fetching jugs of water from a pool to moisten the piles of clay. Next we see them mixing in chopped straw and carrying the material over to the area where it is pressed into oblong forms before being laid out to dry in the sun. Others are carrying the finished bricks on weigh-beams to the nearby construction site of the granaries of Amun, urged on by overseers with sticks. The accompanying captions are exhortations to work carefully and follow the foreman's instructions.

The mason's task may seem simple, but under the scorching sun it must have been exhausting work. Khety speaks of it in the Instruction addressed to his son Pepi: 'I must also talk to you about the bricklayers. Their kidneys suffer because they are out in the sun, laying bricks with no clothes on. Instead of a (proper) kilt they just have a string for a loincloth. Their hands are torn to ribbons by the cruel work; they have to knead all sorts of muck. They eat bread with their fingers, even though they only get a chance to wash them once a day.'

The secret of making clay bricks of a quality to last thousands of years depends on soaking the clay-and-straw mix in water for several days. This partly decomposes the straw, releasing a slime that penetrates the clay, increases its viscosity and ensures its coherence as it dries. Ancient Egyptian bricks came in various sizes, but were generally smaller than the bricks of our times.

Dried bricks were healthier as a house-building material than stone. Being poor conductors of heat they provided better protection from the burning sun, and retained warmth in the house during the cold winter nights. Their only defect, susceptibility to damp, was no bar to their use in a country where rain came seldom and briefly, or not at all.

The bricks were bonded with a mortar made of clay mixed with sand, straw and chaff. Walls were built straight up, slightly tapered and meeting approximately at right angles. The facing plaster, made of a mixture similar to the mortar, was slapped on with a wooden trowel strikingly similar to those in use today. The surface was then smoothed over with a wooden float that had rounded corners and a loop handle. A plumb-line was used to check vertical faces and a wooden try-square with a plumb-line attached for getting horizontal surfaces true. Straight lines were laid out with a stretched cord, as in surveying.

For some simple structures like granaries and pens for small animals walls were built of pressed mud mixed with straw. At the Giza settlement large sheets of mud-and-chaff have been found which may have been used as dividing walls between rooms.

Houses were almost always whitewashed inside and out, whether the walls had previously been plastered or not. The purpose here was hygienic as well as aesthetic. Some of the remains of wealthier houses at Giza bear traces of coloured bands 5–7cm wide, the brown ones with light veins in imitation of wood grain. Perhaps, then, walls were sometimes faced with wooden sheeting.

For the foundations either stone was used, or again brick. In the Giza settlement large foundation blocks have been discovered, covered with pressed mud. Only the richer citizens had limestone doorsills or lintels of the shape familiar from the Giza mastabas; in other houses wooden beams were used instead.

Floors were most commonly made with pressed clay, or with a layer of brick paving-tiles. In the better houses at Giza remains have been found of jointless flooring like a modern terrace. Odd pieces of fired clay and pottery sherds were added to the basic mud mixture and the surface was then sand-ground to a mirror finish. In upper-class dwellings and in the royal palace the floor was finished with a fine mortar, sometimes painted over with stucco. Presumably mats of vegetable material – reed, papyrus or palm-leaf ribs – were laid over such floors; they would be cool to walk on and any dirt or dust would drop through them and not be kicked up.

Right 73 Handsome wooden headrests were made as early as the Old Kingdom. Gurob. 19th dynasty. *University College London, Petrie Museum*

74 A wooden stool with legs carved in the form of lion's paws. New Kingdom. *London, British Museum*

Little has been revealed in the past by excavation about methods of ceiling and roof construction, so here we must rely on extant models of Middle Kingdom houses. Most were covered in with transverse beams laid close together, usually of split or whole date-palm stems, which are useless to the carpenter with their fibrous structure but have excellent power, resilience, resistance and durability. If more than a certain length were needed the date-palm stems could be supported with palm-stem stanchions. The beams were covered in turn with a layer of palm-fronds, papyrus stems or reed bundles, matting, clay bricks or even pressed clay, and over this came an impervious layer of fine mud in a gentle slope for the rain to run off. One could climb up by steps to this flat roof, which was surrounded by a parapet for safety and as a wind barrier, so that the area could be used for storage as well as for working or resting in the open. Less commonly ancient Egyptians made a barrel-vault ceiling out of dried bricks, using wooden supports. Such vaulting is known to have been used also in mastabas and in a few Old Kingdom temples.

Window openings were small, either low and wide, or narrow and upright, in the upper part of the wall. They only let in the necessary modicum of light, but they released warm air from the rooms and warded off the direct sunlight which is so unpleasantly intense in Egypt. Sometimes they were covered with cloth to keep out the sand-laden wind.

Egyptians loved the cool northerly breeze and identified it with the breath of Amun. It is caused by colder, moister air from the Mediterranean being sucked in to replace the rising air-masses in the south as they warm up. Front doors and ventilation holes in the walls were accordingly always made to face north if possible. One avoided by contrast the scorching westerly wind from the Sahara plain which prevails particularly in early spring as a result of disturbances caused by storms over the Mediterranean. This wind was called by the Arabs *khamsin* in reference to the period of 50 days during which it was most prone to occur. It brings with it vast quantities of sand and dust which penetrate everywhere. Those who breathe it in are liable after a time to develop pneumoconiosis, a malady akin to stoneworkers' silicosis, although not as dangerous, due to silica particles of the sand deposited in the alveoli of the lungs. Not surprisingly, evidence of this condition has repeatedly turned up in the lungs of mummies even where there could have been no history of quarry work.

House-doors were made of wooden boards and turned on pegs set in the doorsill and lintel. They were locked with bolts secured with several wooden pins.

The focus of domestic activity for the womenfolk was the fireplace, bricked round on three sides and placed either in the roofless kitchen or out in the courtyard. A kind of portable clay cooker was also known, in the form of a pan with an open conical stem, heated from below with charcoal. Almost every home had an oven for baking bread and a saddle quern for grinding flour from grain. The more affluent possessed a cylindrical clay oven with a door at the bottom for removing ash and a wide opening at the top for putting the fuel in. During cooking, a large utensil would cover the opening completely. Dried manure and vegetable waste, brushwood, timber scrap and the like were all used for fuel. The fire was normally started by spinning a dry hardwood fire drill in a hole made in a piece of softer wood. Smoke from the fireplace often spread into the adjoining rooms and would be inhaled by the inhabitants in large quantities. Anthracosis (soot pigment deposits) has been regularly detected in the lungs of mummies.

Evidence of the intolerable smoke-laden air many people had to breathe comes from Barry Kemp's latest excavations in the workers' walled village south of Akhetaten. He found the undersides of roof beams and the impressions left by beams in the roofing mud to be covered with a black deposit of soot. Ceilings were not thought worth whitewashing.

Not much furniture was to be seen in the houses of simple folk. The living room usually featured a built-in earthenware bench or a low wooden or earthenware table for squatting around. Stools or armchairs were a rarity. There were wooden chests of 74 various sizes and numerous wall-niches for holding sundry possessions. The occupants slept on built-in platforms covered with matting or, in richer houses, on

wooden beds with a wicker cover and mattress.

73   When they went to bed they laid their heads on wooden, bone or stone headrests. These were in common use from the Old up to the end of the New Kingdom and consisted of a crescent-shaped support, its radius only slightly bigger than that of the user's head, joined by a thick support (seldom two) to a broad horizontal base, sometime with decorative carving. The head could be moved around sufficiently for comfort. It is not yet known whether this was an ancient African device, or had on the contrary spread from Egypt to other parts of that continent, where it is still widespread.

With so little light coming in through the narrow windows, illumination was needed as soon as dusk fell. Stone or pottery dishes were used for lamps; these were filled with oil, with a wick of twisted cloth or vegetable material floating in the middle, and placed on tall slender stands of stone, wood or earthenware. A unique specimen has survived among the Tutankhamun treasures consisting of two alabaster dishes fitting together, the inner one being painted with a design that was only revealed when the lamp was lit. The Egyptians also used torches made of wooden splints twisted round a fatty core. These were employed in funeral rites for dispelling the evil spirits of darkness, a custom that gave rise to the 'lamp ceremonies', so popular in Ptolemaic times.

Houses were indispensable for protection against the climate – nights were particularly cold in winter, and in summer the midday heat was intense – as well as providing safety and privacy. On the other hand, they were often uncomfortably overcrowded. One Roman Period source mentions a dwelling with 26 inmates. Given the poor ventilation, people had to breathe an atmosphere heavily laden with kitchen effluvia and the sweat of humans and domestic animals. Not surprisingly, the Ebers medical papyrus includes two recipes for 'improving the smell of houses and clothing'. Overcrowding promoted infectious diseases, particularly infantile disorders and tuberculosis.

Another threat to health came from the ubiquitous insects, especially flies, which came in through doors, unglazed windows and ventilation holes. Flitting from rubbish to food they disseminated intestinal infections, notably amoebic dysentery, typhoid and paratyphoid fevers. Flies were so numerous that people ceased to notice

75 Dogs and goats frolick among shrubs on the outskirts of a village. Incised block (*talatat*) from the temple of Aten, reused in the pylons of the great temple of Amun at Karnak. 18th dynasty. *Luxor Museum*

them and children did not even brush them off their skin or even from their eyes, whence the prevalence of trachoma, leading to a serious condition of the conjunctiva and even blindness. No 845 in the Ebers Papyrus recommends the fat of the golden oriole as an insect deterrent. Cattle were prone to warbles caused by cattle grubs.

Another scourge, mainly in the Delta and in areas that were still marshy, were the mosquitoes which became particularly abundant in October and November as the floods receded. In the Instruction written for his son Pepi, Khety describes the tribulations of a shepherd who went to the Delta to sell his flock and was nearly bitten to death.

Herodotus, too (II, 95), mentions various methods used to deal with this plague ... 'Those who live in boggy places often build towers and sleep on top of them, for the wind prevents mosquitoes from flying at that height. People living in the neighbourhood of water have devised a different solution; they use the nets with which they catch fish by day to drape over their couches and crawl under these to sleep at night ...'

The wooden frame over the bed of Queen Hetepheres, mother of the 4th-dynasty King Cheops, that was discovered in her tomb at Giza, may have served to suspend a mosquito net rather than an ornamental canopy.

Apart from the discomfort of its sting the *Anopheles* mosquito also carried the

76 A tall, narrow 'town house'. The top windows are latticed and the flat roof is enclosed by a parapet. Limestone model. Probably Graeco-Roman Period. *London, British Museum*

Plasmodium vivax organism responsible for malaria. Other species, such as the common gnat *Culex pipiens*, and *Aedes aegypti*, spread the larvae of the nematode *Wuchereria bancrofti* causing a serious affliction of the lymphatic vessels which produces chronic swellings (filariosis). Various prescriptions purported to be effective against mosquitoes, such as spraying rooms with soda solution or the fresh oil from the desert date (*Balanites aegyptiaca*), the 'Egyptian Balsam'.

It can be assumed that Egyptian houses were also infested with bedbugs; spells mentioned in a 3rd century BC papyrus were claimed to be potent against both these and flies. For coping with the fleas that jumped onto people from their cats and dogs the Ebers Papyrus recommends spraying with natron solution or smearing all the rooms with a mixture of fleabane (*Pulicaria dysenterica*) and charcoal.

Living rooms and above all storerooms and granaries attracted rats, mice and other troublesome rodents. Ratholes have been found in the corners of rooms at Illahun which the inmates had stuffed with stones, rags and other oddments. The remains of houses in the Egyptian fortress of Buhen on the Wadi Halfa were found to contain many rodent skeletons. These unwelcome visitors not only ate up food, but might harbour among them the Black Rat, host to the *Xenopsylla cheopsis* flea that can carry the agent of bubonic plague, *Pasteurella pestis*. The occurrence of this high-fatality disease in Egypt, and in Libya too, is testified by the graphic and unmistakable description given by the 2nd century AD writer Rufus of Ephesus. The Ebers Papyrus (No 847) advises: 'To protect things from mice, scatter cat-fat around.' The smell was presumably thought to put them off.

To complete the list of intruders in the home one must mention the ubiquitous lizards and the less common snakes.

Hygienic standards were not improved by the Egyptians' disinclination to dispose of the household waste that continually accumulated. Old rags and shoes, broken pots and tools were relatively harmless, but it was a different matter with food waste, animal and fish bones, soot, ashes and above all animal carcases. Housewives would sweep rubbish out from time to time, but it usually got no further than the nearest roadside where piles grew and attracted carrion-scavengers, especially dogs, hyenas and birds of prey such as the white-headed Egyptian vulture. Sometimes refuse was thrown into nearby holes left after the removal of clay for bricks and homemade ceramics. Or an empty house in the neighbourhood might be used as a dumping ground.

At Illahun there was even an official tip outside the north wall and at Akhetaten a belt of rubbish-piles up to 1.3m high, covering an area of 120 by 180m, was discovered little over half a kilometre from the palace, containing rubbish from there and from the surrounding patrician houses. Here archaeologists found hundreds of fragments of glass vessels, objects bearing the names of members of the royal family, and pieces of valuable imported Aegean ware. At the village of Deir el-Medina waste was taken outside the peripheral mud-wall. It was exceptional for a pile of dried rubbish to be burnt.

Where houses were close to a canal or to the Nile itself some of the refuse would be tipped there, with little harm done. A more dangerous practice was to dispose of it in the village fishponds that were sometimes a by-product of clay-mining. If the natural sanitation process could not cope, the decomposing organic material would produce a stench. Even that did not deter animals from drinking there, or ducks and even children from swimming.

The nastiest and most dangerous waste was of course animal and human excrement. However, droppings that fell in the street or accumulated in animal coops and sheds were meticulously gathered up by women and children, mixed with straw and patted into cakes for drying on the roof as a useful winter fuel. In a land where wood was rare and costly, this was the cheapest and ever-available source of thermal energy.

The common people made little ado about their physical functions, exercising them freely out of doors, and at home using some discreet corner appointed for the purpose. Says Herodotus (II, 35): 'The women pass water standing and the men

77　The granary keeper is carrying what is probably the standard grain measure. Inside the wooden model there are seven bins with sliding traps through which the stored grain and fruit could be removed. Aswan. 6th dynasty. *London, British Museum*

sitting. They go indoors to ease themselves, but they eat their food in the open, saying that indecent needs should be met in private, but decent ones publicly.'

This suggests that there were lavatories in the better-off homes, and some of the model houses in Old Kingdom tombs bear this out: they feature pairs of blocks, originally no doubt of stone, with a space between for a half-filled sand-bucket. Lavatories in dignitaries' houses at Akhetaten were furnished with stone or wooden seats with an opening shaped like a keyhole, or with two parallel dividers and a sand-container between. The tomb of the architect Kha at Deir el-Medina contained a portable wooden chamber-pot.

The earliest evidence of bathrooms comes from the 2nd-dynasty mastabas at Saqqara, which were furnished in imitation of the royal palace. The great houses of Illahun and Amarna had bathrooms leading off from the bedrooms. The walls were faced with stone tiles or finished with a smooth plaster wash. The floor was waterproof, made of a stone slab with a slightly raised border. The waste water drained off either into a vessel sunk in the floor, to be emptied periodically into a lower tank, or else through a soakaway into the street. Piped water supplies being unknown, servants or slaves had to fetch the considerable quantities of water required from the Nile. This alone put bathrooms into the luxury category.

The existence of these facilities in the royal palace is incidentally shown by the title 'overseer of the royal bathrooms', as well as by remains excavated in Merenptah's palace at Memphis and in the harem section of the palace of Ramesses III at Medinet Habu. Small pools for pilgrims to wash in have been found along the procession route to the Great Temple of Ptah at Memphis, and at Dendera there is whole series of earthenware baths lined with fine plaster which were probably used for cures in the 'spa' area of the temple. In describing a model ceramic vessel with a head protruding from the top, Dawson takes this as evidence that bodies were soaked in a soda solution during mummification, but the object more likely represents a living man taking a bath in the waters.

It is curious that no evidence has turned up of sewage systems in households, even in royal palaces, although surface sewers are known from the Old Kingdom in funerary temples and mastabas. Here the water flowed into pits with openings that could be closed with metal bungs, or emptied through a copper-sheet conduit nearly 400m long. Nor are there any traces of urban sewer systems. There was merely an open gully running down the middle of the streets, such as we find even today in remote African villages.

The ancient Egyptians had no means of feeding running water into a house, even a palace. Wells were a rarity because of the cost of sinking them when there was always water near at hand in the Nile valley. They have only been found in upper-class gardens and in a few places far away from the Nile.

In the early morning and late afternoon throngs of women would appear in city and village streets, striding with regal gait and effortlessly balancing great water-vessels on their heads, padded with a soft coil of cloth. The so-called symmetrical atrophy of the skull-bones which occurs more frequently in Egypt than elsewhere has been wrongly attributed to this method of carrying loads. We now know that it is a hereditary condition appearing in susceptible individuals in later life. Other investigators have claimed to find a greater prevalence of vertebral osteophytosis in Egyptian women due to strenuous labour, and in the cervical region these are certainly more noticeable than with the men. It was mainly the women who had to fetch water from the nearest pond or canal, or from the Nile itself, and pour it into the huge ceramic vessels standing by the doorways or in the courtyards of every house. There was a continual demand for water – for cooking, drinking, washing dishes and floors and doing the laundry. Only small items of clothing, of course, were washed at home; for the 'big wash' women went to the source of the water and did the job as a pleasant social event.

In their cramped, unhygienic and overcrowded houses the lives of simple folk could not have been easy. This was the darker side of Egypt's great civilisation, but it makes the achievements of these people even more remarkable.

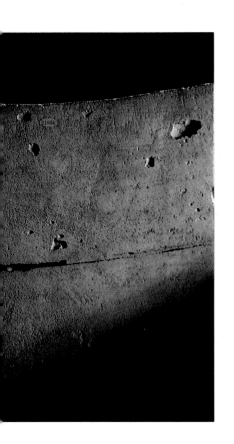

CHAPTER SEVEN

Dress, Adornment and Body Care

Left **78** Sennedjem, one of the builders of the tombs in the Valley of the Kings, wears a pleated kilt. His wife's short-sleeved pleated dress, embellished with a fringe, is pinned on her breast. Underneath she has a close-fitting diaphanous tunic. Both have ointment cones on their heads as they stand in adoration before the shrine with Osiris, Horus and the other gods of the Underworld. Painting on stucco in the tomb of Sennedjem, Deir el-Medina, West Thebes. 19th dynasty

Above **79** Servant girl adjusting the hair of a lady guest at a banquet. Wall painting in the tomb of Djoserkareseneb, West Thebes. 18th dynasty

NO SOONER HAD they stepped outside the dim seclusion of their homes than the Egyptians were exposed to the full impact of the sun. The deep blue sky was seldom hidden by clouds blowing in from the Mediterranean, to be dissipated later over middle Egypt and only rarely reaching into Upper Egypt. The low humidity of the Sahara, the world's largest desert, affected the Nile valley too, so that human body temperature was regulated by the evaporation of sweat even at a time of great physical exertion.

From prehistoric times the climate of the country had forced people to wear light, airy clothes. Heavy perspiration led them to take care of their skin and hair not merely by washing, but by a quite elaborate cosmetic routine. The pioneers in dress and hygiene alike were understandably the women, who learned to enhance the natural beauty of their dark-haired, dark-eyed Mediterranean kind and the charm of their graceful movements by the tasteful lines of their costume, striking coiffure, relative cleanliness and the use of alluring perfumes.

Textile manufacture and dressmaking were indeed the only areas of the economy that remained predominantly in female hands. These were activities pursued in every household, and women were also for a long time paramount in the spinning and weaving shops incorporated in aristocratic houses. The most common material for garments was linen, with wool coming second and cotton added in Ptolemaic times. The dressmaking tools were knives (or scissors) and needles. In predynastic times the knives were made of dressed stone and the needles of bone; in the Old Kingdom both were made of copper, gradually replaced by bronze from the Middle Kingdom on. The eyes of needles, remarkably, were not bored but scratched out with a hard pointed instrument, probably of stone. Thread was made by twisting flax yarn.

Men's skins had since time immemorial been so accustomed to the sun through continual exposure that it represented no problem; they had adapted biologically by increased pigmentation of the lower layer of the skin, acquiring the reddish-brown complexion that became darker further south. The skin colour of the men is faithfully reproduced in tomb paintings.

On some predynastic palettes men are shown naked except for a belt round the loins from which hung either a strip of cloth forming a penis sheath, or else a kilt with a thick fringe made of some plant material. These were probably worn not out of modesty but simply to protect the organs from the elements.

Even in historical times unmarried men still walked around in this garb, especially in the coutryside. The custom is mentioned by Ahmose, the son of Ebana and a participant in the wars of liberation against the Hyksos at the start of the 18th dynasty: 'I did service as an officer in place of [my father] ... though I was still a very

98

young man, had not yet taken a wife and spent each night with my penis sheath tied to my belt.' Similar sheaths are worn by some African natives to this day.

215   The well-known palette of King Narmer, who created a unified Egypt, is the earliest depiction of a king wearing the short kilt with its two ends crossed over and tucked in at the hips under a belt that is tied into a bow at the front. This was to become standard male wear for thousands of years. It was at first very short and remained so among the common people, but in higher circles it gradually lengthened to halfway down the calves and in the Middle Kingdom dropped to the ankles. The upper edge sometimes stood out. The kilt was occasionally supplemented by a strip of linen draped loosely over the shoulder, which in course of time acquired first short, and then long, sleeves. Diaphanous cloaks with short, wide sleeves made of special fine linen (*byssus*) imported from Syria, became fashionable in the New Kingdom.

For working in the fields villagers wore a simple apron, made as a plain triangle of material with a wedge-shaped opening in front and the point hanging down behind over the rump. Boatmen, fishermen and papyrus and reed gatherers wore nothing at all. Villagers only donned the kilt when they were bringing their produce to the granaries or to town, or visiting relatives or temples. They are usually portrayed with kilts, again, when they were bringing funerary offerings. In the course of the Middle Kingdom the kilt became the universal garment in the countryside as elsewhere. During the New Kingdom standard man's dress included a sort of shirt or tunic, very loose-fitting and less easy to see in a picture, but attested by finds and texts.

Aristocrats of the Old Kingdom wore along with the kilt sundry ornaments such as necklaces and breast-pendants of wood or metal, and sometimes also an official badge of office – the vizier, for example, sported a picture of the goddess Maat. Even in this period the kings sometimes had their kilts starched and pleated. The *sem* priests, and aristocrats entrusted with priestly functions, carried slung over their shoulders a leopard skin, dressed but not sewn, including all four legs and the tail. The conspicuous leopard spots proclaimed the wearer's function far and wide. One Middle Kingdom dignitary, Djehutihotep, had himself portrayed in his tomb at el-Bersha wearing a short pleated cloak over his shoulders and a long, wide diaphanous skirt over the usual short kilt.

In the New Kingdom dignitaries of the highest ranks, such as the vizier Rekhmire, the overseer of the physicians Nebamun and the royal herald Intef, sometimes wore a distinctive costume not unlike women's dress – a tunic fitting under the arms, held up by a narrow ribbon round the neck, and reaching to the ankles. Statues of the dead usually show them dressed in this way, whether they were men or women.

The diaphanous tunic worn over the normal kilt by the young nobles shown accompanying the sacrifice-bearer in the tomb of Ramose at Sheikh Abd el-Qurna (18th dynasty) is of slightly different cut – wide at the neck with short sleeves and of calf length.

Other aristocrats under the New Kingdom and later affected either a pleated kilt or an unpleated one with a folded apron over it, and a pleated shirt as well. Both the sleeved tunic and the shirt grew gradually longer, the tunic wider, looser and more comfortable. A further garment was also added now – a short, wide sleeveless cloak with free-hanging edges. Great attention was paid at this time to coloured ornaments and broad inlaid belts. It was naturally the ceremonial costume of the kings that had the most elaborate cut; it was also covered with small symbolic motifs.

Women's dress was less austere than men's and even in predynastic times, though evidence is scanty, probably covered almost the whole body. Presumably women, unlike men, spent most of their time indoors or under the shade in garden or courtyard; even village women only came out onto the fields at harvest-time or to lend a hand with other short-term tasks. Less exposed than the men to intense sunlight, their complexions remained much lighter; tomb paintings depict them in tones ranging from ochre to yellowish.

By the Old and Middle Kingdoms a long, white, smooth and closefitting tunic held up with wide shoulder straps had become standard feminine garb. The upper edge came over, or just below, the bust while the bottom normally reached to the ankles. It

80   Wife of prince Rahotep and 'one known to the King', Nofret is wearing a long mantle and, underneath, a tunic with wide straps. Her own hair is visible under the heavy wig. She wears a wide collar of several rows of beads bordered with pendants. Her husband wears a kilt and a small wig. He has an amulet around his neck and a neatly trimmed moustache. Painted limestone. From the tomb of Rahotep and Nofret at Meidum. Early 4th dynasty. *Cairo, Egyptian Museum*

Left **81** The exquisitely dressed royal couple in a lush garden setting. King Tutankhamun wears a wig with several layers of curls, a large collar and a pleated kilt with a tab and long streamers. On her bejewelled wig Queen Ankhesenamun has a cone of scented fat flanked by two uraei. Wearing a revealing pleated robe, a broad collar and earrings, she is offering bouquets to her husband. Painted ivory panel of a wooden chest. Tomb of Tutankhamun, Valley of the Kings, West Thebes. 18th dynasty. *Cairo, Egyptian Museum*

82 Detail of the statue of the wife of Nakhtmin wearing a seductive tight-fitting dress of fine pleated linen tied under the breast. The twisted locks of her long wig terminate in tightly curled strands. Crystalline limestone. 18th dynasty. *Cairo, Egyptian Museum*

allowed ample freedom of movement and, since the arms were unencumbered, women could dance in it or even execute simple gymnastic figures.

A more convenient costume for dancers, however, was a brief apron usually 46 secured by narrow bands across the bust. Servant girls, too, went about their work as a rule clad only in a skirt or apron.

On cool mornings and evenings women of the wealthier sort covered themselves in a long-sleeved gown that hung in folds and had a wide *décolletage* from the shoulders. This style is exemplified in the famous statue of Nofret, wife of the 4th- 80 dynasty prince Rahotep.

For festive occasions upper-class women would wear nets of red, blue or green cylindrical faience beads across the middle third of their tunics. These restricted movement and made it difficult to sit down. But even in those days, dressing fashionably was important enough to warrant putting up with a little discomfort. Poorer women had to be content with a string of beads round the waist, or a ribbon with coloured stripes to imitate it. One idiosyncratic choice was a tunic painted with a pattern of coloured feathers.

In the course of the New Kingdom feminine fashion became ever more varied and sophisticated. This has been put down to influences from areas of the Near East occupied by Egypt at that time. White remained the most popular colour, only occasionally varied with pastel shades, but dresses were now made of two pieces or more. The outer garments were sometimes smooth, sometimes pleated, made from the finest linen with short sleeves and either pinned together over the bust or tied in decorative folds. They were sheer enough to show off feminine curves, but in fact most ladies still wore the traditional tunic underneath. This was also in many cases diaphanous and skin-tight.

The outer garment varied in length and had narrow lengthwise pleats with fan-pleating at the shoulders, or cross-folds on the sleeves. It was modestly trimmed with coloured braid, ribbons, edging and other embellishments, while metal decorations, embroidery or painted details were added in the Late Period. The neckline was either deep and wide, or narrow, converging down to the waist. Some dresses covered only one shoulder, the other shoulder and breast remaining bare, except when concealed behind a light veil or the edge of wrap or cloak.

The shoulder-wrap or hip-length cloak ended in a fringe tied into little knots. Feminine clothing was becoming subtler and unquestionably sexy during this period, while dancing-girls, singers and musicians, like the young waitresses who served at banquets, walked around with no more to cover them than a string of beads round 142 the buttocks and across the pubis, or perhaps a scanty kerchief for modesty.

Though the inhabited part of Egypt was in those days a green oasis of lush vegetation, the well-trodden paths were dusty and at times muddy. Frequent winds blew up clouds of dust and sand so that long skirts, tunics and cloaks soon became dirty, not to mention sweaty. Frequent changes of clothing were therefore necessary and among the upper classes especially this might be done several times a day. Herodotus (II, 37) writes: 'They wear linen clothes, always freshly washed – and make a great point of this.'

Women washed smaller items at home but assembled for their main laundry on the banks of canals, pools or river, merrily slapping the clothes against boulders or beating them with wooden bats. Noblewomen entrusted their clothes to the professional launderers familiar to us from many pictures and documents. Dirt and 85 grease were dissolved with natron (a natural mixture of sodium carbonate and bicarbonate with various natural additives), and according to Pierre Montet the Egyptians also used a soaplike paste made with ashes, clay and some unknown bonding ingredient that actually produced a lather. The washing was hung up on lines or fences to dry before being laid into wooden boxes. If a dignitary left home for a long period he had to take with him a valet who carried a sackful of fresh clothes.

Simple folk mostly went barefoot. The upper classes of both sexes wore leather or woven papyrus or palm leaf sandals with shaped soles. These were secured with three thongs, one passing between the great and second toes and the other two extending

Left **83** Princess Nefertiabt dressed as a priestess in black-spotted panther skin. Giza. Old Kingdom, 4th dynasty. *Paris, Musée du Louvre*

Right **84** A long diaphanous overskirt worn over a short white kilt, the usual male dress. Painting on papyrus. From the Book of the Dead. New Kingdom or Late Period. *Private collection*

from under the ankles to a point over the instep where all three came together. Priests' sandals had to be white.

It would be hard to enumerate all the fashionable accessories that adorned the clothes not only of women, but of men, especially in affluent circles. There was already a prehistoric tradition of making beads and pendants out of bone, egg-shell, ivory, animal teeth, sea-shells and other organic materials, and the substances used extended later to stone of all kinds, fired clay and faience and, from the Badarian culture onwards, copper.

Bracelets and ankle-rings were fashioned from bone or stone. The necklaces, bracelets and belts in Old Kingdom scenes at Saqqara were also made of gold, silver and semi-precious jewels. It became customary for nobles and their wives to wear
90 wide, many-stranded necklaces of cylindrical beads called *wesekh* and *menat*. The Middle Kingdom saw the introduction of bronze *cloisonné* pectorals inlaid with semi-precious gems and coloured glass. Queen Hetepheres, mother of Cheops, was accompanied to her grave by silver and ivory bracelets decorated with butterflies of carnelian, turquoise and lapis lazuli. Simpler folk had to rest content with ceramic of faience beads in white, red and aquamarine.
88 Girls bound their hair with linen ribbons tied in a bow at the back. These evolved into the coronets and diadems worn in higher circles, with petals round the side and a

lotus blossom in front. Among the very rich these were made of wire or metal strips with ornamental details welded on, notably rosettes for setting gemstones in. Both women and upper-class men wore rings, the cheaper ones of faience, the finer sort of gold and silver, later of bronze and in rare cases iron.

It is curious that in Egypt, unlike other African countries, thousands of years were to pass before jewelry was adopted that required the slightest perforation of the skin – ear-rings, nose-rings or lip-plugs (labrets). The change came in the Second Intermediate Period with the introduction of ear-rings. Some of these were of the clip-on type, but others needed the ears to be pierced. In the course of the New Kingdom heavy rings and studs appeared requiring a much larger perforation, as can be seen in mummies of the period.

Under the New Kingdom and later, upper-class women wore not only bracelets at the wrist but metal bangles round the upper arm, with cloisons for inlays of semi-precious stones or coloured glass. On ceremonial occasions aristocrats wore leather or textile sashes decorated with meshes of beads, fastened in front with an ornamental clasp.

The Egyptians had worn amulets since predynastic times and they became even more popular in the Late and Graeco-Roman Periods. Their function was chiefly magical. Among them were the *ankh*, symbol of life; the *udjat* or Eye of Horus, symbol 272 of protective watchfulness; the Pillar of Osiris or *djed* denoting continuity; the papyrus bundle or *udja* representing youth and good fortune; the Knot of Isis or *tit* standing for the resurrection of the dead, and the Sceptre of Ptah, *was*, emblem of power and prosperity. Protective power was also ascribed in the course of time to scarabs, 168 amulets in the form of the sacred *Scarabaeus* beetle first found in the Middle Kingdom, which were originally used as sealing-stamps.

In earlier times the right to wear gold was restricted to the king, since gold, regarded as the 'flesh of the sun', symbolised immortality. The privilege was then extended by grace and favour to priests and favoured nobles.

In the Ptolemaic Period, traditional Egyptian costume began to give way to Greek fashion which prescribed a loose belted tunic for men and variously cut and decorated dresses, often of ankle length, for women.

Hair and beard style were seen as important not only for general appearance but for setting off clothing and ornaments. In all periods Egyptian men preferred their 80 hair cut short, lying flat and leaving the ears free. Commoners always looked like this until they started losing their hair – a process which (as many illustrations show) began in the front, spread to the middle of the scalp and finally left only a wisp at the back.

There was another hairstyle that featured short curls covering the ears and forming a curve from temples to nape. This is how dignitaries are portrayed at the sacrificial table as well as others taking part in funeral rites such as sacrifice-bearers, cattle-minders, lector-priests and even the servants and butchers preparing to slaughter the sacrificial beasts. Specialists are in doubt as to whether or not these people are wearing wigs. But since even simple folk are shown with this coiffure, many have concluded that they curled their own hair for the occasion.

Moderately long hair divided into locks running down to the neck from the central 78 parting appears both on statues (where it usually covers the upper half of the ears) and reliefs (where the ears are completely hidden). This must usually have meant a wig, since short natural hair is sometimes showing. It was a fashion exclusive to dignitaries and their families, lector-priests and the like. A rare phenomenon in the first four dynasties, it then became the predominant fashion among the nobility for ceremonial occasions, alternating with the curls described previously.

Long hair divided into three parts with one falling down the back and the other two over the bosom was typical for women's wigs. But we also find it on male deities and occasionally in the 6th dynasty on statues of ordinary people. This is not to be confused with the equally long but usually undivided hair in portraits of Asiatics. Short frizzy hair, again, was the mark of a Black. Priests in Egypt came to shave their 241 heads completely and from the 19th dynasty on this was *de rigueur*.

Predynastic figures show that Egyptian men originally favoured full beards. It was not until the start of the historic era that first the nobility, and then the commonalty, began to shave. This was at first done with a stone blade, usually set in a wooden handle, but later with a copper and, from the Middle Kingdom onwards, a bronze trapezium-shaped razor. People either shaved and cut their hair for themselves, or used a barber who visited the aristocracy in their houses but attended to common customers out of doors, for example on a bench in the shade of a spreading sycamore
219 fig. We see such a scene in the tomb of Userhet at Sheikh Abd el-Qurna, where young men are waiting in a row, seated on folding chairs and tripods, while the barber brandishes his razor over a water-vessel at his feet.

From the time of the 3rd dynasty some of the nobility, though not the king, started
80 allowing themselves a modest moustache like Prince Rahotep, beautifully sculpted with his wife Nofret. Others cultivated a short tuft under the chin. A long, narrow beard of several strands plaited like a pigtail with the end jutting forwards (sometimes in statues set with lapis lazuli) became the trademark of divinity. A similar-looking artificial beard, often widening out at the end and secured by a cord round the ears,
10 was reserved for the 'living god', that is the king who, alive or dead, was identified with the god of the dead, Osiris. Men let their beards grow freely at times of mourning,
206 though we sometimes see the same condition in unkempt paupers.

Left **85** A laundryman is wringing cloth to add to the pile at his feet, while another is taking a garment out of a large jar used for boiling or dyeing. Fragment of a wall painting from West Thebes. New Kingdom. *Turin, Museo Egizio*

Above **86** A young woman wearing a large wig and broad collar. Both adornments were very popular in ancient Egypt. Limestone statuette. New Kingdom. *Private collection*

Right **87** Morning toilet and breakfast of Queen Kawit, one of the wives of King Mentuhotep II Nebhepetre. Sitting comfortably in an armchair with a mirror in her left hand, she raises a bowl of milk to her lips while a servant replenishes another. The locks of her wig are being delicately adjusted by a second servant. Detail of the sarcophagus of Queen Kawit. Sunk relief in limestone from the temple of Mentuhotep II. Deir el-Bahari, West Thebes. 11th dynasty. *Cairo, Egyptian Museum*

Women showed more originality in their hair-styles. In their case too the basic preference was for a smooth, close coiffure; only occasionally do we find a natural wave or long ringlets. This applied to all classes insofar as they dispensed with wigs. However, even in Old Kingdom statues and reliefs we find, mainly on noblewomen (but from the 5th dynasty on their maids too) wigs that were usually of moderate length, the hair running from a central parting over the ears down to the chin or to shoulder level. Longhaired wigs in three parts, as described for goddesses, were originally worn only by queens and noble ladies but are later sometimes found on commoners too.

Starting in the 5th dynasty young girls, especially dancers, wore long thick braided
91 ponytails, probably natural; they hung down the back with a disc or ball plaited into the end as a weight. Young children also wore plaits, but these as a rule hung down
25 one side only while the rest of the hair was cut short or shaved right off.

A new model cropped up in the Middle Kingdom: the scrolled coiffure in imitation of the goddess Hathor. Here the hair was combed into two thick tresses ending in spirals, drawn behind the ears and forward over the bust.
86 Heavy wigs with many long tassel-ended tails became popular in the New Kingdom. In the Amarna period, however, shorter and simpler wigs made a comeback and even the queen followed suit.

84

Alongside natural hair cut short, then, it was the various styles of wig that interested women most. They kept them in special chests and could don them at need without tedious combing. The wigs were not only an essential head-cover for ceremonies, banquets and other important occasions, but they protected the wearer against sunstroke – upper-class women in particular were not used to strong sun. In the course of time even village women acquired them for times when they had to spend long hours in the open. Men sometimes protected their heads for the same reason with cloths or horsehair rags wound round like turbans.

Quite a few wigs have survived, especially from the New Kingdom. They were made either by wigmaking specialists or by barbers, usually from human hair, less often from vegetable fibres. In some cases traces of wax have been found on them, used for setting the wave. A scissors-like waving implement for use on wigs was discovered in the New Kingdom settlement of Gurob.

Polish archaeologists recently enlarged our knowledge of Egyptian wigmaking by the discovery of the remains of a workshop in a crevasse overlying the 11th-century temple of King Mentuhotep at Deir el-Bahari. Its date lies somewhere between the 12th and the beginning of the 13th dynasty. Four alabaster vases were found here in a linen sack, containing tufts of hair, tresses strung on threads or bound up with fibres, and a curious thread net which served as the foundation for a wig. There was also a papyrus case with five bone pins in it, a bronze awl and fragments of two flint knives. The most important find of all was a unique model head on which black lines had been traced to show the outline of the wig's attachment and its long and short axes. In further containers there were scraps of textile, leather straps, necklaces of little bone beads and other oddments. On the cosmetic side, the most interesting

85

discoveries were seeds of *Balanites aegyptiaca*, desert date, source of a prized aromatic oil used in perfumes; a brown powder probably for use as hair-dye, and a waxy remnant of hard soda soap which still retained detergent properties.

For all their love of wigs, it must not be thought that the Egyptians took no care of their own hair. A celebrated relief shows the 11th-dynasty Queen Kawit seated in an armchair with a maid curling her hair from behind. While the queen watches the process in a mirror a servant approaches her with a bowl, saying: 'For your *ka* (spirit), my lady, take this drink that I offer you.'

Round mirrors, made from polished copper or silver, were known as early as the Old Kingdom. Special attention was given to the design and decoration of the handles.

Even in predynastic days the Egyptians had wooden or bone combs for their hair, and these materials continued to be used in historic times. There were both single and double-sided combs, some very fine with a long handle, which would have effectively removed dirt – and nits. The latter have in fact been found by Armand Ruffer on the hair of many mummies, and recently again during the Toronto autopsy (1974) of the Theban weaver Nakht. Not only were all lice disagreeable but body lice could be carriers of the organism responsible for typhus (*Rickettsia prowazeki*). According to Herodotus (II, 37) 'the priests shave their whole bodies every other day, so that when they conduct rituals they will be free of lice and other uncleanliness'.'

Washing the hair regularly was another important practice, though how often people did it we cannot be sure. There is plenty of information, however, about the use of oils and perfumes. During New Kingdom banquets servants used to place cones of perfumed fat on the heads of high-born ladies. These would melt in the heat and soak into the hair. They might also run over the ladies' faces and down their dresses; some of the pictures show tell-tale yellow stains on the upper part of their clothes.

Like other people the ancient Egyptians had problems with hair-loss, as we can infer from the recipes for promoting its growth. One of them recommended the seeds of fenugreek (*Trigonella foenum-graecum*), a plant still prized by herbalists and pharmacologists. Hermann Grapow, a specialist in Egyptian medicine, cites '... another hair-restorer, made for Queen Shesh, mother of King Teti: Take the paw of a greyhound bitch, the stone of a date, an ass's hoof: boil [them all] thoroughly in oil in a *djadja* pot and apply liberally.' Another 'guaranteed' remedy for thinning hair, but a more expensive one, was lion's fat.

Greying locks presented no problem either. The blood of a black cow boiled in oil, the fat of black snakes and the contents of raven's eggs would restore their original black gloss ...

However, hair-consciousness was only one aspect of personal hygiene. The Egyptians were well aware of the need to keep the skin clean too. They washed at least once a day, and more often when they got dirty, needed to freshen themselves or had religious rites to perform. There was plenty of water available, even if it was often contaminated. A particular danger was the use of water from stagnant ponds and slow-flowing canals, where snails of the genus *Bulinus* harboured the infectious organism *Schistosoma* whose larvae can penetrate even undamaged skin.

The morning ablution is mentioned in King Akhenaten's famous eulogy of the rising sun: 'Dawn breaks when you come up over the horizon, for by day you are the Sun and dispel the darkness. You cast your rays and the Two Kingdoms bask in festive brilliance. People wake up and start to their feet; it is you who roused them. They wash themselves, pick up their clothes and raise their arms in praise of your appearance.'

Other texts too refer to washing of the face and hands, particularly before and after meals. People were also in the habit of washing their mouths out in the morning with a little natron dissolved in the water, and one document calls this the *sen shem shem*, 'cleansing of mouth and teeth'.

Most common people never saw a bathroom in their lives. They made do with a stone, clay or metal spouted jug, poured water over their hands or other parts and caught it in a wide, deep bowl. There are even references to special vessels for different parts of the body, but these were probably unusual. In one Late Period home a bowl

88 A girl wearing a pretty headband. Fragment of a wall painting. West Thebes. 18th dynasty

89 A stylised lotus blossom was a favourite ornament, here adorning the head. The eye-paint was kohl, made since predynastic times from the sulphide of lead. Mummy mask. 18th dynasty. *Brussels, Royal Museum of Art and History*

was found with the inscription: 'Good health to you when you wash your face, and let your heart rejoice!'

Rich people had servants to pour water over them in their bathrooms, for even they had no bath-tubs. Sometimes the water would be passed through a sieve or basket, producing a kind of shower.

Another hygienic practice was regular rubbing down with unguents, usually made either from the fat of the hippopotamus, crocodile or cat, or from various vegetable oils. The object was to prevent the skin drying up and to keep it soft and supple. Some preparations were thought to be medicinally beneficial too. A supply of massaging-oil might form part of a workman's wages, as documented in the case of the royal craftsmen at Deir el-Medina. In Rekhmire's tomb at Sheikh Abd el-Qurna we can see servants, male and female, massaging their masters. Lidded unguent jars in various shapes have survived, made of pottery, faience, glass, wood or ivory. The contents were applied with a little wooden, bone or ivory spoon, in New Kingdom times often elegantly carved to resemble a girl swimming.

Sundry deodorants are described in the Ebers Papyrus (708 to 711) for dealing with body odour. Alcohol-based perfumes were unknown, but Egyptian women could use fragrant ointments made by leaching the aromatic principles from myrrh, desert date, terebinth or frankincense with a fatty oil. Even the dead had to be sent off on their journey through the underworld with the seven sacred oils that were sprinkled into recesses in a special oblong alabaster palette.

One cosmetic activity much favoured by women, young and old, was shading the eyelids. How ancient a tradition this was in Egypt emerges from the predynastic face-paint palettes that have been found, made of stone (most often slate) in oval form or in the shape of an animal.

Their perfectly smooth surfaces still retain traces of pigments crushed and powdered in oil or fat with a pebble. From historic times there is the famous palette for six different face-paints in Tutankhamun's treasury. If there was any left over it was stored in special little lidded boxes of alabaster (or other stone) or glass, or in phials of alabaster, wood or reed-stem.

Two basic cosmetic pigments were known. One of these, *udju*, was prepared from the green malachite of Sinai, which has often turned up in predynastic tombs. This seems to have been used for eye shadow until about the 4th dynasty, after which there is no more evidence of it.

After the end of the Predynastic Period use was made instead of the black paint *mesdemet* derived either from galena (lead sulphide) or from stibnite (antimony sulphide). There are deposits of galena around Aswan and on the Red Sea coast; it used to be brought by Asiatic bedouin as a tribute to the Egyptian monarch and Queen Hatshepsut's expedition brought back a quantity among the products of the Land of Punt (modern Somalia). It is still used for the same purpose in modern Egypt under the name of *kohl*.

Little canvas or leather bags containing galena have been found in graves from time to time, and it was also stored as a fine powder or paste in conch shells, lengths of hollow reed or small cylindrical jars. Special blue-glazed kohl jars were made from the early First Intermediate Period onwards, and from the 18th dynasty onwards it was kept in glass vessels or slate vessels with a dark-green faience glaze.

Both of these pigments are mentioned among the first-known lists of offerings of the Old Kingdom, along with the seven sacred oils, as prerequisites for eternal life. So the value attached to them in everyday use can be imagined.

Egyptian beauties used to darken their brows, eyelids and lashes with the aid of little splints or miniature spoons made of stone, metal, wood or bone, usually tracing lines from the outer corners of the eyes and eyebrows toward the front of the earlobes, where they met.

Face-paints had a certain curative or prophylactic value as well. Galena has disinfectant and fly-deterrent properties and can protect the eyes from sun-dazzle. The Egyptians seem to have been aware of this, since they prescribed *mesdemet* for eye complaints and even used it in bandages for 'softening the blood vessels'.

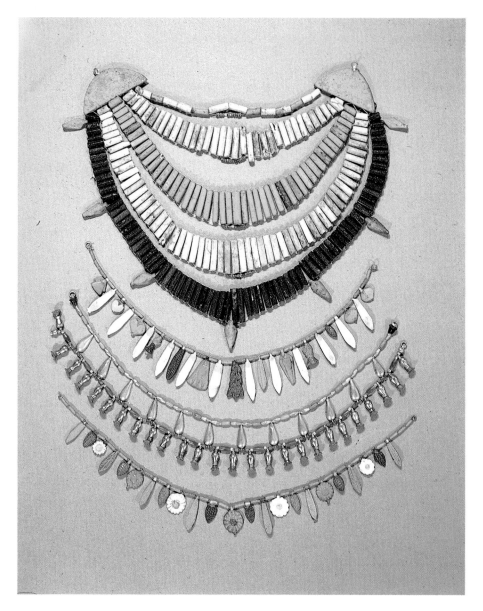

Artificial colouring of lips and cheeks was by contrast a rarity. The scene where the
54 heroine of the Turin Papyrus mentioned in Chapter 4 applies some kind of lipstick
with a brush, spill or spoon is a unique record. The editor of the papyrus states that
her cheeks appear to have been rouged too. Some writers have quoted in this
connection the painted faces of Old Kingdom mummies, but that was probably done
for a quite different purpose – to render the dead more lifelike.

Like Egyptian women today, their forebears coloured their nails, palms, soles and
sometimes hair also with a paste containing the yellowish-red pigment of henna
leaves (*Lawsonia alba*). In evidence of this Édouard Naville cites the reddened finger-
nails of an 11th-dynasty mummy from Thebes, Grafton Smith the distinctly red hair
of the 18th-dynasty female mummy Henutmehet, and Percy Newberry the henna
twigs found in the Ptolemaic cemetery at el-Hawara.

Tattooing was also used to enhance feminine charms. The patterns on some
predynastic and archaic statues are usually regarded as the earliest examples.
Unquestionably tattooed dots in triangles and parallelograms were noted by Winlock
on the trunks and limbs of two girl-mummies found near the temple of Mentuhotep at
Deir el-Bahari, and similar dot-patterns appear on blue faience statues of women of
the same period. An undated and unprovenanced mummy of a singing-girl has
survived with a thigh tattoo of the god Bes, patron of pleasure and lovemaking, and

90 A collar and necklace of glazed
composition beads and pendants. From
Deir el-Bahari, West Thebes. 11th
dynasty. *London, British Museum*

91 A servant girl wearing a wide collar
(*wesekh*), a wig with a plait and a barely
noticeable waistband. Painted wooden
cosmetic spoon. Late 18th or 19th
dynasty. *Paris, Musée du Louvre*

92 A mirror from polished bronze with a handle in the form of a naked girl. Semna, Upper Nubia. 18th dynasty. *Khartoum, Sudan Archaeological Museum*

93 This relief provides evidence of manicure as early as the Old Kingdom. Tomb of Ankhmahor, Saqqara. 6th dynasty

the same deity appears on the thighs of dancers and musicians in some New Kingdom murals. The Egyptian Museum in Berlin owns a New Kingdom ostracon from Deir el-Medina showing a lute-girl with tattooing on her neck and bust.

Excavations by Maspero at Akhmim (el-Hawawish) have yielded several female mummies of the Graeco-Roman Period with tattoo marks on the chin and sides of the nose. French discoveries in Aksha (Nubia) have shown that tattooing was practised there too during the C-Group culture (between the 6th and 18th dynasties), and again in the Meroitic Period (from the 3rd century BC to the 3rd century AD). Some scholars conclude that tattooing came to Egypt from Nubia.

Tattooing involved the subcutaneous injection of a blue-black pigment made of soot and oil with the aid of a sharp instrument with one or several bronze points, or with fishbones set in a wooden handle. The tattooer's chief clients seem to have been dancers, singers, musicians and prostitutes. The erotic overtones of the art emerge clearly from the figures of 'brides of the dead' laid in tombs from the New Kingdom onwards; these were decorated with the familiar tattoo motifs.

Even in ancient Egypt a gorgeous complexion did not last for ever. To treat wrinkles (and freckles) oil of fenugreek was recommended, a plant freely available because of its use as animal fodder. A list of more sophisticated recipes has survived that opens hopefully: 'The beginning of the Book on How to Make the Old Young.' One prescription, guaranteed to get rid of face wrinkles, involves a mixture of terebinth resin, wax, fresh *behen* oil and Cyprus grass, finely macerated and mixed with various plant juices – to be applied daily. Unfortunately its efficacy could not be tested since some of the ingredients have not been identified with certainty.

High-born ladies used to carry around with them numerous toilet articles in special boxes. These included the little metal tweezers also used by priests to remove unwanted hair. Metal, wooden or bone splints were employed for cleaning the nails, and flint (later metal) blades for cutting nails and perhaps shaving off corns.

The depictions of manicure and pedicure scenes at the entrance to the 6th dynasty mastaba of Ankhmahor at Saqqara have often been reproduced. One of them shows a woman manicurist tending her customer's right hand, on another she is dealing with 93 his left foot; both are squatting on the ground. One of the captions has the customer pleading for his nails: 'Don't hurt them!' On another fragment higher up a client is seated between two male manicurists attending to both his hands at once. One of them is saying reassuringly: 'I'll make it enjoyable for you, my dear!'

It might seem from all this that the Egyptians had achieved high standards of bodily care and hygiene all those thousands of years ago. Alas, this did not apply to the common folk, especially the very poor.

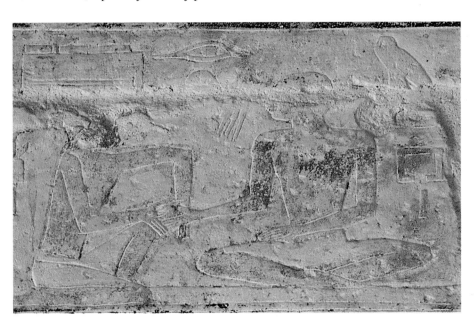

CHAPTER EIGHT

The Bounty of the Black Earth

THE EGYPTIAN LANDSCAPE is scenically among the most extraordinary in the world. A relatively narrow strip of fertile valley spreads out into the Delta in the north, and to the south cuts through the endless expanse of the Sahara. Its fertility does not depend on the amount of rainfall, which suddenly decreased from the end of the Neolithic wet phase (subpluvial, c. 2350 BC) in Upper Egypt and Nubia till it virtually came to a stop. Regular floods bring about the Nile valley's annual miracle, when nature is reborn and the fields turn green and then gradually golden with the harvest.

As early as the fifth millennium BC, the Egyptians realised the extraordinary fruitfulness of their fields and the secret behind it – the deposits of black silt borne down by the river in floodtime. Hence they called the soil of the Nile valley 'black earth' (*kemet*), as distinct from the 'red earth' (*deshret*) of the desert.

In their black land they felt content and safe. They were satisfied that a host of gods, originally regional gods, kept guard over its fertility and that Khnum, the god of the First Cataract, would ensure the punctual onset and adequate height of the flooding. The regular cycle of natural events conferred a rhythm on their lives which was part of the *maat*, the eternal order of things.

The red land, by contrast, was to be shunned as far as possible. From the western wilderness a scorching, destructive wind, the *khamsin* as we now call it, would sometimes blow down on them. Then, as now, it would raise clouds of fine sand and dust, blinding men and animals alike, and sometimes drying out their fields. No wonder they saw the desert as the domain of malignant forces disruptive of the established order and personified in the Late Period by the baneful god Seth.

It was of course the peasant farmer whose links with the soil were strongest. He had learnt to cultivate it to perfection and gradually extended the area of his fields to wherever the annual floods reached. He would clear a course for as much water as he needed and steer the surplus back to its riverbed. In the passage of time the size of his harvests and his herds grew to the point where, even in predynastic times (4000–3000 BC), part of the population could turn to other employment. This second social division of labour (following the first, that between men and women, which went far back into prehistory) continued up to the threshold of the historic period. But even then the majority of the population was still tied to agriculture and the rest of society lived on its produce.

Egypt is the 'gift of the Nile' and her harvests depend on its floodwaters. These were the fundamental pacemaker of the Egyptian farmer's life. It was the farmer, above all, who had vested interest in the calendar, an invention which – thanks to the regularity of natural events – this country was one of the earliest in the world to possess.

The New Year began at the onset of summer, usually around June 19 of today's

Previous page **94** Sennedjem cutting wheat in the fields of the hereafter, where it grew a foot taller. Detail of ill. 97. Deir el-Medina, West Thebes. 19th dynasty

Left **95** This relief of a predynastic king with fan-bearers has been interpreted as a ceremonial start to breaching the first dyke to let water inundate the fields. Detail of a votive mace-head of the so-called King Scorpion. Nekhen (Hierakonpolis). Late Predynastic Period. *Oxford, Ashmolean Museum*

Right **96** Nile god Hapy holding a tray with produce, the bounty provided by the fertile river. Limestone relief in Medinet Habu, West Thebes. 20th dynasty

Gregorian calendar, when after dropping below the horizon for 70 days the star *Sopdet* (Sirius) reappeared at sunrise. People knew from long experience that this was about the time for the level of the Nile to start rising. Just before this, flocks of white ibises would have appeared on the fields as they returned from the south. If they came late or not at all, farmers would see this as a bad omen foreshadowing low floods and a poor harvest. So they regarded the wise bird that knew the secret of this vital phenomenon as an embodiment of the learned god Thoth.

The Nile floods are in fact triggered by sudden monsoon downfalls on the Ethiopian plateau, the source of the Blue Nile, and to a lesser extent by those around Lake Victoria and the Ruwenzori mountains where the White Nile originates. Heavy rain and surging waters bring down the fertile soil which the overflowing Nile then slowly deposits over the fields in its calm lower reaches.

Chemical analysis explains the fertility of the Nile mud, containing as it does all the important ingredients which would otherwise have to be added to the soil by artificial manuring. It has in it about 0.1 per cent of combined nitrogen, 0.2 per cent of phosphorus anhydrides and 0.6 per cent of potassium carbonate. Nitrogen also percolates through the deep fissures in the drying mud, and is fixed by catalysts such as iron oxide.

Egyptian farmers prayed to the hermaphrodite god of the Nile, Hapy – portrayed as

a man with women's breasts in symbolism of the apparently spontaneous fruitfulness 96 of the river and its flood-plain – to ensure that the yearly inundations were just right: not too deep, not too shallow. If they were too shallow, the floods would not reach the thirsty fields, but if too much water came rushing down it would sweep away the laboriously constructed dykes, tear up the fields, overturn ancient trees and even threaten low-lying villages.

The height of the Nile floods was measured in ancient times by the 'nilometers', steps leading down below the water surface and marked with a scale in cubits and fractions of a cubit. On the nilometer at Aswan the optimum high flood level, converted into metres above sea level, is shown as 93m. Whenever it exceeded 94m flood damage would follow, but if it failed to rise above 91.5m famine could be expected. Ancient authors give various estimates of the optimal difference between high and low levels, evidently depending on where it was measured: Herodotus made it 15 to 16, Strabo 8 to 14 and Pliny the Elder around 14 cubits.

One of the key problems in Egyptian history is settling the time when people began consciously to improve the natural effect of the Nile flooding by artificial irrigation, notably by building a canal system. The canals brought the floods to places they otherwise never touched and, when floods were low, made artificial watering easier wherever the canal network was within reach.

According to the theory accepted until quite recently, it was the very need for centrally-managed canal construction and maintenance, and central allocation of water supplies, that played the paramount role in bringing about the rise and continuance of the ancient Egyptian state. This view ascribed the chief decision-making power to the king and his vizier, detailed supervision of the work being entrusted to officials chosen from among the nobility and scribes. It was even proposed by the Polish archaeologist Krzyżaniak that artificial irrigation started as early as the second half of the Predynastic Period. As evidence that canals existed even before the country was unified many writers have adduced the mace-head of King Scorpion, one of the last rulers of a separate Upper Egypt, which may depict him 95 officiating at the ceremonial opening of a new canal.

Recently, however, the evidence for artificial irrigation has been analysed independently by two German archaeologists, Erika Endesfelder and Wolfgang Schenkel. The first-named has noted that pyramid texts (the oldest being on walls of late 5th-dynasty pyramids) do use the terms for 'canal', mer and *henet*, but only in the context of waterway traffic. Schenkel agrees that canals existed in the Old Kingdom for traffic, and possibly also for the drainage of marshes.

The key role played by one such canal in the building of the pyramids has been shown by Gustave Goyon. It extended along the foot of the plateau on which the pyramids and mastabas of the Old Kingdom were built, from Dariut to the edge of the Delta. The only reference to an irrigation function for *mer* canals is in the 'protection decree' issued by King Pepy I, which exempts from taxation the personnel who worked in and for his predecessor Sneferu's pyramid establishment at Dahshur: the canals were described as bringing water to the fields that served the town.

Royal decrees of the 6th and 8th dynasties make no mention of labour squads being seconded for the construction of irrigation canals, but simply make the distinction between two kinds of fields: those that were flooded every year, and higher-lying ones that only came under water in years of exceptionally high flood. Apart from reliefs showing gardeners watering vegetable patches as in the mastaba of Mereruka, there are no scenes in Old Kingdom tombs of artificial field-irrigation or canal- and dyke-building.

It appears indeed that no artificial irrigation was needed as a rule up until the end of the Neolithic wet phase (subpluvial) around 2350 BC. The Nile floods functioned quite regularly, supplemented by occasional rain. It was only a series of low floods during the First Intermediate Period, when rain ceased falling in Upper Egypt too, that famine occurred and radical measures were clearly needed. It is just at this time, around the 9th and 10th dynasties, that we get the first document describing the construction of a canal 10 cubits (5.2m) wide. This is in the tomb of a regional prince,

Khety, at Asyut. Water from this canal would have been distributed over the fields by the system of basin-irrigation to be described later.

It is under the Middle Kingdom that we first come across terms for irrigation-related works: *a* (canal), *meryt* (embankment), *denyt* (dyke) and others.

In contrast to the earlier notion that irrigation was a centralised affair, recent findings show that it was promoted by local initiative which sometimes exacerbated parochial rivalry. Canal-building, maintenance and water allocation were in fact managed by local consortia with no one higher than a regional prince at the head. Nor do any later documents suggest the existence of a central state institution dealing with these matters and we find no relevant titles in the biographies of nobles or priests. On the contrary, every peasant had a share of responsibility for water-management. The Book of the Dead expressly makes it a great offence to obstruct another person in the use of water or illegally to block his supply.

If the central authorities concerned themselves over the height of the Nile floods it was likely to be for fiscal reasons (since it was the basis of harvest forecasting) or religious ones. But they were of course involved in any projects of nationwide importance. Thus some investigators believe that a dam was built below Memphis soon after the town was founded as the capital of a united Egypt. In the course of the 3rd and 4th dynasties the area of land under cultivation grew through 'internal colonisation', namely the draining of the Delta and the utilisation of land previously lying untilled. In the 12th dynasty a vast project was carried out for reclaiming the Faiyum Oasis, in which Lake Moeris (now Birket Qarun) was used as a reservoir. In flood periods water flowed through a canal still extant as the Bahr Yusuf, into a lake which then reached 18m above sea level though its surface is now 45m below. In inter-flood periods water would flow out of this lake onto the surrounding fields through a system of irrigation canals. The extension of cultivated ground in the Faiyum was completed under the first Ptolemaic kings.

The development of an irrigation canal network made possible not only improved supplies of water to fields that had enjoyed Nile flooding in earlier times but, more importantly, an increase in the arable acreage in more remote and elevated areas. While under the Old Kingdom only natural irrigation had existed, in the Middle Kingdom a distinction could be made between low-lying fields flooded by nature and higher land watered artificially. In the New Kingdom two further categories were recognised, of 'used' and 'fresh' fields. The latter, according to Schenkel, yielded two harvests a year. The Wilbour Papyrus from the time of Ramesses V gives the yield-ratio of high-lying, 'used' and 'fresh' fields respectively as $5:7\frac{1}{2}:10$, and this ratio was used for assessing land-taxes. In the same period there are references to still further

97 Sennedjem and his wife Iynefert ploughing and reaping flax and wheat in the mythical fields of Iaru. Painting on stucco in the tomb of Sennedjem, Deir el-Medina, West Thebes. 19th dynasty

98 The women sifting the grain wear head-bands, perhaps to prevent their hair from falling into it. Limestone relief from Saqqara. 5th–6th dynasty. *Cairo, Egyptian Museum*

categories – 'island fields', 'new fields' and 'raised fields' – which are evidently connected with the introduction of a mechanical water-raising device, the *shaduf*.

Butzer has estimated the area of Egypt under cultivation between the Predynastic Period and the Middle Kingdom as 8000 km², with an increase of 10 to 15 per cent after the introduction of the *shaduf* in the New Kingdom and a further increase by as much again after the installation of the cattle-drawn *saqiya* (water-wheel) in Ptolemaic times. (The comparable area today is a little over 40,000 km².)

Herodotus, who had personal knowledge of Egypt in the 5th century BC, evidently saw it during the period of copious flooding. Hence his rosy view of the farmer's life there (II. 14): 'Now, of course, they reap the fruits of the earth with less effort than anywhere else in the world . . . They do not have to plough the furrow or dig the soil, they can dispense with the tiresome labour in the field that other people must endure . . . As soon as the river has risen of its own accord, watered the arable land and receded again, each of them sows his own plot and drives pigs on to it to tread the seed in. Then he awaits the harvest.'

A textbook passage from a scribes' school, by contrast, paints the peasant's lot in much darker colours – exaggerating perhaps by way of propaganda for the happy career of the scribe: 'When [the farmer] returns to his fields he finds them in good condition. He spends eight hours ploughing, and the worms are already waiting. He eats half his crop himself, the rest is taken by the hippopotamus. There are many mice in the fields, and locusts descend on them. Even cattle devour his harvest and sparrows steal it. Alas for the farmer! The little that is left thieves take from his barn. Then the scribe-officer arrives to count up the harvest; he has bailiffs with him who wield sticks, and black men with palm-stalks. "Give us the grain," they say. "There is none." So they hold him by the legs and beat him, then tie him up and throw him in the ditch. His wife is bound too, and his children, and their neighbours make haste to abandon them so as to save their own grain.'

In tilling his land the peasant made do with a small range of simple tools, many of which are used in almost identical form by the *fellah* of today. First and foremost was the indispensable hoe for loosening the soil, its broad, thin sharp-edged blade of hard wood set at an acute angle to the long wooden shaft to which it was bound with plant-fibre cord. This implement gave its shape to the hieroglyph *mer*.

By enlargement and addition of further parts the hoe evolved into the ploughshare, which could more fitly be called a 'plough-hook' since it tore the earth without turning it. The oldest sign of its existence is a plough-shaped heiroglyph of the 2nd dynasty. The plough consisted of a fairly long blade of hard wood fastened at its lower end to a pair of wooden stilts splayed out toward their upper end, on which the

ploughman would lean to drive the blade into the soil to the required depth and guide it along the furrow. A long pole extended from the lower end of the stilts to the yoke over the necks of the draught animals.

For cutting the corn farmers originally used an almost straight or slightly curved wooden sickle with a longitudinal groove in which a row of squarish flint blades were set close together. These were gradually superseded by copper and then, from the Middle Kingdom on, bronze sickles.

For wood-cutting, ground stone axes were used, the heads being tied to J-shaped handles. Other agricultural implements included wooden shovels for tossing grain, wooden pitchforks for loading the sheaves, wooden rakes for collecting the cut ears, plant-fibre nets and bags, leather or canvas sacks for transporting both sheaves and grain, large wooden tubs for measuring grain and cords for field-surveying.

The cereals the Egyptians cultivated were three kinds of wheat (einkorn, emmer and spelt) and several of barley, notably the six-rowed variety. They devoted ample acreage to flax, their main source of textile fibre. For a second crop, or in garden plots, a wide variety of vegetables were grown, including onions, garlic, leek, Egyptian lettuce, radishes, cabbage, asparagus, cucumbers, lentils, peas, beans and many spices. Valuable vegetable oils were extracted from sesame, flax and castor-oil seeds.

The floods meant a period of rest for the farmer, unless the pharaoh called him up into army service or public works. According to Diodorus (I, 36, 11), 'for the duration of the floods the common people, released from their labours, abandon themselves to recreation, feasting without end and freely enjoying every form of entertainment.' At these times the whole landscape disappeared under water with only the villages standing out as islands. People would haul out their papyrus boats and row off to visit friends in other villages, the more devout paying their respects at the shrines of popular gods.

At the height of the floods, usually in mid-August, each farmer would row around his land closing the vents in the surrounding dykes. Then when the Nile subsided the water would slowly run off, deposit all the enriching mud it had brought with it and soak down deep into the soil. After about a month-and-a-half he would come again to release the water, now turned brackish through evaporation. A field irrigated in this natural, but regulated, manner, would of course only yield one harvest a year. To obtain a second harvest in summer the owner would have to resort to artificial irrigation in the later periods of the year.

Once the water had completely seeped away and the ground was firm enough to walk over, the farmer and his family would start hoeing it up again or deep-ploughing it at intervals. Then it was ready for sowing.

The scribe in charge of the granaries would measure out the quantity of grain allotted to each farmer and keep a written record. Then the vizier, through his officials and the town and village headmen, would give the order for sowing to commence.

This involved a ritual in which the king symbolically inaugurated both the earth-breaking and the grain-sowing. The earliest record of this may be the scene on the head of the sceptre of King Scorpion, showing him wielding a hoe while another man scatters seed from a basket.

The ceremony symbolised at the same time the ritual burial of the god Osiris, who had died at the hand of his brother Seth but came to life again thanks to his wife (and sister) Isis. Grain, the symbol of Osiris' body, appears to have no life till it sprouts anew. Hence, in the harvest festivals, the generous praise for Isis, to whom credit was due for the revival of the grain. This popular belief was reflected in the little flat clay figures of the prostrate Osiris which were 'sown'; the appearance of green corn was seen as an analogue to Osiris' resurrection.

So now the farmer could start sowing. With his grain in a leather bag slung across his left shoulder, or in a basket held in his left hand, he would scatter it in wide swathes over the prepared ground. Lest it stay on the surface to be pecked up by birds, he would invite a herdsman to come onto the field with his flock of sheep or goats so that they could tread the grain in with their hooves. In some illustrations we see a

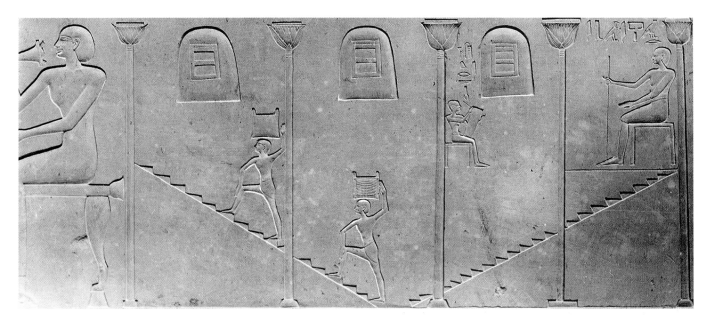

99 A scribe recording the grain being brought into the granary by porters under the supervision of the administrator. Detail of the sarcophagus of Ashait from the temple of Mentuhotep II. Sunk relief in limestone. Deir el-Bahari. 11th dynasty. *Cairo, Egyptian Museum*

young lad coaxing the leading ram of a flock in the right direction with a sprig of fodder, shouting 'Stay close to me!' Some New Kingdom scenes show pigs taking part in the same operation.

The water that had soaked into the ground during the flood season usually sufficed for the grain until it was ripe. But sometimes the sun's heat had drawn off all the moisture before then. This was particularly liable to happen on elevated sites beyond the flood's reach, or in years when the floods were poor anyway. Unlike the Delta and central Egypt, where there would be an occasional brisk shower, usually in November or December, the rest of the valley in Upper Egypt and Nubia had never experienced a proper downfall since the neolithic wet phase. So there was nothing for it but to fetch additional water from the river or the irrigation canals.

During the Old and Middle Kingdoms all a farmer could do in this case was to hitch a yoke over his shoulders and manhandle the water out onto the fields in a pair of wooden or clay buckets. A relief in the 6th-dynasty mastaba of Mereruka at Saqqara 105 shows gardeners with yokes watering lettuce in a garden. When fields or gardens were to be watered they were first divided into square sections with a grid of little dykes. Water was then poured into one section after another, the dykes retaining it just long enough for it to soak in. One can imagine the effort and monotony of carrying water out to the fields in the boiling sun, often from dawn to dusk.

Relief only came with the introduction of the *shaduf* at the end of the 18th dynasty. It evidently came from Mesopotamia, where it is illustrated on an Akkadian cylinder seal dating as far back as 2370–2200 BC. A long wooden beam rocks on a pivot fixed in a supporting tower, usually conical, made of dried mud reinforced with reeds or palm-frond ribs. From one end hangs a leather, wooden or clay bucket, balanced at the other end by a stone or mud-brick weight. By rocking the beam, water could be raised with little effort over a vertical distance of one or two metres and then emptied out into a gully at the edge of the field, whence it flowed to the areas requiring irrigation. The earliest evidence of the use of a *shaduf* comes from the tombs of Neferhotep and Merire II at Akhetaten and from a number of 19th-dynasty Theban tombs. Here we see men irrigating a garden from a square artificial pool, and presumably the same method could have been used for irrigating a field. Though working a *shaduf* was not a strenuous job, it was certainly monotonous and wearisome.

The first mechanical device for conducting water to high-lying fields from the canals dates from the Persian Period (after 525 BC). This was the *tanbur* or Archimedes' screw, a helix that could be revolved inside a sloping cylinder. This provided a many times larger, faster and more continuous flow of water, but as the

tanbur cost more and took more exertion to operate it did not immediately displace the older invention and the *shaduf* continued in use alongside it.

The decisive turn in the technology of water-raising came in the early Ptolemaic Period with the introduction of the *saqiya*, first shown to have been used in the Faiyum around 300 BC. This is a device similar to the water-wheel once familiar in parts of Europe. In *saqiya* the revolution of a horizontal gear driven by an ox walking round a circular track is transmitted to a large vertical wheel with water-scoops hanging around its rim. As they reach the bottom of their orbit these scoops take up water which they tip out when they rise to the top, three or four metres higher, into a wooden channel that leads out onto the field. The *saqiya* not only raises the water by a greater height differential than the other machines but ensures a large and steady flow as well. It proved a most effective way of bringing water to distant and elevated areas, making all-year irrigation possible and enabling second harvests to be reaped on a substantial scale. One such machine is said to be capable of serving as much as 100,000 m² of land every day.

Until quite recently travellers in the Egyptian countryside could see all these irrigation methods still in regular use. Now, however, they have been almost completely replaced by the more efficient engine-driven pumps.

Finally the long-awaited day has arrived. The farmer rubs an ear of the now golden

100 Two baskets of grain are taken to the granary by a donkey, urged on from behind by a peasant with a hoe over his shoulder. When they arrive, porters carry the baskets up the stairs to the charging-hole. In a separate scene three domesticated antelopes are feeding. Painting on limestone from the tomb of Ity. Gebelein. 1st Intermediate Period. *Turin, Museo Egizio*

Right **101** Delinquent farmer being shaken by the tax collector and another being punished with a stick. Painting in the tomb of Menna, Sheikh Abd el-Qurna, West Thebes. 18th dynasty

corn between his fingertips and pronounces it ripe. Harvest-time means mobilising the village's entire labour force, women and children included. From the New Kingdom onwards slaves and violators of royal decrees will have been roped in too, and in an emergency even army units might be detailed to lend a hand.

The start of the harvest involved celebrations in honour of the fertility god Min. These were opened by the king himself, who reaped the first ears of grain with a sickle. Diodorus tells us that even in his day, the 1st century AD, peasants maintained the old tradition of setting up stooks with the first corn harvested, beating their breasts and calling upon the goddess Isis.

Harvest scenes are depicted on the walls of many tombs, nowhere more fully than in the 18th-dynasty tomb of Menna at Sheikh Abd el-Qurna. We shall now take these as a guide.

Before the sickles plunged into the standing corn the assessor-scribes led by the 'Overseer of Fields' turned up to check the position of the boundary-stones and measure the size of the field with a calibrated surveying cord. From these data they worked out the probable yield, which would be compared with the actual yield after the threshing was done. This was clearly done to prevent any part of the harvest being 'mislaid'.

The harvesters usually worked in a straight row, advancing steadily to the rhythm of one of the songs documented for example in the tombs of Ty (5th dynasty) or Mereruka (6th dynasty) at Saqqara. The song-leader was accompanied by a flautist and the harvesters probably chanted in response. (We can hear Egyptian labourers singing today in the same fashion during the tedious work of removing sand from archaeological sites.)

Grasping a bunch of stalks in his left hand the harvester would slice them through at a level just above his knees, then toss the ears aside to be picked up by the helpers. These would pile the eared stalks alternately end to end, so that a compact sheaf formed that required no binding – the Ty relief shows this very clearly. The sheaves

were in turn loaded into nets or baskets to be taken on donkeyback for threshing. Some of the scenes are captioned with words of encouragement such as: 'How now, good people, make haste; the barley [has to be gathered] before the day is out!' Or 'Where are you, who are so good at the job?' – 'Here I am!'

The threshing-floor was sometimes out on the field, sometimes next to the farmhouse. It was a circular arena of trodden clay ringed with a low clay wall. The sheaves would be loosened, the ears thrown on to the ground and cattle or donkeys driven into the enclosure to thresh out the grain with their trampling, while the men stood outside in a circle urging the animals on with cries or prodding them with sticks.

The grain released in this way was still mixed with chaff, straw and other impurities. Cleaning was done on a breezy day on some well-swept piece of flat ground. It was usually a job for young girls, who tossed the corn into the air with short-handled wooden shovels. The wind carried off the lighter chaff and so on while the heavier grain fell back on the ground. This winnowing could also be done by shaking the grain in sieves – usually a man's task. Once again the scribes now came on the scene to measure the volume of grain in standard wooden tubs. Finally it was sacked up and carried, by manpower or donkeypower, to the granaries.

233
100

Right to left **102–4** Gardeners clapping sticks to scare the birds away, watering and cutting the lettuce. Master sketches for the unfinished decoration of the tomb of Neferherenptah, Saqqara. 5th dynasty

105 Gardeners bring water in pairs of jars on yokes to the square lettuce beds formed by a network of shallow trenches. Tomb of Mereruka, Saqqara. 6th dynasty

The oldest type of granary, known from Archaic times, was a round-based cone with a domed top. It was made of seasoned wood, often plaster-lined, or of mud bricks. The largest ones had steps leading up to the filling hole, or else a ladder was laid against them. Once more the scribe checked the number of sackfuls poured in. At the bottom was another opening which could be securely closed; any quantities removed had to be checked again by the scribe.

All grain earmarked for the next sowing was stored in granaries of a different, trapezoidal shape (like the hieroglyph *shenut*) so that there was no danger of it being ground in error.

Among Middle Kingdom models we find another, four-cornered design of granary, standing in a row against one side of a house courtyard. One such granary is shown with a flat roof and five filling-holes through which women are pouring sacks of grain while a scribe, seated nearby, keeps a tally and a guard looks on, stick in hand. This type is often depicted in tombs and at the foot end of coffins.

A huge number of granaries, eloquent testimony to their importance in the running of New Kingdom temples, have survived in the grounds of the Ramesseum, Ramesses II's funerary temple on the west bank of the Nile at Thebes. These consist of numerous rows of long mud-brick corridors with barrel-vaulting and evenly spaced filling-holes at the top.

The system of state and temple granaries was the backbone of ancient Egypt's black-earth economy. As an arm of government these granaries were important at local, provincial and state level; hordes of official scribes answered for their efficient accounting of intake, storage and out-goings of grain. Thanks to them, if floods failed or harvests were poor, there would be enough stocks to stave off famine for several years. One recalls the biblical account of Joseph and his wise leadership during the seven fat and seven lean years. The granaries furnished food for the army, for workers on major construction projects and for the large groups of citizens engaged in non-agricultural activities. In addition to the state and temple grain-stores which absorbed the greater part of each crop, there were large private ones on the big estates and smaller ones in the countryside of humble countryfolk.

Another staple crop, flax, was pulled rather than cut. This was work for a man and his wife side-by-side, as depicted in the 19th-dynasty tomb of Sennedjem at Deir el-Medina. In the harvesting of flax, as Pliny's *Natural History* notes (XIX, 16–18), after removal of roots and seed-heads the stalks were laid to dry in the sun in small bundles for about a week, plunged into water for 10 to 14 days and finally beaten against stones and combed out with a wooden or metal instrument to separate the long fibres. Further processing took place in the weavers' shops or in homesteads.

Completion of the harvest did not mean the farmer could rest. As early as the Old Kingdom it was realised that the interval between the end of harvesting in March or April and the onset of the next floods in July was long enough for a second crop to be cultivated. This was usually a vegetable, most commonly pulse crops which are ideal for alternating with cereals because they enrich the soil with nitrogen. These also bulked large in the Egyptian villager's diet. In the time of Ptolemy III Euergetes there is even evidence of a second cereal crop being sown. There was of course no need in Egypt to allow the ground to lie fallow for a period of recovery. Its rehabilitation would be taken care of by the next Nile flood.

The supervision of the harvest work by the scribes was no hit-and-miss affair, since the fruits of the farmer's toil did not belong to him; the bulk of it had to be handed over to the state. All land in Egypt was the sole property of the king, or of the temples and nobles who received it from the king as a gift. It was in effect a system of large estates tilled by the population at large. Peasants were counted as *meret*, a term usually translated as 'subjects' or less appropriately (since we are not sure whether they were restrained from moving) as 'serfs'; they are also referred to as *ahuty*, field-workers. Each peasant family worked an allotted acreage of soil to which it was tied for life, and handed over most of its produce to the landowner. In other respects peasants enjoyed personal liberty and full civic rights. When slavery spread during the New Kingdom peasants were even able to take on slaves to help them in their work.

If a farmer could not fulfil his quotas he was liable to merciless punishment. The
234 mastaba of Mereruka at Saqqara shows estate stewards leading hunched-up debtors
before a judge and beating them over the back with sticks before they even reach him.
One debtor is sitting tied to a post while a couple of henchmen lambast his naked
101 back. The beating of a prostrate peasant appears also in the tomb of Menna at Sheikh
Abd el-Qurna.

At times when central authority was weakening, especially after the Third
Intermediate Period, several royal or temple priests, army veterans and others were
able to acquire land, initially to cover their own needs for the rest of their lives. This
land could however be passed on by inheritance and in the course of time it came to
be regarded as transferable and then as saleable, the state no longer having enough
authority to re-annex it to the state farming enterprises.

Our account of the blessings of the black earth would not be complete without
some mention of ancient Egyptian gardens. These were planned not only for the
cultivation of fruit and vegetables but also for aesthetic and ritual reasons, not to
speak of the shade they afforded. The Egyptians had a high regard for flowers and
trees and devoted great care to planting, tending and protecting them. To sit in hot
weather under the canopy of a tree was a favourite recipe for relaxing body and mind.

It was popularly thought that trees were the abode of supernatural beings or
much-loved gods. The goddess Hathor enjoyed the title of 'lady of the sycomore'. The
Books of the Dead linked this tree with the rising sun and with the sky goddess Nut, or
at other times with Isis or Hathor. It was thought of as a source of shade and
sustenance for the dead. This reputation was transferred in the second half of the
106 18th dynasty to the date palm. The sacred persea tree (*Mimusops laurifolia*), again,
was regarded as the source of life; the goddess Seshat and the god Thoth were believed
to have inscribed its leaves with the name of the current pharaoh and the duration of
his reign. Various religious sites were linked with the Christ's-thorn tree (*Ziziphus
spina-christi*), and the horseradish tree (*Moringa aptera*) was sacred to the gods
Hetepbakef and Heribakef.

Since Egypt was relatively poor in trees it is no surprise that they enjoyed special
protection. As the home of a god, a sacred tree was not allowed to be felled at all.
Other sorts could only be cut down with the prior permission of the vizier himself. The
103 tree-cutting scene painted in the tomb of Nakht at Sheikh Abd el-Qurna (18th
dynasty) is thus of rare value. It shows a tree-cutter kneeling on his left knee,
clutching in both hands the long-handled, oblong axe with which he has just finished
undercutting a tree about to fall. A second tree has already been felled and a third still
stands in the background.

Left **106** Of ancient Egyptian trees and bushes it is possible to recognise the date palm with its unbranched trunk and small fruit, the doum palm with a forked trunk and big fruit, and the sycomore. Painting in the tomb of Sennedjem at Deir el-Medina. 19th dynasty

Right **107** A kneeling man cutting down a sycomore tree with a bronze axe tied to a wooden handle. Painting in the tomb of Nakht. Sheikh Abd el-Qurna, West Thebes. 18th dynasty

108 This charming sketch of a gardener upset to find a goat feeding on the leaves of a tree, while suckling its kid, may be an example of the subject matter of pictures that decorated private houses. Limestone ostracon. 20th dynasty. *Cairo, Egyptian Museum*

A traveller would have encountered several kinds of gardens in ancient Egypt. The most extensive were sited around the royal palace and the great temples. These are little documented, but the gardens attached to aristocratic residences are well illustrated in the owners' tombs. In the Middle Kingdom they were for the most part modest vegetable gardens entered by steps leading up the banks of canals. But, for instance, in the New Kingdom tombs of Rekhmire, Amenemheb, Qenamun, Menire or Sennefer at Sheikh Abd el-Qurna there are depictions of large gardens surrounded 68 with high brick walls to keep out human or animal intruders. Inside there were straight rows of trees – tall sycomore figs by the wall, date and doum palms closer in, 106 and finally low fig trees growing round a rectangular pool. More sycomore figs alternating with palms fringed the vine-pergolas, lightly built of papyrus stems and trellis. Kiosks and arbours afforded tempting shade and well-stocked fishpools with lotus lilies, reeds and papyrus thickets were a sight to soothe the jaded eye.

Even humble village houses had little gardens next to them. Where buildings were close together the owners might have to be content with a few trees or flower-beds, or simply grow flowers and small shrubs in clay pots or wooden troughs in the courtyard.

A species of great economic importance was the date palm. When the heavy trusses of golden fruit appeared among the crown of fronds, men would clamber up the trunk with knives between their teeth to cut down the strings of dates. There is a painting on the wall of Rekhmire's tomb that shows this being done. Here one man is shown plucking the fruit with both hands and another is carrying it away in pans hung on a yoke. In the royal gardens they even employed tame monkeys for this job. The scribes responsible for grain and food stores also kept a tally of dates garnered in state or temple plantations, and of the quotas handed over by private gardeners. We shall be describing the fruit of other trees in Chapter 10.

An important oil-bearing tree was the *baq*, probably synonymous with the horseradish tree. Apart from cultivated kinds, many valuable trees grew wild, including acacias, tamarisks, mimosas, willows, doum palms and lemon trees.

Most of the native broad-leaved trees yielded only inferior timber that was too knotty, brittle or prone to split for use other than for stanchions, roof-beams and some domestic furniture – chests and coffins. When large-scale construction developed – pyramids, mastabas, palaces and temples – the demand increased for high-quality imported wood, especially coniferous kinds found mainly along the coasts of what are now Israel, Lebanon and Syria. One of the earliest chronicles to mention these is the report of an expedition of 40 ships to Byblos in the time of King Sneferu (4th dynasty), which brought back quantities of cedar, cypress, spruce, pine, fir and juniper logs.

109 Vineyard workers picking grapes. Painting in the tomb of Nakht, Sheikh Abd el-Qurna, West Thebes. 18th dynasty

When Egypt gained control of these lands in the early New Kingdom she developed tree-felling there on such a scale that it helped to denude the entire coastal region. As embalming techniques were refined, resin from the Aleppo and stone or umbrella pines, Cilician pines, various spruces (particularly the oriental spruce) and perhaps from larches was imported from the same area. The cedar produces very little resin. Ebony was imported from the African interior for the manufacture of certain luxury items.

The ancient Egyptians were already experimenting with the acclimatisation of exotic species including the incense-bearing *Boswellia*, specimens of which are shown being brought back by members of the expedition to the Land of Punt on reliefs in Hatshepsut's temple at Deir el-Bahari. There were some gardens, especially among those belonging to temples, that resembled modern botanical collections. One of the most celebrated belonged to Tuthmosis III and is illustrated in the 'botany room' reliefs next to the festival hall in the temple of Amun at Karnak.

Few gardens were without grapevines, which were also grown in separate vineyards. Many Old Kingdom, and even more New Kingdom, tomb murals show 109 bunches of grapes being gathered in baskets and brought to the wine-press. This was 110 a square vat lined with smooth mortar. The grapes were thrown in and the juice trodden out by groups of barefoot men hanging on to ropes suspended from a wooden frame so that they should not lose their balance and tumble into the pressings as they inhaled the heavy vapour. The juice ran out through a wood or metal pipe into a 111 vessel standing underneath. The remaining mass of skins and pips was put into canvas bags with bars fastened to each end; two men would lever these apart so as to squeeze yet more juice out. In Middle Kingdom paintings at Beni Hasan we see an improved version of the technique: one end of the bag was fixed to a wall and pressure was applied to its contents by levering a single bar tied to the other end.

After this the must was filtered through cloth into fermentation vats and left for a time, heat sometimes being applied to speed up the fermentation. When half-fermented, the wine was funneled or siphoned off into tall amphorae and allowed to mature, sometimes over several years.

110 Treading grapes with bare feet shown in the adjacent scene. Both men are holding on to ropes so as not to lose their footing under the influence of the heady vapour. Another man is filling jars from the tap. Painting in the tomb of Nakht, Sheikh Abd el-Qurna, West Thebes. 18th dynasty

Finally the mature wine was again filtered through canvas and improved by the addition of spices or honey, then conveyed throughout the country in wine amphorae whose frequent appearance in archaeological sites shows how popular the drink was, especially from the New Kingdom on and even more so in Roman days. Masses of them were found during the excavation of the Ramesseum storerooms, in the tombs of Theban dignitaries, at Abydos, Tell el-Amarna and other places. Inscriptions on some amphorae give the vintage year, type and quality of grape, locality and owner of the vineyard etc. Wine-making was another concern of the scribes, who impressed their seals on the Nile-mud jar seals while they were still soft. 237

By deciphering the details written on the jars we can reconstruct the map of Egyptian viticulture. The most important centres were the Delta, Lake Marea (now Mariut) near Alexandria, the coast westward to Libya, the oases of the Western Desert (especially el-Kharga and el-Dakhla) and the environs of Kynopolis near el-Maragha in Middle Egypt. Substitute wines were also made by fermenting palm juice, dates, figs or *nabak*, the fruit of the Christ's-thorn tree.

The ancient Egyptians were familiar with many wild shrubs and herbs and used them as drugs, for making dyes and wickerwork – mats, baskets, bed matting, osier stands, sandals and so forth. Many kinds of flowers were tied into bouquets for the living or the dead – cornflowers, poppies, chrysanthemums, mandrakes, mallows, irises, larkspurs, jasmine, ivy and above all papyrus reeds and lotus lilies.

The dense growths of papyrus and lotus in fens and marshes were a typical feature 113 of the Egyptian landscape. Papyrus, particularly common in the Delta, became the heraldic plant of Lower Egypt while the lotus, found all along the Nile, was the symbol of Upper Egypt. The close union of the two parts of the country is proclaimed in reliefs round the plinths of colossal statues of the king, which show the Nile god Hapy tying up bunches of papyrus and lotus together.

Papyrus thickets were also favourite hunting grounds. In the branches of the Nile in the Delta maze little muddy islands developed which continually changed shape or shifted. In mythology the papyrus came accordingly to symbolise the earth arising from the primeval ocean and hence, by a shift of meaning, youth and happiness.

Amulets in the shape of papyrus bundles were popularly worn as a protection for the living, and were credited with magic power to confer eternal youth and everlasting joy on the dead as well. Papyrus bouquets stood for victory and for joy. Papyrus also often accompanies portraits of the gods, such as Horus, Hathor and Udjat. And of course papyrus had a host of other uses in daily life – for writing, wickerwork, boat-building and other activities.

Egyptians were familiar with two lotus species, the white (*Nymphaea lotus*) and the blue (*Nymphaea caerulea*), to which the Indian (*Nymphaea nelumbo*) was added in the Late Period. According to myth the great flower of the blue lotus, from which the sun rose, appeared from the primeval ocean on the first day of the world. The gods accordingly loved it as a symbol of the Creation. The Memphis deity Nefertem, 'lord of sweet smells', is usually shown holding one as his emblem. Lotus blossoms were often laid on graves as a fragrant farewell to those who had left for the hereafter, and they were offered in the temples to the gods. Nor was their heavy scent ever absent from the festivities of the living, such as we see on New Kingdom tomb walls: noble banquets where tables groan under the weight of lotus bunches, women thread them through their hair and every guest holds one to his or her neighbour's nose.

The Egyptians certainly appreciated the black earth that had yielded them so much benefit, and they took care to husband it. New villages were most commonly sited on the very edge of the fertile areas, where the desert sand began, or on flat islands of sand alluvium. In this way the Egyptians minimised the encroachment of damp into their houses, while ensuring that not a scrap of usable soil was wasted.

The Egyptian peasant's habit of working half-naked in the blazing sun, wearing only his short kilt, shows how immune his skin had become to sunburn, and apparently they were not accustomed to cover their heads to avert sunstroke. They stood up equally well to fierce winds, and were resistant to common colds from the alternation of daytime and night-time temperatures. Their diet, based on bread, greenstuff and milk products, was balanced and biologically sound, containing plenty of vitamins and minerals with little animal fat or harmful ingredients. We know from their portraits that they enjoyed slender, wiry frames and athletic physique. They might have been amongst the healthiest people of the ancient world

111 A domesticated baboon stretching the poles in place of the essential fifth man to help the workers squeeze grapes. Painted relief on limestone, tomb of Nefer, Saqqara. 5th dynasty

112 Lotus, an offering to the god Horus. Vignette from the papyrus Book of the Dead of Lady Cheritwebeshet. 21st dynasty. *Cairo, Egyptian Museum*

(as Herodotus (II, 77) reckoned them to be, next only to the Libyans) had it not been for the dangers to which they were exposed at work.

Day after day they would wade through the black mud and often paddled in the shallow waters of canals and gullies. Little did they realise that these places teamed with the larvae of parasitic worms, notably bilharzia worms (*Schistosoma haematobium*), whose eggs had come from the faeces of infected humans and would spend the next phase of their lives in a secondary host, the snails of the genus *Bulinus*. The larvae are able to bore through healthy human skin, migrate up the blood vessels and settle in the urinary passages, where they cause chronic haemorrhaging. The consequent loss of blood can lead to anaemia, decrease of work ability, sometimes even premature death.

Work on the fields also exposed the Egyptian to the bites of any of several dozen species of snakes. The most common of the various vipers, the Sand and Horned Vipers, inject a venom that acts cytotoxically on tissues and blood corpuscles. Especially dreaded were the cobras, the most common being *Naja haje*; its reputation was evidently the reason why it became the symbol of the pharaoh's power over his subjects as indicated by the *uraeus* that adorned the royal crown. The bite of this snake acts neurotoxically, causing spasms, paralysis and death. The myth of Re and Isis includes an accurate description of the effect of cobra venom on the grievously suffering Re. A peasant might also fall foul of one of the several kinds of scorpion that hid under the stones. Their stings also have a neurotoxic effect, like that of the cobra in the larger species, more like a bee's in the smaller ones.

Since neither preventive nor curative medicine of any value was available, people resorted to charms, spells, magic knives and – in the Late and Graeco-Roman Periods – to magic steles on which the god Horus is shown battling victoriously with snakes and scorpions. Perhaps this was why venomous snakes were sometimes embalmed as mummies. In truth most patients could only hope to survive if the snake had already voided some of its poison in biting an earlier victim.

CHAPTER NINE

Stockbreeding and the Hunt

SOME OF THE products of the black earth were destined for use not by the Egyptians themselves but by their constant companions, helpmates and source of sustenance – domestic animals. The green expanses of cultivated lucerne, clover and the chickling vetch *Lathyrus sativus*, provided fodder for cattle especially. Herds and flocks would often wander far off in search of meadows and pastureland as well as clearing up the straw and chaff left in the fields after the corn crop.

The Egyptians probably inherited some of their farmstock in their present domestic forms from Asia Minor, some perhaps via parts of North Africa. Stockbreeding was already a routine activity in the earliest neolithic settlements in the Faiyum and on the western edge of the Delta (Merimda Beni Salama), as we can tell from fragments of bone found in the remains of prehistoric meals. Cave drawings in Upper Egypt and Nubia feature domesticated cattle as well as vivid hunting scenes.

Historic times witnessed a continuous increase not only of agricultural output but in the number and size of herds which, like the soil, belonged to large estate-owners and were tended by professional drovers and shepherds. These men had their own managers and overseers as well as their own assistants such as 'bucket carriers' and 'foddermen'. Each specialised as a rule in one kind of animal – cattle, sheep, goats, pigs, asses, oryx (which they had tried to domesticate during the Old Kingdom), horses (introduced in the New Kingdom), geese and other poultry, and even dogs.

In tomb scenes we can distinguish herdsmen by their very appearance. They were as a rule conspicuously lean; being forever on the move with their charges they had to stint themselves on food and creature comforts. They were usually unshaven, but with little or no hair on their heads. They wore their kilts tucked up and carried over their shoulders a long stick with a roll of matting hanging from it (for protection from wind and sun) and a bundle of pots and food. We see them bringing their animals to 117 the estate-owners or their bailiffs, milking, feeding young stock, helping herds to ford 116 rivers, assisting deliveries and so forth. 115

Every farmer also kept a small number of animals himself to provide indispensable assistance in various tasks, as well as milk, meat and wool.

Foremost among the farm animals were the horned cattle evolved from the pre-historic *Bos primigenius*. The older race, documented in bone finds and drawings of the Predynastic Period and the Old Kingdom, had long lyre-shaped horns such as we still find in Sudan, though no longer in Egypt itself. During the close of the Old Kingdom thinner-legged shorthorn breeds appear. Some experts believe that the long-horned varieties were either displaced by these, or wiped out in some epidemic. There are no ancient Egyptian records of the great black Indian buffalo so common in 114 the country today, though some consider that the water buffalo may have existed, and in earliest times the African buffalo too. The herds contained more cows than bulls; there is no satisfactory evidence that oxen were known.

In the daytime cattle were driven out onto pasture or harvest fields. To ensure that grass was not over-trampled the animals were tethered by thick datepalm-fibre ropes to stones buried in the ground.

To protect them from wild beasts and thieves, cattle were herded each night into palisaded pens or, in the colder winter months, into byres. A wooden model in the 11th-dynasty tomb of the noble Meketre at Deir el-Bahari shows one with two compartments and an interconnecting door. In the rear four cattle are feeding from a trough; in the front half two men are fattening up a pair of cows destined for slaughter, while the ubiquitous guard stands with his stick in the doorway. Animals were tethered to rows of thick wooden pegs like those found during the excavation of the New Kingdom town of Gurob.

Large cattle-herds formed the basic capital of the big estates. This is demonstrated in another wooden model from Meketre's tomb where we see this landowner seated with his son in a pavilion, watching his herds in a kind of march-past. No doubt the occasion was a cattle-census for tax purposes, as indicated by the presence of four scribes, busily recording. A row of herdsmen are steering the cattle into single file;

Previous page **113**   Nebamun hunting birds in the marshes with a throwstick and three decoy herons. His cat has grabbed three birds. Nebamun's wife and daughter are looking on. Painting on limestone. From the tomb of Nebamun, Dra Abu el-Naga, West Thebes. 18th dynasty. *London, British Museum*

Below **114**   Ancient Egyptian breeds are shown in this representation of the sky bull and three of the seven sacred 'Hathor cows'. Painted relief in the tomb of Nefertari in the Valley of the Queens, Deir el-Medina, West Thebes. 19th dynasty

Right **115**   Two men assisting a cow calving. Limestone relief in the tomb of Kagemni in Saqqara. 6th dynasty

235

there are three men counting the numbers aloud while the chief herdsman bows and kneels before the landlord.

Ever since prehistoric times Egyptians had kept flocks of *Ovis longipes palaeoaegyptiaca*, a sheep with long spiral horns spread out horizontally, of tall stature and with a long tail. In the Middle Kingdom another species arrived, *Ovis platyura aegyptiaca*, with spiral horns close to the head, lower build and short fat tails. The former type was seen as the incarnation of Khnum, god of the First Cataract, and a few other deities with ram's heads, while the second was the symbol of the Theban god Amun, who became the chief divinity during the New Kingdom. Despite, or perhaps because of this, sheep's milk and meat did not figure among offerings to the dead. Priests were forbidden, especially during the Late Period, to eat mutton or wear wool.

The domestic shorthair goat, in both short and long-horned forms, can be seen on some tomb murals. It played no part in religious or funeral rites, but it provided skins, milk and meat that even the poorer could afford. Texts indicate that goats were more numerous than sheep up to Ptolemaic times, when the proportions were reversed.

The farm pig is a domesticated form of the wild boar, tamed independently in several places including the eastern half of the Delta as well as in the Crimea,

116 Herdsmen with cattle fording a canal teeming with fish while a crocodile watches. Painted relief in the tomb of Princess Idut, Saqqara. 6th dynasty

108

75

Thessaly, eastern Asia and elsewhere. It was farmed probably in neolithic times at Merimda Beni Salama; it is attested in the 3rd dynasty. Old Kingdom reliefs still show it as a slender animal with long legs, a thick growth of bristle on the back and a long snout, showing that it had not been long domesticated. But both in pictures and in food remains the pig occurs rather infrequently. Only from the 18th dynasty do we have many textual references to large herds of hogs. The noble Renen, for example, is shown on his tomb-relief at el-Kab inspecting his stock and glorying in the possession of 4500 pigs. Thousands of swine were among the property dedicated to the Memphite deity Ptah by Amenophis III.

The value of pork as a food item for Akhetaten emerges from the latest research by Barry Kemp into the walled workers' village south of the city. A number of stone animal enclosures subdivided into smaller compartments, carefully painted in one case with several layers of plaster, were here used – to judge by the bristles and coprolites that have turned up – for large scale pig-breeding. The clean whitewashed areas were no doubt used for butchering the carcasses after the removal of the bristles by steam-scolding. The design and scale of the accommodation suggests that it was not used for village requirements only but was a pork-production centre for the whole city. To spare the villagers the smell, the enclosures had been sited on the south and east sides in the lee of the prevailing winds. Recent examination of bones in waste-tips

117 Herdsmen bringing cattle for the owner's inspection. Painting on limestone. From the tomb of Nebamun, Dra Abu el-Naga, West Thebes. 18th dynasty. *London, British Museum*

Right 118 Grooms with horses. Limestone relief from the tomb of Horemheb at Saqqara. 18th dynasty

has also confirmed the popularity of pig-meat among working-class Egyptians.

A common beast of burden in Egypt (and for a long time the only means of transport) was the donkey. It was domesticated from the Nubian wild ass *Equus asinus africanus* in the fourth millennium BC, probably in North Africa and perhaps, as some believe, in Upper Egypt. Up to the Persian Period Egyptians relied exclusively on the donkey for land travel in their own country and even for long expeditions to Sinai, to the mountain valleys of the Eastern Desert and to distant oases in the west. As the donkey could not survive long without food and water, travellers across the desert had to take fodder with them, and water for their mounts as well as themselves. Their slow speed was another disadvantage. Nevertheless every peasant kept donkeys, since harvest and other field work would have been hard to manage 100 without them.

Wild camels were probably known to the Egyptians from the distant past. There is a camel's grave in the Helwan cemetery (1st and 2nd dynasties) and camel-shaped vases have been found at the Old Kingdom site of Abusir el-Meleq. The bedouin of northern and central Arabia are credited with having domesticated camels in the latter half of the second millennium BC. Authors differ in dating the first occurrence of domesticated camels in Egypt – theories range from 525 BC to the turn of the millennium. With its proverbially modest requirements of food and water, both being stored in its fatty hump, the camel enabled long desert treks to be accomplished much faster and more safely than before.

As regards the horse, originally perhaps domesticated on the steppes of what is now the Ukraine, we know that it first turned up in Egypt in the army the Asiatic Hyksos invaders at the end of the Middle Kingdom. The Austrian Archaeological Institute team recently found a number of horse burials at Tell el-Dab'a, which is probably the site of Avaris, the residence of the Hyksos kings. During the New Kingdom the Egyptians started horse-breeding for themselves, but this was restricted to the stables of the king and the highest dignitaries, where there were special 118 stablemen to look after them. They used to be harnessed to light two-wheeled 126 chariots, in which the king attended ceremonies, hunts and army parades – or rode to war. Some of the pharaohs were so fond of their steeds that they tended them 222 themselves. Amenophis II's affection for horses, for example, is demonstrated on the 223 stele that he had erected in front of the Sphinx at Giza. When the 25th-dynasty king Piankhi had conquered Hermopolis he visited the stables there and found that the horses had starved to death during the long siege, and this caused 'great grief to his heart'. We know that two of Ramesses II's horses were named 'Theban Victory' and 'Mut is Content'. Occasionally senior dignitaries were allowed to own horses; a 128

painting in his tomb at Dra Abu el-Naga shows the 18th-dynasty royal physician Nebamun hunting hyenas in a two-wheeled chariot drawn by a pair of horses with coloured plumes.

The arrival on the scene of man's faithful friend the dog through domestication of the wolf was brought about independently in several parts of the world during the mesolithic age. The oldest domestication sites have been given as Persia, North America and possibly Northeast Africa – though probably not Egypt itself, where the earliest records of dogs are from the Predynastic Period. We find them often on murals, starting in the Old Kingdom.

The only animal we know for certain to have been domesticated by the Egyptians is their cat, descended from the North African wild subspecies *Felis silvestris lybica*; it is attested in neolithic times. Joachim Boessneck concluded that the domestication process took thousands of years, so that we can only speak of tame cats from the New Kingdom onwards. The cat's popularity arose primarily from its capacity for ridding houses of rodents. It was in this protective role that Bastet was honoured, a goddess represented as a cat, or woman with a cat's head. From the New Kingdom the same animal is sometimes associated with the goddess Tefnut, from whom it took over her title of the 'Eye of King Re', personifying the sun's life-giving heat.

Poultry had been kept since time immemorial, notably geese as shown in the celebrated painting in the tomb of Princess Itet of the 3rd dynasty. The birds are here rendered in such faithful detail that experts have been able to identify two species of *Anser* and two of *Branta*, closer to ducks. A fifth native kind, the wild Egyptian Goose, was never farmed. Five species of duck were also bred, notably the pintail.

The domestic hen was introduced to Egypt only later, after the first Persian conquest according to some, according to others not before Ptolemaic times. It seems though that where the report of Tuthmosis III's Syrian expedition speaks of a bird that lays eggs every day, it is referring to the hen. Isolated finds of egg-shell, and what looks like a cock drawn on a New Kingdom ostracon from the Valley of the Kings suggest that the domestic chicken may have been bred even then.

Egyptian poultry scuffled about for food in courtyards or feeding-pens. There were even specialised poultry farms with their own offices, store-sheds and rooms for the staff. But even there birds were never cooped up without a free run. The principles of artificial incubation were also known, though for this purpose eggs were simply buried in dunghills which produced the requisite heat.

Dovecotes were set up either on rooftops or as separate buildings of mud and straw, the variety of design adding a picturesque touch to towns and villages then as now. Their denizens probably included the Rock Dove, ancestor of modern domestic pigeons, but this is not quite certain.

As early as palaeolithic times man had acquired a taste for wild bees' honey, as we know from cave paintings at Bicorp in Spain. The oldest Egyptian drawing of honey being taken from a nest of wild bees dates from the Neolithic Age. The practice continued in historic times; there were professional honey-collectors (*bityw*) who plied their trade along the desert fringes and deep into Nubia.

The domestication of bees, however, goes back at least to the Old Kingdom. A relief in the Sun-temple of King Niuserre at Abusir shows a villager kneeling in front of a row of hives. The work is too damaged for us to be sure whether or not the man is taking a frame out to put in the dish he is holding in his other hand. In the next scene people are pouring honey from a small jar into a storage vessel where it would no doubt be left to mature. Finally we see the contents being decanted into pots with handles, which are then closed for despatch to its destination. The hives were evidently made of reed-bundles and rushes smeared with mud, or else tall vessels were used with openings for the bees on the side and removable caps at the top for taking the combs out.

Wall paintings in the 18th-dynasty tomb of Rekhmire at Sheikh Abd el-Qurna show what progress apiculture had made by the New Kingdom. Hives now consist of vessels lying on their sides, one over another, on a foundation of pressed clay. We see a man smoking the bees out with three candles in a dish while another lays pieces of comb on plates standing ready, his assistants then collecting the honey into large vessels. The jugs near by may have been used for pouring the honey into special jars, which were finally closed and stamped. At the far end of the bee-house wax was poured into triangular moulds.

Beeswax was used to cover wooden tablets for writing notes on, or sketching with a metal scribe; for casting bronze objects by the *cire perdu* method; and as a foundation for pigments. The outline of a bee as a symbol of Lower Egypt formed part of the royal name, as against the reed which denoted Upper Egypt in the same context.

It is interesting to note the attempts made in ancient Egypt to domesticate other wild creatures by snaring them and trying to breed them alongside tame species. We know that this was done with several kinds of antelope and gazelle, with the Nubian ibex, the Barbary sheep and even the hyena, heron and crane. The object of such experiments is clear from illustrations in mastabas where the animals are shown with collars round their necks to which a leash could be fastened. Force-feeding of cranes by stuffing balls of flour down their throats, as with geese, is shown not only in 120 several Saqqara mastabas but also in that of Ptahshepses at Abusir and in the tomb of Djehutihotep at el-Bersha. There is evidence of crane-farming in the Middle Kingdom and these birds feature in a sacrificial procession in the 18th-dynasty temple of Hatshepsut at Deir el-Bahari with their beaks tied for safety to their necks. There are famous portrayals of hyena-feeding in the 6th-dynasty mastabas of Mereruka and 124 Kagemni at Saqqara, where two keepers are having a hard time holding one animal down on his back while they stuff pieces of meat and poultry into its muzzle. The most ferocious specimens had to have their hind legs tied together first. Some writers believe the intention was to train hyenas for taking part in hunts.

A few other animals may be mentioned which kings or nobles kept as pets or curious rarities. There are pictures showing gazelles tied like dogs to a chair that some dignitary is seated on. Ladies liked to take dorcas deer with them for walks. During the

121 Old Kingdom in particular aristocrats amused themselves with the antics of monkeys
122 brought from Nubia or remoter parts of Africa, especially baboons and guenons.
111 There are records of mongoose-breeding in Roman times. Tame cheetahs may have
been used in hunts. One dangerous hobby was keeping a lion about the house. Only a
pharaoh could go in for this, of course; we know that Tutankhamun did, and likewise
Ramesses II, Ramesses III and Ramesses IV.

Queen Hatshepsut had a regular menagerie set up. According to Dale Osborn it
was stocked with animals brought back from the Land of Punt – baboons, giraffes,
cheetahs and exotic birds. In his northern palace at Akhetaten, too, King Akhenaten
had a wild animal enclosure and an aviary.

In the Late and Graeco-Roman Periods in particular Egyptians used to catch, for
ritual purposes, animals that they believed to be the incarnations of various gods.
271 Foremost among these was the falcon, as the incarnation of Horus (though other
birds of prey could be substituted, according to recent research on bird-mummies);
168 the vulture (for the goddess Nekhbet); the sacred ibis (Thoth); the crocodile (Sobek)
and several kinds of fish. At the New Kingdom site of Gurob, William Loat discovered
a unique fish-cemetery where dried Nile perches and other species had been placed in
hollows, wrapped up in dry grass.
32 Other animals, such as baboons and various monkeys (again symbolising Thoth)

122 Nubians bringing a giraffe and long-horned cattle as tribute. A monkey is climbing up the giraffe's neck. In the lower register Syrians bring horses, an elephant and a panther. Painting on limestone. Tomb of vizier Rekhmire, Sheikh Abd el-Qurna, West Thebes. 18th dynasty

Below left 123 Man feeding a piglet. Relief in the tomb of Kagemni in Saqqara. 6th dynasty

Below 124 For a time, ancient Egyptians tried to domesticate the hyena. Here men are force-feeding the fettered animals. Relief in the tomb of Mereruka in Saqqara. Early 6th dynasty

were imported to be kept in temples. Some common animals were also recruited to act as divine reincarnations, such as the cow (mother of the god Apis), the bull (Apis himself), the cat (the goddess Bastet) and the dog (Anubis). Mummified animals, 273 brought along by the devout as sacrifices, were laid in their hundreds of thousands in underground corridors at the sacred-animal cemeteries such as those of Saqqara and Tuna el-Gebel. The custom must have contributed to reduction or extermination of several species in Egypt (falcon, ibis and crocodile).

It must be clear by now that the ancient Egyptians were literally surrounded with animals. Stables and cages jostled with human dwellings and opened onto the same courtyards as were used for cooking and most of the domestic work. It cannot have been unusual, even outside the poorer classes, for humans and animals to share the same room. Herodotus (II, 36) noticed this too. 'The Egyptians,' he observed, 'are the only people who keep their animals with them in the house.'

This coexistence forged strong bonds between animals and people. Those who kept animals knew them well – their mating habits, their diet and growth, their ailments and all their characteristics. They took pleasure in breeding them successfully, but did not see them merely as utilities. We know from many illustrations what care they took of them. When a flock had to ford a canal or creek, the shepherds would pick up the little ones gently in their arms and carry them across. We can see men stroking an animal's muzzle when feeding it. In Kagemni's mastaba in Saqqara we can even see a farmer feeding a piglet from his own mouth. It was part of the moral code that 123 animals should be treated humanely and adequately fed.

A balanced relationship between people and beasts was seen by the ancient Egyptians as one element in the eternal global and cosmic order. Anyone who really knew his animals understood how close they were to him or her, in their physiology, their ailments and, to a degree, their psychology. People could not fail to see moreover the close kinship that much mythology reflected. In contrast to Graeco-Roman civilisation and to Judaic and Christian culture, which placed *homo sapiens* on a pedestal as a privileged being distinct from the rest of creation, the ancient Egyptians saw themselves as children of nature, members of a single, remarkable whole along with the animals and plants.

We should not be surprised, then, by the long catalogue of animal-gods, originally totems, which headed the genealogies of families and tribes who derived their origin from them. In historic times a sizeable proportion of the Egyptian pantheon developed from this ancestry.

The sound relationship between them benefited not only the animals, but humans too. Looking after animals was an antidote to egotism and by instilling consideration

towards other creatures it improved people's relations with their fellows. It would be hard to agree with Dillon Dixon who infers from their overcrowded homes, villages and cities that the Egyptians must have been prone to psychic disturbances and frequent outbreaks of violence. It seems more likely that among the agricultural community the orderly cycle of seasonal work, added to the contact with the animal world, would have had a salutary influence on nerves and spirit.

The symbiosis of humans and animals had admittedly a dark side to it in the increased risk of cross-infection, particularly with bovine tuberculosis, not to mention the chance of injury in handling the more powerful beasts. Beekeepers, again, were exposed to attack by angry swarms, and there is no evidence that they ever wore masks or gloves.

Love of the hunt had come down to the Egyptians from their prehistoric forebears. It had at one time, after all, been the only way of getting meat. In neolithic and predynastic days hunting and fishing were still an important supplement to stockbreeding. A famous hunting scene that has survived from the time of the country's unification shows a party out for lions, gazelles, stags and ostrich. By historic times, however, agriculture and stockbreeding had increased to the point where hunting was losing its economic significance. It gradually became the sport of kings, courtiers and dignitaries, in which they could display their strength and valour. Scholars such as E. V. Cherezov, however, have pointed out that there were even in later times areas of food-gathering and procurement of materials for certain crafts where hunting did not become entirely redundant.

Prehistoric Egypt had been a hunter's paradise. Human settlements were still limited to the edge of the valley where the ground started sloping up to the high plateaus, or to the mouths of the side-valleys; from there the first farmers had only begun gradually to cultivate the fertile alluvium. At that time it was a watery jungle of trees and scrub, mixed with boggy thickets of reed and papyrus, alive with elephants, giraffe, lions, rhinoceros, wild boar, antelopes, gazelles, deer of many sorts, ibex, mouflon, all kinds of birds, fish, crocodiles and hippopotamus. However, the draining of the marshes and extension of the cultivated area during the first three dynasties forced the larger game out of the valley proper.

The decline of the fauna was also hastened by the increasing aridity of northern Africa, starting with the close of the Neolithic wet phase and peaking between 2350 and 2000 BC. In historic times only the few species that were less dependent on water managed to hold out on the grasslands and in the scattered groves beside the fast-drying streams and minor rivers in what is now the Eastern Desert, or on the wide gravel plateaus of today's Western Desert, a part of the Sahara. Swamps only

Below **125** Men harpooning hippopotami from papyrus boats. Locusts and frogs can be seen in the branches of the tree. Limestone relief in the tomb of Mereruka in Saqqara. Early 6th dynasty

Right **126** Ramesses III hunting bulls from a chariot. Relief on the first pylon of his mortuary temple at Medinet Habu, West Thebes. 20th dynasty

Below right **127** A harpooned hippopotamus roaring in a papyrus thicket. Painting from a private tomb, Sheikh Abd el-Qurna, West Thebes. 18th dynasty

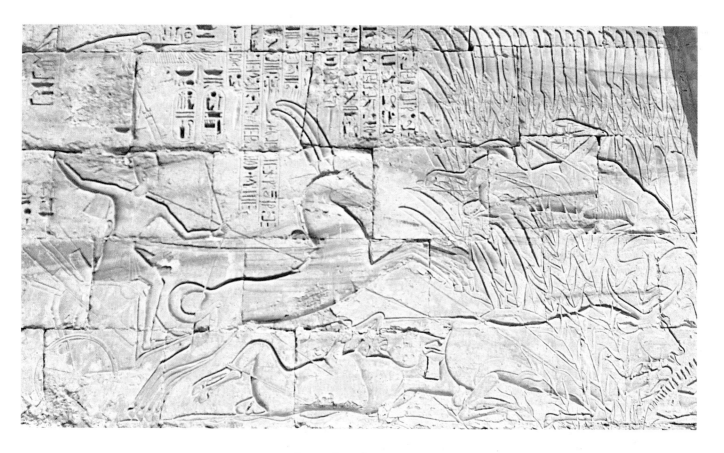

remained in a few places in Upper Egypt and in large areas of the Delta, which continued to grow out seawards as the alluvial soil accumulated.

The siting of royal palaces in the Old Kingdom capital of Memphis indicates that hunting was pursued at the time mainly on the plains beyond the nearby line of pyramid burials. Each of the pharaohs employed a master of the hunt to accompany him, along with a whole troupe of attendants and beaters. The usual quarry were the many species of gazelle and antelope (dorcas, addax, oryx, etc.), ibex, little ox, Barbary sheep and ostriches. A higher degree of skill and courage was demanded for chasing hyenas, lions and leopards. Hyenas abounded in the desert; there were still a fair number of lions, to judge from the frequency with which they appear in Old Kingdom art, but leopards were less common. This can be inferred from the fact that Harkhuf, the Aswan dignitary, cites leopard skins among the rarities imported from lands further south, along with ivory and the giraffes he brought back from his Nubian expedition. Huntsmen were equipped with bows and arrows, lances or spears. There is also evidence for the use of *bolas* in the form of stones attached to a lasso. Antelopes were sometimes driven into lightly fenced traps with the help of trained dogs and even hyenas. Lassoing or trapping enabled animals to be brought back alive and then, as we have seen, fattened or used for experiments in domestication.

Some of the pharaohs set great store by their hunting prowess. Foremost among these were the rulers of the New Kingdom, when love of the chase, associated with successful forays into Nubia or the Near East, flourished and extended beyond the territory of Egypt proper. Thus we find Tuthmosis III boasting that he had hunted down 120 elephants in northern Syria. He came close to losing his life in the process when one large beast, enraged by an arrow the King had let fly at it, came charging in his direction. He was only saved by the presence of mind of one of his soldiers who, the story goes, severed the elephant's trunk with one blow of his sword.

Amenophis II is said to have possessed a bow so mighty that no one but himself could bend it. Modern research has ascertained that his height was 1.70m, slightly above the average for Egyptians at that time. It was his successor Tuthmosis IV who

128 Userhet, Royal Scribe of Amenophis II, hunting gazelles and other desert animals from his chariot. Painting in the tomb of Userhet. Sheikh Abd el-Qurna, West Thebes. 18th dynasty

introduced the safer technique of hunting from a horse-drawn chariot – a style obviously appropriate for royalty. Amenophis III boasted to have slain 200 lions during the first 10 years of his reign alone. He claimed also to have had a large number of wild bulls that were roaming the margins of the land corralled, and then to have done battle with them, dispatching 96.

On one richly-painted chest Tutankhamun is portrayed as a young man chasing lions in a two-wheeled chariot drawn by a pair of horses. Sethos I makes a more daring impression as he dismounts from his chariot to tackle a lion with his lance.

126   Reliefs in the temple of Medinet Habu show Ramesses III hunting wild cattle from his chariot. Another scene shows this same king, after dispatching two lions, turning to confront a third which is just about to attack him. It is hard to believe that as many lions and wild bulls as were allegedly slaughtered by the New Kingdom rulers still survived on the hunting grounds of that time, unless they were bred for that purpose.

That men of influence were loth to be outdone by the pharaohs is apparent from a hunting scene in the tomb of the famous physician Nebamun, shown giving chase in
128 his chariot to spotted hyenas. Likewise Userhet, the great scribe of Amenophis II, is portrayed firing off arrows at a herd of gazelle, who flee in panic.

It must have been a very different experience for these exalted huntsmen to pursue the fauna that abounded in the marshlands. We have reliefs that depict mongoose, chameleons, wild cats (*Felix chaus*), frogs and all manner of wildfowl moving through dense papyrus thickets, and hippos wallowing amid the lotus-lily carpets. Here the hunters would edge slowly forward in their papyrus boats. When a hippopotamus
125 emerged they would harpoon it with a type of spear whose head, when it struck home, broke off from the shaft but stayed tied to a strong rope. There would usually have been several men hunting together, so that the quarry was struck by more than one weapon. At the same time the assailants had to make sure they did not come too
127 close to the writhing giant. Only when its resistance flagged could it be safely hauled out onto the bank.

A more frequent and less dangerous target for boatmen was wildfowl – ducks, geese, herons, cranes, snipe, plovers, quail, pigeons and other sorts. The best season for them was the end of the floods, when the migratory species were making ready to leave and the high water level still made it possible to row up to the concealed nesting places. The marksmen are usually shown standing up, about to aim for the rising bird

with a wooden throwing-stick, a kind of boomerang which, unlike the Australians', 113
never came back. The hunter's family, or servants if he was a nobleman, would help
retrieve the booty from the water.

A more economical technique was fowling in a group with 6, 7 or 8-sided nets
which were first spread out on the ground and sprinkled with corn or maggot bait.
There was a cord running through all the corners of the net. When enough birds had
come to it, the 'overseer of the fowlers' would signal with his hand or kerchief and the
others, by jerking the cord, would close the net with the birds inside. We can see in
some of the illustrations that if the helpers pulled too violently they all tumbled onto
the ground. A relief in the 5th-dynasty mastaba of Ptahhotep at Saqqara shows the
net at the moment when wild ducks and geese have just been trapped in it, only a few
having escaped at high speed. The same situation is depicted rather more realistically
in the 18th-dynasty tomb of Nakht at Sheikh Abd el-Qurna. Here the captured birds
struggle in a confused mass of heads and desperately flapping wings.

There was also a kind of mechanical fowling technique. Middle Kingdom tombs at
Beni Hasan portray smaller nets with sprung frames of flexible wood actuated by a
trigger. Birds were enticed with corn or other bait; when they touched the trigger the
net fell over them.

Birds could also be caught in baited pits dug in the sand. A heavy cover such as an
earthenware tray was placed slantwise over the hole, propped up at one side with
palm-leaf ribs. A bird only had to knock the prop and the cover would fall and trap it.

In another part of the mastaba of Ptahhotep we see captured birds being put into 130
small cages holding four or five at a time; sometimes their wings were broken first.

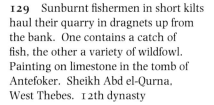

129 Sunburnt fishermen in short kilts
haul their quarry in dragnets up from
the bank. One contains a catch of
fish, the other a variety of wildfowl.
Painting on limestone in the tomb of
Antefoker. Sheikh Abd el-Qurna,
West Thebes. 12th dynasty

They were then taken home to be force-fed in the courtyards till they were fat enough for the table.

A sport that greatly appealed to kings and aristocrats was hunting ostriches. King Tuthmosis III had a scarab made to commemorate the occasion when he hunted a flock of 176 of these birds and bagged 75 of them. On a temple relief at Medinet Habu we see Ramesses III hurtling past a group of ostriches in his chariot. The number of these birds in Egypt declined later, but according to Dale Osborn they never died out completely. A handmade vessel engraved with a group of ostriches was found in a tumulus in Wadi Qitna, showing that they existed in Nubia between the 3rd and 5th centuries AD.

Like fowling, angling was pursued for two purposes, sport and utility. As a sport it was cultivated by aristocrats in the Old and Middle Kingdoms who normally used a harpoon while standing in their papyrus canoes. By the time of the New Kingdom anglers had evidently become lazier; they are now often portrayed with rod and line, sitting in armchairs beside their garden pools.

Economic fishing, with a tradition going back to prehistoric times, was carried out continually by professionals on the Nile and its canals, as well as on Lake Moeris in

130 Trapped fowl are being caged by men who break their wings. Ihy, the overseer of linen, carries away two boxes suspended from a yoke. Painted relief on limestone in the tomb of Ptahhotep, Saqqara. 5th dynasty

131 Two men fishing from a papyrus boat, one with a line and multiple hooks, the other with a net. Painted relief on limestone in the tomb of Idut, Saqqara. 6th dynasty

the Faiyum. The produce not only graced the tables of the nobility but reached humble homes too, where it was a much appreciated source of animal protein.

Fishing seems to have been particularly important during the Middle Kingdom. In several Saqqara mastabas we see fishermen with rods and lines, sitting in their 131 papyrus canoes and waiting for a bite. In Ptahhotep's mastaba an angler is pulling a catfish out of the water, about to stun it. In the tombs of Ty and Mereruka fishes are depicted under water in such detail that Claude Gaillard was able to identify 24 species with certainty, including catfish, eel and Nile perch. Anglers' hooks were made of bone or later bronze, with or without a barb.

Other scenes show fish being caught on a more economic scale in traps plaited out of reed-stems. In Ty's mastaba the position of an underwater trap is shown marked by a buoy. It needed the combined strength of two crews to raise such a trap. Some of their small-talk is reproduced in snappy captions. 'Pull hard on the oars so that we can get on top of them!' With the trap now raised, one of the fishermen gloats: 'Full to the brim! This time we've done it!'

The biggest catches of all were brought in by teams using a large drag-net. This 129 ancient technique can be seen being used by Egyptian fishermen to this day. Clay, stone or metal weights are fastened along one edge so that the net moves over the river bottom while the other side is kept at surface level with wooden floats. Reliefs show such a net being hauled along by anything from three to six men in two boats alongside one another, with another two rowing for all they are worth.

Fishing scenes often contain a tussle between the crews of two papyrus boats. Two 132 fishermen try to knock each other into the water with long poles. We are usually shown one of them in the act of falling in. These were evidently friendly sporting fights serving to break the monotony.

Not even angling was without its dangers, for there was one species of catfish armed with a poisonous spine on its dorsal fin. According to Strabo even crocodiles were afraid of it. On one relief a man is shown sitting on the riverbank, pulling one of these fish out of the catch and extracting the dreaded spine.

Khety's Instruction mentions another peril. 'And now I will tell you about the fisherman, who has a harder time than any. His work takes him to a river infested with crocodiles. When the time comes to count up [the catch], he wrings his hands over it, without even thinking "There might be a crocodile around!" Too late he is gripped with fear. Then as soon as he reaches the water he falls as if struck by the hand of god.' Even if the scribe exaggerates as usual in order to highlight the advantages of his own profession, it was true that if a canoe capsized not even the best swimmer could be sure of escaping the dreaded jaws.

132 A favourite pastime among the crews of the papyrus boats was to stage a mock fight with punting poles on returning from a fowling or fishing expedition. Painted relief in the tomb of Ptahhotep, Saqqara. Late 5th dynasty

CHAPTER TEN

The Ancient Egyptians' Diet

133 A male cook fans the fire in preparation for roasting the duck he holds in his left hand. Painted wood and plaster model. End of 1st Intermediate Period. *Turin, Museo Egizio*

THE READER WILL have gathered from the last two chapters some idea of the wealth and variety of the ancient Egyptian diet. It would be worthwhile, however, to take a look at how meals were planned, cooked and served. Questions also arise about the availability of food to all households, about religious bans on certain food, and whether people were in greater danger of overeating than of starving. The relation between population growth and the quantity of food produced deserves study too.

In the mastaba of the wife of a minor 2nd-dynasty noble at Saqqara, Walter Emery came across a complete set of funerary dishes. All kinds of food were lying not far from the coffin ready to be served on plates and bowls, some of pottery, some of alabaster or diorite. It has been suggested that the food on ceramic utensils was to be eaten hot and that on stone utensils cold. The menu comprised porridge of ground barley, cooked quail, two cooked kidneys, a pigeon stew, boiled fish, beef ribs, little triangular loaves of wheat bread, round cakes, stewed fruit (probably figs) and fresh sidder berries. Bits of cheese were found in some smaller containers and there was a row of large jugs which had probably contained beer or wine.

Stereotyped scenes of funeral banquets occur repeatedly on stelae in noblemen's mastabas from the Old Kingdom and in tomb paintings of later date. The deceased is shown in front of a table piled with various vegetables and fruit, meat dishes, slices of bread and cakes, usually with jugs of beer or wine standing underneath.

For the masses, cereal foods were the basis of daily diet from neolithic times and throughout the historic era. Reliefs and models demonstrate the initial crushing of the grain, usually by men, with stone pestles on flat limestone mortars. The coarse product was then ground again, this time by kneeling women, with a spherical or 137 ovoid roller over a low stone saddle quern with a central depression. In later periods this quern was tilted in a wooden frame with the women leaning over it. For finer grinding tall cylindrical or conical mortars were used, round which both men and women are shown standing with long pestles in their hands. Rotary mills such as were known in Anatolia from the 8th century BC only appeared in Egypt just before the Ptolemaic Period.

Even though it was sometimes passed through papyrus or net sieves, flour made in mortars or crushers contained a good deal of sand and stone impurities. Several samples of ancient Egyptian bread subjected to microscopic, radiographic and petrographic analysis by F. Filce Leek have shown particles of quartz, felspar, mica, ferro magnesium minerals and other foreign bodies in them. The flour was never thoroughly milled or sieved, so that uncrushed germs and even whole grains remained in the bread, averaging about five per cubic centimetre.

Bread was the staple food of poor and rich alike. Until the Second Intermediate

Period it was baked by housewives at home, by servants on the noble estates and by specially deputed workers on the great construction sites and on expeditions. Not till the early New Kingdom were there regular bakeries serving large clienteles.

Breadmaking began with the mixing of the dough, which was kneaded with both hands in a kneeling or bent position on a low, flat stone surface, or else with the feet in a large container. Some yeast, salt, spices, milk and sometimes butter and eggs were added to the flour; after mixing, the dough was left to rise before being put into conical baking-forms or patted into various shapes and baked without a mould.

In the earliest days bread was baked on an open fire, or in the embers. Later on a simple hob was made by setting a large flat stone on top of three upright ones and starting a fire underneath. From the Old Kingdom onwards, thick conical ceramic 'bread-moulds' came into fashion. These were pre-heated on the open fire, then

Above **134** Bakers mixing and kneading dough and filling bread moulds. Painting in the tomb of Qenamun, Sheikh Abd el-Qurna, West Thebes. 18th dynasty

Top right **135** Women filling bread moulds with dough from large jars and stacking them for baking. Wall painting from the tomb of Senet, West Thebes. 12th dynasty

135

Top right **136** Female brewers crushing barley loaves through a sieve. Limestone relief. Saqqara. 5th dynasty. *Cairo, Egyptian Museum*

Above **137** Kneeling woman grinding corn on a quern to make flour. Limestone statuette. 5th dynasty. *Cairo, Egyptian Museum*

wiped with fat and filled with the dough which baked evenly right through, thanks to the accumulated heat.

Middle Kingdom models already feature tall tapering bread-ovens with a firebox at the bottom, a grating and a domed upper compartment that was open at the top. Lumps of risen dough were placed on ledges inside the dome when it was hot.

The variety of loaf shapes in ancient Egypt can be reconstructed from pictures, written descriptions and actual finds. A favourite type in the Old and Middle Kingdoms was the conical white *t-hedj* bread, much used in sacrifices for the dead, often in the form of slices placed vertically. For common consumption bread was made in a pancake shape, whose forming and baking is illustrated in the 12th dynasty tomb of Antefoker at Thebes. Thicker dough-cakes were sometimes made 134 with a hollow in the middle for filling with boiled beans or green vegetables, and there were thin crisp wafers like *eish-shams* of the modern *fellahin*. Large soft griddle-cakes were also made, as in Nubia today. There were round loaves, too, often with deep splits caused by gas escaping during fermentation and baking, not to mention square, triangular, semi-circular and long thin shapes, or flat round ones with a raised edge and a pit in the middle for an egg or other filling. During the New Kingdom dough was also shaped into long or round rolls, or figures of various kinds – a cow, a goat, a woman or a phallus. These were no doubt intended for festive or ritual occasions.

Bread naturally varied according to the flour used. In Herodotus's time Egyptian bread, called *kyllestis* by the Greeks, was made from spelt wheat or, according to Athenaeus, from barley. The grade of milling and the addition of honey or sweet fruit, or of seasoning spices, all contributed to the range available, so it is not surprising that documents refer to 20 named kinds of bread in the Old Kingdom and as many as 40 or 50 in the New Kingdom, though it is hard to tell which names applied to which known varieties.

There was no clear borderline between bread and the various pastries sweetened with honey and flavoured with sesame, aniseed or fruit. Strabo recommends one particular kind, *kakish*, for diarrhoea.

Bread dough was used also in the brewing of beer, which was the favoured drink of the masses in contrast to wine, consumed only by the rich. Beer-brewing and bread-making are almost always shown in the wall scenes side by side. Greek sources say the Egyptians made beer from barley, but analysis of organic remains in beer jugs has usually pointed to wheat.

Beer-making was again women's work as a rule. The grain would be soaked in water for a day, rolled out and left to dry, then wetted again, crushed and trodden in large vats with yeast added. When fermentation was well advanced the mash was

138 Man milking a cow who sheds a tear as she loses the milk intended for the calf tied to her leg. Sunk relief on the sarcophagus of Queen Kawit. Limestone. From the temple of Mentuhotep II in Deir el-Bahari, West Thebes. 11th dynasty. *Cairo, Egyptian Museum*

136 filtered through a sieve or piece of cloth and the filtrate put aside to mature. Stale bread could also be used in place of grain, mashed in a pot of water, boiled and left in a warm place to ferment. The stages most commonly illustrated are the preparation of the mash and its filtration through sieves into tall containers.

Finally the filtrate was seasoned with spices, dates, mandrake, safflower and other additives – hops were unknown. A relief in the Baden museum in Karlsruhe shows dates being trampled out for this purpose in a large tub; the stones are then taken out (by a woman), the flesh rolled into balls (by a man) and put into another container. The dates not only gave the beer a distinctive aroma but speeded the fermentation by increasing the sugar content. Medical papyri list 17 kinds of beer but, as with bread, we cannot attach the names to the known varieties.

Before being drunk, beer was poured through a sieve or fine-meshed cloth to remove remains of the additives and other impurities.

Beer had strong religious associations. One myth tells how the god Re deflected the anger of the goddess Sakhmet by giving her beer dyed red, which she took to be blood, and so saved mankind from destruction. Intoxication led not only to merriment but also to religious ecstasy, for example during the festivals of the goddess Tefnut.

Greek writers credited the Egyptians with having invented beer. It might have been discovered by chance when someone drank the liquid from grain left to ferment for making porridge or bread, and found it exhilarating.

Apart from bread and beer, people lived mainly on vegetables, fruit and fish. Like their descendants today, the ancient Egyptians (as many tomb findings confirm) were happy to make a meal of pulses – beans, chick peas, lentils and green peas.

One of their favourite vegetables was garlic, valued not only for the flavour it imparted to other food but for its smell, which was thought to repel the agents of disease. Onions were likewise prized as tasty, aromatic and medicinal as well. In the preparation of mummies onions were sometimes placed in the armpits, eye-sockets and bodily cavities, as well as in the folds of the wrappings, perhaps in the belief that their odour would stimulate the dead into breathing. Radishes were not much eaten as a vegetable (despite Herodotus's statement that they formed part of the remuneration of pyramid-builders), but their seeds were valued as a source of oil.

102-5 Leeks were popular and so was the Egyptian lettuce, a variety with pointed leaves that grew a metre tall; it is often shown among sacrificial gifts on the tables placed in front of the deceased. It was also believed to promote male potency, associated with the fertility god Min. Cucumbers were among the vegetables grown for their fruit.

Among fruit in the conventional sense the best loved were dates, a rich source of sugar and protein. In humbler circles they were in fact the standard sweetener rather than honey, which only the rich could afford. (The word for 'date' was *bener*, which at the same time meant 'sweet' or 'pleasant'.) Dates were eaten either fresh or in cakes. They could also be softened and pressed, the juice after fermentation yielding date-wine or giving flavour to beer. Dates were also dried to be stored for later consumption. Medicinally, they were thought to clean the intestines and regulate the urinary system. As vaginal suppositories they were supposed to ensure fertility.

The fruit of the argun palm (*Medemia argun*), no longer found in Egypt, was much eaten; it had a sweet taste reminiscent of coconut. The larger fruit of the doum palm was eaten raw, or soaked in water, or used for making syrup. The sweet fruits of sidder were again consumed raw or fermented for wine-making, as is still done by Coptic monks in remote desert monasteries.

Sycomore figs were revered as coming from a sacred tree, and are therefore often found in tombs. They were also used medicinally in treating, for example, an obscure disease described as the 'blood devourer' which Bendix Ebbell argued to be scurvy. Only rarely do we find remains of true figs, though they often appear in illustrations and textual references. Grapes were a popular delicacy and were sun-dried to make raisins.

Water melons have only been found once, in the New Kingdom grave of Nebseni. The fruit of the sacred persea *Mimusops laurifolia*, on the other hand, was often part of the funeral equipment.

The pomegranate is occasionally found in tombs as far back as the 12th dynasty (e.g. in the tombs at Dra Abu el-Naga) and its growing use has been attributed to the expeditions of Tuthmosis III into Syria. It is easily recognised in New Kingdom paintings. Olives probably came to Egypt with the Hyksos in the Second Intermediate Period, to judge from findings from the early 18th dynasty and onwards. The Egyptian plum, walnut and carob pod ('St John's bread') are only known from the New Kingdom, and the peach does not make its appearance until Ptolemaic times.

Spices improved the taste of different foods (and some were used as medicines). Aniseed, cinnamon, coriander, cumin, dill, fennel, fenugreek, marjoram, mustard and thyme have all been found. Pepper was only introduced in Graeco-Roman times.

Meat scarcely appeared on the tables of common people apart from festive occasions, when a sheep or goat might be slaughtered and friends and relatives summoned to share it. In the Egyptian climate it could not be kept for long.

In wealthy circles, however, the regular consumption of meat is evident from the almost invariable inclusion in their tomb-murals of scenes showing butchers at work. Cattle with their legs tied were slaughtered by having their throats cut; with smaller animals the whole head was severed. As the blood ran out it was caught in deep bowls, sometimes tested by a physician to see if it smelled right, and immediately boiled. The animals were then skinned and the hides handed to the tanners waiting for them in the manorial tanneries. The entrails were removed, washed and set aside

139 Butchers slaughtering an ox. Painting from the chapel of Ity, Gebelein. First Intermediate Period. *Turin, Museo Egizio*

140 A servant dressing geese. Painting in the tomb of Nakht. Sheikh Abd el-Qurna, West Thebes. 18th dynasty

for early use. Then the limbs would be jointed with long knives and the trunk meat carved up, the various cuts being hung up on ropes to dry in a well-ventilated store. Sometimes the meat was cut smaller and stewed. The presence of skulls splintered at their base in a 26th-dynasty bulls' cemetery shows that brains were also used for food.

In 1984 a Czechoslovak team digging near the temple of Raneferef at Abusir turned up a unique ritual abattoir, the 'House of the Knife' (*hut nemet*). Here sacrificial animals were tethered to three limestone blocks sunk in the ground in a large open-air slaughtering place. The butchers first cut their throats with stone knives and severed the left forelegs. Then they skinned and quartered the carcases. In one of three adjoining rooms a brick-walled chopping-block was still in position, on which the quarters were carved into smaller cuts to be roasted on the spot or dried. The pieces were then piled in vaulted storerooms that took up most of the abattoir floor. The amount of meat stored in this way can be imagined from a papyrus fragment in the Raneferef temple archive which mentions 130 bulls being sacrificed in 10 days at this sanctuary alone!

It is usually domestic cattle that figure in butchery scenes, though sometimes we see wild game such as antelope, ibex, gazelle or deer. On the other hand we never see sheep, goat or pig carcases being jointed, perhaps because they seldom appeared on the tables of the rich.

Research has shown that in predynastic days pork was consumed on a large scale in Lower Egypt, but only rarely in Upper Egypt. The growing aversion to pork can be explained by the influence of Upper Egypt after the unification of the country. The pig was one of the animals sacred to the Lower Egyptian god Seth, the enemy of Osiris who had originally been monarch of Upper Egypt. In the Late Period a ban was introduced on swineherds entering temples and on priests eating pork, and many of the nobility excluded pork from their tables too.

As against this we know that pigs were bred and pork widely eaten by the people. King Sethos I, whose very name is linked to the worship of Seth, even allowed pigs to be kept inside the temple of Osiris at Abydos, and pork features in many medical prescriptions. Consumption of underdone pork did of course involve the risk of trichinosis, due to the parasite *Trichinella spiralis* forming cysts in the muscles of the host.

We know rather little about how meat was cooked, since none of the scribes thought of recording a single recipe. We do know, however, from several illustrations that in noble houses the work was done by male cooks. We see meat being boiled or stewed and quite often roasted, made into a ragout or fried in oil or fat. A culinary scene on the wall of Ramesses III's tomb in the Valley of the Kings shows a man standing to stir a large cauldron with a ladle, while another stokes the fire beneath; all around lie pieces of meat and a little way off one butcher is holding a bowl to catch the blood from a freshly-slaughtered animal while another is quartering a carcase.

A welcome protein source for the poor was fattened poultry or wild birds – geese, ducks, quails, cranes and other species, and the domestic fowl that were gradually introduced during the New Kingdom. Herodotus (II, 77) tells how they were prepared: 'Of course various birds, quails, duck and small fowl are pickled and eaten uncooked; any other available birds and fish, unless deemed sacred, are eaten roasted or boiled.'

We have several illustrations of poultry being prepared for the table – plucked, drawn, washed and roasted. On one of them we see a man kneeling in front of a large   140 pan on a bed of glowing charcoal. He holds a duck on a long gridiron in his right hand, using his left to wave a large fan either for keeping flies away from the tempting   133 roast or to heat up the embers. Another man is kneeling at a low table, carving. An ostracon from Amarna shows one of Akhenaten's little daughters sitting at a stool laden with food, enjoying a roast duck.

Presumably the Egyptians ate eggs too. Though there is no direct evidence of this, we do, oddly enough, have medical prescriptions that recommend eggs against diarrhoea.

Fish, of which there were many edible and some excellent kinds, afforded nourishment for the poor and an occasional change of menu for the well-off. Fishermen, having caught and killed them, would sometimes scale and clean them in their canoes too instead of leaving this till later. A painting in the tomb of Rekhmire at Sheikh Abd el-Qurna has a seated figure leaning forward over a low table with a board laid across it, taking the head off a fish, carving it lengthwise and discarding the entrails.

Other scenes depict a fish being grilled on a long skewer, with the cook fanning the flames while his assistant rolls the fillets up into balls. A cook in a relief in the tomb of Ty is removing the roe from an opened fish. In the mastaba of Khnumhotep and

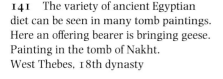

141 The variety of ancient Egyptian diet can be seen in many tomb paintings. Here an offering bearer is bringing geese. Painting in the tomb of Nakht. West Thebes, 18th dynasty

Nyankhkhnum we find fish, or fish soup, being boiled in a cauldron over an open fire.

Most fish, however, were dealt with by being salted and preserved, or dried in the sun and wrapped in ash of burnt grass. Salt fish was much appreciated and constituted an export item.

Certain kinds of fish, however, it was forbidden to eat because of their connection with the myth of Osiris. These included the genera *Lepidotus* and *Phragus* as well as the enigmatic oxyrhynchus, which Gaillard identified with the genus *Mormyrus*. They were reputed to have swallowed the god's penis. In some places people worshipped the Nile perch *Lates niloticus* and abstained from the flesh of this too. The centre of the latter cult was Esna, whose later Greek name Latopolis refers to this fish; thousands of mummified perch and kindred species have been found there. Priests, to be on the safe side, were forbidden to eat any fish whatsoever.

Two kinds of fat were distinguished in the language: *adj*, usually of animal origin, and *merhet*, vegetable fat. In the temple of King Amenophis III in Malqata near Thebes, 91 vessels labelled *adj* were discovered, evidently for storing fat.

In sacrificial inventories four sorts of *adj* are listed: beef fat, goat fat, 'white' and 'melted' fat (perhaps clarified butter). Milk is not mentioned, though quite a few sacrificial scenes show men carrying pots of milk or cream. Milk was given to babies and young children, but was also drunk by adults; milk and dairy products in fact bulked large in the diet of farming people, especially herdsmen.

Even though terms for butter and cheese have not yet been identified it seems probable that the ancient Egyptians were familiar with both. A painting in one Theban tomb from the turn of the 19th dynasty shows a seated woman pulling white cones of what must be butter or cheese out of a large vessel. A man standing next to her is taking them to put into a triangular sack. We see similar sacks being carried on a yoke or transported by donkey. Remains of cheese have been identified in two 1st-dynasty vessels, but otherwise there is no evidence of it until Ptolemaic times.

As for vegetable oils, the language had 21 different names for them. They were

Below **143** A lady guest succumbs to nausea. Fragment of a wall painting. West Thebes. New Kingdom. *Brussels, Royal Museum of Art and History*

Left **142** Elegantly dressed guests, seated on chairs and stools before tables piled high with a variety of food, are offered bowls of wine by servants. Painted relief from the tomb of Nebamun. Dra Abu el-Naga, West Thebes. 18th dynasty. *London, British Museum*

obtained from sesame, from the castor-oil plant, flax seed, radish seed, horseradish tree, safflower and colocynth, the pale-coloured odourless ben oil from the seeds of the horseradish tree being particularly prized. Olive oil was also known, being imported from Mediterranean countries. Not till the 18th dynasty were attempts made to cultivate the tree in Egypt, and olive orchards were founded in the Faiyum in Ptolemaic times.

Oil or fat was used mainly for frying meat and vegetables. Food was also cooked in milk or butter, as is still commonly done in the Middle East. The importance of fats for cosmetics, medicine, religious rites and house illumination is described elsewhere.

Honey was an all-purpose sweetener under the Old Kingdom, but because of its price could only be afforded by the king and his courtiers. Not before the New Kingdom is it included among sacrifices in aristocratic tombs and temples. The common people used dates or various fruit juices instead. Honey was either eaten in the natural state or used in cakes or for sweetening beer and wine. In view of the rarity of dental decay among the ancient Egyptians it seems that even in wealthy circles honey had little deleterious effect on teeth. It was the most common ingredient of medical prescriptions.

Sea salt was regarded as unclean; like everything else connected with the sea it belonged to the domain of Seth, god of evil. But free use was made of salt from the Siwa Oasis and other deposits by everyone except priests, who were supposed to abstain from it on certain occasions. In the Egyptian climate so much salt is lost in perspiration, especially by heavy workers, that a well-salted diet is indispensable for maintaining the density of the body fluids in physiologically well-balanced condition.

Like the daily menu, so the frequency and manner of serving meals differed according to social position. Ordinary people ate twice a day, at sunrise and at dusk, with only the odd snack during the day. Richer folk sat down to an afternoon meal as well. Poor families ate squatting at a low round table, taking their food from common bowls with their hands or with chunks of bread. Before and after eating they poured water over each other's hands, and sometimes rinsed their mouths out. Using common utensils naturally enhanced the risk of spreading certain infections.

Things were very different in patrician households, especially at the luxurious 142 banquets we see depicted on tomb walls. Guests sat on their own mats or stools with little round tables in front of them decorated with flowers, and with their own crockery. Even in these circles, however, there was no cutlery. Servants poured pitchers of water over the guests' hands, sometimes before the meal but chiefly afterwards, brought choice dishes to their tables, served them jugs of fine wine and, in between, sprayed them with perfumes and put cones of ointment on their heads. The diners, after eating and sometimes before as well, would wash out their mouths with water containing a little natron by way of disinfectant. Meanwhile musicians, male and female, and women singers maintained a festive atmosphere while young girls, 45 virtually naked, danced for the company.

Moderation was unfashionable on these occasions. In the tomb of Paheri at el-Qab we see one of the ladies commanding a servant: 'Bring me 18 goblets of wine. Can't you see I am trying to get drunk? My throat is dry as dust.' Not for nothing did the Instruction of Ani include warnings against gluttony and drunkenness. There are even pictures of ladies vomiting, and in the 11th-dynasty tomb of Khety at Beni 143 Hasan we see men carrying their friends out, stiff as rods, alongside scenes of wine- and beer-making.

Are we to assume that the ordinary Egyptian went hungry in the shadow of these ruling-class beanfeasts? Most scholars think not. The soil of Egypt provided ample food for all. Bread, beer, milk, vegetables, fruit, game birds, poultry and fish were within almost everyone's means. Even today, with a population many times greater, the poorest do not starve when they can buy a plate of beans for a pittance. Heavy labourers in the Gebel el-Silsila quarries, according to the stela of King Sethos I, received a daily allowance of around two kg of bread, two bundles of vegetables and a piece of roast meat.

One of the benefits of higher status, however, was a superior and more varied diet.

144 Emaciated man holding a bowl. Wooden statuette. Middle Kingdom. *Berlin, Ägyptisches Museum*

Sethos I's messenger and standard-bearer, for instance, was given every day 'a goodly loaf, beef, wine, sweet oil, olive oil, fat, honey, figs, fish and vegetables'. One consequence of the excessive intake of meat, fat, pastry and honey among the idle rich was obesity. Corpulence could indeed be a visible token of high station, just as in modern Egypt. A classic example is Ankhmahor, portrayed outside the entrance to his 6th-dynasty tomb in Saqqara as a mature and decidedly podgy man, whereas inside he is shown as a lissom youth. Another stout customer figures in a scene in the 6th-dynasty mastaba of Mereruka, taking his ease on a papyrus boat while a slim servant proffers him a drink. Equally ample proportions mark the vizier Ka-Aper whose wooden statue on display at the Egyptian Museum in Cairo is generally known, from the immediate reaction of the workmen who excavated it, as the *Sheikh el-Beled*, the 'Village Mayor'. High personages were of course more susceptible to maladies connected with overeating, such as arterio-sclerosis, biliary or urinary stones, gout or diabetes.

Even if the poor as such were not prone to starve, general famines could strike the whole population, and the poor especially, with catastrophic effect. According to accounts dating from the time of the Ptolemies, Egypt suffered famine as early as the reign of Djoser, around 2700 BC, owing to failure of the floods in seven successive seasons. It was to prevent a recurrence of this that the state maintained an efficient system of national granaries, regularly replenished in good years to tide over the lean ones.

Famines also occurred during the Old Kingdom in the adjoining Eastern Desert, then inhabited by nomadic tribes whom the Egyptians called Medjay. Reliefs on the causeway that leads up to the pyramid of Unas, the last pharaoh of the 5th dynasty, show two rows of emaciated men squatting by the wayside with projecting ribs, hollow bellies and scrawny limbs. In a Middle Kingdom tomb at Meir an obviously undernourished shepherd appears, with the elaborately curled hair-style worn today by the Bishareen bedouin of the Eastern Desert. Evidently we are seeing here the original inhabitants of the mountainous regions to the east of Egypt, who migrated into the Nile valley as a result of rapid desertification between 2350 BC and 2000 BC. Early 12th dynasty reports from the southern frontier fortress of Semna, south of Wadi Halfa, spoke vividly of a 'desert starving to death'.

After the end of the 6th dynasty, around 2200 BC, the safeguard system of state granaries failed, probably through a breakdown in the central administration at critical moments when a worsening climate coincided with inadequate floods. The results were famine, civil war or invasion, and general chaos as described in Ipuwer's account of the collapse of the Old Kingdom.

Calculations of the size of population Egypt could have sustained at various times have largely relied on estimates of cultivated area and yields. A direct palaeo-demographic approach is so far ruled out by the scarcity of dependable anthropological data.

The most comprehensive population estimates to date, based on wide-ranging ecological studies and calculations of the area under cultivation, were published in 1976 by Karl W. Butzer. It is interesting to compare his conclusions with others. He suggests a total of only 350,000 inhabitants for the scattered settlements of predynastic times; 870,000 for the time of Egyptian unification (around 3000 BC); and 1.6 million for the height of the Old Kingdom (around 2500 BC). This last figure lies between the evident overestimate of Reginald Engelbach, 3 million, and the far smaller one of 1 million, proposed by J. J. Hobbs.

The 1.6 million figure has also been put forward by Cyril Aldred, but this time in reference to the 11th dynasty (c. 2000 BC), when Egypt was just starting to recover from the decline caused by the famine in the First Intermediate Period. For the peak of the Middle Kingdom, around 1800 BC, Butzer suggests a population of 2 million.

Thanks to the increase of land under cultivation after the introduction of the *shaduf* device, Butzer reckons that the population would have grown to nearly 3 million by the peak of the New Kingdom around 1250 BC – a modest estimate compared with

145 The tomb owner's fat brother with a duck in his hand being given a drink by a servant. Tomb of Mereruka, Saqqara. 6th dynasty

146 Chief lector-priest Ka-aper clearly enjoyed his food. To the workers who found this wooden statue it resembled the headman of their village – Sheikh el-Beled – the name under which the statue is commonly known. Saqqara. 5th dynasty. *Cairo, Egyptian Museum*

Vercoutter's nearly 4 million and Klaus Baer's 4.5 million, though far exceeding John Wilson's 1.6 million.

For the zenith of the Ptolemaic Period, when the cultivated acreage had risen again through the use of the *saqiya* machine, Butzer suggests a figure of 5 million. Similarly Hobbs notes a rapid increase from 2.4 million at the beginning of the Ptolemaic age to 5 million at its close, that is between the 4th and the 1st centuries BC. A fairly similar figure, 4.5 million, was also proposed by W. M. S. Russell for this latter date. Of the Greek historians living in that time, Diodorus offered an estimate of 3 million according to one version, but made it 7 million according to another. Josephus quotes a figure of 7.5 million.

For comparison it may be mentioned that the 1882 Egyptian census came up with a figure of 7 million, while at the time of writing the country has a population in excess of 55 million.

CHAPTER ELEVEN

Craftsmen at Work

147 A carpenter squatting on a scaffolding is working on a wooden object with his adze. Contrary to custom he is shown dishevelled and unshaven. Painted relief fragment. Unknown provenance. 18th dynasty. *Berlin, Ägyptisches Museum*

A SIDE EFFECT of the great explosion of food production was that large numbers of people were able to engage in non-agricultural work. One important section of these were the artisans who produced goods for the rest of the public. Whether they were simple mass-produced articles for daily use, or artistic luxury items, they were almost always of first-rate design, perfectly finished and tastefully decorated. Not surprisingly, extant specimens are lovingly preserved in museums worldwide as tributes to the skill, care and patience of those ancient master-craftsmen.

We gain an insight into the workshops where these artefacts originated from reliefs and drawings of different periods, and from the wooden models of the Middle Kingdom. The craftsmen made up for the limited range and often primitive nature of their tools by deft and imaginative working methods. In many of the crafts only those with truly 'golden fingers' could have acquitted themselves well. In this field too it was common for the talented son to follow in his father's footsteps, watching and copying the procedures of the proven maestro throughout his apprenticeship.

Most workshops served the needs of their own locality in respect of the range and quantity, and sometimes the style, of their products. As in everything else, design changed over the years as technology developed and fashion dictated, so that archaeologists are often able to date an object by its type or style.

We shall not be concerned here with the artistic quality of the finished products, which are discussed in so many specialised works, but rather with life inside the workshops – the tools and methods that the craftsmen used, the influences that affected them and their position in society. Though most literary sources are silent about these matters, many tomb-walls carry illustrations of the various steps in manufacture.

From these scenes we can gather that most articles passed through the hands of several different craftsmen, each carrying out his own part of the job. It is evident, then, that during the Old Kingdom domestic production by individual workers had already given way to collective production in centres where a number of different craftsmen were concentrated. The producer thus lost his original attitude of ownership toward his tools, materials and products, and became an employee of royalty, priesthood or aristocracy. This loss was outweighed by various gains – improved technology and the opportunity of specialisation in one of the successive stages of production, though this in turn might make for monotony and indifference to quality. However, if we look at the things that have survived we find no trace of slapdash work and can only admire the perfection of detail. In comparison with the domestic manufactures of prehistoric Egypt, the factory system led to greatly enhanced productivity and an upward curve in quantity as well as quality.

When we consider the tomb-wall scenes and Middle Kingdom pottery models we have to realise that they were not designed to leave a scientific record of manufacturing methods, but to ensure the deceased his continued existence in the world beyond. Even after the grave had been furnished with everything the dead man had used on earth, his heirs still had to assume that these artefacts might become worn or fall to pieces with the passage of time. So they would need to be replaced, which not even pious endowments could properly guarantee. Hence the need, it was felt, to provide illustrations of how they were manufactured. It was not merely, then, a matter of decorating the blank walls of the 'eternal abode', but of designing scenes which, while leaving out irrelevant details, included everything essential in the eyes of ancient Egyptians. To bring these scenes to life again all that was needed was for a priest, or the dead man's family, or subsequent visitors to pronounce the reviving formulae.

It would be ideal if one could set the evidence of these tomb-pictures alongside the results of careful excavation. But this is seldom possible, for artisans' shops have been as little studied by archaeologists as the settlements mentioned earlier. So we are restricted to the evidence of murals and models, knowing that they will not answer all our questions, but do reflect reality.

In discussing the various crafts we are necessarily imposing on ancient Egyptian conditions a modern classificatory view based on the materials used and the artefacts produced. In actual fact, however, in various workshops the different skills sometimes overlapped during the course of manufacture of certain products.

The Stone Tool Makers

The art of making tools by stone-knapping had come down from the mists of prehistory. In palaeolithic and mesolithic times they constituted, along with bone and wooden implements, the whole basis of craftwork and their manifold shapes answered to every need.

Every member of the band knew how to make them, either by chipping flakes off one stone with another, or by the method of prepared core. In the course of time even the art of fine-dressing the surface was mastered.

In the Neolithic Age such objects were superseded by stone tools with a perfectly smooth, ground finish. But the little chipped stones of geometric shape which were arranged to form the cutting edge of sickles, remained in use even in historic times.

94
148

The production of chipped knives began in the Predynastic Period. These usually had straight or slightly S-shaped backs and curved cutting edges ending in a sharp asymmetrical point level with the back. At the other end they tapered into a long handle set off in a curve from the cutting edge. Other tools in this category were thick oblong axes and larger, thin, semicircular battle-axes, scrapers and rasps, hollow scrapers for smoothing wooden shafts, pointed blades, saw-blades, daggers, lances and spearheads, arrowheads of many types – three-sided, cylindrical, flat with a stem or with a concave base, geometric microliths and many others.

A number of chipped stone tools survived into the Old Kingdom despite the introduction of copper. In the funerary temple of queen Khentkaus, mother of two kings, and in the temple of the unfinished pyramid of King Raneferef, several dozen stone knives have been discovered in recent years. These were used by priests for ritual purposes, especially the slaughter of sacrificial animals. For circumcision, and for the preparation of bodies for embalming, stone knives were used exclusively throughout Egyptian history. Even in Herodotus' day the *paraschists* or embalmers who removed the entrails from dead bodies used stone knives 'from Ethiopia' for making the incision under the left ribs. Ordinary metal knives were considered unclean for this ritual.

When we come to historical times the untrained worker was no longer able to make stone implements by chipping them: their manufacture became the privilege of specialised artisans, heirs to the ancient craft. It was certainly an uncommon skill, for the demand could be met from a fairly small number of workshops. It is not

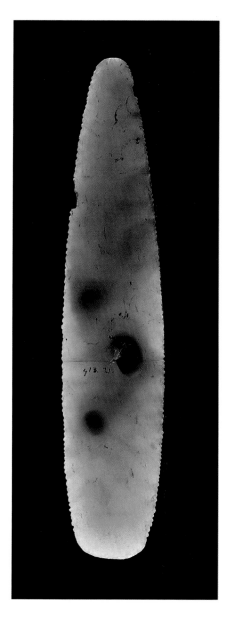

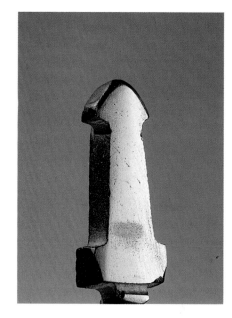

Left **148** A skilfully crafted flint blade. Predynastic Period. *Oxford, Ashmolean Museum*

Below left **149** The phallus was a symbol of the life force, and models like this were believed to aid fertility. Polished stone. *Private collection*

Right **150** Fish-shaped breccia jar for offerings or precious ointments. Thin walls and a fine finish were often achieved by craftsmen using a drill to hollow very hard stone. Predynastic Period. *Berlin, Ägyptisches Museum*

surprising, then, that there are only two extant scenes from the Middle Kingdom tombs at Beni Hasan that show the making of stone tools. There a craftsman can be seen holding a roughly shaped knife-blade in one hand and in the other a stake-like tool with a point evidently made of specially hard stone, set at an angle in a cylindrical wooden handle. He is using delicate pressure to dress the blade, chipping small fragments from its surface and sharpening its cutting edge.

The material employed for making tools by this technique was usually jasper or some other type of quartzite, or less commonly flint. Suitable nodules occurred in vast quantities in terrace formations deposited by the Nile in previous eras.

The Stone Vessel Makers

The manufacture of stone vessels also had a long history in Egypt, going back to the beginning of the Predynastic Period. It provided valuable experience in working all kinds of stone, ranging from soft limestone, alabaster, sandstone and magnesite to the hardest granite, diorite and quartzite. It was a training that produced perfect competence in a wide range of skills, from delicate techniques such as stone bead making to the dressing of huge building blocks and monumental statuary from the 3rd dynasty onwards. Workers in stone and wood, *hemuty*, may indeed have been the first of all predynastic craftsmen to achieve an independent professional identity, since the same term is used in old Egyptian to denote both these, and craftsmen in general.

Depictions of the production of stone vessels are often juxtaposed on tomb-walls with those of sculpture and stone bead drilling. The operations were evidently linked, perhaps because they were all entrusted to fine stone-cutters. Many scenes show holes being bored in large, practically finished, vessels. The boring was done with a drill consisting of a wooden spindle with a handle at the top and a metal or hard stone bit, or a sharpened hollow copper bit. There was no need to press down on the drill as it had a pair of stone weights suspended at the top that acted like a fly-wheel. At the beginning of the work the operator held the vessel in one hand but later, when the drill had penetrated some distance, he held the drill in one hand and turned the handle with the other. On other murals, and on ostraca, we see one or two men smoothing the inner or outer surface of a vessel with an abrasive powder of quartz or other hard mineral. Stonemasons, as we shall see, used the same method to smooth the faces of stone blocks.

Archaeologists have uncovered a large range of stone vessels which show less variation of design from one period to the next than do ceramic vessels. They include 150

151 large flat plates and trays, round-bottomed bowls, jugs, long-necked cans, thick-walled cylindrical vessels, vases resembling a chalice at the top, and many others. There were also smaller vessels for cosmetic and ritual purposes, often designed to hold oils and unguents. One special type of tall vessel with an oval body and a narrow mouth, provided with a separate lid, was the canopic jar, used to hold the entrails removed during mummification.

The Potters

One of the oldest branches of manufacture, going back to the earliest Neolithic Period in Egypt, was pottery. Originally it was the sphere of women who turned out simple hemispherical bowls in their homes. But even in those days more complex designs began to be introduced and attention was turned to decoration by incisions, sometimes filled with gypsum, or painting the surface in white over a dark background – and later in red over white. Even when mass production started, domestic manufacture still held its own and is carried out in remote parts of Nubia to this day.

Depictions of ceramic work are less common than those of stone vessel making, and appear mostly in the tombs of provincial dignitaries of the Middle Kingdom. We often find them close to scenes of baking and brewing; pottery vessels were essential to daily life whereas stone vessels were by then associated more with the cult of the dead.

No one could complain of a shortage of potter's clay in Egypt. The Black Earth itself was the result of fine mud being deposited by the Nile over countless years, and it could be dug up anywhere. In the Red Earth areas, again, there were intrusions of soft marl and shale amongst the limestone. Finished pottery reveals the kind of clay used. Objects made from Nile mud are relatively soft and vary from black to red; those from marl or shale are markedly harder, and pinkish-white or greenish in colour.

The potter's first task was to puddle the clay thoroughly, which according to the illustrations was done by one man, or a pair, treading it out with their bare feet; we also see a smaller lump being kneaded between the hands. Judging from analysis of ceramic ware it was at this stage that roughage was added as a bond – chaff, chopped straw, dung or sand. In another episode a man is shown passing the kneaded clay to a potter squatting in front of his wheel, a device introduced during the first few dynasties. (It is curious that knowledge of the potter's wheel did not lead on in Egypt to the invention of the cart-wheel, even though the military used the wheel in siege ladders.

151 Two alabaster vessels of handsome simplicity. 18th dynasty, possibly the Amarna Period. *Cairo, Egyptian Museum*

152 A red polished clay bowl with four modelled and painted crocodiles separated by diagonal bands of interlocking white chevrons. Predynastic Period. *Berlin, Ägyptisches Museum*

153 Dish with design of hippopotamus, one of the recurring subjects in Egyptian artefacts, reliefs and paintings. Predynastic Period. *Cairo, Egyptian Museum*

An illustration from the time of King Niuserre shows a potter's wheel consisting of a stand surmounted by a revolving disc, which the potter turned quite slowly with his left hand while shaping the clay as required with his right. This method could not yield a very smooth surface, which had to be achieved by hand later.

Not till the New Kingdom was the technique improved. In the tomb of Qenamun, dating from the reign of Amenophis II, two men are shown at the wheel. While his mate, kneeling, spins the wheel fast with both hands, the potter, sitting on a low-backed stool, has his hands free to model the vessel and make it quite smooth.

The last evolutionary stage, with the potter seated and spinning the wheel even faster with his feet, came according to some investigators at the end of the New Kingdom. Others consider that the oldest evidence for it is a relief showing the god Khnum spinning a wheel with human figures on it; this is in the temple at Hibis in the el-Kharga Oasis dating from the time of the Persian king Darius I (522–486 BC).

When ready, the vessels were arranged in neat rows and left for several days to dry out thoroughly. During or after this the surface was given a fresh polishing with pebbles, and painted or treated with a coloured slip of fine clay. Sometimes a pattern would be engraved or painted, or the potter's mark added.

Once dry, the vessels were fired in cylindrical brick ovens as tall as a man. Near the base of each oven was a small opening for fuel (usually wood or dried dung) to be put in and stoked from time to time. Above the fire-chamber was a large upper opening through which the work could be stacked on a perforated clay grid. A wooden block, sometimes with steps, enabled the potter to reach this level. During firing the upper opening was covered except for a small gap to let the smoke out. Modern analysis of vessels made in this way shows that the ovens must have developed temperatures of 600°–800°C.

As soon as the firing-time was up, the potter moved the stepping block close to the lower hole so as to bank the fire down by cutting off the air supply. Later he opened the kiln and passed the finished vessels to his mate, who carried them off on a yoke.

Potters and mud-brick makers were both termed *kedu*, presumably because they all worked with clay. As the Instruction of Khety points out, pottery was not an enviable trade. 'The potter is covered all over with earth, though he is still among the living. He has to grub in it like a pig or worse so that he can fire the pots. His muddy clothes are in tatters. He breathes in through his nose the air that comes out of the oven.' Khety is piling it on as usual, but dirt and smoke must certainly have been the potter's constant companions.

154 During the Middle Kingdom the hippopotamus appeared in the form of small faience sculptures. They were the colour of the water – blue or green – and decorated with lotus blossom and other water plants. *Cairo, Egyptian Museum*

Below **155** Faience dish decorated with a floral design and a girl playing the mandolin. 20th dynasty. *Leiden, National Museum of Antiquities*

The Glass Workers

There is still some doubt as to when and where glass was invented. The tradition passed on by Pliny locates the event on the Phoenician coast, in modern Lebanon, where there later grew one of the most important glass-making centres.

In Egypt, the first glass we know of, as a component of faience ware, dates from as far back as the eneolithic Badarian culture at the turn of the 5th and 4th millennia BC.

Glass is produced from a mixture of silica-sand, lime and soda, coloured with the copper ore malachite and fused at a high temperature. In the oldest Egyptian faience ware a skin of this substance was applied to a core made of silica-sand and clay, or of the stone steatite. This was used at first only for beads, but later on for amulets, 278 *shawabtis* (the little figurines of the attendants of the deceased), other figures and inlays (shapes inserted into the sides of vessels, wooden objects, or into plaster). Particularly in the Middle and New Kingdoms a faience glaze was often applied to 155 complete vessels and statuettes.

Pure glass as a separate material came later, in predynastic times, in the form of 170 translucent beads. In the Old and Middle Kingdoms glass jewellery, amulets, little animal figures, mosaic stones and similar things made their appearance.

Not till the reign of Tuthmosis I in the New Kingdom, however, is there any record of glass vessels being made. The innovation was probably due to Egyptian expansion in the Middle East. There Egyptian soldiers and administrators would have come across advanced centres of glass manufacture and brought back local craftsmen, probably as slaves. This view is reinforced by the fact that production of glass vessels started in Egypt as a royal monopoly serving the court, top dignitaries and the high 156 priesthood. Such 18th-dynasty workshops as have been discovered were very close 157 to royal palaces, such as that of Amenophis III at Malqata or Akhenaten's residential quarter in Akhetaten. Further 19th-dynasty factories have been found at Lisht, Menshiya and possibly Gurob.

Unlike those of other crafts, portrayals of glass production are conspicuously missing from drawings and reliefs. (Alleged illustrations of glass-making that have been reproduced from time to time are in fact metal foundries.) This was no doubt because of the royal monopoly. Since the aristocracy owned no glass workshops, the subject did not feature in their tombs, and in New Kingdom royal tombs non-religious scenes were very rare. The methods of glass manufacture would thus have remained a mystery but for archaeological research and the extant glass vessels themselves.

The glass factory found at Lisht yielded fragments of crucibles, conical clay stands for holding the crucibles during fusing, pieces of slag from the ovens, samples of the

142

156 A small painted core glass vase in the form of a fish, decorated by the application of glass rods of other colours while the vase was still hot.
Tell el-Amarna. 18th dynasty. *London, British Museum*

pigments added to the glass, little discs with well-worn edges used for finishing the surfaces, over 100 glass rods of various colours, pieces of unfinished faience ware and nearly 200 sherds of glass vessels. There are traces on the inside of some vessels of a clay-and-sand core, revealing the technology used.

Manufacture proceeded as follows. The raw glass was heated in pans up to 750°C and then again in crucibles to as high as 1100°C. A clay-and-sand core was made in the shape of the cavity of the intended vessel, covered with cloth and stuck onto a metal rod. This was plunged into the molten mass and given several quick twists to spread the glass evenly over it. (This did not always work out, as we can see from the uneven thickness of some vessels.)

If decoration was required, one or more thin coloured rods were wound spirally over the glass while it was still soft. Before these rods hardened they were moved up and down with metal pins to produce waves, garlands, arches and leaf or feather patterns. Sometimes a comb was drawn across the rods, producing a series of vertical ribs. The whole job was then reheated and rolled over a smooth stone block to produce an even surface. Finally, edge and foot could be pulled out and handles fused on. Once the object was cold, the core had to be scraped out.

157 Three small painted core glass cosmetic vessels. 18th dynasty. *London, British Museum*

Ancient Egyptian glass was usually tinted with pigments added to the raw glass. A milky-white colour was produced with tin or lead oxide, yellow with antimony and lead, or ferrous compounds, red or orange with oxides of copper, violet with manganese salts, greenish blue (in imitation of the prized turquoise) with copper or iron compounds, dark blue (in imitation of lapis lazuli) with cobalt compounds and black with a larger proportion of copper and manganese, or with ferric compounds. The finished artefacts – little bottles, vases, goblets and bowls – were chiefly destined to hold cosmetics and fragrant unguents in the boudoirs of queens and high-born ladies.

The decline of royal power after the end of the New Kingdom put a stop to glass production for a time. Not till the Graeco-Roman Period did new Egyptian glass centres arise in the Hellenistic cities of Alexandria and Naucratis. These enjoyed close links with centres in Asia Minor and their extant Greek-style products show that they followed the international market of their day. Around the beginning of the Christian era moulded glass bowls appear, and another innovation was *millefiori* glass made from variously coloured glass rods fused together.

157

The revolutionary invention of glass-blowing took place, probably in Syria, during the 1st century BC, though the technique did not reach Alexandria until the latter half of the following century. As a rule clear glass was used, either of the natural greenish hue or with additives to make it colourless. It was cut with a copper wheel and ground with emery powder. The new discovery increased production many-fold and glass then ceased to be either a rarity or an upper-class prerogative.

What the social status of glass-makers may have been we can only speculate. It was a highly artistic craft and gifted individuals had a chance to become acknowledged masters. Though the glass-factory employees appear originally to have been slaves, and for the most part foreigners, skilful workers were probably freed at an early stage and imparted their secrets to Egyptian colleagues among the royal artisans.

The work was doubtless strenuous and damaging to the health of its practitioners. The intense heat produced by fusing glass on open fires could injure the body-fluid management; the cornea and retina of the eye suffered from the glare, and skin burns were no rarity. Glass-blowing exerted a back-pressure on the lungs that could lead to emphysema and circulatory trouble at an early age, shortening a worker's life considerably.

158 Two carpenters using wooden mallets and chisels are cutting holes in a beam for a boat. On the left a beam is tied to a vertical pole to allow two-handed use of the saw. Tomb of Ti, Saqqara. 5th dynasty

Carpenters and Cabinet-makers

It was the woodworkers' task to provide the rest of the population with the many objects needed to furnish both their homesteads and their eventual abode – their tombs. What hampered their work was the short supply of good native timber. They accordingly imported soft woods from the Middle East and ebony, 'black ivory', from Africa. This foreign material, however, was only destined for the pharaohs, nobility and priesthood; for other people everything had to be made from homegrown wood. Sometimes the surface would be stained to make it resemble a choicer kind. The cost of high-quality wood obliged the Egyptian craftsman to use up the smallest offcuts, which he managed to do by perfecting the art of dove-tailing.

We can form a fairly detailed picture of their tools and techniques from the numerous illustrations on tomb walls and from surviving models in wood or clay. Like other ancient Egyptian workers, the carpenters and cabinet-makers were content with a small range of tools – the axe, saw, adze, knife, scraper, mallet, chisel and then, starting in the New Kingdom, the drill. Blades made from chipped stone survived into the 3rd and 4th dynasties, when they were displaced by metal ones, first of copper and then, from the Middle Kingdom onwards, of bronze. Mallets, however, were always wooden, and for scrapers flint was the only material.

For rough hewing, the axe was the carpenter's favourite implement. Old Egyptian axe-heads were distinguished by their crescent shape and narrow cross-section. The straight edge was fitted into the cloven end of a wooden haft and carefully bound on to it with cross-wound cords; the rounded cutting edge was sharpened by hammering and honing with sandstone. Axes were particularly useful for lopping 107 branches and for splitting trunks to be used as rafters. We have pictures of carpenters laying a trunk on the ground, planting one foot firmly on the job and bending over it with the axe-handle grasped in both hands.

The next task was to saw the trunk into planks. To avoid having to hold it steady, the carpenter would tie it upright to a pole bedded in the ground, then wind the rope several times round it and secure the lower end with a small bar or stone weight to prevent it working loose. This procedure left both hands free to work the saw, which slid easily down the grain under its own weight. The upper end of a long trunk might be beyond the carpenter's reach, so he would place it aslant with one end tied to a strong pole-trestle and get an assistant to hold the lower end in both hands. Then the trunk could be sawn comfortably from the side.

Planks had to be rid of projecting knots and lumps and made smooth all over. The tool for this was an adze, resembling the farmer's hoe but flatter, and with the slightly 147 arched cutting edge longer and sharper. In one picture we see a worker holding a plank with one hand and planing the surface with powerful strokes of the adze. A colleague is sharpening a blunted adze with a sandstone hone.

Planks were usually joined together with wooden dowels several centimetres long and about one centimetre in diameter, which fitted snugly into the prepared holes. We have no pictures of dowels being made, but we can see holes being bored for receiving them by a worker using a chisel in his left hand and striking it with a 158 wooden mallet. Less commonly, mortice-and-tenon joints were made, to be fixed with a vegetable glue; models of woodworking shops show the glue being heated.

There are many scenes displaying the initial, or more commonly the final, stages in the making of wooden articles. Foremost were the components of house and tomb entrances – door frames, door wings, bolts and pin locks. There is a picture of four men grinding or polishing a frame together. Door wings usually needed two joiners to assemble them; we see one knocking home the dowels while the other holds his mallet on the other side to take the force. Another picture shows the construction of wooden pin locks for holding doors fast from the outside, a simple but effective device that spread from Egypt to other parts of Africa and to Asia Minor, and can be found here and there even today.

The ceilings of large rooms in the wealthier houses were supported with wooden columns whose capitals were carved into lotus, papyrus or palm-leaf patterns.

Illustrations show carpenters forming these with adzes or polishing them with tools whose nature is unclear.

159   There are many scenes showing the construction of furniture, especially bedsteads, which because of their size and complexity usually needed two men to assemble. One is commonly shown smoothing the frame with his adze while the other, with chisel and mallet, cuts out holes for fixing the wickerwork. New Kingdom illustrations show some advance: the holes are now made with a bow-drill instead of being hacked out. This drill consisted of a driving spindle with a metal bit, and a bow whose string was wound round the spindle so that it rotated as the bow was moved to left and right. The bedframe is often shown being polished with pebbles and abrasive powder; one scene shows two men threading long cords crosswise through the holes in the frame to make the inlay.

Elsewhere again we see chairlegs and bedlegs being carved. Furniture meant for 74 royalty had the legs carved as lions' paws or bulls' hooves, in line with the idea that the king was as invincible as a lion and strong as a bull. Later the privilege of sleeping on such beds was extended to the nobility. The beds of simple folk had legs decorated with grooves and projections.

We find examples of completed beds in tombs. They usually slope gently down toward the foot and sometimes have carved or panelled headboards. They are occasionally adorned with figures of Bes and Taweret, guardians of sleep, and there might be a pole-frame over them to support a canopy (or a mosquito net?).

Workers are also shown making chairs and stools of similar design to modern ones. We see for example holes for a reed-wicker panel being drilled in the tall back of a four-legged chair. Chair-backs were made slightly curved for better support of the spine. There were also low-backed chairs for working on, and backless stools with a concave seat made of a single piece of wood, with either three or four legs. Folding chairs were probably designed for nobles and priests on their travels, and there were high chairs with footrests.

Some very simple low stools were made of a round or square piece of wood either with four legs, or only one. In the Ty mastaba reliefs, and in Middle Kingdom clay models of woodworking shops, we find tabletops being ground smooth with pebbles and silica-sand.

Cupboards of our kind were not commonly used by Egyptians, who instead favoured little chests on low or high legs for storing their clothes, shoes, tools and so forth, while wealthy ladies kept their jewellery and toilet paraphernalia in small boxes of wood, ivory or alabaster.

The cabinet-maker also had to provide furniture for temples and tombs, such as the

Left **159** Carpenters shaping a bed and the *djed*-pillar, symbol of power. Painted relief in the tomb of Niankhkhnum and Khnumhotep, Saqqara. 5th dynasty

Right **160** Carpenters and painters finishing two anthropoid coffins. Painting in the tomb of Ipy, Deir el-Medina, West Thebes. 19th dynasty

tall narrow shrines for holding statues of gods and lifesize figures of royalty. For easier transport they were made with a flat base turned up at the front like a sledge. Another type of shrine for holding ritual requisites is characterised by the hieroglyphic symbols cut in fretwork in the sides. Carpenters are shown working on such shrines, burnishing them and painting or coating them with gold foil. Less elaborate chests were used in some periods for storing canopic jars.

Scenes of coffin-making occur less frequently, despite the prime importance of the coffin in funeral ritual. In the Old and Middle Kingdoms coffins were usually rectangular with a flat or slightly convex lid. As a rule they only appear in illustrations at the polishing stage, but there are three unusual New Kingdom portrayals of the final steps in the manufacture of what was by then a popular design 160 – a coffin itself shaped like an embalmed body. Here we are shown the coffins being given a stucco wash, covered with linen, polished, painted with patterns and inscribed. Coffins are usually illustrated with other tomb requisites standing beside them, so it seems there were workshops that specialised in producing everything needed for the dead.

The ancient Egyptian term *medjeh* applied not only to carpenters and cabinet-makers but to other users of wood, such as ship-builders. The illustrations sometimes give their names and affiliation to a particular workshop, or their priestly function, which is in contrast to the normal anonymity of the artisan world. Woodworking must have been a satisfying occupation and a relatively healthy one. An unusual glimpse of an accident at work occurs in the 19th-dynasty tomb of the sculptor Ipy at Deir el-Medina. Here there is a scene of a huge decorated shrine being made. One of the craftsmen is using a probe to remove some foreign body from a colleague's eye – no doubt a splinter that got into it in the course of his work.

The Tanners and Saddlers

In the mists of antiquity the earliest means of shielding the body from the elements was the skin of an animal slain in the hunt. Flaying hides, removing the underlying fat and tanning them were commonplace activities in every prehistoric community. As craft specialisation progressed in Egypt, separate skills evolved among those who processed the raw material on a large scale, the tanners, and the leather workers who made the leather parts of the horse-drawn chariots introduced in the New Kingdom – harnesses, bow-cases, arrow quivers and leather shields.

The best illustration of the stages of tanning occurs on the walls of the 18th-dynasty tomb of Rekhmire at Sheikh Abd el-Qurna. At one point a tanner is seen lifting a raw hide from a vessel evidently containing some curing fluid. (This might have been sesame oil, mentioned in the Instruction of Khety.) Next, the hide had to be thoroughly beaten with stones to let the oil penetrate evenly. This procedure yielded chamois leather. Traces of another agent, tannin, derived from the pods of the Nile acacia, have also been revealed by chemical analysis of ancient Egyptian leather goods.

The most common method of curing, however, was 'tawing' with alum (potassium aluminium sulphate), found in natural deposits in the el-Kharga and el-Dakhla Oases and identified with the Egyptian *ibenu*. There is an interesting depiction in the Middle Kingdom tomb of Iymery at Gebel el-Teir of two tanners standing on either side of a third man who has a leather bag over his shoulder and a lump of something in his hand. One view is that this represents a trading incident, but another expert interprets it as the arrival of a supply of alum.

Only occasionally is a tanner shown scraping the hair or fatty tissue from a hide. Curing was sometimes combined with dyeing, either yellow, with pomegranate juice, or red, with the pigment of the Mediterranean cochineal bug. Curing was followed by stretching the skin out to dry.

Leather cured with alum usually becomes white and stiff. To make it soft and supple again it has to be stretched. This operation is portrayed so often as to be almost emblematic of the tanner's art, with one or occasionally two men pulling the skin taut across a two- or three-legged trestle.

Elsewhere we see the actual production of leather goods, with the craftsman using a special broad-bladed knife to cut the leather into narrow strips, or fashioning sandals. In Old Kingdom scenes he is shown squatting at a low bench, while in New Kingdom times he sits on a stool at a table tilted on a stand.

In Rekhmire's tomb we see several specialists at work. One is stretching out the roughly cut pieces of leather, others are tracing the outlines of sandals, others again are making holes round the sole-edges with an awl or horn, another is cutting out straps which the last of the team is threading through the holes. One of them, having to use both hands to grip the sole, is tugging at the projecting end of a strap with his teeth.

In the same tomb we can see long strips being cut spirally from the edge of a large piece of leather and plaited into a leather rope. Two more workers are twisting and tying the strips. Wider strips were used to fasten the parts of a chariot together, or to bind as tyres round the wheels. Other leather products are shown in their finished state, such as pouches, sacks, bellows, parchment rolls and jackets.

The leather workers were generically known as *tjebu*. Few of them emerge from anonymity like one Weta, who enjoyed special royal favour and the title 'overseer of the secret' – the secret of parchment making, one suspects. It was an arduous profession, not improved by the stench of the curing process. Tanning agents and alum could damage a sensitive skin, and there were no doubt many accidents with the sharp leather-knives.

161 This pleated dress is thought to be the earliest extant garment in the world. Tarkhan. 1st dynasty. *University College London, Petrie Museum*

The Spinners and Weavers

The skills of spinning yarn from plant fibres and weaving cloth go far back into neolithic times. Both were for a long time practised solely by women. Not till the Old Kingdom do we find evidence of textile workshops existing. In examining the linen wrappings which originally enveloped the mummy of Princess Khekeretnebty in her tomb at Abusir (5th dynasty) we came upon a remarkable piece of evidence – a hieratic inscription giving the name of the manufacturer as 'Khenemu, subject of the king ... assistant, superintendent of the weaving workshop ...' The weaving shops were run largely by women and often formed part of a harem, as they certainly did at Gurob during the New Kingdom.

From Middle Kingdom we find models of weaving workshops and also pictures on tomb walls. In a model from the tomb of a noble, Meketre, spinning women are seated on the ground in front of piles of flax, twisting it into balls. Other women are teasing

162 A painted linen mummy shroud in the form of a mummy mask, with a breast plate and a winged scarab below. 21st–22nd dynasty. *University College London, Petrie Museum*

the fibres out of the balls, soaking them in pots of water and winding them onto wooden spindles. Two women then fasten the warp threads onto three pegs driven into the wall. There are two horizontal looms resting on short legs bedded in the floor, with two rows of threads held in the frames, and two women are throwing the shuttle with the weft-thread between them.

A similar weaving shop appears on a painting in the tomb of Khnumhotep at Beni Hasan. One kneeling woman prepares the flax, another feeds it to a rotating spindle and two others, squatting on the floor, throw the shuttle with the weft-thread to each other between the two rows of warp threads in the loom. All these women are working under the watchful eye of a fat male supervisor.

Under the New Kingdom the horizontal loom was superseded by a wider vertical type which survived into Roman times. It consisted of two hanging rods fastened above and below to transverse beams, making a square frame. The Egyptian loom was thus different from the kind used elsewhere, with earthenware weights holding the warp threads down. In vertical looms the weaving was done from the bottom upwards, and the weavers sat more comfortably on benches.

From the New Kingdom onwards more and more men were engaged in this work, till by the Roman Period male-operated looms predominated. In the Ptolemaic Period it was the weaving shops of the great temples that began to acquire importance.

The basic raw material was from the start high-quality Egyptian flax, or less frequently hemp or sheep's wool, which was inferior and often dirty. Only in Roman times did wool gain popularity for weaving coloured designs.

Cotton, originally cultivated in India, evidently reached Egypt in the Saitic Period, for King Amasis was reported as sending the Spartans a cuirass decorated with gold and cotton. The oldest evidence of cotton in Egypt is the sample bundle, evidently used as stuffing, found during the autopsy of the mummy PUM II, dated by radiocarbon to the 2nd century BC. By Roman times cotton was quite common; Pliny the Elder says it was grown in Upper Egypt, Nubia and the Red Sea island of Tyl, and we know from other sources that it was planted in the el-Kharga Oasis. Examination of 3rd- to 5th-dynasty burial grounds in Wadi Qitna and Kalabsha South in Egyptian Nubia showed that the shrouds were most frequently of either wool (44.3 per cent) or cotton (31.8 per cent) or a wool-cotton mixture (5.7 per cent), less often of linen (14.8 per cent) or other fibre (3.4 per cent).

There are no records of silk before the Christian era and it is first mentioned as occurring in the Nile valley by the Roman poet Lucan. This probably referred to silk imported from the Far East; not till Justinian's time (6th century AD) was the silk-worm bred in the Mediterranean area. Goat hair and later camel hair were used for weaving bags and, less often, cloaks.

Specialisation appeared gradually in textile manufacture, especially in terms of the material used. But the traditional predominance of the flax-weavers survived. Makers of carpets and cushions, fullers and dyers all had their own niches; Sir Flinders Petrie discovered a separate dyers' establishment at Athribis in the Delta. One favourite dye colour was the red obtained from safflower.

The Smelters, Metal-beaters and Metal-founders

Ore smelting was invented not in Egypt but in Asia Minor. The earliest copper articles in Egypt were the plain round beads and short pins found in Badarian burial grounds (c. 4000 BC). Metal-working spread rapidly during the Early Dynastic Period and by the 3rd or 4th dynasties copper tools had replaced most of the stone ones.

The importance of metal-working and of metal tools arose from their key role in other developments, whence the frequency of illustrations showing each successive stage: these occupy a considerable proportion of the wall-space in ancient tombs. We shall look at the technology under two main headings, raw material processing and the manufacture of actual metal articles.

The first episode depicted is usually the weighing and issue of the material. Weighing was usually done with a pair of scales whose horizontal beam, with a pan 163

149

163 Weighing metal under the scribe's supervision. From the tomb of Kaemrehu, Saqqara. 5th dynasty. *Cairo, Egyptian Museum*

163 hanging from each end, rested on a vertical support in the middle. The beam is usually shown decorated with a lotus lily at each end, while at the top of the supporting column is a head of Maat, the goddess of truth, as a warranty of fair weight. While one man weighs the goods, another checks and records them. Their titles are often indicated, such as 'overseer of the scales', 'overseer of the metal-workers' or 'scribe and overseer of the funerary endowment'. In New Kingdom scenes three more controllers appear who pick over the material weighed out and allot it to the next workers.

In Old and Middle Kingdom illustrations the material comes in the form of rods, in those of the New Kingdom it consists of rings. What we are looking at, then, is not lumps of ore but material already cleaned and cast where it was mined. Hence the sense of weighing to check the amount of metal issued against the volume of the final products; to have weighed the ore itself would have been pointless because of the amount of waste it contained.

One difficulty with this double-weighing hypothesis is that the weighing of the end-products is seldom illustrated, and then only in sequences where the initial weighing

164 Metal founders smelting ore over an open fire. They hold the crucibles of ore with crossed rods and use foot-bellows to fan the fire. Painting in the tomb of Rekhmire, Sheikh Abd el-Qurna, West Thebes. 18th dynasty

was left out of the story. We assume, then, that it was a convention that the weighing procedure should only be depicted once.

The vital smelting process which features in every picture-series was always carried out in a crucible over an open fire; the Egyptians had no blast furnaces. One unusual picture shows the fuel before it was used, in the shape of round lumps. These are usually identified as charcoal, and there is an interesting theory by David Dixon that the growing demand for this commodity among ore-smelters was the chief cause of the disappearance of once extensive woodland.

For reaching the melting temperature of the metal it was necessary to boost the supply of oxygen to the burning fuel. In the Old and Middle Kingdoms this was done with a blow-pipe made of a hollow reed with a clay nozzle. One pair of lungs would 166 not suffice, so we always see several smelters squatting round the fire, blowing for all they are worth. In the Old Kingdom a round crucible was suspended over the fire with a hole in the side which was closed during the heating and pierced afterwards for pouring the melt out. In the Middle Kingdom a trough-shaped crucible was used.

The New Kingdom brought a revolutionary innovation, the bellows. This 164 consisted of a shallow earthenware dish covered in leather, out of which an air-tube was directed toward the fire. A single worker could operate two pairs of bellows alternately, pressing one down with his foot and raising the other with a string. This

165   In this scene from a metal-vessel workshop the craftsman on the left is chasing a finished vessel with a wooden mallet and metal chisel while next to him another is beating a piece of sheet metal into shape with a hammer-stone. On the right a finished vessel is being carried away. Painting in the tomb of Rekhmire, Sheikh Abd el-Qurna, West Thebes. 18th dynasty

device produced a higher temperature than the blow-pipes, increased productivity and reduced the effort required. The crucible was by now a wide, shallow dish with a spout at the rim. New Kingdom pictures that still feature blow-pipes are probably illustrating either some small-scale operation, or a special process such as soldering.

For the next stage – the casting of the molten metal – we see in Old and Middle Kingdom pictures the red-hot crucible being held between two flat stones and the melt being poured into a flat dish to solidify into a slab. In New Kingdom scenes the smelter grips the crucible with two long flexible rods and empties it through the spout, or a funnel, into a deeper mould or into a flat dish as before.

Then comes the processing of the cold metal. In some cases we see a group of metal-beaters working on a small metal slab as it lies on a low, broad anvil by beating it with smooth oval stones till it is reduced to the required thickness. In others, part of a slab is being beaten into a blade for one of the tools mentioned in connection with other crafts.

In the Old and Middle Kingdoms metal articles were made exclusively by beating. In the New Kingdom other techniques were added, such as casting in a clay mould or using the *cire perdu* method, sometimes combined with beating.

We often see pictures of metal vessels being made, and two distinct procedures were used during the Old Kingdom. The first was to cut the various parts of the job out of the beaten material, bend them into shape, rivet adjacent edges (including any spout or handle) together, and finally rub the seams and the rivet-heads vigorously

with stones until they disappeared. In the other method the job would be laid over a rounded anvil, and while one worker held it and turned it from one position to another the second would beat it out with an oval stone. This latter technique underwent a number of improvements during the New Kingdom until it was possible to use it for large articles up to life-size. The surface would finally be burnished by rubbing with oval stones.

In the New Kingdom metal objects also began to be decorated with hieroglyphs or geometric patterns, special artists being employed for the purpose. One of these, the 165 'chisel-engraver', used a chisel struck with a wooden mallet or stone hammer; another, the 'outline drawer', coloured in the engraved inscriptions or patterns.

The products of the metal-working shops are sometimes shown arranged on shelves. Among Old Kingdom articles we find bowls, jugs, wash-basins (often spouted) and underplates, not to mention the blades for such tools as saws, axes, hoes 92 and adzes, and round metal mirrors.

Foreign influences during the New Kingdom added new lines such as vessels with an animal head on them (usually that of an ibex or a bull) and votive gifts including figures of sphinxes and vultures.

Many actual samples of the metal-worker's art have been dug up on archaeological sites, like the set of miniature, symbolic copper vessels and tools (notably chisels) among Princess Khekeretnebty's funeral equipment in her tomb at Abusir.

The principal metal for all these purposes was for a long time copper, of which there were convenient surface deposits in the valleys of western Sinai. Thanks to the natural admixture of other metals in the ores, ancient Egyptian copper was harder than the highly refined metal yielded by modern extraction methods. Analysis of the copper articles mentioned in Princess Khekeretnebty's mastaba showed naturally occurring traces of arsenic, bismuth, iron, tin, silver, nickel and antimony. Bronze, an alloy of about 90 per cent copper and 10 per cent tin, only appeared in Egypt as an import from Syria in the Middle Kingdom and became generally common during the New Kingdom. Iron long remained a rarity in Egypt, obtained either from abroad or from meteorites. The first evidence of iron-smelting comes from the Greek-colonised town of Naucratis in the 6th century BC.

Not only gold, but especially silver, which had to be imported, and their alloy electrum were expensive, though their cost varied over time. Goldsmiths seldom cast anything from the pure metal; they usually gilded articles made of other metals.

To melt gold required a temperature of over 1000°C. After cooling, it was beaten out on a special trough-shaped stone with a 'guide groove' running lengthwise; by

166   A relief showing craftsmen at work in a precious-metal workshop. A frieze of completed jewellery divides the upper register showing weighing, melting, casting and beating from the lower, where jewellers including several achondroplastic dwarfs are finishing collars and a pectoral. Tomb of Mereruka, Saqqara. 6th dynasty

167 In this jewellery workshop craftsmen bore holes in beads with multiple bow-drills, polish the beads and assemble a broad *wesekh* collar while a metal worker fans the flames. The craftsman on the right holds a piece of metalwork in a brazier, using a blowpipe to increase the heat. From the tomb of Sobekhotep, West Thebes. 18th dynasty. *London, British Museum*

rocking and pressing on a round stone exactly fitting the groove the gold foil could be increasingly attenuated until the extreme thinness of gold leaf was achieved, for gilding wood or other objects. In one scene a metal-beater is seen taking a sheet of gold leaf from a box and passing it to another, who applies it to a wooden cabinet.

Another technique for gilding used on such things as wooden walking-sticks, royal sceptres and copper ornaments, was to plate them by dipping in molten gold.

Casting complete artefacts in gold had to await the new metal-founding technology – and growing prosperity – of the New Kingdom. Such precious objects were designed only for gods and kings. Only a few escaped the robbers, such as the famous statue of Tutankhamun from his tomb treasury or the falcon-figure of Horus from Dendera. The size of these unique creations, understandably, seldom exceeded one royal cubit (525mm). Objects with a gold surface thereby acquired 'divine life' and often featured in religious rites; from the New Kingdom onwards their production was concentrated in the temple workshops.

All metal-workers were denoted hieroglyphically by the stylised symbol of a metal vase, *bedjty*, sometimes with an additional sign to indicate the particular metal. Among them it was the smelters who had the most physically demanding and hazardous work. Like the glass-blowers they were prone to emphysema and circulatory complications when they had to blow down tubes for days on end, so the introduction of the bellows was a prophylactic as well as an economic advance. It also enabled the worker to keep at a greater distance from the glare of flames that could disturb the body fluids management, cornea and respiratory passages. And the danger of burns remained a real one too.

The Jewellers

Tomb scenes show specialised workshops where skilled craftsmen made beads from various kinds of stone and gem, and strung them together. In other workshops they assembled necklaces and other composed jewellery from metal or faience beads made elsewhere. Pictures of the first sort show for the most part the operation of drilling rough stone beads. One Old Kingdom scene shows two jewellers doing this with a hand-drill fitted with a flint bit, such as we have seen used for making stone vessels, but smaller and without a handle or stone weights. Another pair or workers are polishing the beads; captions explain that the material is cornelian and that the men are 'jewellers, makers of decorative stone'.

Some of the New Kingdom scenes show technical progress. Here the beads are embedded in plaster or in the recesses of a wooden slab on the workbench, so that the jeweller can use the bow drill mentioned in connection with woodworking, for which the use of both hands was necessary. A single worker is shown operating even four or five drills with one bowstring. Another scene shows two jewellers at a bench on which a belt of beads lies, hanging over both ends. They are drilling beads at regular intervals and then separating them from the belt. Polishing of the beads, not shown in the pictures, was done manually by rolling them over a flat surface, or in a pit in a whetstone of sandstone or quartzite, or by fixing them to the ends of rods that were then spun between the palms or with the bowstring. Both for boring and polishing finely ground quartz was used as an abrasive. Mass production of beads is known to have taken place at Hierakonpolis at the start of the Dynastic Period.

We can also see the other type of workshop where finished beads were strung into broad collars, *wesekh*. This was very painstaking work, for which achondroplastic dwarfs evidently had a special aptitude. Production can be reviewed in three stages.

The first step was to prepare the strings. A picture from Meir shows one worker holding the string between his soles and twisting with his palms. Elsewhere we see two dwarfs sitting face to face, one holding the end of a string taut and the other splicing its two strands together. The second stage, familiar from Old Kingdom pictures where dwarfs predominate, usually has two of them sitting opposite one another at a low table with an almost finished *wesekh* collar laid out on it, completing the arrangement of the beads and the tying of the threads; in a few cases the tedious stringing of the beads is also shown.

In the final stage the collar is dipped into a bowl or washed with some fluid poured from a spouted jug over a large dish. The captions calls this the 'wetting' or 'anointing' of the jewellery, but the nature of the fluid is unclear. It is usually taken to have been water, designed to shrink the threads and make the collar stronger. But Rosemarie Drenkhahn argues that since the liquid was not disposed of, it had to be either a dye, or some agent for giving the beads a higher and more permanent gloss.

Though the jeweller's job involved no special health hazards it was not without its drawbacks. To quote the Instruction of Khety once more: 'The jeweller has to drill all kinds of hard stones. By the time he has finished an inlay he is tired and weak. He has to sit with his legs folded and back [bent] until sunset.'

The Status of Artisans

The craftsmen of ancient Egypt had no workshops or even tools of their own; these all belonged to members of the ruling class or to the institutions they controlled. So the

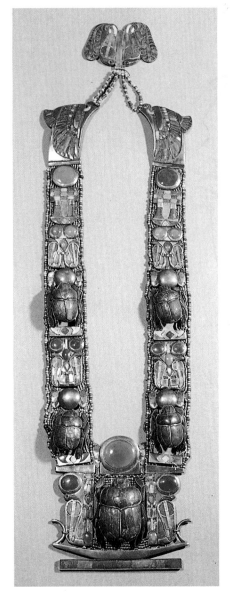

Above **168** A scarab pectoral with articulated straps formed from inlaid plaques with uraei (cobras), scarabs and solar discs, flanked by coloured beads. The straps end with two representations of the vulture goddess Nekhbet and are attached to the counterpoise in the form of two uraei with four rows of beads. From the tomb of Tutankhamun, Valley of the Kings, West Thebes. 18th dynasty. *Cairo, Egyptian Museum*

Left **169** Amuletic jewellery including four gold fish pendants (*nekhau*), two hollow gold sphinx beads and an electrum oyster-shell amulet. Middle Kingdom. *London, British Museum*

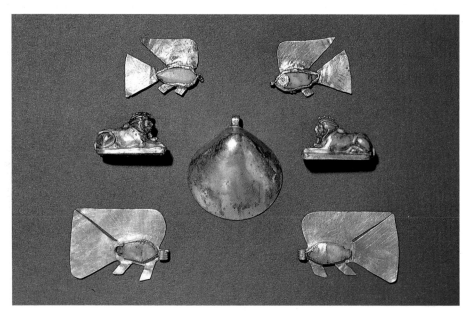

Right **170** Glass papyrus column pendants, glazed composition studs and earrings. New Kingdom. *University College London, Petrie Museum*

social status and prestige of a craftsman depended primarily not on his personal qualities and skills but on the work centre he was attached to.

At the top of the ladder were the employees of royal factories. Oddly enough they are never depicted at work. We see them at feasts, at the hunt, or as funeral priests in the tombs of the mighty, whenever the pharaoh had lent them to some favourite as a sign of appreciation. We know the special titles accorded to royal jewellers, goldsmiths and woodcarvers. Many are known from their tombs, or by their presence in scenes decorating the tombs of the dignitaries they were lent out to, standing in a place of honour beside their new master or at the head of a procession bringing sacrificial offerings. This all demonstrates their high social standing and their master's gratitude for the esteem which the royal loan signified. On a somewhat lower rung were the artisans who worked in the great temples – temples dedicated to gods, or funerary temples for the deceased. There they made the various requisites for religious of funerary rites. At the bottom of the ladder were those who toiled in the workshops of private owners, dignitaries and senior officials; these seldom emerge from anonymity.

Within each of these categories there was a working hierarchy from apprentices and assistants up to master craftsmen, controllers and overseers. It is not known exactly who assigned a newcomer to this or that workshop, but the main principle seems to have been that a son followed his father's calling. It can be assumed that kings and temples poached the best men from the workshops of their subordinates, who were hardly in a position to object. There was nothing in ancient Egypt like the medieval guild to link members of the same craft, and artisans as a whole did not constitute a clearly defined stratum in society.

CHAPTER TWELVE

Immortality through Art

ANCIENT EGYPT HAS has bequeathed us an enormous testimony to the skill and genius of its artists – draughtsmen, painters, relief-carvers and sculptors. The pages of this book testify to their creations, but here we shall focus on the men themselves, their working techniques and conditions, and the place they occupied in society.

It must be stressed at the outset that in their working tools, technical procedures and way of life the artists of ancient Egypt did not greatly differ from the artisans. Woodcarvers shared the tools and techniques of carpenters and joiners, sculptors in stone drew on the skills of stone masons and stone vessel makers, artists who worked with metal learned from the experience of metal-beaters. We often see an artist at work in the craftshop specialising in his chosen medium. The work of the draughtsman and the painter, on the other hand, had a close affinity to that of the scribe.

Works of art, again, did not spring from the hands of single individuals; they were invariably the product of collective effort by a number of men. The contribution of one artist linked up with that of another, a painting or a relief being based on another man's drawing while a sculpture was passed on to the painters to be coloured. It is only for descriptive convenience, then, that we shall be dealing with the various specialisations in terms of present-day classification.

We may well start with the sculptors, as it is they whose working methods are most fully documented. In most cases we are shown a sculptor standing in front of a finished work, normally a lifesize male or female figure, standing or seated, less often the lying figure of an animal. Whatever the medium, any such figure is regularly referred to in captions as *tut*. Often we are shown several figures being sculpted side 175 by side in the same workshop; in the 5th-dynasty tomb of Ty at Saqqara, for instance, there are eight in various stages of completion.

The early stages, by contrast, are seldom depicted. There is one example in the 12th-dynasty tomb of Khnumhotep at Beni Hasan where a sculptor is hacking stone from a block with his long-handled axe to approximate the shape of a statue. And in Ty's tomb we see two men chipping at the surface of an emerging statue with oval stone hammerheads wedged into forked wooden shafts. Sometimes a monumental stone statue would be roughly shaped even while being quarried, like that of Osiris that still lies in the granite quarry where it originated, near Shellal south of Aswan.

The finer work on a sculpture was done with chisel and mallet, the latter club-shaped during the Old Kingdom and subsequently either club-shaped or round-headed. This method made it easier to determine the force of a blow and, by adjusting the angle of the chisel, to alter the thickness of the flakes removed.

To achieve a smooth finish the sculptor used an adze, familiar from our description

171   A masterpiece of sculpture, this majestic statue of King Khephren incorporates the symbolism of the power and protection the god Horus gives to his representative on earth. Behind the throne, Horus is perched to protect the king with his outstretched wings. Diorite. From Khephren's valley temple, Giza. 4th dynasty. *Cairo, Egyptian Museum*

of woodworking, followed by grinding and polishing with the oval stone or with silicate powder, leather and water. The work would then be passed to the painters for polychrome treatment.

It is difficult from extant illustrations to determine the kind of material being used in any given scene. Only occasionally is there a dappled texture indicating granite. Sometimes we can draw conclusions from the juxtaposition of other scenes. Sculptors shown alongside stone vessel makers were probably using stone too, and the linkage is reinforced by the general predominance of stone statues in archaeological finds. Again, the use of carpenters' and joiners' tools will suggest that a soft stone such as limestone was being employed. And this is consistent with the prevalence of limestone, as against the harder granite, diorite, breccia etc., in statues occurring in tombs and temples.

If, however, we are shown sculptors actually working alongside the carpenters and joiners themselves, we can infer that it was wood they were working in. True, far fewer wood than stone statues have been excavated, but this may simply be because a much higher proportion have succumbed to the ravages of time.

Only rarely have metal statues been found. The figure of King Pepy I exhibited in the Egyptian Museum, Cairo, is made of copper plates beaten and riveted together and was made in a metal-beater's shop. Not till the New Kingdom do we find depictions of bronze figures being made.

There are Old and Middle Kingdom reliefs showing statues of commoners being made – the owners of the tombs and their families – but none showing a statue of royalty. In the New Kingdom, by contrast, the bulk of sculpture work shifted to temple studios where numerous figures of kings were turned out both for the temples themselves and for royal tombs.

It was the sculptor's aim in ancient Egypt to reproduce the subject's appearance as faithfully as possible. He did not however have in mind a portrait in the modern sense, exhibiting a particular person at a particular moment in his life, but the presentation of salient features at an ideal age, usually in youth or in full maturity.

The art of making death-masks was known as early as the Old Kingdom. Casts could be used as technical aids in making figures for tombs, particularly for the special chambers called in modern times the *serdab*. These were thought to embody the spirit *ka* of the deceased, the symbol of his individuality, and certain funeral rites accordingly centred round them. Similarly the so-called 'reserve' heads of 4th-dynasty dignitaries from Giza were probably placed in the tomb to ensure that the deceased's likeness should survive even if his mummy disintegrated, and these were executed quite realistically despite a degree of idealisation.

At all periods statues of royalty exhibit, however idealised, characteristic features that enable us to identify the subject. A unique collection of masks, evidently cast from living persons, was found in the studio of the sculptor Thutmose at Akhetaten. They evidently assisted the artist in making realistic or naturalistic portraits, but unfortunately few of these have survived. After a further phase of idealisation the realistic tradition was fully re-established in the Late and Graeco-Roman Periods.

The term *kesty* for sculptors also covered the carvers of stone and wood reliefs. The latter are shown on several fine reliefs chipping away with mallet and chisel on scenes already traced out by draughtsmen. Relief-carving was in fact one of the most frequent commissions given to artists. From the Old Kingdom up to the time of King Sethos I most temple and tomb reliefs were of the raised kind where the figures stood out, fully contoured, with the surrounding areas cut away. In the other, sunk reliefs, also represented in the Old Kingdom, the background is left uncut but the figures are carved in and beneath it. Sunk reliefs dominated temple walls from the time of Ramesses II, and exceptionally deep-cut reliefs are typical of the Ptolemaic Period.

The distinction between draughtsmen and painters is reflected in the ancient Egyptian nomenclature. Draughtsmen are called *sesh kedut*, 'writers of outlines', showing the close affinity between drawing and writing. The old Egyptian script had, after all, evolved through the standardisation of diagrammatic drawings, and scribe

173 Crowned head of Queen Nefertiti who was assured immortality thanks to the art of the sculptor Thutmose, in whose workshop this famous model bust was found. Painted limestone. Tell el-Amarna. 18th dynasty. *Berlin-Charlottenburg, Ägyptisches Museum*

Below 172 An unfinished quartzite head of one of Akhenaten's six daughters. The elongated face and prominent chin are associated with the Amarna style. The features are probably based on those of the King rather than those of his daughter, who may have been quite young when this head was sculpted. Quartzite. Tell el-Amarna. 18th dynasty. *Berlin, Ägyptisches Museum*

and draughtsman used the same instruments. The word for painter, *sesh*, denotes also a scribe.

The activities of draughtsmen and of painters were closely associated. But as their pictures contain no information about their creative environment and methods, we have to rely on archaeological evidence and on partly-finished work.

In addition to possessing originality and a flair for design, the ancient Egyptian artist needed to be fully conversant, not only with objects and events around him, but with various established and immutable religious preconceptions. These included the figures of the gods with all their attributes and the prescribed content of divine, ritual and royal scenes. But he was less bound by stereotypes when it came to portraying the lives of ordinary people.

We get some idea of the artist's preliminary work from the ostraca used for practice
38 by trainee draughtsmen and painters as well as by apprentice scribes. Even qualified craftsmen used them as cheap 'sketch pads' when preparing to work on the walls of tombs or temples, or to write on costly papyrus scrolls.

These sketches furnish more testimony to the creative genius of artists, in fact, than do their final products, subject as these were to meticulous regulation of form and content. They often give a livelier rendering of movement – witness for example the picture of two cheetahs attacking an antelope on an ostracon in the Náprstek Museum in Prague, or the famous figure of a dancing-girl bending over backwards in
46 the Egyptian Museum, Turin. On ostraca there are often sketched (cartoon-like) scenes which illustrate fables. There also occur ostraca with realistic preliminary sketches of human figures, even showing the use of perspective in their drawing, on which the final correction in black line reverts to the normal canonical style, to which we will return later.

Another sketch-pad surrogate consisted of a little wooden board coated in stucco and marked out with a rectangular grid on which the artist made his drawing. In doing so he would adhere to the strict rules and then, having copied the grid onto a wall on a larger scale, transfer the design square by square.
177 Use of a grid also ensured adherence to the basic rules of figure proportion that have been revealed by Erik Iversen and recently revised by Gay Robins. Up to the end of the Third Intermediate Period artists applied the 'first canon of proportion' based on the 'short cubit', that is the distance from the elbow to the tip of the thumb, conventionally set at 45cm. A human figure standing would be drawn onto a grid of 18 squares, each side of a square equalling the width of a clenched fist. Thus the length of a forearm was three squares, of a hand one-and-a-half and so on.

The Saitic Period saw the introduction of the 'second canon of proportion' based on

174 Chief sculptor Yuti painting with his left hand the statue of princess Beketaten. Relief in the tomb of Huye, Tell el-Amarna. 18th dynasty

175 Sculptors working on two statues. Relief in the tomb of Ankhmahor, Saqqara. 6th dynasty

176 A colossal statue of Ramesses II
with a princess, perhaps his daughter
Bentanta, standing between his feet.
Restored and reerected before Pylon II
of the great temple of Amun in Karnak.
19th dynasty

21 squares. This had to do with the wider acceptance of the longer 'royal cubit' (52.36cm from elbow to tip of middle finger) which had previously been used only in architecture. The basic modulus, the width of a clenched fist, remained the same. So there were now three extra squares from top to foot of a human figure, of which one was assigned to the lower leg and two to the trunk, sometimes resulting in an unnatural elongation of the upper half of the body.

In some cases the artist took the risk of sketching the figure straight on the wall-plaster while it was still wet, without a grid. An example occurs on the east wall of the South chapel in the 5th-dynasty tomb of Princess Khekeretnebty at Abusir, where the outline of a seated figure was drawn in white on the dark grey plaster. Usually, however, sketching was done in red, as we see in several scenes planned for the tomb of Horemheb in the Valley of the Kings (18th dynasty). The final drawing was then executed in a strong black line, ready for relief carving or colouring in. There are examples of this for instance, in other parts of Princess Khekeretnebty's tomb, in that of Horemheb and in the fine profile of a young princess in the 18th-dynasty tomb of Kheruef at Asasif on the west bank of the Nile near Luxor.

In addition to the canons of proportion there were other established conventions that the draughtsman had to follow. Successive scenes were arranged according to their content and prescribed order in 'registers', usually several one above another.

180
181

Above **177** Figures from the Underworld in an illustration from the Book of Amduat (Book of What Is in the Underworld). Master sketch for a relief on the wall of the tomb of Tuthmosis III in the Valley of the Kings. West Thebes. 18th dynasty

Left **178** King Akhenaten is said to have taught Chief Sculptor Bak, represented here with his wife. No attempt was made to disguise Bak's obesity. Quartzite stela. 18th dynasty. *Berlin-Charlottenburg, Ägyptisches Museum*

Right **179** Gilded wooden statue of the goddess Nephthys, guarding the canopic shrine of Tutankhamun. From the tomb of Tutankhamun, Valley of the Kings. West Thebes. 18th dynasty. *Cairo, Egyptian Museum*

Figures of important personages, usually the owner of the tomb and sometimes his wife as well, are as a rule drawn several times larger than their children and servants or the offering-bearers, reflecting the hierarchic structure of both family and society.

The human figure is usually represented as seen from several angles, blended into a single form. The head, face and limbs are shown in profile, the eyes and shoulders frontally, while the trunk twists from a frontal view at the top to a profile position below. This was intended to combine the most lifelike aspects of each area of the body, but sometimes produced inaccuracies and blunders.

Instead of perspective treatment, objects were shown overlapping or arranged one above another. Sometimes two characteristic views of the same thing were

combined, eg a front view combined with a bird's eye view from above, or front view with a side view next to it.

Like the scribes, draughtsmen and painters used brushes made of reed stems with one end frayed out by chewing, a palette with six to eight recesses and a conch-shell or ceramic bowl to mix the paint. The choice of colours used also followed rules and had its own symbolism. White (plaster of Paris or chalk) denoted light, dawn, luxury and joy; yellow was used for gold, the bodies of gods and eternity; pale yellow (ochre or arsenic sulphate) for the female complexion and brownish-red (also ochre) for the male; red (ochre with a high ferric content, or haematite) for blood and life, but also evil and violence; green (malachite mixed with lime) for water, turquoise, youth and freshness; blue (copper silicate or cobalt salts) for the sky, the hair of gods and lapis lazuli; black (charcoal and soot) for the black earth, fertility, riches and the life to come. Colours were water-based, with gum arabic and white of egg added as a bond. From the 18th-dynasty beeswax was sometimes used. The finest examples are the encaustic portraits of the Roman Period in the Faiyum.

Drawing was usually followed by relief-carving and then by painting. This sequence was occasionally ignored under the Old Kingdom, but more frequently under the New. Poor quality of the stone probably made relief-carving sometimes impossible, and painting on the flat had to suffice. In that case the rock wall was

Left **180** Unfinished master sketch and relief showing two deities from the Book of the Gates. Tomb of Horemheb, Valley of the Kings, West Thebes. 18th dynasty

Above right **181** A first master sketch with corrections for a relief to be carved in the tomb of Horemheb, showing a man's head and upper body. Valley of the Kings, West Thebes. 18th dynasty

Right **182** Pillared hall in the tomb of mayor of Thebes Sennefer, shown here with his wife being sprinkled with holy water by a priest. Sennefer's short kilt can be seen through the sheer overgarment. West Thebes. 18th dynasty

either smoothed and directly painted over, or covered with a roughcast of mud-clay and chopped straw, followed by a layer of fine white plaster which took the painting.

There are excellent Old Kingdom paintings in the 3rd-dynasty tomb of Princess Itet at Meidum, and in that of Princess Khekeretnebty. Flat paintings predominated in the Middle Kingdom tombs at Beni Hasan and in the mastabas of New Kingdom dignitaries on the West bank at Luxor. The walls of the royal palaces were also painted. In those of Amenophis III at Malqata and of his son Akhenaten at Akhetaten pictorial fragments have survived showing plants (notably papyrus), giraffes, birds and geometric designs.

Painters, as we have said, also found employment in sculptors' studios during the last stage of statue making. There are several fine illustrations that show the artist with a goblet of paint or a palette in one hand and a brush or spatula in the other. Some of the scenes show the front of a statue being coloured, others the back and the column behind with its hieroglyphic inscription. A white stucco undercoat was also used for polychrome work on statuary.

Close though the artists were to the artisans in their technology, they undoubtedly stood higher on the social ladder. This fact was once seen as an acknowledgement of the artistic quality of their work, but more recent research attributes the artist's prestige to his working more specifically than any others 'for eternity'. By making

183 The tomb owner's throwsticks play havoc in the papyrus thicket and the cat presents another threat to the birds. A papyrus stem is bending under the weight of an ichneumon. Detail of an exceptionally lively fowling scene painted in the tomb of Menna. Sheikh Abd el-Qurna, West Thebes. 18th dynasty

likenesses of a tomb's owner he was guaranteeing the person's survival after death. In this way he secured his patron's goodwill, perhaps even his gratitude, like a doctor who has prolonged his patient's existence on earth. This is why the artist is portrayed in the honourable function of offering-bearer in the tombs of commoners, or accompanying the deceased at banquets or in the chase, more frequently than he is shown at work. The figure of the artist is sometimes eloquently labelled 'his [the master's] beneficiary, his beloved, his revered . . .' and so on.

Further evidence of the artist's exalted status in ancient Egypt is that his title never includes the expression *per en djet* (mortuary estate, endowment) so often applied to craftsmen in workshops outside the royal circles. What distinguished the artist was that he worked in his patron's house only for as long as was required to make a statue or decorate a tomb, in contrast to the craftsmen whose wares were indispensable for the everyday running of an estate. The great majority of artists, it seems, worked in royal studios from which the king lent them out to temples or private persons as a mark of favour.

Their status enabled quite a few artists to afford their own tombs and, incidentally, to tell us their names. Sometimes these appear in scenes depicting them at work or at leisure. Even as early as the Old Kingdom the 5th-dynasty vizier Ptahhotep allowed the sculptor who had decorated his tomb at Saqqara to include a portrait of himself in the reliefs and to append his own name. He is shown on a boating trip, being served with food and drink. We also find self-portraits of artists near the edges of some New Kingdom tomb paintings. The creator of the famous scene of the Battle of Qadesh, and the sculptor who carved it in relief in the temple of Ramesses II at Abu Simbel, also put their names to it for posterity. Among the well-known sculptors of the New Kingdom were Thutmose of Akhetaten and the joint occupants of a tomb at Sheikh Abd el-Qurna, Nebamun and Ipuky.

According to their experience and achievement, artists were ranked in categories from the lowest up to the leading masters. Outstanding ones were accorded such titles as 'painter of the palace library of sacred books', or 'chief painter of the temple of Amun'. The pharaoh might even reward them with gifts of land, 'people' (servants or slaves), cattle or treasure. Court records and legacies show that artists often acquired considerable wealth.

It would seem, then, that the life of an artist in ancient Egypt was endowed with the lustre of high status, celebrity, material riches, public honour and, no doubt, work-satisfaction. Apart from the risk of silicosis among sculptors their work was not unhealthy. Only the draughtsmen, relief-carvers and rock-tomb painters of the New Kingdom suffered difficult working conditions in those deep corridors, lit only with dim and primitive candles which used up much of the available oxygen. Their heads must often have ached. The warm Egyptian air, made still warmer by the candles and humidified by the workers' sweat, must have made breathing difficult during the long hours of toil. Yet these inconveniences left no traces in the quality of the works of art created there.

184 Scene from a fable: a typical Egyptian tabby cat equipped like a shepherd with a bag on a shepherd's crook is guiding six geese with whip. The skillful execution suggests that this is a painter's sketch rather than a pupil's practice work. Limestone ostracon. Unknown provenance. 20th dynasty. *Cairo, Egyptian Museum*

CHAPTER THIRTEEN

Quarries, Boats and Pyramids

185 The pyramid of Khephren has retained its casing at the apex. Its inner lining is exposed elsewhere, with limestone blocks as much as 1 metre high. Giza. 4th dynasty

THE CIVILISATION OF ancient Egypt is chiefly renowned for its mighty edifices – pyramids, temples and monumental tombs. The pyramids, the most immense feats of architecture of any time or place, were moreover started a mere three or four centuries after the emergence of a united Egyptian state. It is equally amazing that the technical quality of their construction was such as to withstand the elements for thousands of years.

It is not surprising that ever since modern interest in these colossal works awoke at the end of the 18th century there has been endless speculation on why they were built, on the unaccountable expertise of their designers, on the secrets of the technology used in their construction and even on the status of the men who did the work. For all the accumulated findings of archaeologists, architects, Egyptologists and, latterly, physicists, some of the many theories put forward owe less to research than to the lively imagination of their begetters.

Interest has centred above all on the pyramids and notably on the largest of them, the pyramid of Cheops at Giza, which has often been considered in isolation from the rest. The angles of inclination of walls and corridors and the proportions of internal chambers have been thought by some not only to prove the mathematical knowledge of the ancient priest-scientists but to hold prophetic messages for future generations. Others have claimed that the pyramids were intended as astronomical observatories, huge grain stores or survival-points against the biblical deluge. The authors of these theories were prepared to accept any explanation of the purpose of the pyramids except the one supported by archaeological evidence and historical texts, that they were the monumental mausolea of the king-gods. (Not long ago, Erich von Däniken has even involved the pyramids in speculation about extraterrestrial visitors from some distant planet.)

Rather than join in disputes about the origin and history of the pyramids, we shall examine the other, hidden side of the story – the lives and labours of the men who put them up. We shall look at the tools and technology they used, at how they quarried the blocks, transported them to the site and moved them to the required level and set them in position, at their working conditions and at the range of people involved in the projects.

Their construction obviously required a clear-headed and efficient management team. This was directly answerable to the king and was headed by an 'overseer of all the royal works', often the vizier. It included the most senior state officials such as the 'head administrator of estates' and the 'overseer of the treasury', the mayor of the capital, Memphis, and the high priests both of that city and of Heliopolis, the spiritual metropolis of the Old Kingdom. Together with the king, these were the men who decided on the site, the base dimensions, the elevation of the sides and hence the height, the material to be used and other basic design factors.

The task of elaborating the actual plans fell to the royal architect, whose title *medjeh nesu* ('royal carpenter' or 'woodworker') dated from the time when most buildings were made of wood. (He was also styled 'royal master' and 'royal master-scribe'.) Some of the royal architects are known to us by name. Foremost among these was the inventor of stone-based architecture and creator of Djoser's pyramid **261** complex, Imhotep, who was also a vizier and scion (*iry-pat*) of a noble family. The architect Nefermaat and his son Hemiun designed several pyramids starting with the **187** one at Meidum and ending with the pyramid of Cheops. We also know of the Sennedjemibs, father and son, who built pyramids in the 5th and 6th dynasties. Among the guiding spirits of the great New Kingdom projects was the vizier Senenmut, who by the end of his meteoric career had been honoured with some 80 **10** titles ranging from 'tutor' to the daughter of Queen Hatshepsut to 'chief administrator of estates' and 'overseer of all the Queen's works'. He ensured his immortality by designing the unique terraced temple of Deir el-Bahari.

Unfortunately no technical drawings for the pyramids or the great temples have survived, but we can assume that they once existed since 18th-dynasty papyrus **190** plans have been found for goldmines, the tombs of the Valley of the Kings and for a projected stone *naos*. A few years ago the plan for a late pyramid at Meroe, the capital of the Nubian kingdom of that name, was found by Friedrich Hinkel engraved on the side wall of the chapel of the older pyramid adjoining.

The head architect had to decide on the type and quality of material to be used, work out the quantities required, arrange for it to be hewn in the appropriate quarry and transported to the building site, and estimate the size and qualifications of the labour force needed. Responsibility for housing and feeding the workers and providing them with tools, clothing, footwear and other necessities were delegated to the clerk-scribes.

Before building could start, some other basic decisions had to be taken and preliminary surveys carried out. The king would begin by convening his closest advisors to determine jointly the site of the future pyramid, the size of its base and the slope of its sides.

Astronomers were next summoned to the site to lay down the north-south axis of the edifice. In the course of time they attained an increasing degree of accuracy. In **188** the oldest pyramid, that of King Djoser, the axis was out by three degrees, but the sides of the Great Pyramid of King Cheops are true to within two-and-a-half to five-and-a-half minutes of angle.

Below **186**   The majestic gateway to Djoser's step pyramid and enclosure. Saqqara. 3rd dynasty

Above right **187**   The step pyramid at Meidum was modified into a true pyramid. However, very much later the casing collapsed and exposed the original structure. 4th dynasty

Right **188**   Djoser's step pyramid and enclosure with pavilions, which were used at *sed* festivals, celebrating the King's jubilee. The pyramid's casing was removed later for other building projects. Saqqara. 3rd dynasty

Using a grid the surveyors laid out exactly the length of the side parallel to the north-south axis, and then the length of the sides perpendicular to it. In the case of the Great Pyramid it was fixed at 440 cubits. The cords used for the purpose were no doubt similar to that found at Saqqara in one of the mastabas of the Archaic Period. This was a centimetre thick and made of 190 strands tightly wound so that it would not stretch even when spanning great distances. The success of the operation was proved by Goyon, who ascertained that the actual measurements along the east and south sides were only 7mm and 70mm in excess of the planned length, while those of the west and north sides fell short by 9mm and 131mm respectively.

Levelling was thought by earlier writers to have been achieved by digging ditches, filling them with water and using them like huge spirit-levels. More recent evidence shows that different methods were used. Around the pyramid of Khephren a system 185 of bore-holes was employed, while for those of King Djoser at Saqqara and of 186 Amenemhet III at Dahshur little brick towers were made to carry the points of the grid and height markers. The base of the Great Pyramid of Cheops, despite its enormous area of 53,077m², is almost perfectly level with a maximum error of only 21mm.

Only after these preliminaries, we can assume, did the Ceremony of Cord Stretching take place. The king set off at dawn with his retinue of senior officials to the

site of the pyramid, where they checked its orientation and measurements. Then with the help of assistants representing various gods, notably Seshat, goddess of writing and arithmetic (and hence of major construction projects), he took his golden mallet, drove stakes into the ground where the corners of the pyramid were to be, and stretched a cord between them. Next he dug a short ceremonial trench in line with the cord, threw in a handful of sand to make a neat foundation surface, modelled a symbolic brick out of clay and finally levered the foundation stone into place.

The first step in the actual building was for the stonemasons to hack out the underground rooms. The procedure is well illustrated by the unfinished pyramid of the 3rd-dynasty kings Nebka or Khaba at Zawyet el-Aryan. Here there is a wide cutting with a double stairway leading to an extensive burial-chamber in the middle, down to which a granite sarcophagus had been lowered before the chamber was roofed over.

The construction required vast numbers of stone blocks to be hewn, transported to the site and assembled. The Great Pyramid of King Cheops at Giza with its volume of 2,600,000m³, for example, is estimated to have needed between two-and-a-quarter and two-and-a-half million blocks weighing an average of two-and-a-half tonnes each. Fortunately, not all this material had to be fetched from a great distance. For the core of the pyramid, representing the greater part of its mass, use could be made partly of natural rock outcrops but mainly of locally cut blocks. Superior quality stone from more distant quarries was only needed for the outer casing and to line the walls of the interior rooms and corridors.

For the erection of their monuments the rulers of the Old Kingdom chose a plateau to the north-west of Memphis. It was formed of tertiary nummulitic limestone, a rather inferior, softish material of a yellow or greyish hue. This is laid down in horizontal strata alternating with thin beds of clay, so that a block can be obtained simply by cutting down the sides and inserting levers under the original end-face. The famous Sphinx at Giza was carved from the stratified bluff remaining after blocks had 192 been hewn from the rock around it. One can see how the thickness of the limestone layers diminished downwards, so that blocks cut at the lower levels must have been smaller. If we climb to the top of the pyramid of Mycerinus and look eastward, we can see at several points the regular chequerboard pattern left in outline where blocks were extracted. The greater part of the material for a pyramid, then, was quarried in its immediate vicinity; blocks cut there were also used to make the core structures of the temple walls in the pyramid complexes, and of the tombs of dignitaries that sprang up around every pyramid.

For higher quality material the builders had to use more distant sources. The casing of a pyramid and the wall-facings of temples and mastabas required the finer-grained, harder and less brittle white limestone found on the opposite, eastern side of the Nile in the Mokkatam Hills near modern Tura el-Asmant and Masara. High up in the sides of the quarry the traces left when blocks were cut are still clear. Cuttings were even made deep into the rocks, leaving underground chambers up to 10m high and galleries continuing for as far as 50m.

In Upper Egypt and Nubia the builders exploited the fine sandstone from quarries still visible near Gebel el-Silsila, in the surroundings of Kom Ombo and at Qertassi in northern Nubia. The vertical walls are still criss-crossed by the outlines of various-sized blocks. These sites provided the material for almost all the Nubian temples, apart from those that were carved directly out of sandstone rocks.

The pink granite occurring at various spots around Aswan was used throughout the country. This is a very hard rock found in bizarrely rounded shapes and eroded boulders ideal for block-hewing. Wherever there was a granite plateau, rock was quarried from the surface in one or more layers. Still at the exact spot in the quarry where its cutting was begun, we can see a 36m-long obelisk cut out from all sides except the rear, which remained attached to its matrix. The only reason why the obelisk was not separated was that it cracked in the course of operations. The quarrymen tried to make use at least of the portion beyond the crack by cutting a smaller obelisk, but even this project was never completed.

189   The grandeur of the valley temple of Khephren is enhanced by the rectangular granite monoliths which used to support the roof. Giza. 4th dynasty

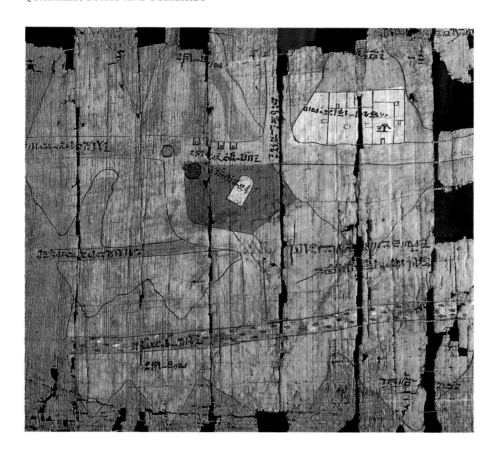

190 The world's oldest extant map shows the gold mines and basanite caves of Wadi Hammamat. Papyrus of Mines. 20th dynasty. *Turin, Museo Egizio*

Another variety of granite was quarried in Wadi Hammamat. Granite from both sites was used for facing the inner chambers of pyramids and for making sarcophagi.

Among other types of building stone used were basalt from Gebel Qatrani in the Faiyum, quartzite from Gebel el-Ahmar near Cairo, diorite from the Western Desert 65km northwest of Abu Simbel, alabaster from Hatnub near Amarna and from the Wadi el-Garawi near Helwan, slate from Wadi Hammamat again, quartzite and porphyry from Gebel Dukhan and Gebel Fatira (Mons Porphyrites and Mons Claudianus) in the Eastern Desert, and dolerite from the Aswan area.

Work in the building-stone quarries was again directed by a staff, sometimes led by functionaries as senior as the vizier or the head administrator of estates, and including the commander of the guard. Staff lists mention in particular specialists such as quarrymen, stonemasons, drillers and 'soft-stone workers', but these – usually around 30 of them – were far outnumbered as we shall see by the unskilled labourers who transported the blocks.

While major projects were in hand some quarries probably worked non-stop for most of the year, including the hottest months.

Quarrymen and masons, like other craftsmen, had to be content with a small selection of implements. Among these was the heavy pointed pick-axe of hard stone – basalt or dolerite – weighing between one and three kilograms and either held in the hands or tied across its saddle to a forked wooden shaft. Chisels made originally of flint or dolerite, but gradually replaced during the Old Kingdom by ever larger and harder copper ones, were struck with a basalt or dolerite hammer weighing between three and five kilograms, or with a wooden conical-headed mallet. The softer rocks were cut with a copper saw whose toothed edge was embedded with grains of sand during the forging.

Once the chosen area of rock had been roughly evened out it was probably strewn with glowing charcoal embers and then cold water was quickly poured over, so that the surface of the stone disintegrated at this point, making the blocks easier to extract. The edges of the desired blocks were then traced out and the side faces cut down to the necessary depth with hammer and chisel. The earlier theory that the blocks were then prised put by inserting wooden wedges and soaking them so that they expanded is not accepted by many experts today. Whenever possible the lower face was made to coincide with an underlying layer of softer rock which was easier to work.

Not till Roman times do we have any hard evidence of a wedge method being used. For this, a series of grooves were excavated along a marked line and metal wedges driven into them. Then a number of iron chisels were simultaneously struck in along the same direction, which usually caused the whole block to break off clean.

For smoothing the faces an abrasive powder of crushed quartzite was used, whose grains were sharp-edged unlike the rounded ones of desert sand.

Both the blocks and the remaining quarry faces were often labelled, probably by the scribes in charge of the work. These standard inscriptions included the name of the king or of the pyramid that the blocks were destined for. We read for example 'It is Cheops there on the skyline', 'Khephren is great' or 'Mycerinus is divine'. In other cases we find data on the size of the block, levelling marks or place directions such as 'For the inner wall' or 'This side up'.

From time to time the king would send a major expedition to bring stone, minerals, timber and other materials. Teams sallied forth, for example, to Wadi Hammamat and Wadi Allaqi in Nubia for gold, to Sinai, the Eastern Desert and Nubia for copper, to the Red Sea coast for lead, to the el-Kharga Oasis for alum, to Sinai for malachite and turquoise and to various places in the Eastern Desert for amethyst, agate, barytes, amazonite, rock crystal and other minerals.

Under the Old Kingdom such an expedition would be headed by a functionary entitled 'the god's seal-bearer of the two great fleets', or simply 'general', to whom other officials were subordinated with naval-style titles such as 'captain', 'ship's captain', 'ship's officer', or 'overseer of quarry work' or 'overseer of the Nubian defence troops'. Skilled craftsmen, notably stone-breakers, were grouped into companies of a 100 and these into units of 10, 5 of whom formed a 'side' like oarsmen. These commandos could involve large numbers of men; one sent to the alabaster mines in Hatnub was altogether 1600 strong.

New Kingdom expeditions were usually commanded by the 'overseer of the treasury', under the Ramessids even of the vizier or the high priest of Amun, and the scale of operations grew enormously. An expedition to Wadi Hammamat in Ramesses IV's reign to procure building blocks had an administrative staff of 170, with 130 skilled stonemasons, 800 Asiatic enslaved prisoners, 2000 temple bondsmen for transporting the blocks, 5000 soldiers and 50 guards. In other expeditions too the largest component were the transport labourers, ranging in number from 350 to 17,000.

191 A man pours water in the path of the sled to make dragging the statue easier on a slippery surface. Limestone relief in the tomb of Idut, Saqqara. 6th dynasty

We have detailed knowledge of the work in the gold mines of Wadi Hammamat and Wadi Allaqi, which were used continually from the Ramessid Period. There even survives a unique map of the site. We know that in the Roman Period the work was done chiefly by slaves who were either prisoners of war or convicts, but also by paupers, often with their entire families. The foremen were astonishingly well informed about the directions of the gold-bearing quartz veins and only mined them as far as their gold content justified. The mining was done in galleries which were sometimes quite wide, but sometimes so narrow that children had to bring out the broken rock. Women crushed the stone in mortars and grinders, then washed the gold out of the grit on basalt tables with grooved ceramic tops, or over stretched sheepskins. The lighter sand was flushed away with the water while the gold particles remained in the grooves or rugosities. However, this could only be done in places like Wadi Fawakhir where there were deep wells and a good water supply. From other mines the rock had to be taken to the Nile, where gold-panning installations have been found, for instance, at the mouth of Wadi Allaqi.

The problem of transporting rock or building blocks over country with a soft subsoil and virtually no hard roads was solved not by the use of the wheel – even though this had been known in principle since the Old Kingdom – but by loading them onto sledges and hauling these over paths paved with transverse logs lubricated with fine mud. The sledges were made of solid baulks of wood, with two runners turned up in front. The method is vividly illustrated in the scene from the 12th-dynasty tomb of the provincial prince Djehutihotep at el-Bersha, showing his colossal statue on the move. The accompanying text states that the statue was carved by the scribe Sipa, son of Hennakhtankh, out of stone from Hatnub (probably alabaster) and was 13 cubits or about 6.8m high. The statue, weighing (it has been reckoned) 60 tonnes, being dragged on its sledge with ropes by 172 men in four files. A man standing at the foot of the figure is pouring water onto the path in front of the sledge, while others urge the team on with rhythmic commands or chants. Three more men are bringing up fresh jugs of water and another three a large beam, probably to use as a lever in case the vehicle stuck. The procession is making towards the front of some building, no doubt the chapel of the prince's tomb.

This was probably similar to the way the Egyptians of the Old Kingdom had moved the stone blocks for pyramid-building. Although those of the Great Pyramid of Cheops weighed anything from 3 to 15 tonnes apiece, their transport was such a routine affair that it was not thought worth documenting. The blocks would have been made fast to sledges with thick ropes and drawn by large teams of labourers. The further the quarry was from the country's main highway, the Nile, the more men had to be used. The shifting of ten $2\frac{1}{2}$m-high granite statues of the seated pharaoh over a distance of 90km from the Wadi Hammamat quarries to the Nile was carried out, we know, by 2000 men. On another occasion it took 4500 men only 14 days to transport 80 gigantic stone blocks from the same site.

As a natural waterway the Nile had played a great part in the unification of Egypt's scattered tribes in a common state and it retained its importance as a communication artery throughout the history of ancient Egypt. Whereas its middle reaches are interrupted by a series of unnavigable rapids, the lower stretch, starting from the First Cataract just above the frontier at Aswan, flows gently down a broad valley with an average gradient of 8cm per km (reduced to 4cm in the Delta) except for a short defile at Gebel el-Silsila near Kom Ombo. The development of Nile shipping was aided by the fact that while the current flows northward the prevailing wind comes southward from the Mediterranean. When there is enough of a breeze, therefore, a ship can sail for most of the way upstream.

We know from rock-drawings and incised pictures on pottery that the Egyptians had built light boats out of papyrus bundles roped together which they propelled with wooden paddles or long poles at least since early predynastic times, that is from the first half of the 4th millennium BC. We can still see such craft today on Ethiopia's Lake Tana, the source of the Blue Nile. During the following half-millennium larger and stronger boats appeared, with high prows, one or two cabins, and long banks of oars.

192 Sphinx and the great pyramid of Cheops at Giza. A king's head on a lion's body symbolised royal power. The sphinx was cut from living rock, perhaps to protect the pyramid complex. 4th dynasty.

As the programme of great stone building projects developed from the 3rd dynasty on, regular Nileside shipyards arose, the property of kings, dignitaries or temples. These employed carpenters and joiners specialising in shipbuilding. The long planks were joined with dowels, resin adhesive and vegetable fibre ropes which shrank when wet and so held the frame of the vessel firm. A rib construction was used for the hulls of larger ships. The mast carried a free-swinging yard at the top for attaching the sail. Along the edge of the deck, recesses were cut for the oars, which sometimes rested in pivoting rowlocks. One or two long oars at the stern did duty for a rudder. Egyptian vessels were relatively broad and tubby, with a shallow draught and no keel because of the many shoals in the Nile.

We gain a good idea of what Egyptian boats looked like from the many extant Middle Kingdom models in wood of vessels large and small, complete with deckhands and oarsmen, but especially from the unique discovery in 1954 of King Cheops' original funeral barge. Altogether 1224 components, mostly of cedar wood, were found lying in one of two trenches near the south side of the king's pyramid at Giza. They were conserved and assembled between 1957 and 1968 by Ahmed Yusuf Mustafa, and the reconstructed ship is now to be seen in a glass pavilion erected over the site of the original discovery.

Cheops' barge is over 43m long, nearly 6m wide and 1.78m high. The wooden planks of its flat, wide hull are strengthened with transverse ribs. There was no keel and the vessel hardly drew any water. It curved up fore and aft into stems with papyrus-shaped capitals. On the deck stood a light structure of poles with papyrus-shaped heads. Here there was room for the captain in the forward section; room for 10 oarsmen to row the vessel, five oars to each side; and for another cabin and anteroom in the rear. Two oars at the stern steered the boat.

Specialists have long disputed the significance of this barge. Was it a symbolic sun-ship in which the god Horus sailed his mythological daily journey across the sky? Was it one of four symbolic boats enabling the King's spirit to travel to the four corners of the celestial ocean? Was it a real boat for conveying the King's remains during the funeral from his residence at Memphis to his pyramid-temple in the valley? Or was it an ordinary travelling boat used during his lifetime? The conservator told us that wooden parts of the vessel were proved by laboratory tests to have been immersed for some time up to the water-line. The recent find of another boat west of the first one adds weight to the symbolic interpretation.

193 A cargo boat with its sail furled carrying a huge block of stone. Limestone relief in the tomb of Ipi, Saqqara. 6th dynasty. *Cairo, Egyptian Museum*

Weni, the 6th-dynasty administrator of the southernmost province, mentions in a report that a boat 31.4m long and 15.7m wide was built in the incredibly short time of 17 days. Vessels of this size might have sufficed for the transport of ordinary stone blocks, but for the great monoliths something larger was needed. The ship that took the obelisk of Tuthmosis I from Aswan to the temple of Amun at Karnak was recorded as having a length of nearly 63m, and the one that carried those of Queen Hatshepsut to her temple at Deir el-Bahari was no less than 82m long.

On the reliefs from the south wall of the causeway leading up to King Unas's pyramid at Saqqara (5th dynasty) we can see columns with palm-frond capitals being transported by water. The inscription reads: 'The delivery of granite columns from the quarries of Elephantine to the pyramid complex 'Beautiful are the Precincts of the Son of Re Unas'.

A wonderful view of the last stage in the journey of Queen Hatshepsut's obelisks from Aswan quarries to Thebes is preserved in the south section of the lower colonnade of the Queen's temple at Deir el-Bahari. The two obelisks are lashed to their sledges, lying base to base on the largest of the ships, which is being drawn by a flotilla of rowing boats in three strings of nine, each manned by 30 to 32 oarsmen together with steersmen, soldiers, officers and a pilot. At the head of the group is a boat with its captain, but the officer in command of the whole manoeuvre seems to be the one shown in the bottom row with a caption describing the scene: 'A peaceful landing at Victorious Thebes; heaven celebrates, earth rejoices – the heart leaps when it sees this monument, erected [by Makare] for her father Amun.' Labib Habachi has proved that there were indeed two obelisks outside the eastern peripheral wall of Hatshepsut's temple, of which only fragments survived. According to a graffito found at Aswan they were carved and transported under the personal surveyance of the architect Senenmut. To make, transport and erect them took only seven months!

We can now turn to the boats used for moving stone building-blocks, and imagine 193 one anchored at harbour with solid wood gangplanks connecting it to the quayside. The sledges, with the blocks roped on to them, could then be taken straight on board with no need to reload them. As soon as they were all in place the captain would give the order to pull away.

The Nile made possible even the longest haul from quarry to building site, the 950km from Aswan to the Giza pyramid plateau taking from one to two weeks. Since the barge was going downstream oars would only be needed in exceptional circumstances, but the skipper or pilot had to keep a continuous look-out for rapids, islands and shoals. At the prow of every boat stood a man who checked the depth of water from time to time with a pole or plumb-line. The boat's minimal draught and the absence of a keel made it possible to negotiate very shallow waters, but the crew had to be quick to react in case of a sudden side wind lest the vessel capsize. Many problems were eased during the flood season when the river flowed fast, wide and deep, but the captain had to know just where the original bed and submerged banks were so that the boat was not stranded in a field.

One must try to picture the countless vessels of all sizes that crowded this unique watercourse, Egypt's busiest thoroughfare. Huge freighters belonging to king, lords and temples would be fetching the harvest in to the granaries or bringing supplies for the builders and quarrymen. Here and there would be a comfortably appointed private vessel, its cabin roof supported on columns with carved bosses, in which a pharaoh, priest or dignitary came sailing by. Dozens of little papyrus canoes would be weaving in and out, with farmers and their crop or anglers bringing their catch home, and villagers setting forth to the nearest market town, visiting friends and relations or making for the temple of a revered deity.

Finally, the plateau with the site of the pyramid looms over the north-west horizon. It will be important to get as close as possible, and most earlier writers assumed that the blocks were only landed in the flood season when the waters came right up to the foot of the plateau. Recently, however, it has been ascertained that by the 3rd dynasty the pyramid-builders had dug a side-canal leading from the Nile in the region of modern Dariut. This canal, which can still be seen running along the foot of the

pyramid plateau, gave all-year access to harbours originally built just below each pyramid site but ultimately incorporated in its valley-temple. In a few temples one can still find stone harbour-ramps and piers, where a boat could anchor and the blocks on their sledges be hauled up on land.

The further transport of the blocks would still have required an approach ramp to the building-site, which lay some 50m higher than the Nile valley. This could have been made out of reliable, light but strong and easily accessible material – sun-dried mud bricks.

Experts are not yet agreed on the number and design of these ramps. Some have pictured slopes of various lengths and gradients leading straight up to the centre of one side, or several sides, of the pyramid as it grew. However, this would have involved continual rebuilding of the ramps with huge expense of material, weakness at the higher points and gradients ever-increasing to a point where haulage became impossible. From traces on the sides of Queen Khentkaus's stepped mastaba Uvo Hölscher deduced that there had been ramps, parallel to the walls, leading up from the lower to the higher step. This idea was then further developed by Gustave Goyon into the theory of a gradually extended ramp encircling the pyramid spirally. This would have led up from each step to the next with much less expenditure of material. It required no rebuilding and no increase in gradient. Goyon suggested that all the pyramids, not merely the oldest 3rd-dynasty ones, had originally been stepped pyramids, but that in the later ones the steps had been eventually filled in and disguised under the skin. Indeed, the stepped pyramid is the determinative of the word *ar*, meaning to walk up, which probably relates to the basic notion of a pyramid as a hill with a staircase for the king's spirit *ka* to walk up on its way to the sun.

A ramp could not be so steep as to prevent the loads being pulled up it, and it would have had to be wide enough for ascending loads to be passed by empty sledges on their way down. In the case of Cheops's pyramid Goyon stipulated a gradient of only 3 inches to 2 royal cubits, little over 4°, and a width of 24m narrowing to 16m at the top. The total volume of such a ramp extending to the summit he estimated at nearly 400,000 cubic metres, or about one-seventh that of the pyramid itself; the total length of the ramp would have come to 2.5km.

Date-palm trunks placed transversely close together would have provided an excellent surface for such a ramp, and spread the weight of the loads over a wider area. The surface would have had to be continually lubricated with water or a thin suspension of mud.

As draught animals were not used during the Old or Middle Kingdoms men had to grapple with the loaded sledges themselves. Assuming a minimum strain of 12kg per

195 Wooden model of a sailing boat with the pilot in the bow and the owner resting under a canopy. 12th dynasty. *London, British Museum*

worker, Goyon calculated that a sledge block would have taken a team of 78 men to draw, or three files of 26. The gigantic blocks used as ceilings for the funeral chambers, to support the overlying mass, weighed up to 40 tonnes and would have needed from 200 to 250 men in four files to haul them.

This idea has been disputed by Dieter Arnold on the grounds that a spiral ramp would not have been stable enough, and by obscuring the corners would have made continuous surveying impossible. Negotiating the 90° corners would have been difficult without, say, some smooth stone disc as a turntable. Again, the spiral ramp assumes the stepped form which has not been demonstrated with certainty for pyramids after the 3rd dynasty. For the later ones, Arnold proposes an internal ramp, 20 to 30m wide, leading to the centre of the structure at a height of 60 to 65m, and then back in the opposite direction for a further rise of 20 to 30m. The remaining 150,000 or so blocks needed to construct the last 50m of the highest pyramids could then have been raised, step by step, up a 'staircase' ramp, or else from layer to layer up the part already built.

In his latest work on the pyramids Rainer Stadelmann suggests that for the first 20 to 25m of height material could have been transported from all sides either up ramps or simply over sand-piles and thereafter (following an older idea of Jean Laurer) up a single long ramp with a gradient of 7° to 12° along one side of the pyramid, up to a height of 100m.

Current opinion has it that each pyramid grew layer by layer, meaning that the internal structure of chambers and passages, together with all the facing, frames and portcullises for preventing access after the king's body had been laid in the sarcophagus, had to be built into the current layer before the next was started.

Specialists have long been worried by the problem of how blocks weighing many tonnes were actually placed in position. The Egyptians were conversant with the lever, inclined plane and roller, but the pulley they knew not, let alone the block-and-tackle. They might perhaps have used a simple lifting device such as a rope slung over a beam held in a wooden support. In several museums there are indeed models of wooden cradles, lifesize versions of which could have played a part in raising or shifting blocks. A still simpler device would have been a fan-shaped arrangement of wooden levers, each held by one worker and lifted simultaneously at a word of command. Ludwig Croon has suggested that the blocks were raised and shifted by a mechanism on the lines of the *shaduf*, but this water-raising invention only came into general use during the New Kingdom. Whatever the truth of the matter, it was no insuperable task to move a block over the short distance from where it was taken off the sledge, as long as the ground was reasonably flat.

It must in any case be borne in mind that no great accuracy was demanded in the fitting of the core of blocks. The builders would have been satisfied with the size, shape and rough finish of a block as it left the mason's hands in the quarry and the final gaps, varying in width, were filled in with a mortar of sand, clay and broken stones and bricks. To enhance the rigidity of the structure a layer of precisely finished blocks, knocked flush against one another, would be interposed from time to time amongst the roughly aligned ones.

It was a different story with the high-quality blocks of white limestone or pink granite used for the casing of the pyramid, and with the ones used to line the inner chambers. The masons managed to face these off so clean and true that as they lie together one cannot put a knife-blade between them. The faces were tested with a pair of flat discs connected by a cord and placed on different areas in turn; sometimes the cord was treated with a red pigment that showed up any projecting spots.

Not even these blocks, however, were made to identical measurements. This was perhaps done deliberately to prevent slippage and by incorporating blocks of different sizes to increase the strength of a wall. The outside face of each block in the skin, added as soon as the corresponding core-layer was complete, was at first left rough-hewn just as it came from the quarry. The faces of the pyramid were dressed from top to bottom, after the uppermost layer had been capped with a pyramidal block or *pyramidion* and as the ramps were being dismantled.

In addition to the standard tools already mentioned in connection with quarry work, stonemasons used symmetrical set squares for checking right-angles, similar squares with a plumb-line for aligning horizontal surfaces, and for measuring short distances a ruler the length of a royal cubit subdivided into seven hand-widths of four finger-widths each.

For every pyramid a number of ancillary structures had to be set up, constituting the 'pyramid complex'. A valley-temple, for funeral rites and embalming, grew up around the original landing harbour, and the old ramp for hauling material up to the pyramid became the causeway, a long stone passage that was left open at first, but it was roofed over from the time of King Cheops. This led up to the funerary temple at the foot of the pyramid itself, where funeral cult of the dead king was observed for many years. Near this temple pits were carved out of the rock to hold the funeral or 'sun' barges.

189   In the floor-blocks of the funerary temple of the pyramid of Khephren there are a number of round holes, 25cm in diameter, believed by some to have served for the rotation of the conical base of a wooden structure with ropes, enabling the builders to erect the pillars round the temple forecourt. Another series of floor recesses, this time square, may have seated the 'claws' of a device functioning as a huge lever for lifting loads.

The same tools and techniques were used for building the New Kingdom temples. Huge statues and obelisks were erected against the façade, or in the forecourts, with the aid of ropes and sand-piles.

There is still dispute over what determined the size of each pyramid, the time allocated for building it and the size of the labour force involved. The size could not have depended on the duration of a pharaoh's reign, since he had to approve the dimensions before work started – usually soon after his accession – without knowing how many years he had before him.

It seems more likely that the size of a pyramid (or in a few cases that of several pyramids erected for the same king) was primarily a function of the state of the country's economy, though it might also be affected by unforeseeable factors such as structural defects. Kurt Mendelssohn, for example, believes that the entire casing of 187 Snofru's pyramid at Meidum collapsed during its construction, and Dieter Arnold argues that interior cracks prevented the use of the pyramid of Amenophis III at Dahshur.

Herodotus, quoting traditional beliefs of Egyptian priests, says that it took 20 years to build a pyramid, and that the 100,000 workers employed were replaced every three months. Croon calculated that if 40 men pulled a block up every four minutes

Above **196** Wooden boats with bipod masts. Wall painting from the tomb of In-Snefru-Ishtef at Dahshur, 5th or 6th dynasty. *Cairo, Egyptian Museum*

Left **197** The funerary boat of King Cheops may have been used in his lifetime for ceremonial journeys during religious festivals. There is a canopy for the pilot and behind it the King's cabin. 4th dynasty. *Giza, Cheops Barque Museum*

on average, 150 of them could have been laid in a day. Thus a medium-sized pyramid containing 1.5 million blocks would have taken 26 years to erect using one ramp, or 13 years using two. In revising these figures Lauer (who had objected that they did not take account of the differential consumption of stone for the upper and lower parts) calculated that King Snofru's pyramid at Meidum would have taken from 8 to 11 years to finish. Recently Stadelmann in turn refined the argument by taking into account inscriptions on the casing of the same king's northern pyramid at Dahshur, and estimated that the completion of 15 stone layers to a height of 13.2m would have taken 2 to 3 years, this constituting about one-fifth of the pyramid's overall volume. Proportionally less material was needed for succeeding layers, but this was outweighed by the greater effort needed to raise it to higher levels. For the largest pyramids Stadelmann reckoned that the volume of blocks laid each day would have ranged from 230 to 420 cubic metres.

Where were the thousands of nameless workers recruited for all the great buildings of ancient Egypt, and what were their working conditions like? Some authors have painted a grim picture of slaves or serfs toiling till they collapsed, whipped on by taskmasters at the behest of despotic rulers, passive automatons resigned to their fate.

Others, impressed by the quality of the results and the radiant scenes depicted on tomb walls, have described the pyramids as 'the work of free men, conscious of performing a unique task' (Goyon). We may be forgiven for believing that the truth lay somewhere in between.

One must first consider how it was possible to marshal such a vast workforce without damaging the country's economy. It would be logical to assume that they were drawn from the most numerous group in the population, the peasantry. Work on the great projects was then a kind of compulsory civilian service, for which physically fit youngsters (*neferu*) and the permanently or seasonally unemployed labourers (*heseb*) were called up.

However, it is now thought more likely that construction work went on all the year round, rather than only in the flood season, considering the magnitude of the projects and the availability of building material at all times. There is further corroboration from the dates inscribed on some of the blocks of one of the Lisht pyramids: Ambrose Lansing found that four of these were carved during the flood period, six in the

198 Landing ramp of the valley temple of the 5th-dynasty pyramid of Unas. In the background is the step pyramid of Djoser. 3rd dynasty. Saqqara

germination season and five at the end of the harvest period. Stadelmann gives grounds for putting the number of workers employed at any one time between 10,000 and 20,000, including 5000 skilled men, with fresh blood being brought in every three or four months – which would have made for greater efficiency as well as coinciding with Herodotus's statement. Certainly no one was condemned to work on the great construction projects all his life.

Recruits were organised in military fashion in teams, *aperu*, divided into five groups (*sa*) each consisting of five 10-man squads under their own leaders. Every *aperu* had its special title incorporating the name of the pharaoh in question, such as 'Cheops Calls for Love' or 'Mycerinus Stands for Joy'.

Though the work was compulsory men did not need, according to some commentators, to be dragooned into it. This seems to be borne out by the inscription in one tomb of Mycerinus' time that reads: 'His Majesty desires that no one shall be compelled to the task, but that each should work to his own satisfaction.' It is even possible that some workers volunteered to take part. Helping to build a residence for the king to reign in for all eternity meant securing a share of immortality for oneself.

A point against the view that pyramids were largely slave-built is the dearth of evidence that there were many slaves at all during the Old Kingdom. Even in that era, it is true, the pharaohs made occasional sorties into neighbouring countries and brought back prisoners who could be made into slaves. But these were still few in number and worked in scattered groups on noblemen's estates, protected by a special statute. They played no great role in the Egyptian economy. Not till the Middle Kingdom did their numbers begin to rise, reaching a peak during the expansive campaigns of the New Kingdom rulers.

Another argument against picturing the pyramid workers as galley-slaves is the small number of men employed to keep order – guards armed with sticks under the Old Kingdom, Nubian and Medjay archers under the New Kingdom. If it had been a question of 'maintaining morale' among downtrodden masses, fully armed military guards would surely have been brought in. And there is no evidence that this ever happened.

The working week in ancient Egypt lasted nine days, the 10th being a day of rest. Every worker was then free to go home to his family, if the distance was not too great.

Workers were quartered in mud-brick and wood buildings, a whole colony of which was found by Petrie to the west of the pyramid of Khephren. There was room in each hut for 10 men's mats or mattresses and the site could have housed 4000 to 5000. Goyon suggested recently that these buildings were in fact stores and offices,

199 The slipway leading to Sahure's pyramid. Abusir. 5th dynasty

and that the workers possibly descended from the pyramid plateau to rest and sleep in nearby villages.

Supplies were organised by the scribes. Grain was got from the royal granaries, meat, poultry, onions, garlic and other greenstuff from the royal estates, some of the tools, clothing and sandals from the royal storehouses and treasury. There were resident cooks, bakers, maltsters and butchers to see that the multitudes were properly fed, and porters to fetch water for drinking, cooking and washing. Storekeepers controlled the issue of kilts and skilled craftsmen produced all the implements required.

Arrangements were similar in the quarries. If these were not near the Nile, it would not be far to the next well where people could draw as much water as they wanted. The stone-workers lived in tent-like huts of canvas-covered wooden ribs over a stone platform.

The vast social difference in ration scales is revealed by a Middle Kingdom inscription on the rocks at the Wadi Hammamat quarries. The leader of the expedition received 200 loaves and 5 measures of beer daily, the overseer of the stonemasons 100 loaves and 3 measures, the overseer of the treasury 50 loaves and 2 measures, a scribe 30 loaves and 1 measure, a skilled mason 20 loaves and half a measure and an unskilled labourer 10 loaves and one-third of a measure.

Construction and quarry work were both highly strenuous because of the crude equipment available. Workers went around in the burning sun from spring to autumn clad only in their mini-kilts. Tough though they might be, and protected from sunburn by their complexion, heat-stroke and sun-stroke must have occurred from time to time.

Stoneworking necessarily produced a dust-laden atmosphere, especially in confined places where there was no through-draught. Sharp silica particles from the harder rocks like granite must have irritated the respiratory linings, stimulating the formation of connective tissue which pushed back pulmonary alveoli and reduced the exchange of gas in breathing (silicosis), impairing the pulmonary, and in many cases ultimately the general, circulation.

The possibility of accidents, sometimes fatal, always hung over those involved in cutting, conveying and above all erecting the huge stone blocks. The low standards of hygiene, nutrition and housing among such large and concentrated numbers meant that infections could spread easily and epidemics break out. Presence of doctors has been proved in the quarries and on expeditions, though not as far as we know on the great building sites. And however well they might have coped with some types of injuries, epidemics would have found them helpless.

CHAPTER FOURTEEN

Builders of the Royal Tombs

WHERE WE COULD only offer a sketchy and largely tentative picture of conditions among the men who built the great monuments of the Old and Middle Kingdoms, when it comes to the New Kingdom village of Deir el-Medina on the west bank of 69 Luxor we have an altogether richer fund of information to draw on. For this we have 203 to thank the French Institute of Oriental Archaeology in Cairo, whose painstaking researches between 1917 and 1951 yielded a great deal of evidence about daily life.

The Czech Egyptologist Jaroslav Černý, who took part in their excavations from the mid 1920s and devoted an entire career to the study of Deir el-Medina and publication of the textual evidence, had hoped to crown it with a three-volume work on this area. His untimely death in 1970 cut the project short, but the publication of the first volume and part of the second in 1973 showed his unrivalled insight into the family and social structure of the community, the way their work was organised, even the history of many individual inhabitants.

This was the village that housed the families of the men entrusted with cutting and furnishing the tombs in the Valley of the Kings and the Valley of the Queens during 207 the 18th to 20th dynasties. Most of the members of the community were skilled stonemasons, stucco workers and plasterers, or artists of several kinds – draughtsmen, relief-carvers, painters.

This community of workmen, artisans and artists occupied a special place in Egyptian society. They belonged to the pharaoh himself, and the vizier administered them on his behalf. As Eugen Bogoslovskiy says they could not be regarded as fully free people, since they were subject to the monarch's will and to that of his senior functionaries. For the most part they were tied all their lives to their place of work, which they were not allowed to leave unless seconded by their superiors to other duties or, where a particular craft was overmanned, demoted to the ranks of the unskilled *semedet* people. Though secluded within their village they could move around freely and there is no firm evidence that they were watched over to ensure that the sites and layout of the various royal tombs remained secret. If the village was guarded and walled off, this was primarily to protect it from thieves and enemies.

Everyone appointed as a craftsman to the royal burial ground immediately received his own house in the village, a hut in the Valley and a tomb, sometimes a storeroom too and other accommodation, together with chattels such as cattle (usually a cow), a donkey, some sheep and goats, and even slaves. Except where these possessions were simply being acquired by a son stepping into his father's shoes, the new appointee also received a plot of land on which he could build in 'the king's time', that is, during working hours. Such property, however, could not be divided nor passed on to an heir. If a worker wished to have full title to a house so that he could divide it at any time, or bequeath it, he had to build it in his own spare time on land not belonging to the community. In the same way, anything he made in his own time with his own tools and material became his private property and he was free to sell it on the local market.

This community, known as the 'Servants in the Place of Truth', was organised not according to skills but on naval lines, and indeed it was also called 'The Ship's Crew'. Just as Egyptian oarsmen were categorised into 'left' and 'right' rowers, so these 'marines' were divided into two 'sides'. (Some investigators believe that this was because each 'side' was responsible for one side of a tomb.)

The number of workers varied as work on the tombs progressed. It was largest at the beginning – usually about 40 men; the maximum – 120 workers – was recorded in the first two years of the reign of Ramesses IV. Numbers thereafter declined, partly because there was less work to do as the tombs were completed, partly by death of workmen. The two 'sides', therefore, were seldom of equal number.

Up until the end of the 19th dynasty the members of the community all enjoyed social equality. From that point on, however, the creative work of the artist began to be more highly prized, whereas the job of a stone-breaker, for example, was in low esteem, and could even be imposed as a punishment in court cases. It was at this time that certain categories – plasterers, blacksmiths, sandal-makers and tomb-guards – were even relegated to the *semedet* people.

Membership of the community also depended on age. Adolescents and *menehu* (according to Černý, young men who were marriageable but not yet married) were counted among the *semedet* people and merely assisted the craftsmen. In the course of time such youngsters usually took over their fathers' jobs. If there was a shortage in a particular skill, young men could be brought in even when their fathers had not belonged to the community. New members were appointed by the vizier on the advice of a scribe and a foreman. Some fathers tried to bribe those with the power of patronage. One of them left it on record that he had given several head of cattle each to the foremen Nekhetmut and Inherkha and to the scribe Harsheri – with what success, unfortunately, we do not know.

Since there were usually several sons in an artisan's family it was normally the eldest who took his father's place, leaving the others to join the *semedet* people or seek their fortunes elsewhere. Thus of the foreman Neferhotep's five sons, the first acceded to his father's position, the second became a soldier and later an officer-scribe, the third became an officer and doorkeeper in the Ramesseum. The vocation of the fourth son is unclear and the fifth was still a young lad at the time of writing.

The discovery of numerous potsherds and flakes of stone used for writing (the equivalent of notepads) shows that there were schools of writing and drawing in the village for bright lads among the community. Even unschooled artisans, like Amennakhte the son of Ipy, and his own son Harsheri, occasionally made it by flair and hard work to the rank of scribe.

Some members of the community were assigned specific functions. At their head were two foremen (the 'Great ones of the Crew'), one for each 'side'. Of 31 foremen attested at various times Černý found that 16 were elected from among the artisans, 12 were sons of previous foremen and 3 cases were uncertain; but they were never 'outsiders'. They could be compared to the modern Egyptian *reis* put in charge of building workers or of labourers on archaeological sites. The *reis* assigned a task to each man and saw it was properly done, checked the condition of implements and exchanged them for new ones where necessary, ensuring good timekeeping and fixing the workbreaks. He enjoyed trust and authority among the men, whom he urged on with shouts and playful taps with his stick. In Deir el-Medina, the foremen spoke for the community vis-à-vis their superiors and corresponded with the vizier, and sent him gifts, through the scribes.

One surprising touch of democracy was the role of the two 'deputies', again one for each 'side'. Out of 24 that we know of, only one was the son of another deputy, 5 were foremen's sons but no less than 18 were ordinary artisans elected to the post. These men continued to do the same work for no extra pay. They acted as representatives

Previous page **200**   Royal tomb builder Pashedu's own tomb contains paintings of outstanding merit. Here the tomb owner is shown drinking from the sacred pool. Deir el-Medina, West Thebes. 19th dynasty

Above **201**   Maia was a distinguished painter who worked at Deir el-Medina during the late 18th dynasty and probably decorated his own tomb. Limestone statue. *Leiden, National Museum of Antiquities*

Right **202**   Sarcophagus of King Merenptah, son and successor of Ramesses II. Pink granite. Tomb of Merenptah, Valley of the Kings, West Thebes. 19th dynasty

and spokesmen for the community, fetched and handed out their rations, answered for their good behaviour and stood in for the foremen in their absence.

The 'Guardians of the Tomb', usually two on alternate shifts, did not appear in the establishment of the group but lived in the same village and enjoyed the same pay until they were demoted to the *semedet* people at the end of the 19th dynasty. Despite their name, they did not guard the tombs but acted as warehouse keepers, guarding material and implements. Under the supervision of the scribes they handed out new tools and passed on old ones to be sharpened or repaired by the smiths, as well as issuing oil, candles and grease, leather bags, painting colours, cloth, sandals and other requisites from store.

The *semedet* people had a definitely lower status than the artisans. They included the unskilled labourers who undertook heavy work such as removing the waste when tombs were being dug, but also certain specialists who did ancillary work for the others – smiths, potters, plasterers, joiners, wood-carvers, laundrymen, gardeners, tomb doorkeepers, constables and those who catered for the village, such as huntsmen, fishermen, wild honey-collectors and food and water-carriers.

It will be instructive to take a closer look, for example, at the doorkeepers and constables. The former, of whom there were either two or three, did 12-hour shifts guarding unfinished tombs and maintaining order in the community; they also acted as messengers and postmen. For ensuring protection of the Valley of the Kings, of the village and the surrounding area there were also units of 'Medjay of the Tomb' with their own headmen. These were descendants of the Eastern Desert nomads who had settled in the Nile valley during the extreme desertification of 2350–2200 BC. At the end of the Second Intermediate Period they had made their mark as mercenaries in the Egyptian campaigns of liberation against the Asiatic Hyksos who occupied the Delta between 1650 and 1550 BC. When that fighting finished they found employment as police units assigned to various towns in Egypt, including the 'Western Town' of Thebes starting in the reign of Tuthmosis III.

On the back of a diary of the 17th year of Ramesses IX's reign kept by the scribes who oversaw operations in the Valley of the Kings we find a name-list of the Medjay on duty there. It ends: 'Six headmen and 18 Medjay, 24 in all', showing, apart from the one-to-three ratio between headman and men, that the establishment was very large. Černý, however, believed that the numbers in this case were higher than usual because of a tomb-robbery that was being investigated, and that the normal complement for policing both village and Valley would have been two headmen and six Medjay. Reports of raids by Libyan tribesmen and Egyptian rebels, as well as of sporadic tomb thefts, start multiplying from the first year of Ramesses IV's reign, and it was then that the Medjay units were enlarged and sometimes stiffened with security guards from the Western Town.

The *semedet* people we have noted are known to have existed as early as the First Intermediate Period, constituting a social stratum intermediate between the artisans and the slaves. According to Bogoslovskiy, their work was assigned to them, and output norms set, by foremen. If they defaulted they were treated like debtors until they had made up the deficit by work or payment. At the same time their obligations were collective, so that one group of the *semedet*, say the water-carriers, could help out another, such as the fishermen. The foreman could switch them at will between different jobs, as they were all considered unskilled.

The *semedet* people did not count as members of the Deir el-Medina community and were separately accommodated in simple huts scattered outside the village walls and in the surrounding countryside (as we know from the house-register of the Western Town). They have left no writings behind as they were probably illiterate. They were never privileged to help in the tomb-digging, except for removing rubble, and were considered as outsiders. Their pay was lower than the artisans' and given out separately. Unlike the artisans they had to do certain jobs even on their days off, such as replenishing the large tank by the northern gate of the village where all the inhabitants drew their water. They were however allowed to own certain personal items such as cattle, to buy and sell at the local market and to give evidence in court on the same footing as the artisans.

Even members of the lowest Egyptian class of all, female slaves, were among the tomb-building population. The records speak of anything from one to 16, but do not say what work they did. From the fact that they always figure in the ration-lists for corn (which was part of the artisans' renumeration), Černý deduced that these were

Above **203** The workers, artisans and artists who created the tombs in the Theban necropolis lived in the village at Deir el-Medina. The foundations of their terraced houses are on the right, their tombs on the left of the photograph. (See also ill. 69.) 18th–20th dynasty

Above right **204** One of the tomb entrances in the Deir el-Medina cemetery

Right **205** This painting in a private tomb shows the tomb owner's and his wife's mummies outside the tomb entrance prior to burial. West Thebes. 18th dynasty

slaves lent out by their owner, the king, to each family in turn for several days to grind their corn ration. The artisans were also allowed to possess or hire slaves of their own. The relief-carver Ken, a contemporary of Ramesses II who was buried in tomb No.4, had as many as a dozen of them.

As we have mentioned earlier, the largely Asiatic prisoners-of-war (*khenetu*) sold as slaves (*hemu* or *baku*) in slave-markets only began to reach considerable numbers during the Middle Kingdom. Their increasing use was related to the development of the irrigation system and the enlargement of the area under cultivation, but some were passed on to nobles and officials by their primary owner, the king, to serve in their households. Their numbers were again swollen by the wars of aggression of the New Kingdom pharaohs, Tuthmosis III acquiring 2000 during his seven campaigns, and Amenophis II allegedly as many as 100,000 in two wars. Amenophis III boasted in one place that his warehouses were 'crammed with slaves – men, women and children – from all the sovereign lands'. Convicted felons also became slaves, as did those who sold themselves for reasons of poverty, debt or indolence to some highly placed person or to a temple in the hope of lifelong sustenance and protection.

To quote Zbyněk Žába, the slaves were 'on the same legal footing as cattle or inanimate objects; they could be owned, sold, given as presents and bequeathed, and their labour could be hired out.' Hans Schneider even maintains that they were labelled by being branded with their owner's name. The Egyptian moral code nevertheless required that they should be treated humanely and there is documentary evidence that they were allowed, with their master's consent, a modicum of personal property. A slave could always be freed or adopted by his owner and thereby acquire full civic rights.

Most investigators agree that slaves did not form an important component of society even as late as the New Kingdom and the Late Period. Not till the Ptolemaic age did Egypt join in the international slave trade, and only then did their labour contribute substantially to the economy.

The artisans of Deir el-Medina, then, divided their time between their village homes and their worksite in the Valley of the Kings – a hollow hidden among the hills west of Luxor and approached from the Nile by a winding cliff-path that had to be broadened at one point to allow the passage of the royal funeral procession with all the paraphernalia destined for the tomb. During the 18th dynasty it was the burial place not only of every king but of his queen (occasionally of her parents too) and of the princes. From the 19th dynasty the queens and members of the royal family had their own cemetery in the Valley of the Queens, about a kilometre south of the artisans' village. 208

Each king, soon after he ascended the throne, chose the site for his future tomb 207 after consultation with the vizier and with a commission sent to the Valley to look for suitable places. The royal architect then drew up an initial plan which became binding for the artisans' work. Once the tomb had been completed, the vizier came to check it and had a final plan made of the actual layout. Two such have survived: the project for Ramesses IX's tomb (No.6) on Ostracon No.25184 in Cairo's Egyptian Museum and the final plan of Ramesses IV's tomb on the back of Papyrus No.1885 in the Turin Egyptian Museum. Both of them reproduce the ground-plans of the tombs and the papyrus gives the Egyptian names of the various passages, halls, burial chambers, side storerooms and so on.

During the period that passed between the initial project and the final plan the artisans were working full out. From the records of candle issues Černý was able to calculate that the working day was split into two equal parts. Since the number of candles allocated for whole days was always divisible by eight, and that for half-days (when afternoons were free) by four, it seems that morning and afternoon stints were four hours long. (The Egyptians divided both day and night into twelve hours, the length of an 'hour' consequently varying throughout the year. At the summer solstice when the sun rose at about 5am by our reckoning, and set at 7pm, each daylight 'hour' would be 10 minutes longer than at the spring and autumn equinoxes, while in midwinter it would be 10 minutes shorter. The 'eight-hour' shift at the height of summer, then, really meant nine hours and twenty minutes, which was probably near the human limit among those sun-scorched rocks.)

For their mid-day and night-time breaks the workers would rest in a hut reserved for the purpose, on simple couches; 78 such huts have been found on the fringe of the Valley.

In building a new tomb the stone-cutters had the first task. It must have been a strenuous and time-consuming challenge, considering that the length of a tomb could be as much as 100m (Sethos I) or even 210m (Hatshepsut). (Tutankhamun's was exceptionally small by contrast.) There is a unique sherd in the Fitzwilliam 206 Museum, Cambridge, that shows one of the masons at work. We see a bald, muscular man with stubby face and half-open mouth, prising a rock apart with his long metal chisel and pear-shaped wooden mallet. The hewn material was broken up into smaller pieces to be taken off in wicker or leather bags by porters to a dump near the tomb entrance. Other workers would be levelling the steps and chamber walls and making all the right-angles true. Any remaining cracks and irregularities would be filled by the stucco-workers. The plaster was originally made by the stoneworkers themselves, but from the 20th dynasty this was the province of *semedet* 'plaster makers'. After the plaster had been applied it still needed to be pebble-smoothed and sometimes whitewashed.

Once a surface was ready the artists could begin. Draughtsmen divided each area with red lines into registers and traced a rectangular grid, onto which they trans-ferred outline designs (also in red) from their small-scale models, and columns of hieroglyphic text. They might also use designs from copy books for religious texts such as the Book of Amduat, which showed the progress of the sun through the underworld by night. The chief draughtsman would then make corrections in black, or draw in contours such as we see in the tomb of Sethos I. From various references Bogoslovskiy compiled a list of 97 painters and 5 assistants, but these were only a fraction of the total number. He found that the decoration of Ramesses II's tomb, which took 40 years to build, involved between 20 and 30 draughtsmen, though probably not all at one time. About 15 took part in the latter half of the work on Ramesses III's tomb, and on Ramesses IV's more than 20 were engaged simul-taneously.

177 The next step was to colour the pictures and hieroglyphs, as in the tombs of
180 Haremheb and Ramesses I, or, more frequently, to carve the reliefs which were
181 painted afterwards.

251 Černý judged the reliefs in the tombs of Sethos I, Horemheb and Sethos II to
212 represent the finest work, while those of Ramesses III and X were of lower standard.

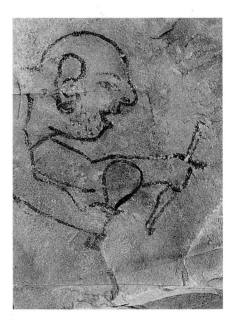

206 A grumpy unshaven stone-mason hard at work. Painted ostracon. Deir el-Medina. 20th dynasty. *Cambridge, Fitzwilliam Museum*

Left 207 Tomb entrances in the Valley of the Kings. Virtually all the pharaohs, and some queens, of the New Kingdom are buried here, starting with Tuthmosis I. West Thebes. 18th–20th dynasties

Right 208 The cliffs of the Valley of the Kings

Comparison of style shows that the same group of artists had in succession decorated the tombs of Ramesses IV (who reigned for 6 years), Ramesses VI (10 years) and Ramesses VII (7 years). If we add to these the 10-year reign of Ramesses V, whose tomb has not yet been identified, the artists in question must have worked together for 33 years on end. 209

As work progressed further into rock artificial lighting became necessary. Reflecting sunlight from a copper disc would only have helped for a limited distance. Yet no soot traces from smoking lamps have been found on the ceilings. However, we have already mentioned that candles were issued. These consisted of canvas twisted into lengths of about 35cm, spirally bound with strips of webbing. They contained no wax, but are described in the records as 'smeared' with fat, presumably sesame oil or butter.

As these were edible fats they could only be used 'in the presence of scribes', and the issue of candles 'from store' had to be carefully noted down. The oil was apparently mixed with salt to absorb moisture from the material; this would have prevented it smoking and depositing soot on walls and ceilings. The burning candles could not be held in the hand, so they were stood singly or in bunches of three in goblets or vases, as illustrated in some of the Deir el-Medina tombs, and put into special niches in the walls. The number of candles issued varied according to the distance of the job from the tomb-entrance and the size of the working party. One ostracon lists 22 days on which 32 candles were expended daily, while on 3 other days (evidently when afternoons were free) between 12 and 18 sufficed. Two other ostraca, dating from the 5th year of a king whose name is illegible, record a consumption of $52\frac{1}{2}$ to $58\frac{1}{2}$ candles, presumably when work was being done at a greater depth.

Provided the team managed to finish a tomb while the king was still alive, they had time to clear all the waste stone from the corridors and around the entrance. Sometimes, however, operations would be interrupted by a message from the vizier that 'the falcon has flown up to heaven, and another has taken his place'. Then the workers only had the 70 days standard embalming period in which to do whatever was most urgent. Often they had to leave large areas of decoration unfinished, or projected chambers unexcavated. When Horemheb died in the 27th year of his reign, to quote Maspero, 'the workmen did not trouble to remove the stone debris and 212 assorted rubbish littering the floor . . . They simply cleared a path across the chamber so that the bearers bringing the mummy and sacrificial gifts could reach the sarcophagus.'

On the day of the funeral all work ceased in the Valley. Only the chanting of priests and the wailing of mourners accompanied the procession. The accession of the new king, by contrast, would be the sign for three days of wild merry-making.

The craftsmen spent their free days – every 10th day, and the holidays – back in their village. The scribes' diaries tell of other reasons for absence too: a family event such as a birth or wedding, a relative's burial, the worker's illness or his child's, an injury, a snakebite, temple duty, or even such a bizarre reason as having to brew beer at the end of the week or take a sick donkey to the vet. Men would start off home at noon on the day before their leave, taking a path that snaked over the ridge between the Valley and the Deir el-Bahari basin and then, amongst the noblemen's tombs, to the col overlooking the village. It could have been done comfortably in about an hour.

The reason why Amenophis I, the probable founder of the artisan village, later venerated as true god and patron of the burial sites at West Thebes, chose a rather distant concealed side-valley instead of a site nearer to the royal burial ground was probably religious. It was not proper that a village of the living should disturb the tranquillity of the god-kings. There was also a security consideration. The village formed an autonomous part of the 'Western Town' of Thebes, a group of scattered settlements for priests and employees of the king's funerary temples, together with some farming hamlets. When first built it comprised 21 houses, but by the time it ceased to exist at the end of the 20th dynasty this had increased to 68, on a relatively 69 small terrain measuring 48 by 130m. Its brick wall, over two metres high, had to be 203

Previous page **209**   Sixth section of the
Book of Caverns on the wall of the
sarcophagus hall of the tomb of
Ramesses VI. The two lions represent the
horizons on whose backs descend and rise
the barques of night and day. Valley of
the Kings, West Thebes. 20th dynasty

210   Painting of the goddess Neith on
a pillar in the outer hall of the tomb
of Nefertari. The exceptional beauty of
the decorations suggests that among the
wives of Ramesses II she was his
favourite. Painted relief on plaster.
Valley of the Queens, Deir el-Medina,
West Thebes. 19th dynasty

211 The austerity of the burial chamber of Tuthmosis III is in complete contrast with the exuberant colours in the tomb shown opposite. Its architecture and drawings on smooth plaster are part of an innovative, highly effective overall geometric scheme. On the walls is the first full version of the Book of Amduat (The Book of What is in the Underworld) which sets out the spells and charms necessary to defy evil forces during the 12-hour night journey to the other world. Some of the scenes on the columns show Tuthmosis III with his queens. Valley of the Kings, West Thebes. 18th dynasty

Overleaf **212** The artist did not have time to finish this fine painting of the god Osiris before King Horemheb's funeral. This is Horemheb's second tomb. He had one built in Saqqara while he was still a general. Valley of the Kings, West Thebes. 18th dynasty

shifted several times in the course of its growth. At the western edge a cemetery 204 gradually arose with tightly-packed graves marked by miniature pyramids.

In their leisure time the artisans could rest in the bosom of their families. Many of them exploited their spare time by making funerary wares or objects of general utility in their homes, or they would get friends to help them construct and decorate their own tombs. As some of them were spare-time minor priests they were allowed to join ceremonial processions carrying figures of gods, including the deified Amenophis I. The procession usually halted at a place to the northwest of the village for the statue to utter, as it was believed, prophetic messages.

In return for their help in securing the king's eternal life the artists could expect a royal reward. Their emoluments measured up to this in two respects – in their scale, and in the fact that they came from the king's treasury. As coinage did not exist before the 26th dynasty they were paid primarily in grain. The vizier and the superintendent of the royal treasury were responsible for its disbursement, one of the scribes handing it out and keeping a careful record. Thanks to this we know the exact monthly allocations of grain – wheat for baking bread and cakes, barley for brewing beer – in dry measure units, one *khar* (k.) equalling 76.89 litres.

If we accept the interpretation of Jacob Janssen, the wage differentials among the various categories of workers were not over-great. A foreman received $5\frac{1}{2}$k. of wheat

197

and 2k. of barley, a rank-and-file artisan 4k. and 1½k. with no distinction between artists and manual workers. In the extant sources the pay of a scribe is given as only half that of a foreman, which seems absurd in view of his managerial and auditing responsibilities. But Janssen points out that the same scribe worked for both 'sides' of the 'crew' and was therefore paid twice over, or exactly as much as a foreman. Again, a doctor's pay is given as 1k. of wheat and ¼k. of barley, but Janssen believes this was a supplement over and above the regular craftsman's wage which he received as well. He makes the same assumption for the 'tomb doorkeeper's' remuneration of 1k. plus ½k., but this small amount may on the contrary have reflected the relegation of doorkeepers to the *semedet* people whose pay (not recorded) would have been well below that of the artisans'. Young unmarried men also received the modest quantities of 1½k. of wheat and ½k. of barley, as did any artisans who had missed a substantial amount of working time. In addition to the grain, artisans and to a lesser extent the *semedet* people received irregular allowances of bread, cakes, beer, oil, fish, vegetables, dates, meat (rarely), not to mention pottery, clothing (at least once a year), sandals (whenever required), firewood and other things.

The sources say that wages were meant to be paid out regularly, on the last working day of each month, but in fact they were always in arrears by half a month on the average and on one occasion by half a year. These delays led to the world's first recorded strike, in the 29th year of the reign of Ramesses III. There is a detailed account of it by the scribe Amennakht in the Egyptian Museum in Turin.

The artisans downed tools and eventually established a camp outside the walls of several funerary temples in the Western Town, hoping to receive grain and other supplies from the granaries and warehouses there. In an encounter with the high priests and the scribe Hednakht they complained: 'Hunger and thirst have driven us here. We have no clothing, oil, fish or vegetables. Write about it to our good lord the pharaoh, write about it to our master the vizier, and ask them to give us something to live on.' Though the authorities tried to break the strike with promises, and the scribe Amennakht resorted to threats, the men remained united in their struggle, conscious that they 'have been done an injustice on royal ground'. The vizier might have settled the matter promptly, but he had gone off to the Delta to take part in the *sed* festival in honour of the pharaoh's 30th year of rule. The strikes continued on and off for at least seven months. Finally the scribe Hori obtained half of the delayed wages and announced: 'Half of your dues will now be given to you. I shall hand it out myself.'

The papyrus is damaged and incomplete, so we do not know how the dispute ended. As Isidor Lurye has put it, the strike 'was clear evidence of the conflicts in ancient Egyptian society between the various strata of the free population', and demonstrated 'the economic chaos which afflicted the country during the 20th dynasty and led to its collapse'.

The previous figures show that the artisan's ration of grain came to about 215kg a month, which would have milled down to far more flour than a whole family could consume. A good proportion of it, then, would have been exchanged for other goods.

It needs to be stressed that until the Late Period Egypt had nothing like a market economy with prices set by supply and demand, or independent merchants operating a money system. The state machine simply collected most of what was produced and rationed it out to non-producers.

This system was supplemented by the bartering of goods, either informally between individuals, or at market stalls in the towns and larger villages. Farmers customarily traded their surplus crops and farmstock, and artisans part of their corn ration and their home products such as furniture, coffins, wooden statuettes etc., in return for livestock, food, oil, clothing, walking-sticks and the like. Employees of the kings and dignitaries and temple staff (including artisans), were glad to take on other work in return for payment in kind – bread, beer, clothing or whatever.

Despite this non-monetary system of direct exchange, values were expressed in a comparable unit, the *shat*, originally denoting a flat silver disc (silver having been more precious than gold until the 18th dynasty or, according to some, until Graeco-Roman times).

Because of the barter economy the *shat* itself was not in current use, but the word was needed to express values in contracts and bookkeeping. During the New Kingdom it corresponded to 7.5 or 7.6g of silver. The next higher unit, by a factor of 12, was the *deben* (90–91g of silver). At the end of the 18th dynasty a goat, for example, cost ½ *shat*, a cow 8, a bedstead 4 and a house 10. A male slave could be bought for 7 *deben* of silver, a girl-slave for 4. One *arura* of land (2756sq.m.) went for a mere 2 *shat*.

In the course of Ramesses III's reign the *shat* disappeared, to be replaced by a new unit, the *kedet*, worth one-tenth of the silver *deben* or 10 times as much as the copper *deben* – showing that the ratio in value of silver to copper was 100:1. (By the time of Ramesses IX it had fallen to 60:1.) Janssen found 1250 prices of various items, from the Ramessid era, listed on ostraca and papyri from Deir el-Medina. For example, in terms of copper *deben*, a goat or sheep was worth 1–3, a pig 3–5, an ass 25–40, a head of cattle 20–150, a chair 12–30, a bed 12–25, a table about 15, a casket between ½ and 10 according to size, a garment 5–25, a pair of sandals ½–3, a leather bag ½–3, a razor 1–2 and so on.

For corn, the unit both of value and dry measure, the *khar*, was divided into 4 *oipe* (19.22 litres) each of 40 *hin* (0.48 litre). In the Ramessid period, 1 *khar* was conventionally valued at 2 copper *deben*.

During the New Kingdom free trade began to emerge between Egypt and the more advanced regions of the Middle East, instead of commerce being a royal monopoly. Scenes from the tomb of Qenamun, the harbourmaster of Thebes, show goods being taken on board by Syrian merchants. Egypt's main export was grain, but also included cloth, parchment and dried fish. The country received in turn copper from Cyprus, timber from the Middle East, metal ware from the Aegean, myrrh from the Land of Punt and ebony, ivory, cattle and exotic animals from the south. Crete and the Middle East supplied weapons and other military equipment. Internal trade also increased as a consequence, the 20th-dynasty Lansing Papyrus enthusing: 'Merchants sail upstream and downstream, eager to convey goods from one place to another and to supply whatever is needed anywhere.' There are more and more frequent records of commercial deals sworn under oath before the courts.

Deir el-Medina itself had a local court staffed by foremen and scribes who heard complaints, arbitrated in disputes, ensured the execution of court decisions and witnessed contracts. The guardians and the doorkeepers led in suspects or prisoners, and gave evidence. Constables made preliminary investigations, gave evidence and carried out sentences. This court dealt mainly with minor offences against private property and only had to impose mild penalties, usually the return of stolen or embezzled goods with a fine of twice their value. Corporal punishment could mean 100 or 200 strokes of the cane, in serious cases with 5 bleeding cuts added, or 10 brands as a sign of permanent dishonour. Court officials were also required to inspect tombs.

The gradual impoverishment of the workers toward the end of the 20th dynasty, reflected in the building of much smaller tombs and the re-use of old ones, sometimes led to one of the most heinous crimes – robbing tombs in the Theban burial-ground. We know from court records and scribes' diaries that not only several artisans and *semedet* people were implicated, but also some scribes and even priests from nearby temples. Sentences for serious crimes against the state or religion were handed down by the king or vizier. Offenders were punished by mutilation – the cutting off of a hand, tongue, nose or ears – by being exiled to Nubia or some Western oasis, or sent to forced labour in distant mines or quarries. Capital punishment was inflicted by impalement on a stake, burning alive, drowning, decapitation and, in Roman times, by throwing the condemned to wild beasts. Penalties were accompanied by loss of job-rank, forfeiture of property and, as a rule, by the deletion of the offender's name from the tomb he had made himself. It was also generally believed that any offence against the prevailing order (*maat*) would earn divine retribution too, in the form of failure, poverty, sickness, blindness, deafness or death, with the final settlement awaiting the Court of the Dead.

CHAPTER FIFTEEN

The Fortunes of War

213   Tutankhamun's army wreaking havoc among his Nubian enemies in an imaginary battle. Detail of casket. Wood, stuccoed and painted. Tomb of Tutankhamun, Valley of the Kings, West Thebes. 18th dynasty. *Cairo, Egyptian Museum*

Below 214   Fallen Asians, most probably Assyrians. Fragment of a painted limestone relief found at Deir el-Bahari, West Thebes. 11th dynasty. *London, British Museum*

WARLIKE ENCOUNTERS HAVE characterised the history of the human race from the earliest times, certainly since groups of people began consciously to feel ownership of the land on which they fished and hunted or, at a later stage, grew their crops. Stronger groups have always seized the territory of weaker ones: the Egyptians were no exception, however much some writers may insist on their peace-loving nature.

The earliest evidence of conflicts between bands of hunter-gatherers in Egypt comes from a cemetery of the Qadan culture (12th to 10th millennia BC) at Gebel Sahaba to the north of Wadi Halfa, where flint arrowheads were found embedded in some of the male bones.

Local communities began to form in predynastic times, finally coalescing into the independent kingdoms of Upper and Lower Egypt. We can tell that the unification process was not always peaceful from the oldest preserved wall-paintings in the mud-brick tomb (or cult building) at Nekhen (Hierakonpolis), the modern Kom el-Ahmar. Here for example, close to a group of six large ships, we see a warrior despatching three kneeling enemies; at another point two pairs of men are fighting, one man depicted upside down to show, presumably, that he has been killed. Another has his club raised against an opponent whose figure is missing. There were no armies at this time; if an attack was planned, or invasion threatened, the chief summoned all fit men to take up arms, and when everything was over they went back to their work.

Fighting intensified when the Two Kingdoms were joined together at the beginning of historic times, as is illustrated in contemporary artefacts like the magnificent carved ivory knife-handle found at Gebel el-Arak. Its upper part depicts a fight between two ranks of nine almost naked men, while the lower part shows four bodies floating – evidently down the Nile – between two lines of boats. On the famous Battlefield Palette a mighty king is symbolised as a huge lion springing onto his foe as 218 he falls; one of two men in the picture has his arms tied behind his back, in the manner used later on prisoners-of-war; in the foreground birds of prey are swooping down on four corpses.

A palette of the first recorded king of a united Egypt, Narmer, shows him standing 215 with the crown of Upper Egypt on his head, clutching by his hair an enemy (distinguished by his long locks and beard) whom he is about to smite with his mace. Above the kneeling man is an oval outline with six papyrus reeds radiating from it, and a human head with a rope through its nose, held by a falcon. Most scholars believe that all this represents the triumph of the king of Upper Egypt (and of the associated god Horus) over the Land of the Papyrus, Lower Egypt. Underneath we see more battle casualties – two naked bearded men with limbs spread out, evidently floating dead on the water. On the other side of the palette the King appears as a bull, trampling his enemies and piercing the battlements of a city with his horns.

At the very beginning of the historic period, then, an unknown artist here portrays a powerful king in triumph over his defeated foe, creating a symbolic scene that will appear constantly in royal buildings and temples throughout the existence of the Egyptian monarchy. In ever-increasing numbers we meet with captured enemies whose features, hair or beard, and clothing identify them as Nubians or black Africans infiltrating from the south, or as Libyans and Asiatics threatening the country from the north.

There is no evidence of a permanent military establishment or organisation during the Old Kingdom. When the need arose, as before Uni's campaign on behalf of Pepy I in Palestine, provincial governors, temples and estates provided units under the command of higher local officials. The only professional soldiers were the Nubian mercenaries, attested during the 6th dynasty at the latest. The only region under serious threat at the time was the Delta, since the rest of the country was shielded by the increasingly arid desert, and sparsely populated Lower Nubia presented no danger to the Egyptians. It was the Egyptians who tried to conquer Nubia in several attested campaigns as early as the 1st dynasty, later during 4th dynasty when they founded their stronghold Buhen, and again in 6th dynasty for the purpose of securing the supply of luxury goods from the African interior. It was not until the Middle Kingdom that the native Cushite empire, with its capital in modern Kerma, became strong enough to endanger Egypt's border.

Mounting evidence of a military profession originates from the turbulent times of continuous armed conflict in the 1st Intermediate Period. The Middle Kingdom that followed had a permanent royal army led by professional officers. Supported by provincial governors and their units the army occupied Lower Nubia, which became a heavily militarised zone. Special units of hunters patrolled the adjacent desert, and a chain of mighty forts protected the Egyptian army from the menace of attacks from the south and from resistance of the population. Back in Egypt, references to a variety of military titles increased towards the end of the Middle Kingdom.

During the New Kingdom a large professional army with a fully developed hierarchy made possible Egypt's expansion into the coastal lands of the Near East. Rather than enumerate all the battles and campaigns we shall instead look at the organisation of the army and the life of its soldiers – their training and equipment, their fighting methods and consequent risks to life and limb, awards given for bravery, and care for veterans. Particular engagements will only be mentioned by way of illustration.

In early times most young men need not fear that they might be conscripted into the army, but many second and subsequent sons, unable to follow their fathers' profession, volunteered for the sake of a career and a secure livelihood.

During the New Kingdom, when the armed forces were demanding more and more recruits, young men were sometimes levied against their will. This emerges from letters written by the scribe Djehutimose, who accompanied the general and vizier Piankhi on his Nubian campaign, to his son Butehamun, a scribe in the royal artisans' village at Deir el-Medina. Djehutimose instructs him to 'take good care of the conscripts', ensure they are well fed and see that they do not abscond. However, many men did not wait to be conscripted but disappeared in good time.

As soon as they were in barracks, the recruits faced a hard school of discipline and toughening up. Their 'uniform' was a short kilt or merely a penis sheath, with a feather in the hair for ornament. Physical exercise and wrestling alternated with weapon training. For breaches of discipline the commander would order a thrashing; we read of an offender being beaten by his fellow-recruits 'like papyrus' – an allusion to one stage in the preparation of Egyptian writing material. Military reviews were held on state holidays or after the return of a victorious army, in the presence of the king (and gods), to the accompaniment of trumpets, fifes and drums.

The size of the armed forces during the Old and Middle Kingdoms is uncertain, but they were far smaller than under the New Kingdom. One can infer this, for example, from the Middle Kingdom wooden model of a military detachment found in the tomb

215 King Narmer, identified as king Menes, unifier of Upper and Lower Egypt, about to smite with his mace a kneeling prisoner, probably from Lower Egypt. Detail of the Narmer palette. Greywacke. Nekhen (Hierakonpolis). Protodynastic Period. *Cairo, Egyptian Museum*

216 The king, wearing the Red Crown of Lower Egypt, is escorted by men bearing standards representing different regions to the temple of Horus, to inspect his slain enemies. Detail of the reverse of the Narmer palette. Greywacke. Nekhen (Hierakonpolis). Protodynastic Period. *Cairo, Egyptian Museum*

of Mesehti, prince of the province of Asyut. It represents 2 companies, each of 40 men marching in 4 platoons of 10. One company consists of well-tanned Egyptians in white kilts, with spears in their right hands and shields on their left arms. The second company is made up of darker-complexioned Nubians in motley kilts, each holding a bunch of four arrows with broad flint tips in the right hand and a plain curved bow, tapering at each end, in the left.

From the start of the New Kingdom, when the Egyptian army had emerged from a tough war of liberation against the Asiatic Hyksos and was about to push northwards and southwards, its basic unit was the division of 5000 men. Up to the time of General (later King) Horemheb at the end of the 18th dynasty we know of two divisions existing; by the time of Sethos I there were three, and by that of his son Ramesses II, four.

The division was divided into about 20 companies of 250 men and each of these into 5 platoons of 50. Each division had its own title, the four divisions under Ramesses II being named after the gods Amun, Ptah, Seth and Re respectively. The army had had its own ships for patrolling the Nile and transporting troops and equipment ever since the Old Kingdom, and in the New Kingdom the traditional spearsmen and archers were joined by a new arm, the cavalry.

The forces were organised on strictly hierarchical lines. They were under the command of the king, who had an advisory council made up of the vizier, the generals and the most senior functionaries. Divisions, regiments and companies had 'overseers' equivalent to modern officers and NCOs. As in every other sphere there were army scribes, officials charged with unit administration including enlistment, indenting for weapons and equipment and registering casualties, booty and prisoners.

During the Old Kingdom the Egyptian army had been largely a national one, but with the gradual subjugation of neighbouring peoples foreign auxiliary units began to be formed. Even during the Old Kingdom the Nubians were valued as archers (whence the Egyptian name for their country, the Land of the Bow), and from the Second Intermediate Period use was made of the Medjay who had acquitted themselves so well in the struggle against the Hyksos. In the New Kingdom there were units from various nations of Asia, the Mediterranean and Libya. From the time of Sethos I there appears a contingent of the Sherden, always pictured with swords, helmets and shields; their origin is obscure, but they are thought to be the people who colonised Sardinia and gave the island their name. It was not unusual for a foreign mercenary to reach the senior ranks or even join the king's élite bodyguard; Amenophis III's guard was composed of Nubians.

The weapons the Egyptians used were simple but effective enough. For hand-to-hand fighting there was the stick, club, flint knife, battle-axe and spear. Chiefs, kings and high-born commanders used the dagger or, after Ramesses III, the sword. For action at a distance there were lances, boomerangs and, above all, bows and arrows.

The oldest means of defence was the shield; a late predynastic painting at Hierakonpolis shows hides stretched over a wooden frame. Later on shields were made of wood covered with leather. These were used first by infantry; in the New Kingdom the driver of a war-chariot held one to protect the archer standing beside him. It was in this period that some troops acquired helmets of bronze or leather in imitation of Asiatic models, and others shirts made of leather strips sewn together in rows. Armour made of iron lamellae appeared in the reign of Shoshenq I (22nd dynasty).

Weapons were manufactured in the workshops of the royal palaces and the great temples. There are few illustrations from the Old and Middle Kingdoms, mostly of bows and spear-shafts being smoothed. We can see a man doing this, for example, in a 6th-dynasty tomb at Zawyet el-Maiyetin, holding the wood upright on the ground or laid across a trestle. There was a special device for bending bows. Drawing the arrow can be seen in Middle Kingdom reliefs at Beni Hasan.

There is more plentiful pictorial material in the New Kingdom, showing such things as a craftsman straightening the shaft of a spear over a fire after wetting it from a cup of water beside him, a bow being tested for resilience, arrows being made, metal helmets weighed, bow-cases sewn up with an awl etc. A recently published block from an unidentified tomb of the 18th dynasty at Saqqara shows an arrow being checked for straightness by one workman, while a second uses an adze to plane out another arrow resting on his knees.

In the previously mentioned letters exchanged between the scribes Djehutimose and Butehamon we read that General Piankhi, for his Nubian operations, required from Deir el-Medina 'fresh supplies of copper spear-heads' made by the local coppersmiths, and also spare parts for war-chariots, new material for clothing and old material 'for bandages' – a rare sign of concern for the wounded, unless they were wrappings for the dead.

During their fierce encounters with the Hyksos the Egyptians adopted from the superior military technology of their enemies the horse-drawn war-chariot, thereby adding the important facility of surprise encirclement to their tactical repertoire. Warfare now became more rapid, sudden and pitiless. The new vehicles could break through serried ranks of infantry. Light and easy to manoeuvre, drawn by two horses, they had room in the body for a bowman-warrior as well as the driver with a shield to cover both of them. There were at least 50 such chariots to each division and their crews were the élite of the forces. The kings had magnificently carved and gilded 226 specimens, but it is not certain whether these were used in action or only for 227 ceremonial and triumphal purposes.

In several New Kingdom tombs there are illustrations of carpenters, joiners and 224 leather-workers all working on a chariot together. In addition to wood they required large amounts of leather for fastening parts together, covering the body, tyring the wheels and making reins, blinkers and bits. We see the final smoothing of wheels, yokes and shafts, and a worker testing the flexibility of a shaft by jumping on it. In amongst the wooden components we see strips of leather used for binding the wheel-felloes, tying the spokes to the rims and hubs, and joining the whole vehicle together. One saddler is winding leather round a wheel-rim while another fastens a shaft to the carriage-body and his mate attaches the reins to the shaft.

Rosemarie Drenkhahn noticed that all the workshop scenes shown in Theban tombs between the reigns of Queen Hatshepsut and Tuthmosis IV feature the workshops of the Great Temple of Amun at Karnak. Of the six occupants of tombs in which they appear, four held high office in that temple. It may be asked why temple workshops should have been used for making military vehicles that were seemingly not designed for ritual purposes. Drenkhahn suggests that this was because their manufacture required high-quality exotic timber such as came to the temples in large

217 Bound captives escorted by standards of deities represented by a hawk and an ibis. The obverse of the 'Battlefield' palette. Predynastic Period. *Oxford, Ashmolean Museum*

218 Lion and vulture preying on slain enemies. The lion probably represents the king. Detail of the 'Battlefield' palette. Predynastic Period. *London, British Museum*

amounts by way of trade or of royal gifts, or else because the temples may have employed more of the skilled foreigners familiar with chariot technology.

After the end of the 18th dynasty we find many similar scenes in the Saqqara tombs whose owners – bearing such titles as 'overseer of the artisans in the army smithy' or 'overseer of the artisans-armourers' – were clearly employed in the royal armouries at Memphis. It has been suggested that the military workshops of the old Egyptian capital continued operating throughout the New Kingdom and were directly controlled by the royal treasury, the office in charge of the country's economy and finances.

It is from murals that we also gain most enlightenment about weapon usage and tactics. Up to the 5th dynasty there is little to show. Egypt seems to have been living at peace with its neighbours; efforts were concentrated on the great pyramids, with only occasional sallies into Nubia that met with slight resistence. The first battle-scene relief occurs on an isolated block that originally formed part of the wall of the causeway at Saqqara leading to the pyramid complex of Unas, the last 5th-dynasty king. This shows Egyptians, armed with bows and daggers, fighting with enemies who from their long hair and beards must be Asiatics.

The rock-tomb of Inti at Deshasha, assigned by Petrie to the second half of the 5th dynasty but by W. Stevenson Smith to the middle of the 6th, has a lively scene of the

breaching of city fortifications, evidently somewhere in southern Palestine. On the left we see preparations under way before the ramparts, where a unit of archers is assembling; other soldiers armed with battle-axes are attacking some men with clubs who have emerged from the fortress to fight in the open. Two Egyptians are leading off a file of prisoners, including women. While this is going on the Egyptians are making ready to take the bastion, some digging underneath the wall, others bringing up a ladder to scale it.

The right-hand part of the scene shows the tense situation within the walls. At the bottom a man is crouching to listen where the battering-rams are at work and raising one hand to make the others keep quiet. Higher up we see a group of women thrashing some cowardly men who had tried to hide away. The despairing commander is tearing his hair, oblivious of a young woman at his feet who is trying to console him. Another woman is in tears while an old man takes her child off to safety. The hopeless plight of the defenders emerges in the top register, where a warrior signals surrender by breaking his bow before the eyes of his wife and their little son.

The later stages of a siege appear in the 6th-dynasty tomb of Khaemweset at Saqqara. Egyptian soldiers are scaling the walls with a siege-ladder mounted on wheels for easier handling (showing that the wheel was known in principle during the Old Kingdom), while hand-to-hand fighting goes on in their rear. A little way off is

219 In the top register an officer is addressing recruits; in the bottom register others are having their hair cut among sycomore fig trees. Two recruits have dozed off. In the middle register the remaining recruits are biding their time, seated on low stools or squatting on the ground. Tomb of Userhet, Sheikh Abd el-Qurna, West Thebes. 18th dynasty

220 Light infantry on parade, carrying standards, battle-axes and palm fronds. They wear wigs and uniform kilts with frontal tabs. Painted relief. Temple of Queen Hatshepsut at Deir el-Bahari, West Thebes. 18th dynasty

a shepherd leading his flock to safety, while at the edge of the picture women and children are in hiding.

Another siege episode appears in the 11th-dynasty tomb-chapel of General Intef in West Thebes. We are shown Egyptians in heavy armour marching towards the walls, infantry with axes, clubs, daggers and long spears or lances, and Nubian troops with their bows and arrows. Other troops are already climbing up a wheeled siege-tower. The Asiatic defenders are raining arrows down from the high walls, but many have already been hit by the Egyptians and some are hurtling down to the ground, head foremost. Inside the walls, meanwhile, the Egyptians are winning the hand-to-hand fighting, the defenders are fleeing ignominiously with their women and children, and a row of prisoners is being marched off. General Intef, bow and arrows in hand, is shown in personal command of the operation.

There are similar pictures on the walls of 12th-dynasty tombs at Beni Hasan belonging to Amenemhet, Khnumhotep, Baqet III and Khety. Here the ramparts, over 10m high, have a projecting sentry-path near the top with holes in its floor through which the defenders could fire arrows, or pour boiling liquids onto their assailants, as well as shooting from the battlements. The Nubian archers advance by leaps and bounds, standing or kneeling to shoot, with aides carrying their quiverfuls of arrows. Behind them come the heavy infantry with individual shields, or large ones shared between two or three men, anticipating the Roman *testudo*. Two men carry a ram designed to break through the wall. Hand-to-hand combat is under way nearby and the piles of corpses are growing. Some of the survivors are taking the dead men's weapons and at one place a victor is ripping the kilt from his defeated opponent.

221 Two soldiers wrestling, apparently in the presence of the pharaoh. The inscription indicates the sporting nature of the fight. It reads: 'Behold, I let thee tumble softly before the pharaoh.' Sketch on limestone. 20th dynasty. *Cairo, Egyptian Museum*

In these scenes, significantly, there are Egyptians fighting on both sides. They may represent episodes from the wars of unification in the middle of the 11th dynasty, when the north was ranged against the south. The Beni Hasan tomb paintings may also refer to local strife between the Oryx province and forces from other districts.

Egypt waged several campaigns against the Nubians under the 12th dynasty, a war of liberation against the Hyksos around the middle of the 16th century BC, and the first of a series of wars of conquest against Asiatic and Nubian neighbours during the New Kingdom leading to the annexation of their lands and the creation of an Egyptian empire, but there are no extant portrayals of any of the battles involved.

Only at the end of the 18th dynasty do we suddenly find that large numbers of battle scenes with explanatory texts start to appear. But by now these are only found in temples, not in tombs. They no longer glorify particular generals but put out state propaganda for the omnipotent pharaoh. They usually start off with the preparations for war, with arms being issued and troops marching off to fight. The climax comes in 226

227 the heat of battle, dominated by the king firing from his chariot into a mass of enemies
228 or trampling over their corpses and tying up prisoners. Then comes the victory
parade, with high officials and crown princes leading files of prisoners before the king
and presenting him with the spoils, while scribes count up the severed hands or
uncircumcised genitals of the slain foe. The cycle usually ends with the king
presenting prisoners as a sacrifice to the triad of gods, Amon-Re, Mut and Khonsu, to
work as slaves in the temple fields and workshops.

These elaborate battle-cycles, often covering huge wall areas, then for a
considerable period took over from the traditional stereotype of a king standing and
smiting his enemies on the head with his sceptre. This sudden change, which took
place in the reign of Horemheb, the last king of the 18th dynasty, is probably
connected with the events of the preceding Amarna period when the notion of an
omnipotent god-king had received a severe jolt. Scenes of the monarch's domestic life,
it will be recalled, showed him as a simple mortal. But when the old order was
restored the king had once more to be portrayed as an invulnerable, ever-victorious
deity – and battle-scenes served that propaganda purpose admirably.

It would be outside the scope of this book to enumerate the pictures of each king's
battles with this or that enemy. They add little, in any case, to our knowledge of
fighting methods. What is of interest, however, is the fate of the wounded. Pictures of

222
223

Left **222** Egyptian and Hittite war chariots clash at Qadesh. Relief in the rock temple at Abu Simbel. 19th dynasty

Below **223** Ramesses II smites a Hittite in the heat of battle at Qadesh, trampling on the body of another. Relief in the rock temple at Abu Simbel. 19th dynasty

224 Wheelwrights making a chariot wheel. Relief from the chapel of Min, Saqqara. New Kingdom. *Cairo, Egyptian Museum*

Horemheb's battles with the Nubians from his rock-temple at Gebel el-Silsila, for example, show Nubians collapsing and dying in agony, one of them trying to wrest an arrow from his chest. An analogous picture of Ramesses II, three pharaohs later, doing battle with the same Nubians shows two men carrying a wounded comrade from the field.

A cycle devoted to Sethos I's campaign against the Asiatic Shasu bedouin, which decorates the outside of the northern wall of the great hypostyle hall of the Karnak temple, includes a battle fought in the desert on the way to Palestine. Here too there are large numbers of enemy wounded, dying or surrendering, and heaps of bodies beside them. In another scene the people of the city of Jenoam emerge with their hands over their heads, burning incense as a sign of capitulation.

However much the artist strove to glorify the triumphant, invulnerable king and his heroic deeds in contrast to the confused hordes of his nameless enemies, the bloody nature of the battle could not be disguised. Though the scenes tactfully omit to show them, Egyptian losses and suffering must have been heavy too.

One battle does deserve closer attention as a cardinal event in ancient history. This was the engagement between Egyptian forces under Ramesses II and the armies of the Hittite king Muwatallis outside the Syrian fortified city of Qadesh (today Tell Nebi Mend) on the river Orontes (now Nahr el-'Asi), around 1285 BC. We know the details very well, thanks to an epic poem copied by the scribe Pentawer and to the official report that accompanies the wall-reliefs of the battle carved in the temples that Ramesses had erected in Upper Egypt and Nubia. They are best preserved on the pylon of the temple at Luxor, on the first and second pylons of the Ramesseum, and on the north wall of the Great Hall of the great rock temple at Abu Simbel.

Ramesses drove off to battle from the coast of what is now Lebanon along the River Litani with four divisions of men, placing himself at the head of one consecrated to Amun. As the poem says:

> Now his majesty had made ready his infantry and his
> chariotry, and the Sherden in his majesty's captivity
> whom he had brought back in the victories of his strong
> arm. They had been supplied with all their weapons, and
> battle orders had been given to them. His majesty journeyed
> northward, his infantry and his chariotry with him,
> having made a good start with the march in year 5, second
> month of summer, day 9

Having been misinformed that the Hittite armies were on the move far away from

Qadesh, Ramesses advanced quickly to the northwest of that town with the aim of attacking it from there without waiting to concentrate all his divisions.

The relief depicts final preparations in the Egyptian camp before the city gates. Round the camp is a square palisade of shields driven into the ground close together, with just two gaps for entry and exit. The dominating feature is the royal tent, surrounded by the smaller ones of the staff officers and princes. Soldiers are unloading or shoeing their horses, fetching water, distributing fodder, piling up food supplies, operating a field kitchen, arranging their quarters, checking their weapons and maintaining guard. There are horses, cattle – and the King's tame lion – to be seen in an improvised stable.

Ramesses is seated in his tent on a gilt throne, conferring with his staff. His war chariot and his bodyguard of Egyptians and Sherden await him nearby. In the foreground two Hittite spies, who had infiltrated the encampment and been caught, are being given a thrashing. Under duress they have revealed the awkward news, for Ramesses, that the Hittite forces are in fact encamped close by, to the northeast of Qadesh, and ready to do battle.

> His majesty had arrived at the town of Qadesh, and now
> the vile Hittite foe had come and brought together
> all the foreign lands as far as the end of the sea.
> The entire Hittite land had come.

It was in vain that the King immediately despatched his vizier and chief aide to speed the arrival of the outlying division. The Hittite cavalry, under the command of their royal princes, had already set out for battle, crossed the Orontes below Qadesh and attacked the Egyptians' Re division which had approached Ramesses's camp. Caught by surprise, its men started to flee toward the base. But the Hittite cavalry gave chase and even assaulted the camp itself. Confusion ensued and the Egyptians rushed panic-stricken in all directions.

> Then his majesty drove at a gallop and charged the forces
> of the Hittites, being alone by himself, none other with him.
> His majesty proceeded to look about him and found 2500
> chariots ringing him on his way out . . .

225   These three gold flies were part of an award for valour. They were buried with Queen Aahotep at Dra Abu el-Naga, West Thebes. 18th dynasty. *Cairo, Egyptian Museum*

Left 226   King Sethos I about to smite a Libyan whom he is holding with his bow. Libyans were depicted with a pigtail and a feather on their head. Relief on the western part of the northern wall of the hypostyle hall, great temple of Amun, Karnak. 19th dynasty

227 More than once Ramesses III had to defend Egypt against foreign invaders. This is a scene from his second Libyan campaign. Relief on the wall of the temple of Ramesses III at Medinet Habu, West Thebes. 20th dynasty

The reliefs show the King with his bodyguard. He stands up fearlessly in his chariot, surrounded by the enemy everywhere. Thanks to his godlike power he is able not only to save himself but to emerge the victor. The enemy are shown falling to the ground, dying, fleeing towards the city or disappearing under the waves of the Orontes ...

Other scenes feature the Hittite commanders too. On the second pylon of the Ramesseum we see two soldiers holding the prince from Aleppo head down to make him disgorge the water he had swallowed when the furious Ramesses hurled him into the river. On the same relief the walled city of Qadesh is shown encircled by the waters of the Orontes, which in fact flows only round one side of it. A little way off stands the Hittite king Muwatallis with his footsoldiers and chariots.

What in truth saved Ramesses and procured his victory was the involvement of a fresh Egyptian contingent, the *naren* or 'Young Troops'. According to R. O. Faulkner, these were commandos whose job was to cover the marching army on the flanks and from the rear. It was their sudden onslaught that turned the tide of battle. The Hittite ruler had to throw in another thousand chariots, but by then the Ptah division had also arrived and the fortunes of war turned in favour of the Egyptians.

The men of the fleeing Amun and Re divisions returned by cover of night and on the next day, when the Hittite king attacked with his infantry, a second engagement took place that ended with Muwatallis suing for an armistice. The battle was naturally publicised throughout Egypt as a victory, even though it failed in its object of taking Qadesh and thereby halting the Hittites in their plan of overrunning the Levant. The outcome was in fact the reverse, for as soon as the Egyptians left the

whole region of Upe, which had previously acknowledged Egyptian sovereignty, passed under Hittite rule. Despite these awkward facts the reliefs include the usual scenes of triumph and the one at Karnak shows the presentation of prisoners to the triad of Theban deities.

In Egypt, with its convenient waterways, the army as we have mentioned always had ships on the Nile for patrolling and transporting troops and supplies. Although during the Asiatic campaigns infantry and chariots often advanced overland, reinforcements, weapons and food were taken by ship to Byblos and other ports. Naval vessels were almost as large as cargo ships, with the added features of cabins for officers and wooden parapets along the decks, with gaps for oars, to protect the rowers from enemy arrows. This made rapid manoeuvring feasible even in the course of battle. Warships had grand names such as *Star of Egypt, Soul of the Gods, Wild Bull, Beloved of Amun* or *Tuthmosis Appears in Memphis*. Their prows were decorated with meaningful carvings, like the head of a lioness devouring an Asiatic.

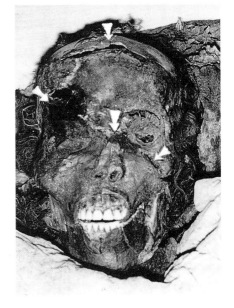

The oldest evidence of naval warfare was, as we have seen, on the Gebel el-Arak knifehandle. But the first portrayal of ships actually engaged in battle is in General Intef's tomb, where each of the three registers shows an oared vessel with soldiers on board, about to jump on land or onto an enemy ship. They are armed to the teeth with battle-axes, or firing arrows.

228 Defeated Philistines being led into captivity. Relief on the wall of the temple of Ramesses III at Medinet Habu. West Thebes. 20th dynasty

There is a unique relief showing Ramesses III's battles with the 'Sea Peoples' in 1174 BC, on the outside of the northern wall of the royal mortuary temple at Medinet Habu. One scene has the King standing on the shore over the bodies of fallen enemies, shooting in company with four other archers (presumably princes) at approaching ships. The caption states that the enemy had 'infiltrated through canals in the mouth of the Nile' onto Egyptian territory. Another scene shows a battle on the Levantine coast; there are nine ships in three rows, four Egyptian and five enemy ones with bird-head prows. The enemy crews, composed of Philistines and Sherden, are faring badly under a cascade of Egyptian arrows; some of their men have been pierced through, some are falling headlong into the water. One enemy ship has capsized. A little way off we see an Egyptian craft leave the battle with a full load of prisoners.

Foreign expeditions and action against an attacker were only one aspect of military life. Peace-time defence and guard duty were important too. As early as the Old Kingdom Egypt had set up a forward base at Buhen in Nubia, and her defence system was completed under the Middle Kingdom with a whole cordon of fortresses in the region of the Second Cataract. At one of these, Mirgissa, a cemetery has been excavated where Egyptian soldiers who died on defence duty were buried.

The army also had a considerable role to play in maintaining public order and royal authority inside the country, and large military contingents were used to guard commercial and exploratory missions.

Both officers and other ranks could receive 'Gold of Bravery' awards for valour on the field and other military virtues, consisting of decorated weapons, usually axes, daggers or swords. Other trinkets – such as little golden lions and gold flies – can be 225 regarded as the world's oldest medals. The lion symbolised bravery, the fly perseverance in the attack. Additional rewards were shares in the booty, prisoners (male and female) to be kept as slaves, and – in later times – the grant of a plot of land.

Not everyone, of course, returned from the wars alive and healthy. Casualties were considerable. Many a hero ended up scarred, blinded or with a limb missing. Two adult male skeletons have been described where the lower end of a forearm had been severed, either by an enemy sword or as a punishment for theft. Every group of skeletons excavated yields several cases of skulls afflicted by cutting or stabbing wounds or by blows from blunt instruments, and fractures of limbs and vertebrae are commonplace. The largest concentrations of these have turned up in our examination by 3rd- to 5th-century remains from Sayala in Nubia excavated by Austrian archaeologists. The population involved were probably Blemmyans, the dreaded race of former Eastern Desert nomads who took to making raids on Upper Egypt.

Even kings sometimes displayed personal courage and gave their lives in battle. This was confirmed by the examination in 1974 of the 17th-dynasty mummy of King Seqenenre which the author carried out with Manfred Bietak in Cairo. Of his five fatal 229 skull fractures two proved to correspond exactly to the cross-section of a type of battle-axe used by the Hyksos, with whom the king had gone forth to battle.

229 Fatal injuries to the forehead and face of the mummified head of King Seqenenre Tao caused by cutting blows. He met his end bravely resisting the Hyksos invaders who occupied the Delta during the 2nd Intermediate Period. 17th dynasty. *Cairo, Egyptian Museum*

Those defeated in warfare had to expect unpleasant consequences. The victorious side would carry off many of the men and women into slavery, loot their houses, steal or destroy their crops and cattle and cut down their trees, and sometimes it was the Egyptians themselves who had to suffer this fate.

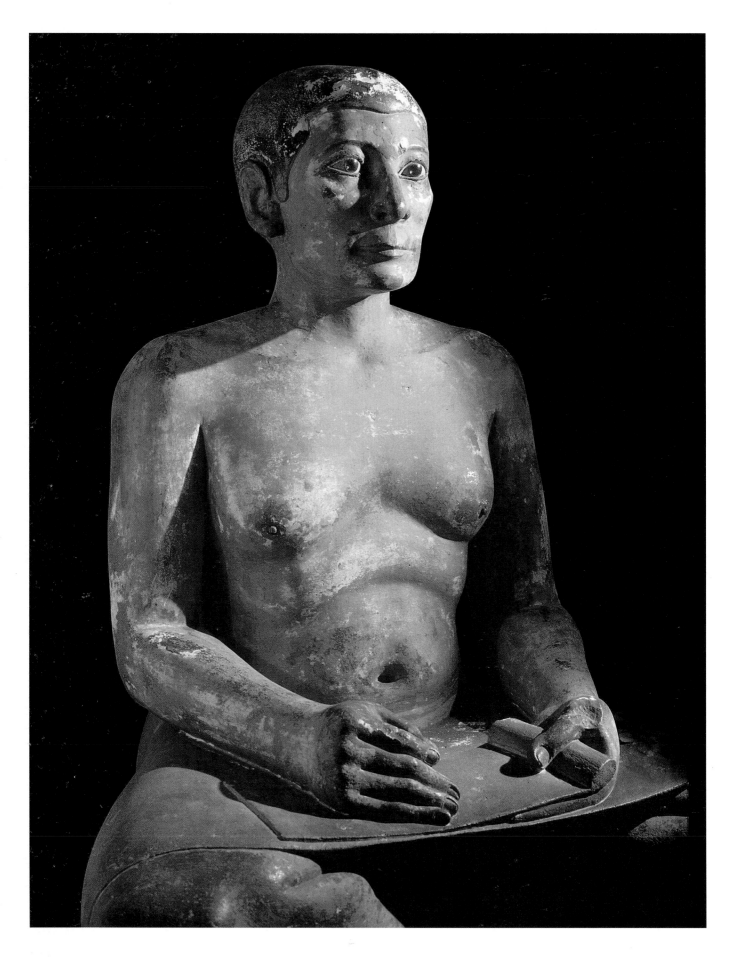

CHAPTER SIXTEEN

Administrators and Managers

Left **230** The high regard in which scribes were held is best expressed in this masterpiece. Although sculptures of scribes squatting with a roll of papyrus on their knees were by no means uncommon, none can compare with the Louvre Scribe. The eyes are of ebony with a crystal pupil inset in a copper capsule. Painted limestone. Saqqara. Late 4th or early 5th dynasty. *Paris, Musée du Louvre*

231 Scribes rendering accounts. Fragment of a sunk relief from the Amarna period. 18th dynasty. *Detroit Institute of Art*

WHATEVER SPHERE OF ancient Egyptian activity we examine – on the farms, in the workshops, in army units, temple offices or departments of state – we invariably bump into the ubiquitous scribe, the *sesh*. He belonged to a well-defined and rather exclusive caste, standing out from the surrounding illiteracy by his command of the secret skills of reading and writing. These qualifications were considered a privilege, and perhaps a mystery, shared only with the rulers and the gods.

Writing things down was only one aspect of the scribe's profession. He was in effect a civil servant of the king, dignitary or temple institution, fully competent in his particular field, equipped for independent thought, decision-making and management. The records he kept enabled him to make judgements designed to bring order into every field, to ensure that things ran smoothly and would continue to do so.

Along with the higher-ranking priests and some of the educated dignitaries, the scribes constituted the intelligentsia of ancient Egypt. They occupied the upper rungs of the social ladder to the very top, and enjoyed due recognition accordingly. We are indebted to their industry in leaving behind a wealth of documentation, from everyday reports to literary texts of high merit.

The scribes were well aware of their status and guarded their professional secrets jealously. Free from physical labour, they had soft hands, clean clothes and minds unencumbered by bodily fatigue. They were the managers who gave orders, checked results, took records, granted or withheld permission. The ordinary Egyptian turned to them for all kinds of help, from drawing up a will or a marriage contract to simply reading and writing letters.

Scribes were usually the sons of scribes and few members of other professions, or even their offspring, managed to penetrate the group. It was perhaps to make his calling even more attractive to his son Pepi, who had just left his birthplace in the Delta to attend the palace school for scribes in the capital, that Khety in the early 12th dynasty wrote his famous Instruction, also known as the Satire on the Trades. Khety paints the dark side of various callings in turn so as to highlight the glory, and the advantages, of his own. For 'it's the most important of all occupations,' he says. 'There is no other like it in the whole country.' And above all

> There's no job without an overseer
> Except the scribe's: he is the overseer.
> Hence if you can write,
> You will be better off
> Than in those professions I've told you about.

Thus Khety concludes, and Pepi no doubt took it to heart like all the other boys who

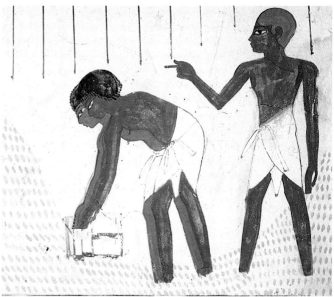

diligently copied out the Instruction on tablets and ostraca in the scribal schools. Other textbooks for aspiring scribes strike a similar note:

> It is the scribe who imposes and collects taxes in Upper and Lower Egypt; it is he who keeps account of everything there is. He organises every unit in the army. He brings city and village delegations before the king and guides each individual at every step. It is he who gives orders to the whole country and keeps watch over all proceedings.

Novices are encouraged in these terms:

> Become a scribe so that your limbs remain smooth and your hands soft, and you can wear white and walk like a man of standing whom [even] courtiers will greet.

Is it any surprise that some scribes were so dazzled by the prestige and exclusiveness of their profession that they were inclined to lord it over their fellow-citizens and even to squabble among themselves? Thus in the Papyrus Anastasi I we find the scribe Hori taunting his colleague Amenemope, whose letter he found below standard, with being unable to work out food rations for labourers digging a trench, the right number of bricks for building a ramp, the weight of an obelisk or the number of men it will take to shift it.

The Greeks called the ancient Egyptian picture-writing 'hieroglyphic', meaning sacred, because when they first arrived in the country and saw it used on tombs and temple walls they assumed it had a secret religious significance. It developed from a system of simplified, carefully stylised pictures of actual objects. The original hieroglyphic symbols, with some new ones added in the course of time, were used in monumental inscriptions throughout the history of ancient Egyptian civilisation, and as temple or tomb carvings have lasted for centuries beyond.

Both for everyday records and for extended literary texts, on the other hand, the simplified cursive form or 'hieratic' script was required, in which the original pictures were mostly simplified beyond immediate recognition. This was the form of writing used by scribes from the Old Kingdom up to the 8th century BC, and for religious texts up to the last centuries of the pre-Christian era. Until the Middle Kingdom texts were written in vertical columns from top to bottom, but from the New Kingdom in rows from left to right.

Starting in the 8th century BC the spoken language was recorded in a still more cursive script, called 'demotic' or popular, in which often groups of symbols, now

Above left **232**　Surveyors measuring the grain crop. Wall painting in the tomb of Menna. Sheikh Abd el-Qurna, West Thebes. 18th dynasty

Above **233**　Two men scooping grain under strict supervision. Wall painting in the tomb of Menna, West Thebes. 18th dynasty

234 Farm managers rendering accounts. Relief in the tomb of Mereruka, Saqqara. 6th dynasty

unrecognisably simplified, were merged in quite new complex symbols, phonograms.

In the Ptolemaic Period the court used the Greek language and alphabet. It was then that the need for translations arose, as illustrated *par excellence* by the Memphis Decree of the time of Ptolemy V Epiphanes (196 BC). It was this decree, engraved on a basalt slab in Greek, Egyptian demotic and Egyptian hieroglyphic, that was found by Captain Bouchard, a member of Napoleon's expeditionary staff, near the Delta town Rosetta (Rashid). It enabled Champollion to decipher the hieroglyphic script in 1822.

Laborious carving in stone or engraving on clay tablets, as practised in ancient Mesopotamia, was unsuitable for either of the cursive scripts. But for these nature provided in Egypt an easily obtainable, superior and easily portable medium – papyrus.

The word is also the name of the paper reed *Cyperus papyrus*, from which the material was made, a plant which then abounded in the marshes around the branches of the Nile, especially in the Delta. The traveller will seek it in vain today. Its complete extinction in the natural state in Egypt was evidently accelerated by its popularity, not only as a writing medium, but for making boats, mats, baskets and other wickerwork, sandals, kilts, ropes and so forth. It has not yet been understood whether climatic, ecological or other factors contributed. To see it in Egypt today one must resort to the plots maintained in artificial pools in front of the Egyptian Museum and the Agricultural Museum in Cairo, though it still survives wild in the wetlands of Bahr el-Ghazal in the southern Sudan and along the Blue Nile in Ethiopia.

The word papyrus is of ancient Egyptian derivation (*pa-puro* in Coptic) and meant something royal, which itself implies that the pharaohs enjoyed a monopoly in its manufacture, as documented specifically from Ptolemaic times. The word then passed into European languages via Greek and Latin as *paper*, even though the wood-pulp from which this is now made has no connection with papyrus itself.

To make writing material the Egyptians had to slit the papyrus stem into thin strips which were laid close together and then covered with a second layer running at right-angles to the first. These were sprinkled with water and beaten hard with stone hammers, not only to flatten them but to release the natural viscous juices that bonded them together into a strong but pliant sheet, usually between 15cm and 50cm wide. Once dry, the white surface could be written on without the ink running or fading for a very long time. The sheets were finally glued together in strips and wound cylindrically on wooden rods. The resultant scrolls were often of considerable length, as much as 40m and more for literary texts.

A less common medium for writing was parchment, made of specially cured hides stretched out thin and treated to make them perfectly white.

In ancient Egypt a scribe was instantly recognisable from the wooden or stone 258 tablets that he carried on a cord over his shoulder. These were 'palettes', each with two recesses – one for black ink (made from soot bonded with papyrus juice) and the other for red (made from finely ground burnet ochre, similarly bonded). Along with these went a little leather bag with a drawstring, containing a phial of water for mixing the colours. Each palette also had a groove to hold a brush made from a rush stem (*Juncus maritimus* or *J. rigidus*), the tip of which had to be frayed by chewing before use. From Ptolemaic times reed pens were more common, made from the stems of *Phragmites aegyptiaca* cut to a point and split at the end like quills. Pens were kept in a leather case tied to the palette with a strap.

Thanks to Egypt's hot, dry climate, papyrus documents have survived for thousands of years despite their fragile cellular structure. Among several papyrus collections discovered in modern times is the celebrated temple archive from Abusir, found by Ludwig Borchardt at the beginning of the 20th century in the ruins of the 5th-dynasty funerary temple of Neferirkare's pyramid and published in 1976 by Paule Posener-Kriéger. Further valuable finds were made at Abusir by a Czechoslovak team led by Miroslav Verner, in the funerary temple of Queen Khentkaus in 1980, and two years later in the temple of the unfinished pyramid of King Raneferef. The latter was a cache of some 150 papyrus fragments of varying length which have greatly enlarged our knowledge of the organisation and economy of such temples in a wide historic context.

Many papyri have turned up in urban rubbish dumps. Others, unfortunately, had been used as fuel for bread ovens and pottery kilns, as in the grounds of King Tuthmosis III's treasury south-east of the temple of Amun at Karnak.

Scrolls bearing texts of the Book of the Dead, which accompanied mummies into their tombs, had a better chance of survival. One unexpected source of papyrus documents proved to be the 'cartonnages' used as cheap coffins in the Late and Graeco-Roman Periods. These were made of several layers of linen cloth, sometimes interleaved with used sheets of papyrus. Discarded papyri and cloth were used to stuff the mummies of sacred animals, particularly crocodiles.

For short records and notes, accounts, certificates and draft texts the scribes also resorted to a cheaper material – fragments of broken pottery or limestone sherds, *ostraca*. These were sometimes used for more permanent records too, such as inventories, but even private legal records and contracts.

From texts and from numerous tomb-wall illustrations we can visualise how the managerial and auditing functions of the scribes entered into people's daily life. All kinds of routine records, for the most part lists and summaries, were their doing.

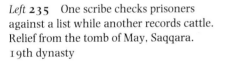

Left **235** One scribe checks prisoners against a list while another records cattle. Relief from the tomb of May, Saqqara. 19th dynasty

Right **236** A scribe hard at work in his 'office'. Relief in the tomb of Princess Idut, Saqqara. 6th dynasty

Everything, it seems, had to be noted down, from the number of bags of grain harvested to the size of herds, amounts of seed-grain and materials issued from store, types and quantities of objects manufactured, building supplies, tools and artisans' requisites. Records were kept of work attendance, wages paid, kinds and quantities of booty seized, numbers of hands and phalluses cut from the bodies of fallen enemies – all as punctiliously as the inventories of gifts that followed the deceased into the next world or were daily sacrificed in his honour by the funerary priests.

The precision with which quantities are reckoned, impressive even to a modern reader, shows that a good scribe had to be good at arithmetic. Calculations of labour and material needed for the construction of canals, ramps or monumental buildings also display a degree of algebraic skill that must have been invaluable in the planning stage. Even the pedantic lists of all and sundry were far from being the pointless whim of soulless bureaucrats. By giving senior officials an oversight of the country's total stocks it made possible their orderly distribution, the creation of reserves and planning for special projects.

Other documents from the scribe's pen include regulations issued by various bodies, court proceedings and records of private contracts dealing with sale and purchase, loans, hire, financial arrangements between spouses, inheritance, receipts, taxes, accounts and so on.

We also find many documents of a private character, such as letters. Where the writer is the scribe himself, his own name appears on them. We possess for example a set of 54 letters, in whole or part, exchanged between the scribe Butehamun in the artisans' village of Deir el-Medina and his father Djehutimose in far-off Nubia. Scribes also penned letters, in return for payment, on behalf of illiterate clients.

Writing, and in particular the copying out of literary texts was another important field of activity. Among such texts were biographies, instructions, literary, historical, political and propaganda writings, short stories, fairy tales, fables, travellers' tales, poems, chronicles, 'stories of kings' and 'stories of great men', public announcements written on scarabs, scientific, didactic and religious literature, and dramas.

The diligence and concentration of the scribe at work is nicely caught in pictures like those in the 6th-dynasty mastaba of Mereruka at Saqqara. There we see them squatting in a row with their heads down, copying texts onto papyrus rolls on their laps. Behind the last scribe in the row stands an apprentice with a blank roll, ready to be handed to whoever needs it. The novice is shown bowing slightly in deference to his masters and preceptors.

The care with which scribes followed harvest operations emerges from paintings in
232 the tomb of Menna, a scribe to the estates of Tuthmosis III, at Sheikh Abd el-Qurna (18th dynasty). Here we see them, tablet in hand, noting down the figures supplied by surveyors for the area of a standing crop so that they can estimate the yield for later comparison with the amount actually harvested. Meanwhile their master, presumably Menna himself, has climbed up onto a pile of sheaves for a better view. Elsewhere scribes are writing down the number of sacks that the farmers are emptying into the granary – one of many figures which, when totalled up, will have enabled the top administrators to know how much there was in the state granaries.

In one Middle Kingdom model from the 11th-dynasty tomb of Meketre the landowner is shown seated in a pavilion with four scribes on his right. These are busy counting the cattle as they are led past by the herdsmen. This ritual was part of a general cattle census, which gave an overview of the animal herds in different regions, and on which planning could be based for consumption levels, temple sacrifices and so on.

Equal importance attached to the work of the scribes in the craft shops, especially those dealing with metal. In the Egyptian Museum in Cairo there is a 5th-dynasty
163 relief from Saqqara where an official is weighing material in a hand-held pair of scales, a steelyard. One pan contains the weights, the other a number of long objects, presumably the raw material. A scribe is jotting the figures down on a scroll. A further weighing ensued after processing so that the scribe could compare the two results and ascertain whether the wastage was within approved limits.

237 Scribes recording jars of newly-made wine. Painting on limestone in the tomb of Userhet. Sheikh Abd el-Qurna, West Thebes. 18th dynasty

This routine weighing operation reappears in the many portrayals of the Judgement of the Dead. In these we see the heart of the deceased being balanced 287 against the propriety of his deeds during life, this being represented by an ostrich feather – symbol of the Goddess of Truth, Maat – or by a seated figure of the goddess herself. The recording scribe in this case is Thoth, patron of scribes and scholars.

In the royal artisans' village of Deir el-Medina originally two, and from the end of the Ramessid period four scribes were employed. Together with the foremen and one of the draughtsmen they belonged to the management group known as the 'Overseers of (the crew's) Work in the Place of Truth'. They reported directly to the vizier, as implied by their title, 'King's Scribe in the Place of Truth'. They lived either in the artisans' village itself, as Wennefer and Horisheri did, or close by. Among the tombs of the artisans we have found those of two scribes, Amenemope and Ramose, which are equal in size, decoration and furnishing to those of the foreman.

The main responsibility of the scribes in this community was to organise, check and record work progress on the tombs of the Valley of the Kings. At the start of each day they noted whether everyone had turned up for work, and the reasons for any absence. Remarks about various aspects of the work were put down on limestone sherds and later compiled into a ledger on scrolls kept in the scribe's office for future reference. From these a report was written up at regular intervals for the vizier.

The scribes had to draw all kinds of material from the royal warehouses – copper implements, plaster, charcoal, structural timber, cloth, candle grease and so on. These they held in their own storerooms, keeping a careful record. All tools and material issued to workers by the 'Guardians of the Tomb' had to tally with the scribes' records, not only as a check but as the basis for requisitioning fresh supplies from the appropriate warehouse.

It was the same with the grain stocks from which the scribes gave the workers their wages in kind. When deliveries were held up by the breakdowns in central government that occurred during the 20th dynasty, the scribes tried to cope with the emergency by touring the surrounding villages with a couple of stick-toting tomb-doorkeepers and levying grain for their community from the farmers. The scribes also shared responsibility with the foremen for ensuring public order and security both on and off the worksites.

Inside the artisans' village, too, the scribes made their impact by helping to solve any problem that required a document to be written or read. People came to them with their private complaints and quarrels, and brought suspect individuals for preliminary questioning. Where only minor offences, or *semedet* people matters, were involved, the scribes would try to settle the issue on the spot. Weightier ones were dealt with by the 'Court of the Tomb' on which the scribes also sat. Where human justice failed, the scribes would seek divine aid by placing written questions before the statue of the deified king Amenophis I, asking for his ruling to be announced by oracle.

Among other functions the scribes fulfilled those of the professional writers such as we can still see in countries where illiteracy persists. They drew up, and sometimes witnessed, all kinds of legal contracts, wrote letters to dictation, or read them for those who could not manage it themselves. They also wrote the funerary inscriptions on the coffins of deceased community workers and their families, and supplemented their incomes by doing the same service for clients outside the community. The tomb scribe Horisheri, for example, earned 95 copper *deben*, a considerable sum in 20th-dynasty Thebes, for his work as 'scribe and painter' on three coffins for Tanodjmet, a female singer in the service of Amon-Re.

Though their activities served the purposes of the élite, the majority of scribes functioned as hardworking, patient and efficient organisers of the everyday life of society. They constituted a fairly numerous network of educated men, contributing to the advancement of culture. Despite their numbers and their omnipresence in every branch of life they can hardly be considered as a brake on progress, analogous to 'bureaucracy' in its pejorative sense. Without their efforts the monuments of Egypt would only bear silent witness to ancient times.

CHAPTER SEVENTEEN

Inside the Temples

Left **238** Interior of the hypostyle hall of the great temple of Amun, Karnak. Upward view through the papyrus bud columns towards the window openings with a stone grille. 19th dynasty

Below **239** The dignity and authority of priesthood was perfectly captured by the sculptor who made this quartzite statue of chief lector-priest Petamenope. Karnak, 26th dynasty. *Cairo, Egyptian Museum*

EVERY VISITOR TO Egypt is intrigued by the large number of ancient temples, mostly of mammoth proportions. On their thick stone walls, massive gateways and slender sky-scraping obelisks the relief-carvers left forever the evidence of an ideology whose religion, with its pantheon of revered gods, secured the maintenance of cosmic order and of harmony between humans and the natural world all around them.

The very ubiquity of the temples shows how essential they were to the society of their day. But their religious purpose was not the whole story. Their sheer size, whether they were dedicated to gods or to the spirits of dead kings, hints at the ceaseless activity that went on inside their walls. Created though they were for religious ends, the temples had their estates and workshops, their libraries and the Houses of Life, all of which played a major part in the economic and intellectual life of the country. And often one temple was so close to another that whole temple complexes, even temple cities, arose like Giza, Abusir and Saqqara under the Old Kingdom, or the Western Town of Thebes, or Karnak, under the New.

The priestly caste with its rigid structure was a very numerous one. Thanks to all manner of privileges conferred on it by the king, the economic and hence the political influence of its leaders, the high priests, grew continually. They played an increasing role in government and in some periods, such as the end of the 20th dynasty, the High Priests of Amun aspired to and even attained the power of a pharaoh. So our picture of ancient Egyptian life would not be complete without some attention to the organisation of the priesthood and the daily life of its members.

We must begin by stressing the deep differences between the functions of the Egyptian priesthood and the Christian clergy. The Egyptian priest was no messenger of revealed truth, for the traditional view of the world as created, ordered and governed by the gods was handed down from generation to generation and permeated every aspect of everyone's life. Nor was he a preacher seeking to convert people to the faith or guide them toward the good life, for no one doubted the validity of the traditional religious ideology – if we except the heresy of Akhenaten, which was perhaps only a variant of the same dogma. People tried to live good lives in the hope of earning merit for the life to come, of whose reality they were mostly convinced. Where, in Christian devotions, believers worship a god who bestows his grace on them, the Egyptian priest rendered material and magic services to the god of his particular temple. In so doing he strove to ensure that god's presence on earth and, as a consequence, maintain the harmonious order of the world as the gods had created it. This was why the priests called themselves 'servants of the god' or 'slaves of the god', or in the Greek period 'prophets'.

In serving the gods the priests were acting on behalf of the king whose decisions

implemented the will of the gods on earth, and who was alone entitled to immediate contact with them by means of religious offices. This is why, in every period of Egyptian history, we find temple-wall reliefs forever repeating the motif of a king 7 standing face-to-face with this or that god, to whom he is making an offering. Being 243 himself a 'living god', he is drawn on the same scale as the supernatural being in front of him, with whom he is essentially on a par.

In view of the great number of deities and their temples the king could not cope alone with all the duties ensuing from his privileged status. Accordingly he devolved them on the priests, who day by day performed religious rites on his behalf through-out the realm. If we consider the creative energy and material resources that went into the running of the temples, we cannot avoid the conclusion that they were a considerable burden on the economy.

Before a priest could enter the innermost parts of the temple, where the god was pleased to reside with one part of his being in a statue in the dimly lit sanctuary, a complex purification procedure was necessary. This was not, as in Christianity, a

240 First pylon with an entrance into the temple of Isis which was recently transferred from the island of Pylae to the island of Agilkia. Ptolemaic Period

Right **241**   Tanefer, the Third Prophet of Amun, pouring libation and burning incense at a table laden with offerings of bread, wine, meat, fruit and flowers in honour of Osiris. Drawing on papyrus from the Book of the Dead of Tanefer. 21st dynasty. *Cairo, Egyptian Museum*

Below **242**   Sacrifice bearer with lotus and a crane. Painted limestone relief. 20th dynasty. *Cairo, Egyptian Museum*

spiritual act involving the avoidance and forgiveness of sins, but a sequence of physical operations. The largest group of low-ranking priests were in fact styled 'the purified ones'.

A basic precondition for ritual cleanliness was circumcision. If this had not been done in youth, the novice had to undergo the operation before he could be accepted into temple society. Herodotus (II, 37) remarks: 'They practise circumcision for the sake of cleanliness; for they set cleanliness above seemliness.'

A further requirement for priests was that their entire bodies should be clean-shaven. We have already quoted Herodotus's report (II, 37) that they did this every third day to avoid the danger of 'lice or any other uncleanliness'. This is why they always appear in illustrations bald-headed and without eyebrows or lashes. Even a foreigner inquiring into the secret sciences studied in the temples, like the Greek travellers Eudoxus of Cnidus, had to have his hair and eyebrows shaved off.

Priests also had to abstain from certain foods. Greek writers give a long list of banned items, such as the meat of a cow, pork and mutton, pigeon, pelican and fish (especially sea-fish), beans, garlic and all greenstuff. They were forbidden salt, and wine was allowed, if at all, only in small quantities. One might be tempted to feel sorry for the starving priest, but Herodotus (II, 37) paints a different picture: 'They neither consume nor spend aught of their own; sacred food is cooked for them, to each man is brought every day beef and geese in great abundance, and grape-wine too ... They may not eat fish.' It seems likely in fact that in each temple usually one or only a few items were forbidden, namely the kinds of meat or vegetables rejected by its particular god. Priests were also forbidden the meat of any species seen as an incarnation of the god, and therefore sacred.

Priests normally married and enjoyed family life, but according to Diodorus were only allowed one wife (though we know of exceptions to this rule). For several days before entering a temple they had to eschew sexual contact, and within the temple there was a ban on intercourse with priestesses or temple dancers, singers and musicians. Herodotus (II, 64) says that priests were forbidden to have intercourse inside a temple or to enter a temple after intercourse without first washing.

Their garb also distinguished priests from the rest of the population. In order to be ritually pure their clothes had to be woven from clean, fine linen thread and cut to a conservative Old Kingdom pattern. Whereas common folk went barefoot, the priests

241

wore white sandals. Lector-priests usually wore a ribbon across the chest. The higher ranks were favoured with special robes such as the leopard-skins worn over the shoulders by the *sem* priests; the high priest of Heliopolis had a dress sewn out of leather stars and his colleague of Memphis was adorned with a special necklace and a long plait fastened to his head.

After complying with all the requirements a priest still had to undergo the prescribed ritual ablution before he entered the inner sanctum. With large temples, we find on the inside of the periphery wall a capacious stone pool with a long set of steps leading down to the water so that the priest can sprinkle himself with it. Lesser temples had small pools or cisterns for the same purpose. The ablution was intended not only to wash away all the dirt of the home and the street, but to fortify the priest with the fresh vigour imparted by water as the cradle of life and the source of the sun's perpetual renewal. Herodotus claims (II, 37) that the priests washed 'twice a day and twice every night, in cold water'. Washing was supplemented by swilling out the mouth with a solution of natron and rubbing the body with oil, large quantities of which were consumed in the temples.

Ritual purification contributed no doubt to the priests' relatively high standard of health. If one also takes into account their relative affluence, adequate diet and housing, and tranquil mode of life under a strict regime that avoided crises,

Above **243** Ramesses II burning incense in honour of Amun in his sacred boat carried by priests masked as mythological creatures. Bas-relief, later reworked as sunk relief on the inside of the wall of the hypostyle hall of the great temple of Amun at Karnak. 19th dynasty

Right **244** The sacred lake was an important place at all large temples. Here the priests took part in ritual purification and held ceremonies involving the sailing of the barque of the god or goddess of the temple. Karnak

excitement or exertion, they enjoyed every prospect of a long and trouble-free existence.

As well as being clean in body the priests were supposed to abide by a strict code of ethics, though how far they respected it we cannot be sure. 'Never enter a temple in a state of sin or impurity', they were warned. 'Lay no false charges, be not desirous of profit, accept no bribes, spurn not the lowly in favour of the mighty, use no false measure or weight, tell no gossip about the rites you perform, for these are secrets peculiar to the temples.'

In contrast to Christian practice laymen could only enter the forecourt of an Egyptian temple, the inner parts being reserved for the priesthood. It will be useful to imagine ourselves watching a temple service.

After the heavy gates have been opened each morning the priests advance into the great hypostyle hall whose ceiling rests on great columns with capitals carved in lotus or papyrus patterns. Some of the priests carry plates of food or jugs of drink, others boxes with toiletries, still others water and incense. As they make their way one room succeeds another, each with its ceiling lower than the last, so that less and less light filters in through the ventilation holes and the air of mystery deepens. The procession comes to a halt before the closed doors of the central chapel. A clay seal, which has preserved the god's privacy all night, has to be broken and a bolt drawn. Then the leaves of the door swing open.

At the exact moment when the sun appears over the horizon the priests intone the dawn hymn 'Awake in peace, great god . . .' In the gloom of the chapel, lit only by a flickering candle, the most senior priest approaches the *naos* or sanctuary (a special structure, usually of basalt or granite), breaks its seal and opens it: the statue of the god is revealed. The priest stretches out a hand to 'give the god back his soul' and reassert his earthly shape, while he recites a prescribed prayer four times over. Amid the smell of incense the priests lay on the altar a breakfast of bread and cakes, meat, vegetables and fruit, not forgetting jugs of wine and beer. It will of course suffice the god (or, in funerary temples, the deceased) to consume the spiritual essence of these sacrifices, so that the material 'remainder' can be removed later and shared among the priests and the temple workshop staff. To ensure supplies of food for god and priests, every temple has its own estate, given to it by the king.

After breakfast follows the god's morning toilet. This is entrusted to the stolist-priest (*medjty*), who removes the old garment from the god's statue, washes the statue, rubs it with oil and dresses it in fresh clothes. This attire, like that of the priests, is made of finest linen from the temple's weaving shops and kept in a special storeroom. Every day four lengths of cloth, white, red, blue and green, are in this way

sacrificed for the god. Next the stolist makes up the god's face, anoints his forehead with *medjet* oil (using the little finger of his right hand) and recites sacred formulae. Finally he sprinkles the statue and the whole sanctuary with water, lays five grains of natron and resin on the floor in front of it, and envelopes it in more clouds of incense. Then the doors of the sanctuary are closed and resealed, the procession departs and each man goes about his further duties.

This ceremony was repeated each noon and dusk, but with the chapel and sanctuary remaining closed. The evening rites, similar to the morning ones, were performed in one of the side chapels; the noon service consisted only of sprinkling and infusing with incense the central chapel door and surrounding area.

Festival rites conducted on holidays were of quite a different kind. At these times the god's statue was taken out of the temple and carried in procession, or transported down the river, so that everyone could see it and even put questions to it. For such occasions it was richly adorned with jewellery from the temple treasury – magnificent necklaces, bracelets, sceptres, amulets and trinkets of gold or silver encrusted with lapis lazuli, enamel, glass and semi-precious gems which, glinting in the sun, underlined the god's greatness and majesty.

The statue was then put into a wooden shrine of the same shape as the stone sanctuary, standing in the centre of a light wooden barque. There was one of these in every temple on a stone platform beside the sanctuary or, in the case of large temples, in an open-sided chamber of its own. (In the temple of Amun at Karnak it was actually housed in a separate building.) The larger the temple, the bigger and heavier the barque, so that it might take several men to carry it on a sledge-shaped stretcher over their shoulders; sometimes it needed as many as 30 bearers walking in pairs, with poles resting on their shoulders. In front of the boat walked a priest with smoking incense, while other priests and onlookers followed behind. A less usual procedure was for the statue, like that of Min in the Delta town of Buto, to be conveyed on a cart drawn by men or by a pair of horses.

The cortège would halt from time to time to allow the bearers to rest and the priests to carry out the prescribed rites, burning incense, making offerings of food and drink, reciting more formulae and so forth. This also gave an opportunity for the god to 'respond' by oracle. If his reaction to the question put was favourable, the bearers would bow or proceed; if negative, they drew back.

For lengthy journeys the barque was put onto a real ship, often as much as 120 or 130 cubits long, which would touch at every harbour to be greeted by waiting crowds. It was on one such vessel that the statue of the goddess Isis was taken regularly from her seat on the island of Philae to various temples scattered throughout Nubia.

Another elaborate procession took place during the days of the *opet* festival at Thebes. This was during the joyful season of the Nile flooding and the holiday gradually grew from 11 days in the time of Tuthmosis III to a full 27 in that of Ramesses III. On these occasions the god Amun in the temple of Karnak was taken to visit his 'southern chapel' at Luxor. The ceremony can be seen on reliefs carved in the 'processionary colonnade' in the central section of the Luxor temple. The western wall there shows the god's journey from Karnak to Luxor; his return trip appears on the eastern side.

The cycle starts with the rites conducted before the barque containing the Amun statue inside the temple of Karnak; King Tutankhamun is shown in charge. In the next scene the barque is being carried on its stretcher by six rows of three or four priests, led by two *sem* priests. One priest strides in front of the vessel to clear the path, another wafts incense over it and a third sounds a trumpet. Behind Amun's barque other priests are carrying similar vessels with the figures of the god's son Khonsu, his wife Mut and Tutankhamun himself. Originally, as we know from reliefs in the chapel of Queen Hatshepsut at Karnak, the procession went overland from Karnak to Luxor, along an avenue of sphinxes with halts at six resting places. From Tutankhamun's time or even earlier, however, it only went as far as the harbour at Karnak where all the barques were loaded onto special Nile barges.

245 Painting of offerings on the wall and the night sky on the ceiling of the chapel of Anubis in the temple of Hatshepsut at Deir el-Bahari, West Thebes. 18th dynasty

243

Now follows the voyage along the Nile, shown in the relief as only a narrow strip of
248 water. The barques of Amun and of the king are placed on a large barge called
Userhet, while those of Khonsu and Mut are carried on a second vessel. The barges are
hauled, partly by a flotilla of sailing-boats, partly by groups of men with ropes along
the bank, for whom this task is a great honour. Many spectators are to be seen,
among them soldiers with their officer, men carrying standards, others praising
Amun and prostrating themselves in the dust, three Nubians dancing to the rhythm
250 of a drum, with clubs in their hands, two Egyptians and five Libyans dancing and
banging with sticks, some women shaking their sistra and a group of priests clapping
time.

In the next scene priests are carrying the barques on their shoulders up from the
harbour to the Luxor temple. Meanwhile eight bulls have been ritually slaughtered
on the river bank and six men are bringing the legs to the temple for sacrifice. In three
of the northwestern chapels of the first forecourt the barques are now shown resting
safely on their stands, and the king is making his offerings to the gods.

It would appear that the purpose of Amun's visit to Luxor was his mystic marriage.
This is indicated by the prominent role of the high priestess as 'wife of the god' in the
processions portrayed in the temple itself, and by the siting of the chamber designated
as the resting-place for Amun's barque next to the 'birth chamber' where the divine
conception of Amenophis III is depicted. The Egyptians evidently believed that Amun
had begotten the future king during one of his sojourns in Luxor. The old name for
Luxor, Ipet-reseyet or 'Harem of the South', also has to do with this sacred union.

The festival ends with the return voyage, portrayed by similar pictures in reverse
order. But the king accompanying the procession is this time Amenophis III, and
there is no need now for the barge to be pulled as it is floating downstream.

Commoners were allowed to put questions to a god also in his temple and for this
purpose, exceptionally, were admitted to special audience rooms. The priest would
intone the answers either through a concealed window high up in the wall, or from
inside a hollow statue. Questions could also be put in writing, as we know from short
texts preserved on ostraca at Deir el-Medina, asking for example: 'Is the calf good
enough for me to accept?' or 'Good master, is one of my goats with Ptahmose?' The
god's reply was usually a laconic Yes or No. Auguries were also taken from sacred
animals that were regarded as incarnations of the god. The bull of Apis, for example,
might be let out of its stall for its behaviour to be scrutinised.

Judicial functions were also performed by the priests at the temple gates. In the Late
Period there are frequent references to 'the gate that delivers justice'. People with a
guilty conscience would come to ask for a ruling, which the priest then pronounced

246 The ritual boat journey to the tomb
of Osiris at Abydos was undertaken by
pious Egyptians, although not necessarily
in their lifetime. Their great wish was to
be buried as close as possible to Osiris.
Tomb painting from Deir el-Medina.
West Thebes. End of 18th dynasty

247 Hymn to Amun, carved on the wall of the tomb of the vizier Ramose. West Thebes. 18th dynasty

in the god's name. We have no further information about these courts or the kind of cases they dealt with. Priests, moreover, sat on the bench at lay trials, which were often held in or near temples. This demonstrated the particular god's role in maintaining the rule of law on earth.

Many duties fell to the priests on connection not only with running the temples but with organising the operations of the temple workshops and farmlands, and the building or rebuilding of houses. They also spent time studying theology, law and other subjects in the temple libraries and Houses of Life, while at night they would climb up to the flat roof of the temple to observe the movements of the stars.

One often saw a priest bound on official business outside his temple. He was usually on a religious errand such as taking part in major festivals of neighbouring temples and shrines dedicated to the same deity as his own, or to that deity's spouse. The statue of the goddess Hathor, for example, would be taken by priests of her temple at Dendera 150km upstream to the temple of Horus at Edfu for a 'good meeting', in which the goddess could enjoy two weeks with her divine husband.

The highest-ranking priests attended councils of state in the royal palace and accompanied the king during his jubilee celebrations or on trips abroad. In the Ptolemaic Period priestly delegates, who had previously only met when the occasion demanded it, began to hold regular annual 'synods' to discuss matters of common interest under the chairmanship of the overseer of the 'Prophets of the Two Lands'.

The priest's profession conferred not only, as we have seen, social standing and an assured livelihood, but also a share in the life of the gods and consequently spiritual armour against any perils that loomed. So it is not surprising that the priesthood was a rather tight society into which few entered from non-priestly families. Herodotus states baldly (II, 37) that 'when a priest dies, he is succeeded by his son'. The steles of some Late Period priests carry lists of up to 17 generations of forebears who had served the same god. Succession was of course not automatic, since it required not only the royal assent (usually a formality) but approval by all the other priests of the temple in question.

If there were no other suitable candidate to fill a vacancy the priests would choose a young man from outside the caste, usually no doubt one whose father had benefited the temple in some way or performed honorary functions as a layman. A third method of succession was the purchase of a priestly function. There are occasional records of this from the Middle Kingdom, but in the Roman Period it became quite common.

We do not know precisely how novices were trained. They presumably had to master writing and learn various religious manuals by heart so as to acquire a

248 The sacred boat with Amun's tabernacle afloat. Relief on a block from Hatshepsut's Red Chapel, demolished by her successor Tuthmosis III. Karnak. 18th dynasty

grounding in theology. The attainment of priests probably varied enormously. Some were barely able to read, write and follow the services, but there were others whose intelligence broke through the closed system of traditional ideas and helped them lay the foundations of science. Every novice started his career with an inaugural ceremony in which he was purified with water, had his hands anointed and was then inducted before the god in his sanctuary. He was 'filled with awe at the god's might', we are told. This may have been the occasion for initiating him into the various temple secrets and magic incantations.

The strict hierarchy of functions that we have seen in other callings was nowhere more elaborate than in the priesthood, at least in the larger temples – in small ones the personnel was limited to a few men.

At the top of the pyramid, for each particular god, was his High Priest or 'First Prophet'. In the New Kingdom it was the High Priest of Amun of Thebes who exercised supreme authority and who was chosen by the king himself, usually from among subordinate priests of the temple of Amun, senior courtiers or army generals.

The appointment of the High Priest by Ramesses II, for example, was announced as follows: 'His Majesty has given Nebunef two gold rings and his electrum staff. He has been named High Priest of Amun, Overseer of the Twin Houses of Silver and Gold, Head of the Twin Granaries, Overseer of Works and Overseer of Artisans in Thebes. The King has sent his messenger to inform the whole land that he has been given the House of Amun with all its estates and people.' Similar fanfare attended the appointment of the High Priest of Re at Heliopolis, 'who is permitted to gaze on the Great (God Re)', and that of Ptah at Memphis, entitled 'Supreme Head of the Artists' because of his control over the extensive studios there.

Deputy High Priests ('Second Prophets') were responsible in particular for temple property. The Second Prophet was chief administrator of the estates, workshops and stores where all the gifts and spoils of war dedicated to the temple's god were kept. He had under him the respective overseers of the estates, scribes, soldiers, herds, fields, wheat and barley granaries, treasury and 'everything kept under the seal of Amun', plus the chief steward and other officials. And each of these officials had at hand a staff of scribes – specialists and assistants – to keep the economy of the temple running smoothly.

The largest ecclesiastically-controlled economic unit in the country was the estates and workshops of the temple of Amun at Karnak. A papyrus of the reign of Ramesses III says that it comprised 2393km² of arable land, 433 orchards, 421,362 head of livestock, 65 villages, 83 ships and 46 workshops or building sites, with a total labour force of 81,322.

The temple of Re at Heliopolis, again, owned 441km² of arable land, 64 orchards, 45,544 head of livestock, 103 villages, 3 ships and 5 workshops or building sites, with a personnel of 12,693. Thanks to the scribes' conscientious records we can see what a cardinal role temple estates must have played in the national economy.

Intermediate between the small club of high-ranking priests and the innumerable lower ranks were those whom Serge Sauneron classified as specialists, in that they had a clearly defined field or activity. These included the stolist-priests mentioned above, who looked after the cloth and jewellery belonging to their god, dressed and washed his statue every day and painted his face. Then there were the scholars who worked in the Houses of Life. The lector-priests (*khery-heb*) or 'reciters of the god's book', *pteroforoi* (winged ones) to the Greeks because of the two feathers they wore attached to their shaven heads, were essentially scribes who performed administrative duties, and recited ritual texts. As experts in magic medicine, charms and spells they 'performed rites pleasing to good spirits' at funerals. Another category were the *sem* priests, whose name originally denoted the first-born son responsible for his father's funeral. In the 3rd dynasty this became the official term for any layman performing the son's office at a funeral. In the New Kingdom this function evolved into a priestly office for the conduct of important rituals.

Doubt still surrounds the position of the 'hour-priests'. Some authorities believe they were laymen who ministrated for a limited period during temple services and

249 An alabaster offering table with two stylised lions supporting a tray sloping towards the deep vessel at the back, where the blood of the slaughtered animal was collected to avoid desecrating a holy place. Saqqara. End of 2nd–beginning of 3rd dynasty. *Cairo, Egyptian Museum*

250 Men performing a ritual dance at a festival. Relief in a private tomb. Sheikh Abd el-Qurna, West Thebes. 18th dynasty

were often rewarded with honorary clerical titles. Sauneron, however, thought they were practising astronomers who, by observing the movements of the sun and stars, were able to state the precise time when a service was due to begin.

Very different was the role of the *horoskopoi* (as the Greeks called them), versed in the mythological calendar with all its lucky, indifferent and unlucky days. They provided this information to all enquirers, for example at the birth of a child – whence the 'horoscopes' of later times. There were also interpreters of dreams, *oneirocrites*, with their own consulting rooms in the temples where, in the Late Period and after, clients were put to sleep so that they could receive advice from the god through oracular dreams.

Among the specialist priests we may also include the temple choristers and musicians who sang ritual texts, usually to a harp accompaniment. These were recruited from the musical sons of poor families who offered them to the temple to ensure them a better livelihood. Their status and income improved during the Graeco-Roman Period.

This last category sometimes included women. We can see them on many reliefs 64 singing, shaking tambourines or plucking stringed instruments. In temples dedicated 65 to goddesses the priestesses – usually priests' daughters or high-born ladies – were 66 allowed to hold other offices too. In the case of the temple of Amun at Karnak, as we 83 have seen, there was even an earthly consort of the god, the 'God's wife of Amun', a role enacted at ceremonies by a queen or a princess, or between the Third Intermediate and Saitic Periods by a royal virgin dedicated to Amun.

For routine temple activities there were usually four groups of priests, working in shifts for a month at a time. At the end of each shift there was a stocktaking of ritual requisites, everything being recorded on papyri or wooden tablets.

The most numerous groups of all priests were the low-ranking 'purified ones', *web*. These included the porter-priests who carried the sacred objects, the priests who sacrificed animals by ritually correct methods, the carriers of the sacred barque, the head gardeners and overseers of the temple draughtsmen, painters and scribes. The embalming priests had their own separate hierarchic structure.

The temple estates and workshops employed many laymen of various trades alongside the clerics. Old people, too, sometimes sought refuge under the wing of a temple, acquiring in return for an initial donation and casual help a place to live in for the rest of their days.

Temples, finally, were the cradle of the Egyptian theatre. On important feast-days religious plays were performed outside the gate of the temple at Abydos, relating the life, murder, resurrection and deification of Osiris, patron of the dead.

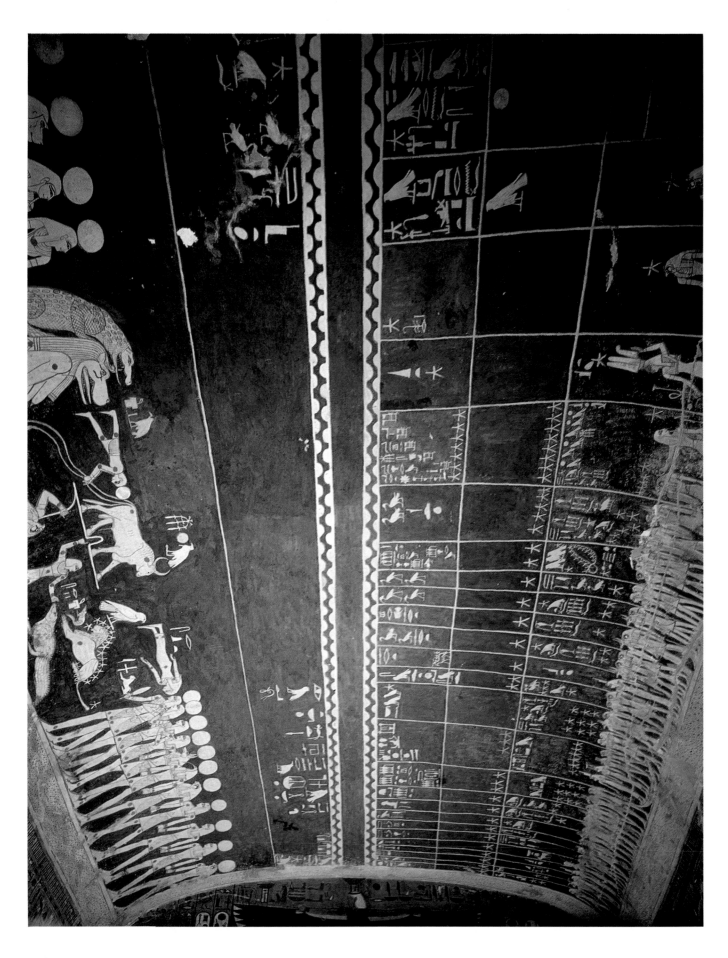

CHAPTER EIGHTEEN

The Scribes of the Houses of Life

Left **251** Ceiling of the sarcophagus hall in the tomb of Sethos I with the list of Northern Constellations and stars. Valley of the Kings, West Thebes. 19th dynasty

Above **252** A female hippopotamus with a crocodile on her back was one of the Northern Constellations. Detail of the ceiling in the tomb of Sethos I. Valley of the Kings, West Thebes. 19th dynasty

IN ATTEMPTING TO describe what the ancient Egyptian *per ankh* or House of Life really was and how it operated, we have to admit to an embarrassing lack of information. They are frequently referred to in ancient texts but we are seldom given any details about their organisation or function. All we know for certain is that they were closely linked to the major temples, which maintained them and benefited from their activity.

Houses of Life are known to have existed at Memphis, Akhetaten, Akhmim, Abydos, Koptos, Esna and Edfu, and probably elsewhere too. They seem to have comprised offices, planning rooms, laboratories and observatories where scribes wrote down, authenticated and copied religious and technical documents for various purposes, as well as textbooks incorporating empirical scientific findings to a greater or lesser extent.

It is easy to picture the *per ankh* scribes, whom the Greeks were to call *hierogrammatikoi* or experts in sacred texts, poring over their papyrus rolls. According to several sources the majority of them were indeed priests, yet the secular titles given to some of them show that some laymen were allowed to collaborate. Without a doubt they were the most educated men in the land, and in some fields they achieved remarkable results. Not surprisingly, it was from among these scribes that representatives of the priesthood were chosen at the king's behest to act as his advisors. One such was Petiese, a *per ankh* scribe selected to hand the bouquet of Amun to King Psammetichus II in 591 BC, on the grounds we are told that 'one could ask him anything' and he always knew the right answer.

Another institution closely connected with the House of Life was that of the temple archive or library, sometimes called the House of Books, dark little chambers whose walls were lined with recesses for papyrus rolls. Remains of rolls were found during the excavation of one such room in the little town of Tebtunis in the Faiyum. The walls of temples at Tod, Edfu, Esna and Philae are inscribed with title-lists of 253 documents originally housed in their libraries. One of the oldest libraries was at Hermopolis parva in the Delta. They were veritable treasure-houses of precious learning gleaned by the scribes from the wide-ranging culture of ancient Egypt and committed to writing.

The Egyptians' prowess in sacred scholarship was deeply admired by the learned men of ancient Greece, who looked upon Egypt as the cradle of science. They acknowledged the Egyptians as masters of theology, history of ancient kings, geography, astronomy, geometry, herbal medicine, the diagnosis and treatment of diseases and even in the techniques for invoking rain and soothsaying. Many Greeks accordingly went on research attachments to the *hierogrammatikoi*.

Thus we find Thales of Miletus pursuing astronomy and geometry in Egypt. Democritus spent five years there studying the same subjects. Plato lived among Egyptian priests for 13 years, reading geometry and theology, and came to admire their astronomy.

We learn some interesting facts about Pythagoras's stay in Egypt from his biographer Porphyry (AD 233 to c. 304). After being amiably received by King Amasis the scholar was sent first to the priests of Heliopolis, then to Memphis and finally to Thebes; there he was given a permanent position (to please the King) but treated with an offhandedness that showed he was no welcome guest. Despite the snubs, Pythagoras displayed such zeal in his studies that he won admiration and respect, and was even allowed to participate in sacrifices to the gods – an unheard-of honour for a foreigner. So he was in no hurry to return home and his attachment is said to have been extended to a full 22 years.

Yet however remarkable the discoveries made by the ancient Egyptians in several fields, there was a profound difference between modern science and the sacred learning of the Houses of Life. Where the modern scientist tries to get to the bottom of things by experiment, analysis and a continual process of advancing hypotheses which either prove inadequate and are replaced by others, or else lead to a general theory or to conclusions of wider application, the ancient Egyptian savant clung as a rule to the works of his predecessors, the magic authority of the written word.

This cannot always have been the case, however. At the start of the Old Kingdom in particular there seems to have been an exceptional wave of scientific discoveries. But as soon as a body of knowledge had been accumulated which satisfied daily needs, it was regarded as sufficient, binding and largely immutable. If some serious incident or catastrophe occurred where accepted wisdom offered no help, the priest-scholars, rather than trying to find out the reason, would turn to the writings of their distant predecessors to see how they had coped with some analogous situation.

It seems amazing to us that with such homage paid to authority and tradition, science was able to make any progress at all. When it did, it was usually not through any doubt being cast on previous views but empirically, by checking the results given by current methods and coming up with alternative solutions that were often better. So it was the pressure of practical needs that sometimes forced the scribes to lay their scrolls aside and look for new approaches to new problems.

An essential feature of ancient Egyptian science was its close ties with theology and with the prevailing notion of a world created in its entirety by the gods, perfectly ordered and unchanging. Their science was therefore concerned primarily with theological problems and questions arising from religious practice. The priests were forever copying out old texts, correcting errors and filling gaps. Thousands of copies were made of the Book of the Dead which guided the deceased on his journey to the hereafter. Other scribes provided the captions and draft sketches for artists working on the walls of tombs and temples. Philosophical debates arose from the various religious systems worked out in the principal temples of each important god, since they often gave conflicting explanations of how the world-order was created and maintained.

For 2000 years the priests continued in all their activities to use the 'classical' liturgical language, regardless of the growing gap between that and the popular tongue. For another eight centuries they wrote in the hieratic script, even though the still newer demotic script was being used in public administration since the 8th century BC. The time-lag shows how conservatively the priesthood adhered to the letter of their original texts.

Theology went hand-in-hand with magic, command of which gave one power over living beings, cosmic forces and even the deities themselves. It was by uttering spells that the priests kept their god resident in his statue and shielded him from the machinations of demons. Extant library lists mention books for 'capturing people, safeguarding the king in his palace, averting the evil eye, overthrowing Apophis, the enemy of Re and Osiris . . . dispelling evil spirits' and so forth.

Original works of literature did sometimes come from the Houses of Life, but most of

253 The library was located in the eastern section of the vestibule in the best preserved temple in Egypt. The temple of Horus at Edfu was begun in 237 BC and finished in 57 BC. Ptolemaic Period

them originated in all probability outside the temples, for instance in the schools for scribes. Only in the Late, and especially the Greek, Period did the temples embrace this activity too. The temple library of Tebtunis was found to contain several literary texts, a few copies of the Books of Instruction and three onomastic papyri, listing words according to their meaning.

The only history books in ancient Egypt were bare chronicles. The oldest such document is the so-called Palermo Stone with its 5th-dynasty inscription recording the names of predynastic and Old Kingdom kings, the height of the annual floods, dates of commercial and military expeditions and other major events of each reign. 257 The Turin King List, a papyrus from the time of Ramesses II, gives the length of each reign, to a very limited extent groups the kings into dynasties, and gives total figures for the duration of historic periods. In the temple of Sethos I at Abydos the King is shown making sacrifice to the 76 royal predecessors he recognised, starting with the legendary Menes, unifier of the two halves of Egypt and presumably identical with the historically documented Narmer. The first attempt at real historiography, albeit with quite a few mistakes, was the work of the priest Manehto in the reign of Ptolemy II. Priests were of course aware of many historical facts from the inscriptions on temple walls.

Geography was a subject in which the *per ankh* scribes were more successful in assembling data. There are some temples where the lowest register on the walls shows processions of sacrifice-bearers from the various provinces. Male figures with female breasts signify the Nile, purely female figures denote fertile tracts. Each figure carries local products and has the name of the province written over its head. The sequences were probably designed by priests with geographical knowledge. The most complete list, in the temple at Edfu, gives the names not only of the provinces but of 256 their capital cities and of the locally worshipped gods and goddesses. In addition we find the names of the chief priest and musician-priestess, of the sacred barque and the canal it was usually floated along, of the province's tree, the main holidays and religious bans on particular acts and foods, the name of that part of the Nile flowing through the province and the generic name of its fields and its *pehu* (probably the untilled wetlands). In a way, it is a religious almanac of the country.

238

Left **254** The divine union of earth god Geb and sky goddess Nut which preceded the creation of the world. Sarcophagus of Butehamun, scribe of the royal necropolis in Thebes. 21st dynasty. *Turin, Museo Egizio*

Right **255** In the act of creation the air god Shu holds aloft the sky goddess Nut, separating her from Geb. Sarcophagus of Butehamun. 21st dynasty. *Turin, Museo Egizio*

The Jumilhac Papyrus in the Louvre provides in addition to similar information, a list of all temples in the 18th province of Egypt, with inventories of sacred objects and records of associated mythology, holidays observed and productive property owned. There were probably analogous compilations for every province. A fragment of one has been found for the 3rd province of the Delta, and a list of holy sites in the province of Dendera, found in one of the crypts of the temple in the capital, was no doubt based on another. Some temple walls display even lists of distances and of the areas of provinces; the little alabaster temple of Sesostris I at Karnak is an example.

Royal exploits in Asia and Nubia extended the *per ankh* scribes' knowledge of geography outside Egypt. The plinths of the royal colossi in front of the temple gateways of Karnak and Luxor, for instance, display lists of the lands and cities conquered by Amenophis III, Ramesses II and Shoshenq I. Temples at Dendera and Edfu enumerate areas in Asia and to the south of Egypt which were being visited by prospecting and mining missions. The names of Asiatic and Nubian kings and princes hostile to Egypt appear on ceramic vessels and figures representing prisoners, designed to be smashed or used in black magic rituals.

Remarkable progress was made in astronomy by observation of the sky, notably

256 Figures representing different regions bearing local produce. Limestone relief. Birth-house (mammisi) of the temple at Kom Ombo. Ptolemaic Period

from the flat roofs of temple pylons. This was not done purely out of scientific curiosity but to meet the practical requirements of telling the time for temple services to begin, matching the public calendar with celestial time and correctly orienting sacred buildings such as temples and pyramids.

Ancient Egyptian astronomers were familiar with five planets: Mercury (*Sebegu*), Venus (as Evening or Morning Star), Mars ('Horus the Red'), Jupiter ('Bright Star') and Saturn ('Horus the Bull'). These they aptly characterised as 'the stars that know no rest'. The fixed stars were grouped in constellations, different from ours, which were evidently borrowed from the Babylonians; they are shown on the ceilings of some of the royal tombs, as in the Golden Hall of the tomb of Sethos I.

251
252

Special importance among fixed stars was assigned to Sirius, 'the Dog Star', equated with the goddess *Sepdet* (Sothis). With their remarkable talent for observation the astronomers of the Houses of Life had noted that this bright star, after being hidden below the Egyptian horizon for 70 days in the year, reappears in the morning sky just before sunrise at the beginning of the Nile floods, around 19 July by our reckoning. They accordingly made this day the start of the new year.

In popular usage the year was divided into three seasons of four lunar months each: the flood season, *akhet*, approximately July to October; the sprouting season, *peret*, November to February, and the harvest season, *shemu*, from March to June.

However, since the moon takes about $29\frac{1}{2}$ days to go round the earth, 12 lunar months only came to 354 days as against the solar year of just under $365\frac{1}{4}$ days.

Alongside the lunar or 'natural' calendar, therefore, the astronomers established for administrative purposes an artificial 'public' calendar in which there were also 12 months, but each of 30 days, to which 5 extra holidays (epagomenal days) were added corresponding to the 'birthdays' of the gods Osiris, Seth and Horus, and of the goddesses Isis and Nephthys.

This calendar was found to lag behind the solar year by about one day in every four years, so that it would in theory take 1460 years for the two to coincide again. The public calendar had therefore to be repeatedly shifted forward in relation to the natural one. It was not until the reign of the Emperor Augustus that the adjusted Alexandrian or Julian calendar – still observed by the Copts – was introduced. It had first been proposed by the synod of Egyptian priests in 238 BC, but was not adopted at the time. This calendar included a sixth 'extra' day every fourth year – our Leap Year.

The reconstruction of ancient Egyptian chronology by modern historians was based on this coincidence of the solar and public calendars every 1460 years, since Egyptian dates were only given in terms of the reigns of successive pharaohs.

At night, the time was determined by the aid of 'decans' listing the rising, culmination and setting of various stars during 36 ten-day periods in the year. Such tables can be seen in the tombs of Sethos I and Ramesses IV.

Eclipses of the sun, which in other countries inspired fright as divine interventions, were seen by the astronomers of the Houses of Life as perfectly natural 'meetings of the Sun and Moon'. A fragmentary document from the reign of Tuthmosis III describes the unique appearance of a bright body in the southern sky. This is one of the earliest reports of a comet, probably Halley's.

Just why the Egyptians were so concerned to have their sacred buildings oriented in a precise direction we do not know. Evidently there were underlying religious motives, the East being seen as the place where Horus was reborn while the West was where the Kingdom of the Dead lay, the domain of Osiris. Certainly they made every effort to achieve maximum accuracy; we have already seen that the axis of the Great Pyramid at Giza is aligned only a few minutes of arc from the geographic (not magnetic) north pole. How were the Egyptians able to do this? They could not have used what we now call the Pole Star in the constellation of the Plough, since in ancient times the earth's axis pointed not to this but to the star Alpha Draconis, and some modern writers have suggested that this was the one the Egyptians used to find true north. However, Zbyněk Žába has pointed out that Alpha Draconis was only exactly in the north in 3440 BC and again in 2160 BC, not during the period 2700 to 2400 BC when most of the pyramids were being built.

257 Part of the list of the kings of Egypt. Kings of the 18th dynasty are named in the upper row; the names of Ramesses II are repeated in the lower row. Painted relief from the temple of Ramesses II in Abydos. 19th dynasty. *British Museum*

Žába suggests that the astronomers used another method, observing the maximum deviations of the star Pi Ursae majoris and determining true north by splitting the difference. For this they could have used the *merkhet*, a primitive astrolabe with an L-shaped frame. A weighted cord was suspended from the short arm, which was pointed upwards. While one man held the long arm horizontal, another could determine direction from a certain distance through a notch in a palm-rib. Gustave Goyon has noticed, when looking from the Great Pyramid at Giza, that the north-south axis might have been in line with some significant point on the horizon such as a tower or tall building in Khemu (Letopolis), the capital city of the Delta's 2nd province.

The scribes' skill in arithmetic and geometry was of great practical value. They used the decimal system of numbers that comes most naturally to man as a creature with 10 fingers. Several mathematical treatises have survived – including the Moscow, Berlin, Kahun and Rhind Papyri. These do not contain any general definitions, rules or equations showing a theoretical grasp of the subject, but only practical hints for solving particular problems, and exercises for students.

For measuring the Egyptians used, as we have seen, the royal cubit (52.36cm) composed of 7 hand-widths, each of 4 thumb-widths. For field surveys larger units were needed – the *meh-ta* (*ta*) equal to 100 royal cubits and for areas the *setjat* (later called *arura*) of 100 cubits square.

In geometry the Egyptians knew that a triangle whose sides are in the ratio 3:4:5 has a right-angle opposite the hypotenuse, and some authorities believe that they knew the principle of Pythagoras's Theorem. They were able to calculate areas of triangles and quadrilaterals, and they made an effort to get closer to the area of a circle by using for *pi* first of all 3, but later the square of sixteen-ninths or just over 3.16 – very close to our customary approximation 3.1416. They calculated the angle of the face of a pyramid from the ratio of its height to half its base; in the case of the Great Pyramid this was 14:11, giving an angle of 51°52'. A recent study by Jaroslav Švastal suggests they may have worked out the angle by a geometric function using the Golden Section.

The most important of the mathematical treatises is the Rhind Papyrus, copied around 1660 BC by the priest Ahmose from an older, 12th-dynasty work. In its 84 exercises fractions with numerator 1 are in common use, and there is a special table giving the values of fractions with numerator 2. It seems that the Egyptians were able to solve equations with one unknown, as in the following problem: 'A certain quantity (*hau*, "what is sought") plus one-seventh of it equals 19. Find *hau*.' This is solved by regarding *hau* as 7 parts and adding another to make 8, then dividing 19 by 8 to get $2\frac{1}{4}+\frac{1}{8}$ and multiplying this by 7 to find *hau* equal to $16\frac{1}{4}+\frac{1}{8}$...

To ensure supplies of fragrant unguents for the statues of their gods the priests had to know the recipes. In the temple of Edfu the walls of one room, now called the laboratory, are covered with hieroglyphic instructions for preparing sacred perfumes: the basic ingredients, the quantities of each additive, how long to boil and cool them. The library of the same temple contained a book with 'all the secrets of the laboratory'. In other temples too, such as at Karnak and Esna, there were little rooms for making and storing fragrant substances. It is no doubt in such places that drugs for human and veterinary medicine were made out of mineral, vegetable and animal materials, including the herbs mentioned in chapter 8.

Some of the *per ankh* scribes and the stolist-priests had considerable zoological knowledge. According to Herodotus (II, 38) they tested the ritual cleanliness of bulls and had strict rules for selecting new specimens to succeed sacred animals such as the falcon at Edfu and Philae, the bull of Apis at Memphis, the ram at Mendes and the crocodile at Crocodilopolis.

A list of Egyptian priests' books compiled by Clement of Alexandria does not mention any works on medicine. However, the discovery of medical texts amongst other papyri in the temple at Tebtunis, and the medical titles accorded to many priests, show that medicine was one of the subjects studied in the Houses of Life, as discussed in the following chapter.

CHAPTER NINETEEN

For Every Malady a Cure

OF ALL THE branches of science pursued in ancient Egypt, none achieved such popularity as medicine. Homer put it aptly in the Odyssey (IV, 229–232):

> That fecund land brings forth abundant herbs,
> Some baneful, and some curative when duly mixed.
> There, every man's a doctor; every man
> Knows better than all others how to treat
> All manner of disease . . .

There was even a degree of specialisation quite remarkable for the time, if we are rightly informed. Herodotus (II, 84) asserts that 'The practice of medicine is so divided among them that each physician treats one disease, and no more. There are plenty of physicians everywhere. Some are eye-doctors, some deal with the head, others with the teeth or the belly, and some with hidden maladies . . .'

The usual term for a doctor was *sunu*, written with an arrow-shaped symbol that, it had been suggested, was an allusion to the use of arrowheads to lance abscesses.

Some doctors belonged to the priesthood, including priests of the goddess Sakhmet, patroness of diseases, remedies and physicians, and of the lector-priests (*khery-heb*). Some again were counted among the scribes, as shown in such titles as 'chief doctor and scribe of the word of god'. Many enjoyed ecclesiastical as well as lay titles.

Like other professions doctors had their hierarchy. Besides ordinary doctors there were senior doctors, inspectors, overseers and masters of physicians and the 'Chief of Physicians of the South and the North', a kind of minister of health. Royal and palace doctors had their special hierarchy and titles.

The Belgian scholar Frans Jonckheere counted 82 doctors known by name, many with titles suggesting specialisation in some defined area. Hermann Grapow, however, is probably right in thinking of them as simply exemplifying the various skills which the doctor might possess. Thus the 6th-dynasty court physician and high priest Pepyankh, known as Iry, was not only 'doctor to the king's belly' and 'shepherd of the king's anus', but also 'the king's eye-doctor'. There has been much dispute recently as to whether dentistry ranked as a separate calling; there are only five references to it in the Old Kingdom and another isolated one in the 26th dynasty. Nor has it yet been settled whether any of the doctors known to us conducted research.

There were no female nurses to help the doctors, but we do know of male nurses, dressers, masseurs and lay therapists.

It would be wrong to see connections between the medical profession and that of the embalmers, priests of the god Anubis. Contrary to older ideas that Egyptian doctors took part in the preparation of mummies to improve their knowledge of

258 Chief of Dentists and Physicians Hesire was an important dignitary who had several other titles. He is shown with inkwells in a palette, a pen case and a bag over his shoulder. In his left hand he is holding a staff and the sceptre symbolising his authority. Wooden panel. 3rd dynasty. *Cairo, Egyptian Museum*

243

anatomy, it must be re-emphasised that most of their information came from ancient texts in which descriptions of the internal organs were based on analogy with animal bodies. The embalming procedure had nothing in common with medical autopsies.

The physician learnt his trade in the Houses of Life, notably at Per Bastet in the New Kingdom and at Abydos and Sais in the Late Period. He was no doubt given some practical experience, but chiefly he had to study what was already written. As the Ebers Papyrus says: 'His guide is Thoth, who lets the scrolls speak for themselves, compiles treatises and expounds knowledge to the savants and doctors who follow in his path.'

Diodorus too confirms this (I, 82, 3): '[They] administer their treatments in accordance with a written law which was composed in ancient times by many famous physicians.' From his further statement that 'on their military campaigns and on their journeys in the country they all receive treatment free of charge', it appears that for some people, at least, there was a system of free medical aid, such as we know existed also at Deir el-Medina. But on other occasions doctors expected to be handsomely reimbursed, as we can tell from a scene in the 18th-dynasty tomb of the doctor Nebamun at Dra Abu el-Naga. There we see a patient, supported by his wife, (both dressed in Syrian style), being handed some medicine by Nebamun's orderly. Behind this group and on another register is a file of servants bringing the doctor his fee – a copper ingot, a set of vessels (full, no doubt) and several little slave-girls.

The medical texts were not only the fount of professional knowledge but an insurance against possible failure. Diodorus saw this clearly (I, 82): 'If they follow the rules of this law as they read them in the sacred book and yet are unable to save their patient, they are absolved from any charge; but if they go contrary to the law's prescriptions they must submit to a trial with death as the penalty.'

Of the eight extant medical compendia the most important is the Ebers Papyrus, a collection of about 700 prescriptions for treating internal diseases arranged according to the organ concerned. This was built up between the 4th millennium BC and the New Kingdom through the continual addition of fresh material. The Hearst Papyrus, by contrast, probably represents the memoranda of a practising doctor of the 18th dynasty in which he had written out remedies from other works, the Ebers

259 A blind harpist playing at a banquet. Detail of a wall painting in the tomb of Nakht, Sheikh Abd el-Qurna, West Thebes. 18th dynasty

Below left 260 The Queen of Punt and her husband, the Chief of Punt, receive members of an expedition sent by Queen Hatshepsut. The representation of the excessively obese Queen shows clear signs of lipodystrophy or Decrum's disease: steatopygia, pronounced curvature of the spinal column, and folds of fat on her arms and ankles. Fragment of a painted limestone relief from the Temple of Hatshepsut at Deir el-Bahari. 18th dynasty. *Cairo, Egyptian Museum*

Right 262 A pot-bellied black dwarf supporting a nude child who is astride his back. The hieroglyph meaning 'protection' on top of his head suggests that the object had a magical purpose. Late Period. *New York, Norbert Schimmel Collection*

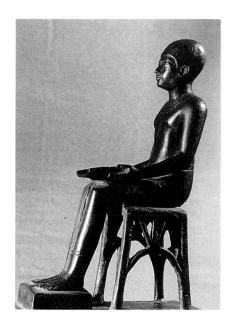

261 A votive statuette of Imhotep, the architect to Djoser who built the world's first monumental stone building, the step pyramid. He was revered for his healing skills, and was later deified as the god of medicine and healing. *St Petersburg, Pushkin Museum*

Papyrus among them. The Edwin Smith surgical papyrus shows a profound empirical knowledge of the different types of injuries and how to treat them: this is a copy from the Second Intermediate Period of a work at least 1000 years older. Other medical documents include the Great Berlin Papyrus, the London Papyrus, Chester Beatty Papyrus No. VI, Papyrus Ny Carlsberg No. VIII and the Kahun Papyrus, the last dealing with gynaecology. These are largely copies of Old Kingdom treatises made during the Middle and New Kingdoms.

Examination of both medical and non-medical documents has convinced many investigators that the ancient Egyptians knew their anatomy in fair detail. In addition to externally visible features there are many names of internal organs well known from butchery and cooking.

Notions of physiology and disease were all anchored in the concept of the heart as the centre of the organism. It was the site of the soul, the reasoning faculty, qualities of character, and emotions. It was through the heart that god spoke, and the Egyptian received knowledge of god and god's will. The heart was one's partner; it spoke to a person in his or her solitude. It was at the same time the engine of all the bodily functions, not only of one cardinal function, the circulation, as modern science revealed. From the heart proceeded channels (*metu*) linking all parts of the body together. These channels, the Egyptians believed, conveyed not only the blood, but also air (reaching the heart from the nose, they thought), tears, saliva, mucus, sperm, urine, nutriment and faeces, as well as harmful substances (*wehedu*) conceived to be the agents of pain and illness. Not only blood vessels were considered as *metu*, but also the respiratory tract, tear duct, ducts of various glands, spermatic duct, the muscles, tendons and ligaments. The female organs were likewise seen as tubes open into the internal cavity; the eye was supposed to communicate with the ear and the only purpose of the brain was to pass mucus to the nose, with which it was also thought to be connected. The Egyptian idea of the human body, then, was as a network of interconnecting channels and analogous to the branches of the Nile and the artificial canals of their own country.

It was soon realised that in some of the *metu* the heart 'spoke' and a doctor could 'measure the heart' from this beat. But he could only tell if the heart was going faster or slower by comparing the patient's pulse with his own. The concept of circulation was still beyond the Egyptians' knowledge, since they did not distinguish between arteries and veins, nor appreciate that the blood returned to the heart.

The precondition of good health, they thought, was free flow through the *metu*; ailments arose when they became blocked, just as with irrigation canals. Thus if a woman was infertile this was because the sexual channel was closed, and constipation or accumulation of the blood were likewise causes of disease.

Harmful substances might find their way into the *metu* through the natural orifices, mainly by the ingestion of bad food. But they could also originate inside the gut, and doctors were therefore much exercised to ensure its regular evacuation. Sometimes seeing worms in the stool, they deduced that these too might have come into the body through the mouth and cause a disease. They gave them various names, such as the '*hefet* worm in the stomach', and the '*pened* worm', and attributed toothache to the *fenet* worm gnawing at the tooth.

With externally visible damage like wounds and fractures the causes were often obvious. But with many internal ailments doctors were at a loss, so they imputed them to irrational influences, usually gods – either hostile and malignant deities, or well-intentioned ones who sent down plagues as a punishment for wrongdoing. Sickness might also be the work of evil demons, or of an envious neighbour's evil eye.

It would far exceed the scope of this chapter even to enumerate the diseases of ancient Egyptians that our researches have so far revealed. The evidence comes from several sources; from identification of their names and from their description in the texts, from their characteristic appearance in portrayals of the human body, from the study of pathological tissues in mummies and, in the case of diseases of bones and teeth, from the examination of human skeletal remains from burial sites. The study of all these sources constitutes the recently defined discipline of paleopathology.

263 Achondroplastic dwarf Seneb and his family. Seneb was Chief of all the Dwarfs of the Clothing. His wife shows her affection for him. By placing the children in front the sculptor succeeded in making Seneb's deformity less conspicuous. Painted limestone. Giza. 4th or early 5th dynasty. *Cairo, Egyptian Museum*

According to medical texts the ancient Egyptians recognised some 200 types of sickness, though there is no mention of diseases of the lungs, liver, gall-bladder, spleen, pancreas or kidneys – the symptoms evidently eluded them. We can of course never be sure what any named disease refers to unless its symptoms or recommended treatment are mentioned in the same context.

The descriptions of external lesions and in particular of wounds are fairly clear. A wound is said to have a 'mouth' and 'lips' and may 'go as far as the bone'. It is usually accompanied by bleeding, which in the case of severe injuries to the skull, may come from the nose and ears too. The Ebers Papyrus (Case 8) mentions that a skull fracture haemorrhaging into the brain can cause paralysis, on the same side of the body it says, not the opposite side – perhaps this was a copyist's error. The Smith Papyrus (Case 7) quotes a man with a gaping head-wound as showing the symptoms of tetanus: 'His mouth is locked tight . . . his brow is convulsively contorted and he has the expression of a man crying.'

The Egyptians distinguished simple fracture, *sedj*, where the bone is broken in two, and complicated fractures, *peshen*, resulting in numerous fragments.

Conditions characterised by a bulging of the affected part were classified either as *shefut*, commonly translated as 'swellings' but in view of some scholars references to a liquid content possibly including abscesses too, or as *henhenet* and *aat*, thought

to denote tumours. The former were treated with dressings, the latter by excision.

Most of the ophthalmic and internal maladies mentioned in the texts are difficult to identify with certainty. The only unambiguous ones are constipation, inflammation of the rectum, cystitis, and blood in the urine, usually due (in Egypt) to bilharzia, equated by Ebbell and Jonckheere with the disease *aa*.

We are on safer ground where we can find illustrations drawn by artists with a feeling for characteristic changes of appearance. The Queen of Punt, familiar to us from a relief in the temple of Hatshepsut at Deir el-Bahari, suffered from abnormal obesity, probably lipodystrophy. The eunuchoid appearance of Akhenaten towards the end of his reign suggests Fröhlich's syndrome resulting from malfunction of the pituitary gland or of the mesencephalon, most probably due to a tumour. There are many depictions of dwarfs, distinguishable from the ethnic pygmies of Africa by their abnormal proportions. Among hunchbacks one can distinguish angular deformation, resulting from tuberculosis of the spine, from curvature brought on by bad posture, rickets, ankylosing spondylitis and so on. Atrophy of the lower part of the right leg in the priest Remi as shown on his stele in the Ny Carlsberg Glyptotek in Copenhagen was evidently an after-effect of poliomyelitis. The 5th-dynasty mastabas of Ptahhotep and Mehu at Saqqara show a number of men with umbilical or scrotal hernias. Portraits of blind harpists, or of the blind man walking behind a field

260
264
262
263
268
265
259

264 The acromegalic and eunuchoid features of Akhenaten could have been connected with Fröhlich's syndrome, due to disturbance of the hypophysis or the mesencephalon. This is one of several such heads which belonged to colossal statues of the King in the peristyle court of the temple of Aten built near the great temple of Amun at Karnak. Sandstone. 18th dynasty. *Cairo, Egyptian Museum*

Right **265** Priest Remi depicted with a shorter and thinner right leg, apparently the result of poliomyelitis contracted in childhood. His wife and child are with him. Funerary stele of Remi. 18th dynasty. *Copenhagen, Ny Carlsberg Glyptotek*

surveyor in the tomb of Menna, suggest the widespread occurrence of trachoma, which often ends with blindness.

The study of pathological conditions in mummies has been going on for about 170 years. As early as 1825 A.B. Granville diagnosed a malignant ovarian tumour in the mummy of an elderly woman of the Ptolemaic age. Microscopic examination of another elderly female mummy, carried out by Jan N. Czermak in Prague in 1851, revealed arteriosclerosis. After the turn of the century autopsies of mummies began giving way to X-ray examinations which do not damage the mummy, and these have now been conducted in many of the world's collections. In Czechoslovakia alone the author was able to examine 170 Egyptian mummies and mummy-fragments in this way between 1971 and 1974 in collaboration with the radiologist Luboš Vyhnánek and others. Since the 1970s practice has partly reverted to autopsies, this time aimed at removal of tiny tissue samples for examination by modern techniques. All these findings have greatly enlarged our knowledge of ancient Egyptian pathology.

One important achievement has been the examination of fragments of lung tissue overlooked by the embalmers when they were removing the soft parts from inside the body. It has shown that Egyptian lungs, like ours, contained coal dust in the lymphatic nodules (anthracosis), probably through inhaling smoke from open fires. Hypertrophied connective tissue between the alveoli, and the lymphatic vessels of other mummies proved to contain minute sharp-edged particles of silicates, felspars and other granite minerals (silicosis). In other cases lungs were found to be covered with dust of fine desert sand (pneumoconiosis). Other mummies again showed changes characteristic of pneumonia, sometimes complicated by pleuritis or pericarditis. One proven case of pulmonary tuberculosis and numerous findings of spinal tuberculosis attest that the disease in general must have been widespread.

Microscopic investigation of other organs has confirmed the high incidence of parasitic diseases, especially those caused by worms – bilharziosis, trichinosis and infestations of thread-worms, tape-worms, liver-flukes, *Strongyloides*, *Trichuris trichiura*, *Ancylostoma duodenale* and *Dracunculus medinensis*. Amoeboid cysts have also been described. All this indicates the poor standard of hygiene, especially in the countryside where people were accustomed to go barefoot through mud and water, to drink polluted water and to eat unwashed fruit and vegetables.

Enlargement of the spleen, which might be due to malaria or to the intestinal form of bilharziosis, was found in the 19th-dynasty mummy of a poor weaver called Nakht, whose entrails had been left in.

Of the major infectious diseases, small-pox and poliomyelitis have been found in mummies. Metabolic disturbances leading to gallstones have so far only been shown in three instances, but stone in the urinary tract has been found quite frequently. A great surprise has been the discovery of arteriosclerosis in 10 to 20 per cent of all adult mummies, which hardly accords with our notion of the Egyptians' tranquil life-style and healthy diet. Evidently the middle and upper classes – those whose bodies were customarily embalmed – were far from abstemious, enjoyed animal fat, and were subjected to stress from time to time.

Several series of skeleton finds have thrown light not only on the pathology of bones and teeth, but sometimes also on skeletal reaction to disease in the adjacent soft tissues which had long since decomposed. The large numbers of investigated individuals have made statistical conclusions possible on rates of prevalence and age-correlation. These skeletons have also provided our only data on health conditions among the poor, who could only afford partial mummification or none at all.

A common phenomenon was the growth of marginal excrescences on the vertebral bodies (spinal osteophytosis), starting before the age of 30 and found in almost every individual in the 40–50-year age group, often very long, and sometimes tending to fusion. That this condition occurs much less frequently in mummies is explained by the fact that people affluent enough to afford embalming did not have to exert themselves as much as the rest of the population whose spinal wear-and-tear was very considerable. Total rigidity of the spine (ankylosing spondylitis) resulting from inflammatory disease (Bekhtyerev's disease) has turned up relatively rarely, in

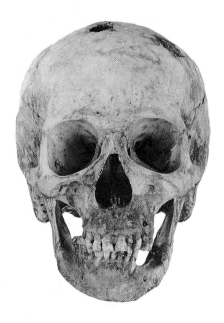

266 Two metastatic lesions on the top of the skull of a 35–45-year old woman most probably caused by carcinoma of the breast. Christian cemetery at Sayala in Egyptian Nubia. 6th–11th century AD. *Vienna, Naturhistorisches Museum*

267 The cranial base of a 40–50-year-old male destroyed by the invasive growth of a nasopharyngeal carcinoma. Cemetery at Naga el-Deir. 6–12th dynasties. *Berkeley, Robert H. Lowrie Museum of Anthropology*

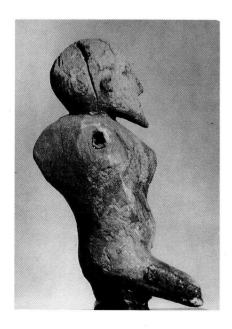

268 Sharp angulation of the spine of a hunchback suggests affliction with tuberculosis. Wooden statuette. *Brussels, Royal Museum of Art and History*

Below 269 The last four thoracic and the first lumbar vertebrae of Khuyankh, an official and probably priest of the royal necropolis, were damaged by tuberculosis, producing a sharply curved deformation, but completely healed. Abusir. Middle Kingdom. *Excavations of the Czechoslovak Institute of Egyptology*

Below right 270 Calcified myoma of the uterus, a benign tumour, found in a 35–45-year-old woman. Sayala, Egyptian Nubia. 3rd–5th century AD. *Vienna, Naturhistorisches Museum*

contrast to over 30 described cases of spinal tuberculosis, often with vertebral collapse and angular deformation.

In several series of skeletons examined wounds and fractures were common. They occurred almost entirely among adults, three times more frequently in men than in women, reflecting their greater liability to accidents at work or in combat. The fractures present a surprisingly favourable picture of subsequent knitting without marked deformation or pseudoarthrosis except in fracture of the femur, where the powerful muscle tension often led to shortening and formation of substantial calluses. Degenerative disease of the joints (arthrosis) was found commonly, inflammatory changes (arthritis) only rarely.

Benign bone tumours occurred in almost every series of skeletons, whereas in the literature only seven cases of malignant growth have been described to which we can add one cancer we found in a 40–50-year-old man in the Old Kingdom cemetery at Naga el-Deir. This tumour, probably arising in the naso-pharyngeal epithelium, had destroyed most of the facial skeleton and the front half of the cranial base. In recent excavations of Late to Ptolemaic cemeteries at Abusir and Saqqara we came upon four skulls with numerous small round osteolytic lesions, due either to metastatic carcinoma or to a primary bone tumour (myeloma multiplex). The small number of tumours found in general is a function of the short average life-span of the Egyptians, and perhaps also of inadequate effort devoted to looking for them in the past.

266

The incidence of gout is still an open question; only one definite case has been proved, in a 6th-century AD cemetery on the island of Biga near Philae. The same applies to leprosy, reported once from the same site and period, though more recently Tadeusz Dzierzykray-Rogalski found four skulls with bone damage in the upper jaw, which might have been due to leprosy in a Ptolemaic cemetery at Balat in the el-Dakhla Oasis.

The most serious congenital abnormality recorded is no doubt achondroplasia, a failure of ossification producing dwarfs. Kent R. Weeks described nine skeletons of this type from different periods confirming the iconographic evidence that it was relatively common, being no doubt maintained in the population by inbreeding.

166
263

Dental disease is a story of its own. The main problem in ancient Egypt was not decay, but the rapid and intense wear of teeth. This led to the crowns being flattened with possible exposure of the pulp, a danger to which the organism reacted by forming 'secondary dentine'. If the speed of abrasion exceeded that of the defence mechanism, the pulp was finally exposed and inflammation followed. Infection then often passed down through the roots to the socket, causing abscesses that destroyed the attachment of the tooth. The contents of the abscess would then be released either

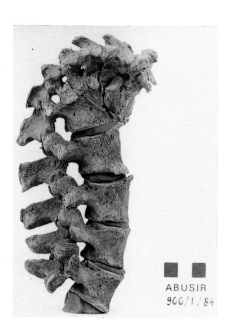

ABUSIR
900/1/84

through a bone fistula or by the tooth falling out. Most investigators attribute the rapid wearing-down of Egyptian teeth to the heavy consistency of their diet and the presence in it of fine silicate dust, either from the flour grinders or wind-borne from the desert.

It is not surprising that due to poor oral hygiene periodontitis and tartar were found frequently in every series.

Among the orthodontic defects found were minor anomalies such as prognathism, protruding teeth, crowding of the lower incisors and canines, displacement and rotation of teeth, impacted wisdom teeth (and occasionally other teeth), adult retention of milk teeth and the like.

Though we have not mentioned all the conditions identified, and many others no doubt remain to be found, enough has been said to show that the ancient Egyptian physician had plenty to do. It is time to consider whether he had the knowledge and the means to give useful treatment.

Over 200 remedies are mentioned in the texts, but not all of them would have been pharmacologically effective. They were derived from about 70 species of animals, 25 plants, 20 minerals and a number of common foodstuffs, drinks and secretions. Among them were the flesh, fat, blood, milk, gall, faeces and urine of animals and humans, and the leaves, fruit and powdered roots of such plants as henbane, thorn-apple and mandrake, to mention only the three most likely to have produced results. Some of the less convincing remedies were fresh dew, lumps of Nile mud, dirt from a patient's finger-nails and mouse excrement. The active ingredients were mixed by the doctor himself with bases such as milk, honey, sweetened beer or oil, and for ointments oil or fat. There is no evidence of specific pharmaceutical equipment, so presumably household vessels, mortars, rods, spoons and so on were used.

Enemas and vaginal douches may well have been administered through an animal horn with the tip cut off. Believing that noxious substances enter the body in food, or arise in the digestive tract itself, the Egyptians 'look after the health of their bodies by means of enemas, fasting and emetics, sometimes every day and sometimes at intervals of three or four days. For they say that the larger part of the food taken into the body is superfluous and that it is from this superfluous part that diseases are engendered,' to quote Diodorus (I, 82, 1). Modern dieticians will no doubt applaud.

Eye-drops were administered with a vulture's quill. Inhalations were prepared by heating a given substance on a hot stone, the vapour being breathed in through a reed coming out of an inverted pot placed on top. For genital fumigation women sat on a pot in which the recommended substances were similarly heated.

Surgery was performed with knives, forceps, and wooden or metal probes. A relief in the Ptolemaic temple of Kom Ombo shows a case of instruments which might have been used for surgical, dental or cosmetic purposes, though some commentators suggest that they were objects ritually deposited at the foot of the foundation wall when the temple was being built.

For dressing wounds ordinary linen bandages, sutures, nets, pads and swabs were used. In setting fractures recourse was made to palm ribs, strips of bark, reeds or wooden splints bound with canvas or plant fibre.

Treatment of wounds was something Egyptian doctors were quite skilled in. References to 'threads' in this context suggest that they may have sewn them sometimes, but normally they drew the edges together with bandages. For the first day they would cover a wound with fresh meat, then on each of the following days apply a dressing soaked in oil or honey. Severe or inflamed wounds were left uncovered, drenched in oil, kept cool and allowed to dry.

The Edwin Smith Papyrus shows how competently they dealt with dislocations.

> If you have to treat a man whose lower jaw is dislocated, so that
> his mouth stays open and he cannot shut it, you must place
> both forefingers on the ends of the arms of the jaw-bone
> inside his mouth and both thumbs under his chin. Then you must
> draw [the heads of the dislocated bone] downward until they

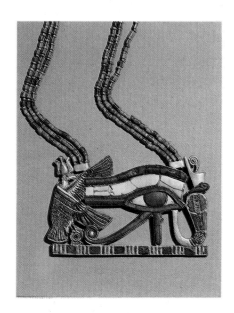

are resting in their right place. At the same time you must say: 'A man with a dislocated jaw – that is the sickness I shall treat.' Then you will put on a poultice with *imeru* and honey each day until it is better.

When knives were used for opening 'tumours' – the same word applied to abscesses – they were first heated over a fire so that they would staunch the bleeding; unwittingly, of course, the physician had thereby sterilised them too. Blisters and warts were pierced with glowing splints or red-hot metal probes. The medical texts make no mention of any more sophisticated surgery, and yet 10 cases have been described of skulls that had been trepanned, in four cases demonstrably for medical reasons, and probably in the others too. The operations had in all cases been carried out on living patients who survived them for long periods, as the extensive subsequent healing shows.

No dental fillings have been found; there was a recommended mixture, of resin and malachite, but this was probably short-lived. Of 16 dental prescriptions mentioned in the papyri seven are for treating loose teeth by enclosing both tooth and adjacent gum area in a casing made from wheat-grains, with ochre or honey (the same as was applied to splints for supporting broken bones). Some of the remedies mentioned in the Ebers Papyrus for dental treatment contained copper sulphate, an astringent still used for chronic gum inflammation.

If a tooth fell out, Egyptian dentists were able to fasten it to its sound neighbours with gold or silver wire; five examples of such 'bridges' have been recorded so far.

Where rational medicine failed, magic stepped in. Indeed, some of the medicines could only work by magic, as when baldness was treated with a mixture made from a rook's vertebra, a burnt ass's hoof and the lard of a black snake. The repellent nature of some prescriptions, such as faeces, urine or blood, was supposed to exorcise the demons that had caused the disease. Consumption of medicine, application of dressings and the preparation of drugs were all accompanied by the recital of magic spells.

At other times people turned to those gods credited with healing power, either by 59 praying to them or writing them letters. The gods in question included Amun, Thoth, 7, 32 Min, Horus, Isis and Serapis. Three mortals were also promoted into their company, 271 namely Imhotep, vizier and architect to King Djoser and identified by the Greeks with 261 Aesculapius; Amenhotep, son of Hapu, who was an architect and senior officer in the 274 reign of Amenophis III, and finally Antinous, the Emperor Hadrian's lover.

Magical cures also took place in some of the temples. The oldest evidence is from the Ramessid period at Deir el-Medina, other sites being the upper terrace of Hatshepsut's temple at Deir el-Bahari, the Serapeum and Anubieion at Saqqara and the temples at Canopus and Abydos. Remains of a sanatorium have been found on the grounds of the temple of Hathor at Dendera, where patients stayed isolated in small rooms recalling monastic cells, praying, meditating and benefiting from healing sleep, during which truths would be revealed to them in dreams. The use of bathing pools fed from the temple's sacred lake was also part of the cure.

There were always magicians at hand to rid the patient's body by incantation of demons that had caused his disease. People also sought to ward off these demons by wearing amulets, one of the most popular being the Eye of Horus, *wedjat*, the 'moon 272 eye' which Seth had injured in combat with him and Thoth had restored to health. This story was connected with the phases of the moon, which Seth caused to wane and Thoth to wax again. Protection against snake bites, scorpion stings and crocodile attacks was conferred by a stele showing the god Horus doing battle with these dread creatures. It sufficed to pour water over the stele, catch it as it ran off and drink it . . .

In sum, an Egyptian who fell ill could always rely on some cure being available, whatever the problem. The most rationally based branch of medicine, incomparably more advanced than that of other countries at the time, was certainly surgery. When it came to internal medicine there were some potentially beneficial drugs, but most prescriptions could only have psychotherapeutic effect.

CHAPTER TWENTY

. . . Whence No Traveller Returns

273 The dead man praying to Anubis, god of mummification, asking for admission to Abydos, to be near Osiris whose tomb was believed to be there. He hopes to be resurrected like Osiris. Vignette from the Book of the Dead of Neferrenpet, 'The Spell for the Admission of the Dead to Abydos'. Papyrus. 19th dynasty. *Brussels, Royal Museum of Art and History*

THE STAGES IN the life of an ancient Egyptian were summarised by a writer of the Ptolemaic age, and preserved in the Insinger Papyrus (17, 22 to 18, 3), in these words:

> [A man] spends ten [years] as a child before he understands death and life.
> He spends another ten [years] acquiring the instruction by which he will be able to live.
> He spends another ten years earning and gaining possessions by which to live.
> He spends another ten years up to old age, when his heart becomes his counsellor.
> There remain sixty years of the whole life which Thoth has assigned to the man of god.

From the age of 40 to the expected 100, then, a man could enjoy the best years of his life, using the fruits of his labour and knowledge. The Egyptians regarded the attainment of this age as evidence of special divine favour and the reward for blameless behaviour. Old people were respected for their experience and sagacity, and their 'wise advice for living' received close attention. One of the authors of the Instructions, Ani, gives formal expression to this respect in his injunction: 'Never remain seated if a man older than yourself is standing.'

It is curious that there should be hardly any realistic portraits of elderly people in Old and Middle Kingdom art. One cannot infer from this that no one reached a ripe age in those days. It was simply that youth and maturity were thought the ideal subjects to depict.

In the New Kingdom, however, we start finding pictures of bent figures with round backs, folds of fat on the chest and belly and wrinkled faces, leaning on sticks – this latter being the determinative sign in the word denoting old age.

The Instruction of the vizier Ptahhotep vividly describes the troubles of the old.

> Age is here, old age arrived,
> Feebleness come, weakness grows,
> Childlike one sleeps all day,
> Eyes are dim, ears deaf,
> Strength is waning through weariness,
> The mouth, silenced, speaks not,
> The heart, void, recalls not the past,

The bones ache throughout.
Good has become evil, all taste is gone,
What age does to people is evil
in every way.

To reach full years one had to live a just life in harmony with nature, other people and the eternal order or *maat*. Everybody also had to be aware of his or hers auspicious and inauspicious days and to be guided by magic formulae, for it is written in the Coffin Texts that 'He who understands life will live to a hundred and ten.'

One hundred and ten, then, was the somewhat puzzling Egyptian figure for the ideal life-span. Joseph Janssen has counted 27 places in documents where the figure crops up, showing that it was a current notion in the Old Kingdom and enjoyed its widest acceptance in the 19th and 20th dynasties. One man reputed to have reached that age was the 6th-dynasty king Pepy II, and since we know of events happening in the 94th year of his reign, perhaps he did. Ptahhotep, vizier to the penultimate ruler of the 5th dynasty, Djedkare Isesi, and two other individuals were also credited with reaching 110. The other 23 citations only refer to 110 as a desirable age to attain.

What, then, was the average length of life in reality? The obvious place to look for an answer would be in the life histories which, from the 4th dynasty on, prominent persons had engraved on their tomb-walls or on the steles in their tomb chapels, the equivalent to modern gravestones. From the Middle Kingdom we find biographical details on temple statues as well. These sources give names, titles of active and honorary offices held, the name of the reigning monarch and, starting in the New Kingdom, such further information as participation in campaigns and expeditions or involvement in major building projects. But there are no dates of birth or death, and no clues to a person's age at death beyond vague references to a 'long life'. It is quite exceptional to read, for example, that 'Amenhotep, son of Hapu, lived to 80' or 'Amenemope reached the age of 88.'

The picture only changes when we come to the Ptolemaic Period and biographies now include the date of birth, father's name and profession, date of marriage, name of spouse, number of children and date of death – sometimes of burial too. On the basis of 14 male and 5 female life histories Grapow calculated the average age at death as 54 for the men and 58 for the women. These figures are surprisingly high, but the sample was a very small one and excluded entirely individuals under 25, the minimum age that entitled a person to a biography.

François Baratte and Bernard Boyaval have tried to extract more reliable statistics from the wooden tags hung round the necks or chests of mummies in the Roman Period. Each tag bears the name of the deceased, written in black. In the set of mummies, examined in the Louvre, most of the names were Egyptian, only a few were Greek and still fewer Roman. The tags also state the place of birth (which in all cases was the district of Panopolis) and profession, with priest as the most common, followed by artisan or peasant, less often official or soldier. They state the year in the current king's reign but without identifying the king except in 20 cases where a Roman emperor – from Augustus to Aurelian – is cited. Out of 1211 tags only 279 mentioned the age at death, but this is an impressively large sample of a fairly homogeneous cross-section of society. From these data the mean life-span comes out as a mere 25.4 years, the men alone dying on average at 27, the women at 22. Children under 5 are in this case well represented (18 per cent) while persons over 60 account for less than 5 per cent. The author obtained a very similar figure, 25.2 years, on the basis of ages quoted on 43 out of 58 recently oublished steles of the 2nd and 3rd centuries AD from the necropolis of Terenouthis (Kom Abu Billo) in the Delta.

The ages attained by the various Egyptian kings have usually been calculated from the documented lengths of their reign, combined with their conjectured age at accession. The Turin Royal Canon from the time of Ramesses II mentions for all the kings figures higher than the known length of their reigns, leading some commentators to conclude that they refer rather to the lengths of the kings' lives.

274 This statue of Amenhotep, son of Hapu, as an old man bears an inscription stating that Amenhotep was 80 years old when it was made, and that he hopes to live to the age of 110. Grey granite. Karnak. 18th dynasty. *Cairo, Egyptian Museum*

Below **275** A female mourner. Detail of a master sketch on stucco for a relief in the tomb of Horemheb. Sheikh Abd el-Qurna, West Thebes. 18th dynasty

More recently, Edward Wente collated all the data for royal mummies in the Egyptian Museum at Cairo and found, out of 26 kings and queens, only three kings who reached an advanced age (Ramesses II, max. 92; Merenptah, max. 70; Tuthmosis III, between 55 and 66) and three queens (Henttawy, max. 91; Nodjmet, max. 60; Teye, max. 59). All the others died between the ages of 20 and 50, or even under 20, as in the case of Siptah. Of rulers not covered by this survey, Smenkhkare lived to about 30 and Tutankhamun died when he was only 16–18.

X-ray examination of the same mummies by James Harris and his team produced a surprising result. Death at an 'advanced' age (over 55) was only apparent in the single case of Ramesses II, and between 40 and 50 in only three others (Merenptah, Ramesses IV and Amenophis II). All the rest, from the X-ray evidence, died between 20 and 40. From the individual data we calculated an average life-span of just under 35 years, quite close to the 38.1 years (39.8 mean for men, 35.2 for women) based on 53 mummies in Czechoslovak collections. The mummies, then, showed an average age at least 10 years higher than the figures derived from the written evidence mentioned earlier. But it must be remembered that they included very few children, since these were rarely mummified.

Whereas the statistics mentioned so far cover the upper, and uppermost, strata of society, we can use skeleton findings to tell us more about the life expectancy of common folk. In a sample of 296 individuals from the secondary cemetery of the Late to Ptolemaic Periods in the mastaba of Ptahshepses at Abusir we found the mean age at death to have been only 19.5 years, and about two years higher for men than for women. The picture was not much better in the set of 609 skeletons in the 3rd- to 5th-century AD tumulus cemetery at Wadi Qitna in Nubia, with a mean age of 20.1 years and only a slight sex difference. The corresponding figures for the secondary burials in Horemheb's tomb at Saqqara for a sample of 225 persons were 23 years, the men living nearly four years longer than women.

Even though these figues seem low, it must be added that the deaths of babies under one year old seem to be under-represented, accounting as they do for 7.1, 14.5, and 13.6 per cent of the remains at Abusir, Saqqara and Wadi Qitna respectively, as against the 20 to 25 per cent which demographers say is typical for pre-industrial cemetery populations in general. So if one made allowance for the missing infants, the mean age at death calculations for the series mentioned above would have to be reduced by another one or two years.

For the common people, then, life expectancy at birth (similar to the quoted mean age at death) was a mere 20 to 25 years, and the hope of living longer was one of the more important privileges of the upper classes. The chief reason for the contrast was no doubt the different standards of diet and infant care, while the relatively short life-span of Egyptians in general must be laid at the door of poor hygiene, high incidence of endemic diseases, occasional epidemics and the futility of much medical treatment.

However, the very high infant and premature adult mortality were matched by the high birth-rate, so that despite everything the population slowly increased. With generation succeeding generation so rapidly, the population remained predominantly young. If we put a generation at 20 years, and the average population for simplicity at 3 million, it follows that 5.25 billion individuals must have existed on Egypt's soil during the 3500 years of its ancient civilisation, ignoring the unknown multitudes of prehistoric and predynastic times.

Living as they did with the threat of death constantly hanging over them, it is not surprising that Egyptians sought comfort in their conviction that it was possible to prolong their lives, albeit in a different form, in the world to come. When their ancestors' bodies had been buried in the hot desert sand, they noticed that they survived and retained their outward appearance for a very long time. So the preservation of the body itself came to be regarded as a precondition for the return of the soul that had been sundered from it at the moment of death.

Their belief in resurrection arose from observing many natural phenomena. The sun dies in the west each day, only to be reborn in the east next morning. A kernel of grain cast into the earth appears dead enough, but it soon sprouts into fresh life. The same idea was reinforced by myths, especially those surrounding the good king Osiris, murdered by his envious brother Seth who scattered parts of his body over the length and breadth of Egypt. It was Osiris' faithful wife Isis, we recall, who gathered the parts together and, with the help of other gods, brought them to life again.

Rich or poor, Egyptians loved their paradise valley along the Nile and were never happy living anywhere else. So they wanted to remain at home even when they died, and if death came to an Egyptian abroad his relatives made every effort to fetch his body back. They hoped their dear ones would continue living, beyond the grave, in the same surroundings they had been used to on earth and even created the 278 *shawabtis*, those little figures of 'helpers' who would work for the deceased in the hereafter and allow them to enjoy its pleasure without interruption.

Belief in life after death was deeply ingrained in everyone; rarely, in the later periods, do we hear a note of doubt as in the Despairing Man's Dialogue with his Spirit. And even there, after the spirit (*ka*) has argued that all the funeral ritual is vanity, it is confidence in the bliss to come, in the company of the gods, that wins the day.

Every man of means, then, as soon as he had secured a settled life around the age of 20 to 25, began preparing a tomb for himself and his family to serve as their 'real and everlasting abode'. A male heir was accordingly welcomed not only as someone who would take over one's job and keep the family going, but who would also conduct the

276 Mummified head of Nebera, chief of the royal stables of Tuthmose III. Tomb of Nebera, Valley of the Queens, Thebes. 18th dynasty. *Turin, Museo Egizio*

Above **277** The lid of the canopic jar of Nebera bears some resemblance to him. Tomb of Nebera, Valley of the Queens, West Thebes. 18th dynasty. *Turin, Museo Egizio*

Below left **278** *Shawabti* statuettes were placed in the tomb to work for the deceased. 18th dynasty. *St Petersburg, Pushkin Museum*

Right **279** A priest wearing the mask of Anubis, the jackal-headed god of embalming, leans over a mummy in its anthropoid coffin, resting on a lion-shaped bier, to perform the ritual of Osiris prior to the burial. Tomb of Sennedjem. Deir el-Medina. West Thebes. 19th dynasty

funeral rites when the time came. Even the poorest, who could not afford the luxury of a stone tomb at the edge of the desert, hoped that if their bodies were laid out in the hot sand, wrapped in matting, cloth or leather, they would stay intact for their descendants to perform an occasional libation and recite a magic spell over them.

Yet despite all these precautions Egyptians still saw death as a tragedy. 'Death is an evil thing, the cause of tears and sorrow, snatching a man from the circle of his kin and casting him into a desert grave . . . Never again will you step into this world and see the light of the sun!'

Death, whose herald was the same goddess Sakhmet we have met as patroness of medicine, marked the beginning of that perilous interregnum when the soul, *ka*, had left the body and was living apart. Only after priests and family had ritually purged the body, rescued it from decay by embalming, and buried it, could the soul enter it again. The whole ceremony lasted 70 days – exactly the length of the period for which the foremost star in the Egyptian firmament, Sopdet, 'died' and disappeared under the horizon.

The whole elaborate ritual varied according to the social standing of the deceased, and differed from place to place. Tomb-walls often depict this or that episode, but never all of them in the proper order. Among Old Kingdom tombs the one that gives the fullest account is that of Pepynakhtheni (6th dynasty) at Meir, while the most complete in the New Kingdom are those of Nebamun, Amenemhet and Rekhmire in West Thebes. Several specialists have tried to reconstruct the sequence and distinguish anything from 13 episodes (Gaballa) to 16 (Altenmüller). We shall focus on the most important ones.

In the opening scene we see the lamentations of the afflicted household. The mourners are usually women, some swooning with grief, others supporting them. A daughter wails: 'Oh, my father, my beloved master!', while another woman assures the deceased: 'Anubis will make you beautiful!' Herodotus (II, 85) relates: 'When a

man of any importance in an upper-class family dies, all the women of the household spatter their heads and even their faces with mud and then, leaving the deceased at home, run around town mourning, with their clothes tucked up and their breasts bare, and their relatives likewise. The men also join in the mourning with their kilts tied up.'

In the next scene the coffin is brought down from the house to the canal, where the boats are waiting. It is usually carried by three men, with a procession of others who may include a symbolic impersonator of the king, an embalmer-priest impersonating Anubis and the funeral priest, the *sem*. In the next episode the coffin is taken along the Nile or canal, this being described in the Old and Middle Kingdoms as its 'conveyance to the purification tent' or in New Kingdom illustrations as the 'river journey to the hall of Anubis'. The sarcophagus, or sometimes a shrine with statues of the deceased, stands under a baldachin in the middle of the boat, which has the same form as the funerary barque of the kings. At this stage it is only accompanied by the priests and embalmers.

In front of the 'purification tent', a light wooden temporary structure open at both ends, two groups of six men await the arrival of the boat so that they can perform the ritual washing of the body. Next, the procession carries it to the embalming workshop or *wabet* ('clean place'), also known as the 'good house' or 'divine hall of Anubis', usually situated on the west bank of the Nile where the desert came down to the valley.

The embalming workshops were permanent buildings of mud-brick or stone, surrounded with a high wall to shield them from unauthorised eyes. In later periods there existed also light travelling *wabets*, but we do not know what these looked like. Those designed for embalming the Old Kingdom pharaohs were situated on the terraces of their valley-temples. We know little of their interior furnishing; the picture in Pepynakhtheni's tomb shows them with a large main entrance and a smaller exit. One passed through an L-shaped room into a smaller one and from that into the 'central court', a large rectangular working area.

The ruins of the embalming workshop at Deir el-Bahari contained several small chambers where pots and packets of natron were kept, along with vessels full of straw for stuffing the mummies, fragments of papyri and other things.

The 12th-dynasty tomb of Ipy at Deir el-Bahari contained a wooden embalming table with traces of resin and natron still on it, but how it came to be there is unclear. Around it were wooden blocks, on which the body would have been placed during mummification. At Memphis there was a special place for the embalming of sacred bulls; here there were alabaster tables with slightly inclined tops and outlet holes at the end for the waste fluids, decorated with standing lions carved on the sides.

The embalmer's tools included a spirally curved copper hook for breaking through the lamina cribrosa of the ethmoid bone to remove the brain, a large flint or obsidian knife used traditionally for religious reasons, to open the abdomen below the left ribs, an ordinary metal knife for cutting up the entrails and tongs for inserting subcutaneous stuffing through short incisions in the skin.

Far from being a mere technical operation, embalming was a complex ritual reflecting the stages by which Anubis made ready to resurrect Osiris. As such it was an essential part of the funerary ritual. Each action was accompanied by recitation of appropriate texts, which were as important as the operation itself.

Depictions of the embalming process are always symbolic, the actual technical details being evidently regarded as a close secret. Alongside the embalmer, leaning 279 over the body where it lies on a couch and wearing a mask of Anubis, a lector-priest is sometimes shown reading from a scroll.

Two papyri in hieratic script in the Cairo museum and the Louvre, both 1st century AD copies of very ancient texts, unfortunately describe only the closing stages of the embalming. Each of the 11 extant paragraphs mentions first the operation about to be performed, and then the magic formulae to be read aloud.

The embalmers, known in the Graeco-Roman Period as *taricheutai*, belonged to a special caste of the priesthood. The most senior was known as the 'Overseer of the

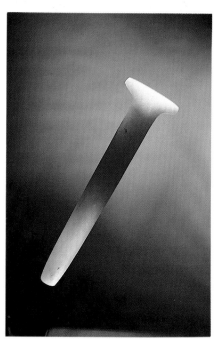

Top **280**   The purpose of the ceremonial Opening of the Mouth was to restore to the deceased the use of the senses, bringing him or her to life. Here a priest wearing the mask of Anubis is proffering to the mummy a bowl of holy water. Tomb of Inherkha. Deir el-Medina, West Thebes. 20th dynasty

Above **281**   One of the tools used in the Opening of the Mouth ceremony. *Private collection*

282   The bereaved sprinkle sacred water in a last purification ceremony at their parents' burial. Wall painting in a private tomb, West Thebes. 18th dynasty

Secrets of the Place', and also as 'Anubis' since it was on behalf of that god that he conducted the rites to transform the deceased into the immortal Osiris. The chief 'operating' embalmer had the title of 'Chancellor of the God' and was supplied with a number of assistants to prepare unguents, fetch water, natron, resin and other requisites, wash the body and entrails, fill the body with packets of natron, wipe it over with resin and wrap it in linen bandages. These assistants were the 'Children of Horus' or 'Children of Khenty-irty'. Beside the 'Chancellor' stood one or more lector-priests reciting sacred texts. Statements by Greek writers that the *paraschistai*, the specialists who made the incision in the body, were stoned for their trouble probably refer to a symbolic ceremony in which Seth was chastised for harming a body that was about to change into Osiris. Graeco-Roman authors who wrongly described the embalmers as social pariahs were probably just giving vent to their own revulsion at the practice.

Embalming technology went through a long evolution starting in the earliest historic times, when the rise of a centralised state and a class society led to kings and aristocrats being buried in large hollow tombs. Bodies placed in these did not normally last as well as those that had previously been left in hot, dry sand. Attempts were therefore made to prevent decomposition by first drying the body in the sun and covering it with tight bandages. Later, recourse was had to salt, in imitation of fish-curing, but this destroyed the skin, so embalmers tried covering it with plaster and painting in the features. Mummies of this period look like polychrome statues.

When around the 4th dynasty the ritual position of the body changed from flexed to extended, it was realised that decay could be prevented by removing the internal organs, and that the best drying agent was not salt but natron.

Embalming methods still continued to be improved. Recent finds enabled the author to show that the technique of removing the brain was known at the latest in the Middle Kingdom, not the New Kingdom as commonly stated. In the Third Intermediate Period embalmers started restoring even the outward features of the deceased with subcutaneous packing, insertion of artificial eyes and other devices. The skill declined continuously from the Late Period until Roman times.

The only historic sources of information about embalming techniques are the testimonies of Herodotus and Diodorus, written when the art was already in decline. In recent times it has been possible to check their statements, rectify certain mistakes and correct the order of operations as they described them. We shall try now to reconstruct the whole procedure as performed when the technique was at its peak in the Third Intermediate Period.

First, the body was carefully washed and all hair removed. Then a hook was inserted in the nasal passage and a hole made in the lamina cribrosa of the ethmoid bone through which (according to Herodotus) part of the brain was removed while the rest was dissolved with 'drugs'.

In view of the small size of this hole in mummies we have examined it seems impossible that the brain could have been cut up and removed through it by means of any instrument, however long. In any case, examination of mummy PUM II at

Below left **283** Scenes from a funeral procession. In the upper register the favourite bull of the deceased is driven in front. Five men carry the barque with the gilded sarcophagus containing the anthropoid coffin past the three lamenting mourners. In the lower register men carrying offerings and funerary equipment encounter a group of female mourners. Wall painting from the tomb of Amenemhet, Deir el-Medina, West Thebes. 18th dynasty

Above **284** Part of the funeral procession of the vizier Ramose. Painting in the tomb of Ramose, West Thebes. 18th dynasty

Detroit and more recently of Czechoslovak mummies, using computerised tomography, showed that in many cases collagenous membrane in the brain cavity, such as the falx cerebri and tentorium cerebelli, which any mechanical dissection would have ruptured, were preserved intact.

What 'drugs' were used for liquefying the brain we do not know. Nor is it particularly important. For the brain is known to liquefy rapidly, if exposed to air, especially in the high temperatures that would have existed in the *wabet*. All that was necessary was to turn the head round so that the fluid ran out of the hole already made.

The chief *paraschistes* then made the abdominal incision in the left flank and, according to Goyon, inserted his left hand through the small gap – only a few centimetres long – deep into the belly and then, after penetrating the diaphragm, into the chest cavity. The various organs were found by feeling around and cut free with a metal knife, usually in a very crude fashion: there was no question of proceeding systematically. The kidneys usually remained in place, being fixed behind the parietal sheet of the peritoneum, where the groping hand no doubt missed them, and so did the heart which was not supposed to be taken out since the soul was thought to reside in it. If it was taken out by mistake with the other thoracic organs, it was simply put back again. The urinary bladder also sometimes escaped the attention of the embalmers.

The entrails that had been removed were next washed in natron solution, dried and usually covered in resin before being stored in wooden caskets with separate compartments, or in miniature wooden coffins or, most frequently of all, in canopic jars. These were named by early Egyptologists who thought them to be the jars with human heads described by classic writers as representing Canopus, the pilot of Menelaus, buried in the Delta port of Canopus, who became a local deity. There were four such jars, each corresponding to one of the four sons of Horus and symbolising the four elements. From the New Kingdom onwards the lids of the vessels bore carvings to represent the gods: the vessel with a human head (the god Imset) received the liver; the one with the jackal head of Duamutef was reserved for the stomach; that with the baboon-head of Hapy was for the lungs and the intestines were consigned to the falcon-head vessel of Qebehsenuf.

In the Third Intermediate Period the entrails were tied up in four oblong packets, sometimes carrying wax figures of the respective gods, and put back into the body cavity or, in the Late Period, between the thighs. By this time the canopic vessels, if still placed beside the coffin, were purely symbolic and not even hollow.

In Herodotus's account the next operation was to cleanse the body and fill it with aromatic substances. But what in fact followed the removal of the entrails was the desiccation process. By what method it was done was for a long time the subject of

learned argument. Earlier in this century Warren Dawson and others still accepted Herodotus's statement that the body was first immersed in natron solution for 70 days.

Since linen bags of dry natron were kept in the embalming workshops, however, and since there is no trace of containers large enough for the immersion of an entire body, it seems that what the embalmers did was to fill the whole body cavity with natron and lay packets of natron all around the body. This view has gained weight from experiments in embalming pigeons, which worked with dry natron that absorbed the moisture from the tissues, but not with the solution. The effect of the natron could have been increased by exposure to the sun and, if necessary, to an open fire. The length of this drying process – the most important part of embalming if the body was to be successfully preserved – was probably put more accurately by Diodorus at 30 days, rather than Herodotus's 70.

Once the desiccation was complete any remaining organic matter or drying material was removed and the body wiped clean with spiced and perfumed palm wine and fumigated with incense. Then, according to Herodotus, it was filled with 'fresh powdered myrrh, cassia and other sweet-smelling things' and the embalmer's incision sewn up. However, the Greek historian left out several other stages. The whole skin was painted several times with fragrant oils to make it supple again. Warm fluid resin was poured into the brain cavity where, with the head supine, it normally solidified at the back of the skull with a horizontal level. Sometimes strips of cloth, or clay, were used in place of resin. The belly and chest were usually stuffed with pieces of cloth soaked in resin, or with sawdust, clay, lichen or straw, sometimes after being first wiped out with oil or partially filled with resin.

As for Herodotus's statement that the original incision was sewn up, this has only been confirmed in rare cases. As a rule the edges were pushed together but the cut remained gaping. In mummies of later periods the incision is sometimes covered over with a wax plaque, or in the case of kings and nobles with a plate of precious metal.

Various organs and external features were sometimes treated further to make them lifelike. Artificial eyes were supplied, made of glass, stone, bone or wood, or sometimes of little rolls of linen with the details painted on in black. In the Third Intermediate Period the custom was introduced of making short superficial incisions for packing the skin of the face and neck with materials similar to those used for the main body cavity. The skin was also sometimes painted a reddish-brown colour for

285 The anthropoid coffin being carried into the tomb, preceded by a priest burning incense. Inside the tomb the coffin is laid to rest on a bier with an emblem of a lion's head. The soul, *ba*, rises from the coffin in the form of a bird with a human head. Painting from the tomb of Amenemone, Qurnet Murai, West Thebes. 19th dynasty

286   Sennedjem at the gate of the Other World. Painting in the tomb of Sennedjem, Deir el-Medina, West Thebes. 19th dynasty

men, or light ochre for women, and women's eyes might be outlined with black *kohl* pigment. Attempts were made to fasten the nails on with linen thread.

The next stage in preparing a mummy was described in the documents mentioned earlier. It took 17 days according to two 18th-dynasty papyri found by A.H. Plind. For a start the head was painted with oil, the whole body perfumed and the back massaged. The body was then wrapped in a winding-sheet of red or yellow linen. The fingers were swathed separately with narrow bandages and, if they were a king's, sheathed in gold. The head was now oiled a second time and bound round in a process taking seven days. After a third oiling of the head the limbs were enclosed in spiral bandages and the legs bound together. Finally, a wider bandage was wound round the whole body, the arms being either left straight with the hands alongside the legs or over the lap, or folded across the chest. Protective charms and scarabs were sometimes tucked into the bandages, in particular 'heart scarabs' engraved with the 30th chapter of the Book of the Dead. Each layer of wrappings, according to Herodotus, was smeared with 'a kind of paste used . . . as an adhesive', which was no doubt resin again. In the case of kings, the face was now covered with a golden mask.

Mummies were variously prepared not only in different periods, but in different social groups. Herodotus speaks of three 'classes' of embalming, of which the first, involving the complete procedure, was reserved for the very rich. Second-class embalming omitted the removal of the brain and instead of the body being opened, the entrails were dissolved by cedar oil being injected through the rectum. Class three treatment amounted to little more than washing the body and drying it with natron.

287 On the Day of Judgement in the Hall of Osiris, Thoth weighs a dead person's heart. A crocodile-headed monster is ready to devour it should it be found wanting. A vignette from the Book of the Dead of Kenna. Papyrus. West Thebes. 19th dynasty. *Leiden, National Museum of Antiquities*

According to Diodorus, the first class cost one talent and the second 20 min; the third was 'very cheap'.

Once the embalming was over the burial rites could proceed, and these again are plentifully portrayed. The mummy was placed on the barque again, or on a bier, and offered food or a freshly-killed animal. During the Old Kingdom this sacrificial ceremony took place in the *wabet* itself, but under the New Kingdom it was held in a special 'reunion hall'.

Up to the 5th dynasty an exclusive feature of any royal funeral was the ritual river voyage to various holy cities – northward to Sais, home of the goddess Neith, to Buto (modern Tell el-Farain), the former capital of the Delta and seat of the goddess Wadjet, to On (Heliopolis) and other sites or southward to Abydos. With the 'democratisation' that started in the early 6th dynasty such episodes came to feature in the iconography of dignitaries' tombs as well. But whereas a dead pharaoh might actually make the pilgrimage on his barque, lesser mortals probably had to be content with token representations of the holy places set up along the way from the 246 *wabet* to the tomb, or else scenes of the journey were simply incorporated in the tomb decor and had symbolic ritual value even if the voyage had never taken place.

The most vivid illustration of a funeral procession is perhaps the painting in the 284 tomb of Akhenaten's vizier Ramose at Sheikh Abd el-Qurna. Here we see a priest conducting the ceremony with a papyrus scroll in his hand, while behind him is a train of bearers carrying fragrant unguents, wine, fruit, meat, bread and vegetables. Some have caskets full of the vizier's personal belongings, others little round tables with all the things laid out that the dead man will need in the hereafter. Other priests are cleansing the area with water or wafting incense, while behind them professional mourners raise their arms in gestures of sorrow. High officials are shown striding slowly along, and four men with a sledge are hauling a strange object like a huge scarab, the *tekenu*, symbolising the 'sun in bull's form'. A second sledge carries the

288 Hathor in the form of a sacred cow licks the arm of the dead man to reassure him. Papyrus. 18th dynasty. *Cairo, Egyptian Museum*

coffin and mummy inside a wooden gilt shrine and on another is a shrine containing the canopic vessels, watched over on either side by the four tutelary goddesses Isis, Nephthys, Selkis and Neith, with further priests in the rear ... There are even dancing-girls in the cortège, clapping their hands, moving in rhythm, beating their bosoms and shaking their heads so that their hair falls down in front. This was the *muu* mourning dance with its strict rules, attested as far back as the pyramid-building days and performed up till Graeco-Roman times.

Once the procession had reached the tomb entrance the mummy was stood upright on the ground in its coffin. Weeping women hurled themselves at its feet 205 while the lector-priest recited eulogies of the deceased and another priest began the 282 cleansing ceremony.

Now followed the most important part of the whole ritual for the mummy's life to come – the ceremony of the Opening of the Mouth. This was the *sem* priest's task. He would touch the mummy's face twice with an adze and once with a chisel, then rub 280 its face with milk. The purpose of this was to renew all the senses and bodily functions of the dead person. Then the priest embraced it, so as to bring back its temporarily departed soul. Only now could the feast be set before it on the sacrifical table: bread, meat, beer, wine, fruit and vegetables. The deceased was invited by the priest to consume them with the words: 'Arise, Osiris, take your seat before these myriad offerings.' And he or she could now see all the other gifts destined to furnish the tomb.

The time had come for the members of the family to take their leave. In some pictures we see the widow trying to hold the priest back as he makes to pick the coffin up and take it to the tomb. But finally the priests and bearers together carry the coffin 285 and all the gifts right inside, while chanting such words as 'Westward, westward, to the land of the just, now that the glorious funeral is complete!' There are more libations, incense-waving and rhythmic beating with sticks to the cry of 'The god is coming!' – identifying the deceased with Osiris himself.

265

At royal funerals the Opening of the Mouth was carried out on the king's statue in the 'golden house', the sculptor's workshop. The placing of this statue in the tomb was likewise preceded by a ceremonial 'voyage to Abydos', that having been the traditional burial site of kings during the earliest dynasties.

Finally the family and guests would betake themselves to a funeral banquet prepared in the old home, with the deceased present as an invisible guest. Like other feasts, it would be enlivened with music and dancing-girls.

Care for the departed did not end with the funeral. Continued obsequies for kings were conducted by their funerary temples, maintained by endowments set up for the purpose. These had their own staff of 'soul servants' (*hemu ka*), funerary priests who looked after the burial ground, set food and drink on the altar-table each day for the deceased, made libations, burnt incense, recited sacred texts and administered the endowments.

More modest funerary cults were kept up, particularly on feast days, by the families of important men in their tomb-chapels. In case this aftercare for the dead were ever abandoned, there was still the reliable magic of the scenes depicted on the tomb-walls, scenes which could come alive rather than that the deceased should suffer hunger, thirst, or deprivation of whatever he or she needed. For the still graver contingency that the mummy might not withstand the ravages of time, there was a statue of the tomb's occupant either in a special closed chamber, the *serdab*, or in a recess in the tomb-chapel. His or her portrait was also on the stele over the false door by which the soul, *ba*, could freely depart from the tomb and return to it. When sacrifices were being accepted, the statue or portrait deputised for the deceased and ensured that the returning soul would recognise the body it belonged to.

In humble circles the eldest son, at least, with some other relatives, would come to the burial place sometimes, and certainly on its official feast-days, to make a libation and bring some modest gift to his late father.

That the dead would attain eternal life was a universal creed. But it was to be no simple matter. According to ancient Egyptian ideas the soul had a difficult journey to accomplish in the underworld, and many obstacles to overcome with the aid of instructions and formulae provided by the Pyramid and Coffin Texts and the Books of the Dead.

All souls had moreover to face the judgement of the dead under the severe gaze of Osiris, god of the underworld, when the heart of the deceased with the burden of all his or her deeds on earth would be weighed in the scales against Maat, goddess of truth. Blessed were they who could then say, with a clear conscience, that they had lived right all their lives by the strict moral code of ancient Egypt.

Perhaps it was because they were so mindful of the ever-present risk of death and spent their lives preparing themselves for an assured future in the next world, that the Egyptians so appreciated this one with all its delights. As the Harper's Song in the tomb of King Intef succinctly puts it:

> None comes from there
> To tell of their state,
> To calm our hearts
> Until we go where they have gone.
>
> Hence rejoice in your heart ...
> Make holiday, do not weary of it.

289 Body and soul reunited: the *ba* bird returns to the body. A vignette from the Book of the Dead of Neferrenpet. Papyrus. 19th dynasty. *Brussels, Royal Museum of Art and History*

287

Chronology of Ancient Egypt

NEOLITHIC PERIOD

5000–4000 BC

PREDYNASTIC PERIOD

About 4000–3000 BC

ARCHAIC PERIOD

3000–2840 *1st Dynasty*
Narmer, Aha, Djer, Djet, Den, Anedjib, Semerkhet, Qaa

2840–2700 *2nd Dynasty*
Hotepsekhemwy, Raneb, Nynetjer, Peribsen, Khasekhem, Khasekhemwy

OLD KINGDOM

2700–2600 *3rd Dynasty*
Sanakhte, Djoser, Sekhemkhet, Nebkare, Neferkare, Khaba, Huni

2600–2500 *4th Dynasty*
Sneferu, Cheops (Khufu), Radjedef, Khephren (Khaphre), Mycerinus (Menkaure), Shepseskaf

2500–2350 *5th Dynasty*
Userkaf, Sahure, Neferirkare, Shepseskare, Neferefre (Raneferef), Nyuserre, Menkauhor, Djedkare, Unas

2350–2190 *6th Dynasty*
Teti, Userkare, Pepy I, Merenre I, Pepy II, Merenre II

1ST INTERMEDIATE PERIOD

2190–2160 *7th–8th Dynasty*
2160–2106 *9th Dynasty* (Herakleopolitan)
2106–2010 *10th Dynasty*

MIDDLE KINGDOM

2106–1963 *11th Dynasty*
Inyotef I, Inyotef II, Inyotef III, Mentuhotep I, Mentuhotep II, Mentuhotep III

1963–1786 *12th Dynasty*
Ammenemes I, Sesostris I, Ammenemes II, Sesostris II, Sesostris III, Ammenemes III, Ammenemes IV, Sobkneferu

2ND INTERMEDIATE PERIOD

1786–1633 *13th Dynasty*
1786–1602 *14th Dynasty* (West Delta)
1648–1540 *15th Dynasty* (main Hyksos)
17th cent. *16th Dynasty* (local Hyksos)
1633–1550 *17th Dynasty* (Thebes)

NEW KINGDOM

1550–1295 *18th Dynasty*
Amosis, Amenophis I, Tuthmosis I, Tuthmosis II, Hatshepsut, Tuthmosis III, Amenophis II, Tuthmosis IV, Amenophis III, Amenophis IV/Akhenaten, Smenkhkare, Tutankhamun, Ay, Horemheb

1295–1186 *19th Dynasty*
Ramesses I, Sethos I, Ramesses II, Merneptah,
Amenmesses, Sethos II, Siptah, Twosre

1186–1069 *20th Dynasty*
Sethnakhte, Ramesses III, Ramesses IV,
Ramesses V, Ramesses VI, Ramesses VII,
Ramesses VIII, Ramesses IX, Ramesses X,
Ramesses XI

LATE PERIOD: 3RD INTERMEDIATE PERIOD

1069–945 *21st Dynasty*
Smendes, Psusennes I, Amenemope, Osorkon I,
Siamun, Psusennes II

945–715 *22nd Dynasty* (Libyan)
Shoshenq I, Osorkon II, Takelothis I,
Shoshenq II, Osorkon III, Takelothis II,
Shoshenq III, Pami, Shoshenq V, Osorkon V

818–715 *23rd Dynasty* (various contemporary rulers)
Pedubastis I, Osorkon IV, Peftjauawybast

727–715 *24th Dynasty* (Libyan)
Tefnakhte, Bocchoris

747–656 *25th Dynasty* (Nubian or Cushite)
Kashta, Piankhi, Shabaka, Shebitku,
Taharqa, Tanutamun

LATE PERIOD

664–525 *26th Dynasty* (Saitic)
Necho I, Psammetichus I, Necho II,
Psammetichus II, Apries, Amosis,
Psammetichus III

525–404 *27th Dynasty* (1st Persian)
Cambyses, Darius I, Xerxes I, Artaxerxes I,
Darius II

404–399 *28th Dynasty*
Amyrtaeus

399–380 *29th Dynasty*
Nepherites I, Psammuthis, Akhoris,
Nepherites II

380–343 *30th Dynasty*
Nectanebo I, Teos, Nectanebo II

343–332 *31st Dynasty* (2nd Persian)
Artaxerxes III Ochus, Arses, Darius III
Codoman, Khababash

GRAECO-ROMAN PERIOD

332–323 *Macedonian Dynasty*
Alexander III the Great, Philip Arrhidaeus,
Alexander IV

323–30 *Ptolemaic Dynasty*
Ptolemy I Soter I, Ptolemy II Philadelphus,
Ptolemy III Euergetes I, Ptolemy IV
Philopator, Ptolemy V Epiphanes, Ptolemy VI
Philometor, Ptolemy VII Neos Philopator,
Ptolemy VIII Euergetes II, Cleopatra III
and Ptolemy IX Soter II, Cleopatra III and
Ptolemy X Alexander I, Ptolemy IX Soter II,
Cleopatra Berenice and Ptolemy XI
Alexander II, Ptolemy XII Neos Dionysos,
Berenice IV, Cleopatra VII, Ptolemy XIII,
Ptolemy XIV, Ptolemy XV Caesarion

30–AD 641 *Roman and Byzantine Age*
Roman emperors

AD 641 *Arab Conquest*

Bibliography

ABBREVIATIONS

BIFAO	Bulletin de l'Institut français d'Archaeologie Orientale
IJHM	Indiana Journal for the History of Medicine
JEA	Journal of Egyptian Archaeology
JNES	Journal of Near Eastern Studies
ZÄS	Zeitschrift für ägyptische Sprache und Altertumskunde

ALDRED, C. The Egyptians. London 1966.
ALDRED, C. Akhenaten, Pharaoh of Egypt. London 1968.
ALDRED, C. Jewels of the Pharaohs. London 1971.
ALLAM, S. 'Zur Stellung der Frau im Alten Ägypten in der Zeit des Neuen Reiches', Altertum, 16–1970: 67–81.
ALLAM, S. 'Quelques aspects du mariage dans l'Égypte ancienne'. JEA 67–1981: 116–135.
ALLAM, S. 'Wie der Altägypter in der Zeit des Neuen Reiches kaufte und verkaufte'. Altertum 27–1981: 233–240.
ALLAM, S. 'Eheschliessung und Scheidung in Altägypten'. Altertum 29–1983: 117–123.
ALLAM, S. La vie quotidienne en Égypte ancienne. Guizeh 1983.
ALLAM, S. 'Women as owners of immovables in Pharaonic Egypt'. In: Lesko, B.S. (edit.) Women's Earliest Records from Ancient Egypt and Western Asia. Atlanta, Georgia 1987, pp.123–135.
ALTENMÜLLER, H. Darstellung der Jagd im alten Ägypten. Hamburg 1967.
ANDERSON, R.D. Musical Instruments. Catalogue of Egypt. Antiquities in the British Museum, vol.III. London 1976.
ARNOLD, D. (edit.) Studien zur altägyptischen Keramik. Mainz/Rhein 1981.
BADAWY, A. A History of Egyptian Architecture: The Empire (the New Kingdom). Berkeley and Los Angeles 1968.
BADAWY, A. The Tomb of Nyhetep-Ptah at Giza and the Tomb of Ankhmahor at Saqqara. Berkeley, Los Angeles, London 1978.
BAINES, J., MALEK, J. Atlas of Ancient Egypt. Oxford 1984.
BAINES, J. 'Practical religion and Piety'. JEA 73–1987: 79–98.
BARATTE, F., BOYAVAL, B. Catalogue des étiquettes de momies du Musée du Louvre. CRIPEL 2–1974: 155–264.
BARDIS, O. 'Circumcision in ancient Egypt'. IJHM 12/1–1967: 22–23
BARDIS, P. 'Contraception in Ancient Egypt'. IJHM 12/2–1967: 1–3.
BARDIS, P. 'Incest in Ancient Egypt'. IJHM 12/2–1967: 14–20.
BAUD, M. Le caractère du dessin en Égypte ancienne. Paris 1978.
BIETAK, M., STROUHAL, E. 'Die Todesumstände des Pharaohs Seqenenre (17. Dynastie)'. Annalen des Naturhistorischen Museums Wien 78–1974: 29–52.
BIETAK, M. Zu den nubischen Bogenschützen aus Assiut. Mélanges Gamal eddin Mokhtar, Bulletin de l'Institut d'Égypte 97–1985: 78–97.
BIETAK, M. 'Zur Marine des Alten Reiches'. In: Pyramid studies and other Essays presented to I.E.S. Edwards (J. Baines et al., edits.), London 1988, pp.35–40.
BISSING, F.W. Altägyptische Lebensweisheit. Zürich 1955.
BISSING, F.W. Die Kultur des alten Ägyptens. Leipzig 1913.
BLACKMAN, A.M. The Story of King Kheops and the Magicians. Transcribed from Papyrus Westcar (Berlin Papyrus 3033). Reading 1988.
BOAK, A.E.R., PETERSON, E.E. Karanis. Topographical and Architectural Report of Excavations during the season 1924–28. Ann Arbor, Mich. 1931.
BOESSNECK, J. Die Haustiere im Altägypten. München 1953.
BOESSNECK, J. Studien an subfossilen Tierknochen aus Ägypten. München 1982.

BOGOSLOVSKIY, E.S. 'Hundred Egyptian Draughtsmen'. ZÄS 107–1980: 89–116.
BOGOSLOVSKIY, E.S. 'On the System of the Ancient Egyptian Society of the Epoch of the New Kingdom'. Altorient. Forschungen 8–1981: 5–21.
BOGOSLOVSKIY, E.S. 'Drevneyegipetskaya ekonomika na puti k vozniknoveniyu deneg'. Vestnik drevney istoriyi 159–1982: 3–12.
BOGOSLOVSKIY, E.S. Drevneyegipetskiye mastera po materialam iz Der el-Medina. Moskva 1983.
BORCHARDT, L., RICKE, H. Die Wohnhäuser in Tell el-Amarna. Berlin 1980.
BORCHARDT, L. 'Eine Holzschachtel mit Darstellung einer ländlichen Szene in Nubien'. In: Studies presented to F.Ll. Griffith. London 1932, pp.257–262.
BOURRIAU, J. Umm el-Ga'ab. Pottery from the Nile Valley before the Arab Conquest. Cambridge 1981.
BREASTED, J.H. The Edwin Smith Surgical Papyrus. 2 vols. Chicago 1930.
BROTHWELL, D.R. 'Notable Examples of Early Trephining'. Man 59–1959: 93–96.
BROTHWELL, D.R., CHIARELLI, B.A. (edit.) Population Biology of the Ancient Egyptians. London, New York 1973.
BROTHWELL, D.R., MØLLER-CHRISTENSEN, V. 'A Possible Case of Amputation, Dated to c.2000 BC. Man 63–1963: 192–193.
BROTHWELL, D.R., SANDISON, A.T. (edit.) Diseases in Antiquity. London 1967.
BRUNNER, H., Altägyptische Erziehung. Wiesbaden 1957.
BRUNNER, H. 'Vita brevis, ars longa'. ZÄS 107–1980: 42–45.
BRUNNER, H. Altägyptische Weisheit. Lehren für das Leben. München 1988.
BRUNNER-TRAUT, E. 'Der Tanz im alten Ägypten'. Ägyptologische Forschungen 6, Glückstadt 1938.
BRUNNER-TRAUT, E. 'Die Wochenlaube'. Mitt.d.Inst.f.Orientforsch. 3–1955: 11–30.
BRUNNER-TRAUT, E. 'Das Muttermilchkrüglein'. Welt des Orients 5–1969–70: 145–164.
BRUNNER-TRAUT, E. 'Buchmalerei und Bildostraca', In: Propyläen Kunstgeschichte, Band 15, Berlin 1975, pp.338–348.
BRUNNER-TRAUT, E. Egyptian Artists Sketches. Istanbul 1979.
BRUNNER-TRAUT, E. Die Alten Ägypter. 3.Auflage, Stuttgart etc. 1981.
BRUYÈRE, B. Rapport sur les fouilles de Deir el-Médineh, 17 vols. Cairo 1924–1953.
BRUYÈRE, B. 'Les fouilles de l'Institut Français à Deir al-Medineh de 1914 à 1940'. Revue d'Égyptologie 5–1946: 11–24.
BUTZER, K.W. Early Hydraulic Civilisation in Egypt. Chicago 1976.
BRYAN, C.P. The Papyrus Ebers. London 1930.
CENTRE DE DOCUMENTATION ET DES ÉTUDES SUR L'ANCIENNE ÉGYPTE: Dress in Ancient Egypt. L'Agriculture dans l'Égypte Ancienne. La Chasse et la Pêche dans L'Égypte Ancienne. L'Armée dans l'Égypte Ancienne. Le Mobilier dans l'Égypte Ancienne. Le Caire (not dated).
ČERNÝ, J. 'Questions adressées aux oracles? BIFAO 35–1934: 41–58.
ČERNÝ, J. 'Consanguineous Marriages in Pharaonic Egypt'. JEA 40–1940: 23–29.
ČERNÝ, J. Ancient Egyptian Religion. London 1952.
ČERNÝ, J. 'Prices and Wages in Egypt in the Ramesside Period'. Cahiers d'histoire mondiale 1–1954: 903–921.
ČERNÝ, J. 'A Community of Workmen at Thebes in the Ramesside Period'. Bibliothèque d'études 50, Le Caire 1973.
CHAPELAIN, J.R. La pathologie dans l'Égypte ancienne. Coulommiers 1920.

CHEREZOV, E.V. *Tekhnika sel'skogo khozyaystva drevnego Yegipta*. Chernovtsy 1969.

CHEVRIER, H. 'Technique de la construction dans l'ancienne Égypte'. *Revue d'Égyptologie* 22–1970: 15–39.

CLAYOVÁ, J. 'Váhy a vážení ve starém Egyptě'. *Listopad 1977 v Náprstkově muzeu v Praze*, 1–6.

COCKBURN, T.A., BARRACO, R.A., REYMAN, T.A., PECK, W.H., 'Autopsy of an Egyptian Mummy'. *Science* 187–1975: 1155–1160.

COCKBURN, A. and E. (edits.) *Mummies, Disease, and Ancient Cultures*. Cambridge 1980.

COLE, D. 'The Role of Women in the Medical Practice of Ancient Egypt'. *Discussions in Egyptology* 9–1987: 25–29.

CROCKER, P.T. 'Status Symbols in the Architecture of el-Amarna'. *JEA* 71–1985: 52–65.

CZERMAK, J. 'Beschreibung und mikroskopische Untersuchung zweier ägyptischen Mumien'. *Sitzungsberichte d.K.Akad.d.Wissensch., Mathem.-Naturwiss. Classe (Wien)* 9–1852: 427–469.

DARBY, W.J., GHALIOUNGUI, P., GRIVETTI, L. Food: The Gift of Osiris. 2 vols. London, New York, San Francisco 1977.

DARESSY, G. *Ostraka. Catalogue général des antiquités égyptiennes du Musée du Caire*. Nos. 25001–25385, Le Caire 1901, p.35.

DAUMAS, M. *Histoire de la Science*. Paris 1957.

DAUMAS, F. 'Le sanatorium de Dendera'. *BIFAO* 56–1957: 35–57.

DAUMAS, F. *La vie dans l'Égypte ancienne*. Paris 1968.

D'AURIA, S., LACOVARA, P., ROEHRIG, C.H. *Mummies and Magic. The Funerary Arts of Ancient Egypt*. Boston, Mass. 1988.

DAVID, A.R. (edit.) *The Manchester Museum Mummy Project*. Manchester 1979.

DAVID, A.R. (edit.) *Science in Egyptology*. Manchester 1986.

DAVID, A.R., TAPP, E. *Evidence Embalmed*. Manchester 1979.

DAWSON, W.R., GRAY, P.H.K. *Catalogue of Egyptian Antiquities in the British Museum. I. Mummies and Human Remains*. London 1968.

DEINES, H. von, GAPOW, H., WESTENDORF, W. *Grundriss der Medizin der alten Ägypter*, vols.IV–IX, Berlin 1958–1973.

DESROCHES-NOBLECOURT, C. '"Concubines du Mort" et mères de famille au Moyen Empire'. *BIFAO* 53–1953: 7 ff.

DIODORUS SICULUS, *Library of History*, vol.I. New York 1933

DIXON,, D.M. 'The Disposal of Certain Personal Household and Town Waste in Ancient Egypt'. In: UCKO, J., TRINGHAM, R., DIMBLEBY, J. (edit.) *Man, Settlement and Urbanism*. London 1972.

DIXON, D.M., 'Population, Pollution and Health'. In: COX, P.R., PEEL, J. (edit.) *Population and Pollution*. London, New York 1972, pp.29–36.

DRENKHAHN, R. *Die Handwerker und ihre Tätigkeit im alten Ägypten*. Wiesbaden 1976.

DRIOTON, E. 'Une représentation de la famine sur un bas-relief égyptien de la Ve Dynastie'. *Bulletin de l'Institut d'Égypte* 25–1942–43: 44–45.

DUCHESNE-GUILLEMIN, M. 'Music in Ancient Mesopotamia and Egypt'. *World Archaeology* 2–1980–81: 287–297.

EBBELL, B. *The Papyrus Ebers, the Greatest Egyptian Medical Document*. Copenhagen 1928.

EBBELL, B. 'Die ägyptischen Krankheitsnamen'. *ZÄS.* 63–1928: 71–75.

EDWARDS, I.E.S. *The Pyramids of Egypt*. London 1961.

EGGEBRECHT, A. 'Schlachtungsbräuche im Alten Ägypten und ihre Wiedergabe im Flachbild bis Ende des Mittleren Reiches'. PhD Thesis, München 1973.

EGYPTIAN CIVILISATION: Daily Life. Egyptian Museum, Torino 1988.

EL-AGUIZY, O. 'Dwarfs and Pygmies in Ancient Egypt'. *Annales du Service des Antiquités d'Égypte* 71–1987: 53–60.

EMERY, W.B. *A Funerary Repast in an Egyptian Tomb of the Archaic Period*. Leiden 1962.

ERMAN, A. *Aegypten und aegyptisches Leben im Altertum*. Berlin 1887.

ENDESFELDER, E. 'Sklaven in der Nekropole von Deir el Medine'. *Altorientalische Forschungen* 5–1977: 17–24.

ENDESFELDER, E. 'Zur Frage der Bewässerung im pharaonishen Ägypten'. *ZÄS* 106–1979: 37–51.

ENDESFELDER, E. 'Bemerkungen zur Entstehung und zum Charakter des Beamtentums im alten Ägypten'. *Altorientalische Forschungen* 9–1982: 5–11.

ERMAN, A. *Life in Ancient Egypt*. London 1894.

ESTES, J.W. *The Medical Skills of Ancient Egypt*. Canton, Mass. 1989.

EYRE, C.J. 'Crime and Adultery in Ancient Egypt'. *JEA* 70–1984: 92–105.

EYRE, C.J. 'Employment and Labour Relations in the Theban Necropolis in the Ramesside Period'. PhD Thesis, The Queen's College, Cambridge.

FAKHRY, A. *The Pyramids*. Chicago 1961.

FEUCHT, E. 'Geburt, Kindheit, Jugend und Ausbildung im Alten Ägypten'. In: *Zur Sozialgeschichte der Kindheit* (J. Martin and A. Nitschke, edit.), Freiburg and München 1986, pp.225–265.

FIELD, H. 'Body-Marking in Southwest Asia'. *Papers of the Peabody Museum, Harvard University* 45/1–1958, Cambridge, Mass.

FISCHER, H.G. 'The Trumpet in Ancient Egypt'. In: *Pyramid Studies and Other Essays presented to I.E.S. Edwards* (J. Baines et al., edits.) G.A., *Narrative in Egyptian Art*. Cairo 1976.

FISCHER, H.G. 'Women in the Old Kingdom and the Heracleopolitan Period'. In: Lesko, B.S. (edit.) *Women's Earliest Records from Ancient Egypt and Western Asia*. Atlanta, Georgia 1987, pp.5–24.

GABALLAH, G.A., *Narrative in Egyptian Art*. Cairo 1976.

GAILLARD, C. 'Les tatonnements des Égyptiens de l'ancien empire à la recherche des animaux à domestiquer'. *Revue d'Ethnographie et de Sociologie* 3–1912: 329–348.

GAMER-WALLERT, I. *Fische und Fischkult in Ägypten*. Wiesbaden 1970.

GARDINER, A. 'The House of Life'. *JEA* 24–1938: 157–179.

GARDINER, A. *Egypt of the Pharaohs*. Oxford 1961.

GERMER, R. *Flora des alten Ägypten*. Mainz/Rhein 1985.

GHALIOUNGUI, P. *Magic and Medical science in Ancient Egypt*. London 1963.

GHALIOUNGUI, P. 'The Persistence and Spread of Some Obstetric Concepts held in Ancient Egypt'. *Annals du Service des Antiquités de l'Égypte* 62–1977: 141–154.

GHALIOUNGUI, P. *The Physicians of Pharaonic Egypt*. Cairo and Mainz/Rhein 1983.

GHALIOUNGUI, P., EL-DAWAKHLY, Z. *Health and Healing in Ancient Egypt*. Cairo 1965.

GILLINGS, R.J. *Mathematics in the Time of the Pharaohs*. Cambridge Mass. 1972.

GOYON, G. *Le secret de bâtisseurs des grandes pyramides Khéops*. Paris 1977.

GOYON, J.C. *Rituels funéraires de l'ancienne Égypte*. Paris 1972.

GRANVILLE, A.B. *An Essay on Egyptian Mummies*. London 1825.

GRAPOW, H. *Grundriss der Medizin der alten Ägypter*. Vols.I–III. Berlin 1954, 1955, 1956.

GRIFFITH, F.Ll. *Beni Hasan, Memoir 5*, London 1896.

GRIFFITH, F.Ll. *Hieratic Papyri from Kahun and Gurob*. 2 vols. London 1898.

GRUNERT, S. *Thebanische Kaufverträge*. Berlin 1981.

HAFEMANN, I. 'Zum Problem der staatlichen Arbeitspflicht im alten Ägypten', II. *Altorient.Forsch.* 12–1985: 179–215.

HARRIS, J.R., WEEKS, K.R. *X-Raying the Pharaohs*. New York 1973.

HARRIS, J.E., ISKANDER, Z., FARID, S. 'Restorative Dentistry in Ancient Egypt: an Archaeological Fact'. *Journal of the Michigan Dental Association* 57–1975: 401–404.

HARRIS, J.E., WENTE, E.F. (edit.) *An X-Ray Atlas of the Royal Mummies*. Chicago, London 1980.

HARTMANN, F. *L'agriculture dans l'ancienne Égypte*. Paris 1923.

HAYES, W.C. 'Inscriptions from the Palace of Amenhotep III'. *JNES* 10–1951: 82–112.

HELCK, W. 'Die Tochterheirat ägyptischer Könige'. *Cahiers d'Égypte*. 87–1969: 27–59.

HELCK, W. OTTO, E. *Kleines Wörterbuch der Ägyptologie*. Wiesbaden 1956.

HEPPER, F. N. *Pharaoh's Flowers. The botanical treasures of Tutankhamun*. London 1990.

HERODOTUS *History*. Vols.I, II (A.D. Godley, transl.), Cambridge (Mass.) 1926.

HICKMAN, H. 'Altägyptische Musik'. In: *Orientalische Musik*. Leiden, Köln 1970, pp.135–170.

HINKEL, F.W. 'Ancient Scheme to Build a Pyramid at Meroe'. In: *New Discoveries in Nubia*. Leiden 1982, pp.45–49.

HOBBS, J.J. 'Sands of the Shore: Animals in Egyptian Life'. M.A. Thesis, University of Texas, Austin 1972.

HOFFMANN-AXTHELM, W. *History of Dentistry*. Chicago etc. 1981.

HOOPER, F.A. *Funerary Stelae from Kom Abu Billou*. Ann Arbor 1961.

HOOTON, E.A. 'Oral Surgery in Egypt during the Old Empire'. *Harvard African Studies* 1–1917: 29–32.

HORNUNG, E. 'Zum Turiner Grabplan'. In: *Pyramid Studies and other Essays presented to I.E.S. Edwards* (J. Baines et al., edits). London 1988, pp.138–142.

HÖLSCHER, U. *Das Grabdenkmal des König Chefren*. Leipzig 1912.

HURRY, J.B. *Imhotep, the vizier and physician of King Zoser*. Oxford 1928.

IVERSEN, E. *Canon and Proportions in Egyptian Art*. 2nd edit. Warminster 1975.

JAMES, T.G.H. *An Introduction to Ancient Egypt*. London 1979.

JAMES, T.G.H. *Pharaoh's People. Scenes from Life in Imperial Egypt*. London 1984.

JANSSEN, J.J. *Commodity prices from the Ramessid Period*. Leiden 1975.

JANSSEN, J.J. 'The Day the Inundation Began'. *JNES* 46–1987: 126–136.

JANSSEN, J.J. 'Marriage Problems and Public Reactions'. In: *Pyramid Studies and other Essays presented to I.E.S. Edwards* (J. Baines et al., edits.). London 1988.

JANSSEN, J.J. 'On Prices and Wages in Ancient Egypt'. *Altorientalische Forschungen* 15–1988: 10–23.

JANSSEN, J.M.A. 'On the Ideal Lifetime of the Egyptians'. *Oudheidk. Medelingen Rijksmuseum Oudheden* 31–1950: 33–43.

JONCKHEERE, F. *Une maladie égyptienne: L'hématurie parasitaire*. Bruxelles 1944.

JONCKHEERE, F. *Le Papyrus médical Chester Beatty*. Bruxelles 1947.

JONCKHEERE, F. 'La circoncision des anciens Égyptiens'. *Centaurus* 1–1951: 212–234.

JONCKHEERE, F. La "mesdemet". Cosmétique and médicaments égyptiens'. *Histoire de la médecine* 2/7–1952: 1–12.

JONCKHEERE, F. 'L'eunuque dans l'Égypte pharaonique'. *Revue d'Histoire des Sciences*. 7–1954: 139–155.

JONCKHEERE, F. 'La durée de la gestation d'après les textes égyptiens'. *Chronique d'Égypte*. 30–1955: 19–45.

JONCKHEERE, F. 'Un chapitre de pediatrie égyptienne: l'allaitement'. *Aesculape* 36–1955: 19–45.

JONCKHEERE, F. *Les médecins de l'Égypte pharaonique. Essai de prosopographie.* Bruxelles 1958.

KATSNEL'SON, I.S. (edit.) *Kul'tura drevnego Yegipta.* Moskva 1976.

KAMAL, H. *Dictionary of Pharaonic Medicine.* Cairo 1967.

KANAWATI, N. 1977 *The Egyptian Administration in the Old Kingdom. Evidence of its Economic Decline.* Warminster 1977.

KEIMER, J. *Remarques sur le tatouage dans l'Égypte ancienne.* Le Caire 1948.

KEMP, B.J. 'Tell el-Amarna as a Source for the Study of Urban Society in Egypt'. *World Archaeology* 9–1969: 123–139.

KEMP, B.J. 'The Harim-Palace at Medinet el-Ghurab'. *ZÄS* 105–1978: 122–133.

KEMP, B.J. *Amarna Reports III.* London 1986.

KEMP, B. 'Large Middle Kingdom Granary Buildings (and the archaeology of administration)'. *ZÄS* 113–1986: 120–136.

KILLEN, G. *Ancient Egyptian Furniture.* Vol.I. Warminster 1980.

KITCHEN, K. A. 'The chronology of ancient Egypt'. *World Archaeology* 23–1991: 201–208.

KOROSTOVTSEV, M.A. 'Was ist ein Sklave?' *Altorientalische Forschungen* 5–1977: 5–15.

KROMER, K. *Siedlungsfunde aus dem frühen Alten Reich in Giseh.* Wien 1978.

LACOVARA, P. 'The Hearst Excavations at Deir el-Ballas: The Eighteenth Dynasty Town'. In: *Studies in Ancient Egypt, the Aegean and the Sudan. Essays in honor of Dows Dunham.* Boston, Mass. 1981, pp.120–124.

LASKOWSKA-KUSZTAL, E. 'Un atelier de perruquerier à Deir el-Bahari'. *Études et Travaux* 10–1978: 83–120.

LAUER, J.P. *Histoire monumentale des pyramides d'Égypte.* 2 vols., Paris 1962.

LEAKE, C.D. *The Old Egyptian Medical Papyri.* Lawrence, Kansas 1952.

LEBEN IM ÄGYPTISCHEN ALTERTUM. Literatur, Urkunden, Briefe aus vier Jahrtausenden, Staatl. Museen zu Berlin 1977.

LECA, A.-P. *La médecine égyptienne au temps des Pharaons.* Paris 1971.

LECA, A.-P. *Les momies.* Paris 1976.

LEEK, F.F. 'Observations on the Dental Pathology seen in Ancient Egyptian Skulls'. *JEA* 52–1966: 59–64.

LEEK, F.F. 'Bread of the Pharaoh's Baker'. *American Research Center in Egypt Newsletter* 77–1971: 2–4.

LEEK, F.F. *The Human Remains from the Tomb of Tutankhamun.* Oxford 1972.

LEEK, F.F. 'Teeth and Breath in Ancient Egypt'. *JEA* 58–1972: 126–132.

LEEK, F.F. 'Did a Dental Profession exist in Ancient Egypt during the 3rd Millennium BC?' *Medical History* 16–1972: 404–406.

LEEK, F.F. 'A Third Millennium BC Dental Profession in Egypt: Fact or Fiction?' In: *Paleopathology Association 3th European Meeting,* Caen 1980, pp.43–49.

LEFEBVRE, G. 'Tableau des parties du corps humain mentionnées par les Égyptiens'. *Suppl. Annals du Service des Antiquit.* 17, Le Caire 1952.

LEFEBVRE, G. *Essai sur la médecine égyptienne de l'époque pharaonique.* Paris 1956.

LEFEBVRE, G. 'L'âge de 110 ans et la vieillesse chez les Égyptiens'. *C.R.de l'Acad.des Inscr. et Belles Lettres* 1944: 106–119.

LEFEBVRE, G. 'Lait de vache et autres laits en Égypte'. *Revue d'Égypt.* 12–1960: 59–65.

LEFF, S., LEFF, V. *Von der Zauberei zur Weltgesundheit.* Berlin 1958.

LEWIN, P., MILLS, A.J., SAVAGE, H., VOLLMER, J. 'Nakht, a weaver of Thebes'. *Rotunda* 7/4–1975: 14–17.

LEXA, F. *La magie dans l'Égypte antique de l'ancien empire jusqu'à l'époque copte.* 3 vols. Paris 1925.

LEXA, F. *Papyrus Insinger. Les enseignements moraux d'un scribe égyptien du premier siècle après J.-C.* 2 vols. Paris 1926.

LEXA, F. *Výbor ze starší literatury egyptské.* Praha 1947.

LEXA, F. *Výbor z mladší literatury egyptské.* Praha 1947.

LEXA, F. *Veřejný život ve starém Egyptě.* 2 vols. Praha 1955.

LEXIKON DER ÄGYPTOLOGIE (W. Helck, W. Westendorf, edit.). Wiesbaden I–1975, I.–1977, III–1980, IV–1982, V–1984, VI–1986.

LEXOVÁ, I. *O staroegyptském tanci.* Praha 1930.

LICHTHEIM, M. *Ancient Egyptian Literature: a Book of Readings.* Vols.I–III. Berkeley 1975–1980.

LISOWSKI, F.P. 'Trépanation en ancienne Egypte'. *VI Congrès fédératif internat. d'anatomie.* Paris 1955, p.143 ff.

LUCAS, A.L. 'Cosmetics, Perfumes and Incense in Ancient Egypt'. *JEA* 16–1930: 41–53.

LUCANUS, M.A. *De bello civili libri X* (C. Hosius, edit.) Leipzig 1905.

LUCAS, A.L. 'The Use of Natron in Mummification'. *JEA* 18–1932: 125–140.

LUCAS, A., HARRIS, J.R. *Ancient Egyptian Materials and Industries.* 4th edit. London 1962.

LUCAS, A. 'Poisons in Ancient Egypt'. *JEA* 24–1938: 198–199.

LURYE, I.M. 'Zabastovka remeslennikov Fivanskogo nekropolya vo vremeni Ramese III'. *Vestnik drevney istoriyi* 35/1–1951: 221–232.

LURYE, I.M. *Studien zum altägyptischen Recht des 16. bis 10. Jahrhunderts v.u.Z.* Weimar 1971.

LÜDDECKENS, E. *Ägyptische Eheverträge, Ägyptologische Abhandlungen* 1–1960.

MANNICHE, L. 'Egyptian Sexual Life'. *Acta Orientalia* 38–1977: 11–24.

MARRO, G. 'Contributo alla patologia del sistema osseo negli Egiziani antichi'. *Memorie della Reale Accademia delle Scienze di Torino,* ser.II, tomo 70, parte I, pp.119–140, 1946.

MARRO, G. 'Documentazioni morbose finore ignorate nell'antico Egitto'. *Minerva Medica* (Torino) 42/39–1952: 1–14.

MASALI, M. 'Dati sulla mortalità infantile nell'Egitto dai reperti della collezione "G. Marro"'. *Rivista di Antrop.* 54–1967: 171–173.

MATIEGKOVÁ, L. 'Vyšetřování egyptských mumií'. *Anthropologie* 7–1929: 237–253.

MATIEGKOVÁ, L. *Dítě ve starém Egyptě.* Anthropologická knihovna Praha 1937.

MENDELSSOHN, K. *The Riddle of the Pyramid.* London and Cambridge 1974.

MIDDLETON, R. 'Brother-Sister and Father-Daughter Marriage in Ancient Egypt'. *Amer. Sociol. Review* 27–1962: 603 ff.

MILLET, N.B. 'The Narmer Macehead and Related Objects'. *Journal of the Amer. Research Centre in Egypt* 27–1990: 53–59.

MILLER, R.L. 'Hogs and Hygiene'. *JEA* 76–1990: 125–140.

MONTET, P. *Les scènes de la vie privée dans les tombeaux égyptiens de l'ancien Empire.* Strasbourg et Paris 1925.

MONTET, P. *La vie quotidienne en Égypte aux temps des Ramsès.* Paris 1946.

MOODIE, R.L. 'Roentgenologic Studies of Egyptian and Peruvian Mummies'. *Field Museum Nat.History Memoir* 3. Chicago 1931.

MORENZ, S. *Gott und Mensch im alten Ägypten.* Heidelberg 1963.

MORENZ, S. *Egyptian Religion.* Ithaca 1984.

MOUSSA, A.M., ALTENMÜLLER, H. *Das Grab des Nianchchnum und Chnumhotep.* Mainz/Rhein 1977.

MÜLLER, W.M. *Die Liebespoesie der alten Ägypter.* 2nd edition. Leipzig 1932.

NAVILLE, E. 'Figurines égyptiennes de l'époque archaique'. *Recueil des Travaux* N.S.5–1899: 212–216, N.6–1900: 65–71.

NEWBERRY, P.E. *Beni Hasan, memoirs* 1–2. London 1893.

NOLTE, B. 'Die Glassgefässe im alten Ägypten'. *Münchner ägypt. Studien* 14. München 1968.

OCKINGA, B.G. 'On the Interpretation of the Kadesh Record'. *Cahiers d'Égypte* 123–124-1987: 38–48.

OMLIN, J.A. 'Der Papyrus 55001 und seine satirisch-erotischen Zeichnungen und Inschriften'. *Catalogo del Museo Egizio di Torino.* Vol.III Torino 1973.

ONASCH, A. 'Werde Schreiber!' Schulen und Schüler im alten Ägypten. *Das Altertum* 31–1985: 204–212.

ONASCH, A. 'Zur sozialen Stellung der ägyptischen Beamten im Neuen Reich'. *Ethnogr.-archäologische Z.* 26–1985: 281–290.

PAVLOV, V.V., KHODZHASH, S.I. *Khudozhestvennoye remeslo drevnego Yegipta.* Moskva 1959.

PECK, W.H., Ross, J.G. *Egyptian Drawings.* New York 1978.

PEET, T.E. 'Excavations at Tell el-Amarna: a preliminary report'. *JEA* 7–1921: 169–185.

PEET, T.E. *The Great Tomb-Robberies of the Twentieth Egyptian Dynasty.* Oxford 1930.

PETERSON, B.E.J. 'Zeichnungen aus einer Totenstadt'. *Medehavs Museet Bulletin* 7–8. Stockholm 1973.

PETRIE, W.M.F. *Kahun, Gurob and Hawara.* London 1890.

PETRIE, W.M.F. *Illahun, Kahun and Gurob.* London 1891.

PETRIE, W.M.F. *Athribis.* London 1908.

PETRIE, W.M.F. *Arts and Crafts of Ancient Egypt.* Chicago 1910.

PETRIE, W.M.F. *Social Life in Ancient Egypt.* London 1923.

PETRIE, W.M.F. *Objects of Daily Use.* London 1927.

PLINY *Natural History.* 10 vols. (H. Rackham et al., transl.) Cambridge (Mass.) 1938–1990.

POLÁČEK, V. 'Randbemerkungen zum Sklaventum im Alten Ägypten'. In: BECHER, W.G., SCHNORR VON CAROLSFELD, L. *Sein und Werden im Recht. Festgabe Ulrich von Lübtow.* Berlin 1970: 153–172.

POLLAK, K. *Wissen und Weisheit der alten Ärzte.* Düsseldorf 1968.

POSENER, G. 'Sur l'attribution d'un nom à un enfant'. *Revue d'Égyptologie* 22–1970: 204–205.

POSENER, G., SAUNERON, S., YOYOTTE, J. *Knaurs Lexikon der ägyptischen Kultur.* München, Zürich 1960.

POSENER-KRIÉGER, P. *Les archives du Temple funéraire de Neferirkare (Les papyrus d'Abousir).* 2 vols. Le Caire 1976.

POSENER-KRIÉGER, P. 'Remarques préliminaires sur les nouveaux papyrus d'Abousir'. In: *Ägypten. Dauer und Wandel.* Mainz 1986, 35–43.

PUSCH, E.B. 'Das Senet/Brettspiel im Alten Ägypten', I and II. *Münchner ägyptologische Studien* 38, Munich–Berlin 1979.

RACHELWILTZ de, B. *Black Eros.* London 1968, chapter II.

REINEKE, W.F. 'Wissenschaft und Wissenschaftler im alten Ägypten'. *Altorient. Forschungen* 9–1982: 13–31.

RIAD, N. *La médecine au temps des Pharaohs.* Paris 1955.

RIEFSTAHL, E. 'An Egyptian Portrait of an Old Man'. *JNES* 10–1951: 65–73.

RIZQALLAH, F., RIZQALLAH, K. *La préparation du pain.* Cairo /1978.

ROBINS, G. 'The Physical Proportions and Living Stature of New Kingdom Pharaohs'. *J. of Human Evolution* 12–1983: 455–465.

ROBINS, G. 'Natural and Canonical Proportions in Ancient Egyptians'. *Göttinger Miszell.* 61–1983: 17–25.

ROBINS, G. 'Ancient Egyptian Sexuality'. *Discussions in Egyptology* 11–1988: 61–72.

ROBINS, G. 'A critical examination of the theory that the right to the throne of ancient Egypt passed through the female line in the 18th dynasty'. *Göttinger Miszelleen*. 62-1983: 67-77.

ROBINS, R.G. 'Some images of women in New Kingdom art'. In: Lesko, B.S. (edit.) *Women's Earliest Records from Ancient Egypt and Western Asia*. Atlanta, Georgia 1987, pp.105-116.

ROWLING, J.T. 'Pathological Changes in Mummies'. *Proc.Royal Soc.of Medicine* 54-1961: 409-415.

RUFFER, M.A. 'Study of Abnormalities and Pathology of Ancient Egyptian Teeth'. *Amer. J. Phys. Anthrop.* 3-1920: 335-382.

RUFFER, M.A. *Studies in the Paleopathology of Egypt*. Edited by R.L. Moodie. Chicago 1921.

SALIB, P. 'Orthopaedic and Traumatic Skeletal Lesions in Ancient Egyptians'. *J.Bone and Joint Surgery* 44 B-1962: 944-947.

SAMEH, W. *Alltag im alten Ägypten*. Munchen 1963.

SANDISON, A.T. 'The Use of Natron in Mummification in Ancient Egypt'. *JNES* 22-1963: 259-267.

SAUNERON, S. *Les prêtres de l'Ancienne Égypte*. Paris 1962.

SAUNERON, S. 'Les dix mois précédant la naissance'. *BIFAO* 58-1959: 33-34.

SAWI, A., BOUZEK, J., VIDMAN, L. 'New Stelae from Terenouthis Cemetery in Egypt'. *Archív Orientální* 48-1980: 330-355.

SCHEEL, B. 'Studien zum Metallhandwerk im Alten Ägypten'. I, *Studien zur Altägyptischen Kultur* 12-1985: 117-177.

SCHENKEL, W. *Die Bewässerungsrevolution im Alten Ägypten*. Mainz/Rhein 1978.

SCHNEIDER, H.D. 'Shabtis'. *Rijksmuseum van Oudheden te Leiden*, part I. Leiden 1977, pp.13-17.

SCHOTT, S. *Altägyptische Liebeslieder mit Mächen und Liebesgeschichten*. Zürich 1950.

SCHOTT, S. *Das Schöne Fest vom Wüstentale. Festbräuche einer Totenstadt*. Wiesbaden 1952.

SCHOTT, S. 'Aufnahmen von Hungersnotrelief aus dem Aufweg der Unaspyramide'. *Revue d'Égypt.* 17-1965: 7-13.

SCOTT, N.E. *The Home Life of the Ancient Egyptians*. New York 1947.

SCOTT, S. *Altägyptische Liebeslieder*. Zürich 1950.

SHAABAN, M.M. 'Trephination in Ancient Egypt and the Report of a New Case from Dakhleh Oasis'. *Ossa* 9-11-1982-84: 135-142.

SHATTOCK, S.G. 'Microscopic Sections of the Aorta of King Merneptah'. *Lancet* 1-1909: 318.

SHAW, I. *Egyptian Warfare and Weapons*. Princes Risborough 1991.

SHORTER, J. 'A Magical Ivory'. *JEA* 18-1932: 1-2.

SLOMANN, H.C. 'Contribution à la paléopathologie égyptienne'. *Bull. Soc. d Anthrop. Paris*, sér.8, tome VII-1927: 62-86.

SMITH, G.E. 'The Most Ancient Splints'. *Brit.Med.J.* 1-1908: 732-734.

SMITH, G.E. *The Royal Mummies. Catalogue général des antiquités égyptiennes du Musée du Caire* 59. Cairo 1912.

SMITH, G.E., DAWSON, W.R. *Egyptian Mummies*. London 1924.

SMITH, H.S. *A Visit to Ancient Egypt. Life at Memphis and Saqqara*. Warminster 1974.

SO LEBTEN DIE ALTEN ÄGYPTER. Katalog. Museum Basel 1976.

STADELMANN, R. *Die ägyptischen Pyramiden*. Mainz/Rhein 1985.

STAEHELIN, E. *'Untersuchungen zur ägyptischen Tracht im Alten Reich'. Münchner Ägypt. Studien* 8. München 1966.

STEINMANN, F. 'Gab es im alten Ägypten Sklavenarbeit in der Späre der handwerklich-künstlerischen Produktion?' *Altorient. Forschungen* 5-1977: 25-31.

STEINMANN, F. 'Die gesellschaftliche Stellung der ägyptischer "Künstler" im Neuen Reich'. *Altertum* 24-1978: 36-43.

STRABO, *The Geography of Strabon* (translated by H.C. Hamilton and W. Falconer). London 1881.

STROUHAL, E. 'Tumours in the Remains of Ancient Egyptians'. *Amer.J. Phys. Anthrop.* 45-1976: 613-620.

STROUHAL, E. 'Maternity in Ancient Egypt'. In: DOLEŽAL, A., GUTVIRTH, J. (edits.) *Anthropology of Maternity*. Prague 1977, pp.287-292.

STROUHAL, E. 'Ancient Egyptian Case of Carcinoma'. *Bull.N.York Acad.Medicine* 54-1978: 290-302.

STROUHAL, E. 'Queen Mutnodjmet at Memphis: Anthropological and Palaeopathological Evidence'. In: *Égyptologie en 1979, Axes prioritaires de recherche*, tome II, Paris 1982, pp.317-322.

STROUHAL, E. 'Paleopathology of Dentition of the Ancient Egyptians from Abusir'. *Garcia de Orta, sér.antropobiol.* (Lisboa) 3-1984: 163-172.

STROUHAL, E. 'Anthropology of the Late Period Cemetery in the Tomb of King Horemheb at Saqqara (Egypt)'. *Internat.J.of Anthrop.* 1-1986: 215-224.

STROUHAL, E. 'Adaptation of the Late Period Population of Abusir (Egypt)'. *Anthropos* (Athinai) 11-1986: 94-103.

STROUHAL, C.L. 'Embalming Excerebration in the Middle Kingdom'. In: *Science in Egyptology. Proceedings of the Science of Egyptology Symposia* (A.R. David, edit.). Manchester 1986, pp.141-154.

STROUHAL, E. 'Three Figured Ostraka from the Ancient Egyptian Collections of the Náprstek Museum'. *Annals of the Náprstek Museum* 15-1988: 47-68.

STROUHAL, E. 'Life of the Ancient Egyptian Children according to Archaeological Sources'. In: *Children and Exercise* (G. Beunen et al.,

edits.). Stuttgart 1990, pp.184-196.

STROUHAL, E. 'Vertebral Tuberculosis in Ancient Egypt and Nubia'. In: *Human Paleopathology. Current Syntheses and Future Options* (D.J. Ortner and C. Aufderheide, edits.). Washington 1991, pp.181-194.

STROUHAL, E., JUNGWIRTH, J. 'Ein verkalktes Myoma uteri aus der späten Römerzeit in Ägyptisch-Nubien'. *Mitteil.d.Anthrop.Gesellsch.*, Wien 107-1977: 215-221.

STROUHAL, E., JUNGWIRTH, J. 'Paleopathology of the Late Roman-Early Byzantine Cemeteries at Sayala, Egyptian Nubia'. *J. of Human Evol.* 9-1980: 61-70.

STROUHAL, E., VYHNÁNEK, L. 'New Cases of Malign Tumours from Late Period Cemeteries at Abusir and Saqqara (Egypt)'. *Ossa* 8-1981: 165-189.

STROUHAL, E., VYHNÁNEK, L. 'Results of Examination of the Mummy of Qenamun'. *Anthropologie* (Brno) 13-1975: 219-221.

STROUHAL, E., VYHNÁNEK, L. 'Egyptian Mummies in Czechoslovak Collections'. *Acta Musei Nationalis Pragae* 35 B, 1979.

ŠVASTAL, J. 'Beitrag zur Erforschung der Geschichte der Vermessungskunde im Alten Ägypten'. *Acta Polytechnica – Práce ČVUT v Praze* 13-1983: 69-80.

THIERFELDER, H. *Die Geschwisterehe im helenistisch-römischen Ägypten*. Münster 1960.

THOMAS, A.P. *Gurob: A New Kingdom Town*. Warminster 1981.

THORWALD, J. *Macht und Geheimnis der frühen Ärzte*. München, Zürich 1962.

TIETZE, C. 'Amarna. Analyse der Wohnhäuser und soziale Struktur der Stadtbewohner'. *ZÄS* 112-1985: 48-84.

TIETZE, C. 'Amarna (Teil II) Analyse der ökonomischen Beziehungen der Stadtbewohner'. *ZÄS* 113-1986: 55-78.

TOUNY, A.D., WENIG, S. *Der Sport im alten Ägypten*. Leipzig 1969.

VACHALA, B. 'Ein neuer Beleg der Polygamie für das Alte Reich?' *ZÄS* 106-1979: 87-88.

VACHALA, B. 'Ein interessantes Relieffragment mit Familienszene aus Abusir'. *ZÄS* 107-1980: 88.

VACHALA, B. 'Neue Salbölpaletten aus Abusir'. *ZÄS* 108-1981: 61-67.

VACHALA, B. 'Die Kriegsgefangenen im Lichte der schriftlichen Quellen des Alten Reiches'. In: *Akten des vierten internationalen Ägyptologen Kongresses München 1985. Band 4*. Hamburg 1992, pp.87-93.

VALBELLE, D. *'Les ouvriers de la Tombe'. Deir el-Medineh à l'époque ramesside*. Cairo 1985.

VANDIER, J. *La famine dans l'Égypte ancienne*. Le Caire 1936.

VANDIER, D., ABBADIE, J. *Catalogue des objets de toilette égyptiens*. Paris 1972.

VERCOUTTER, J. 'Les femmes et l'amour au temps des Pharaons', *Miroir de l'Histoire* 186-1965, June, p.32 ff.

VERNER, M. 'Periodical Water-Volume Fluctuations of the Nile'. *Archív Orientální* 40-1972: 105-123.

VERNER, M. 'The Seal-Bearer Qenamun'. *ZÄS* 100-1974: 130-136.

VERNER, M. 'A Slaughterhouse from the Old Kingdom'. *Mitteil.d.Dtsch.Arch.Inst.Kairo* 42-1986: 181-189.

VILÍMKOVÁ, M. *Egyptian Jewellery*. London 1969.

VYHNÁNEK, L., STROUHAL, E. 'Arteriosclerosis in Egyptian Mummies'. *Anthropologie* 13-1975: 216-221.

VYHNÁNEK, L., STROUHAL, E. 'Spondylosis and Arthrosis in Ancient Egyptian Mummies from Czechoslovak Collections'. *Acta Facult.Rerum Natur.Univ.Comen.-Anthropologia* 23-1976: 319-324.

WATERMANN, R. 'Paleopathologische Beobachtungen an altägyptischen Skeletten und Mumien'. *Homo* 11-1960: 167-179.

WEEKS, K.R. 'The Anatomical Knowledge of the Ancient Egyptians and the Representation of the Human Figure in Egyptian Art'. Ph.Dissert., Yale Univ., University Microfilms International, Ann Arbor, Mich. 1981.

WEINBERGER, B.W. 'The Dental Art in Ancient Egypt'. *Amer.Dental Assoc.J.* 34-1947: 170-184.

WEINDLER, F. *Geburts- und Wochenbettdarstellungen auf altägyptischen Tempelreliefs*. München 1915.

WENIG, S. *Die Frau im alten Ägypten*. Wien, München 1969.

WILKINSON, G. *Manners and Customs of Ancient Egyptians*. London 1837.

WILKINSON, G. *Second Series of the Manners and Customs of the Ancient Egyptians ...* London 1841.

WILSON, J.A. 'Medicine in Ancient Egypt'. *Bull.Hist.Medicine* 36-1962: 114-123.

WINLOCK, H.E. *Models of Daily Life in Ancient Egypt from the Tomb of Meket-Re at Thebes*. Cambridge 1955.

WIPSZYCKA, E. 'L industrie textile dans l'Égypte romaine'. *Archiwum filologiczne* 9-1965, Wrócław, Warszawa, Kraków.

WOLF, W. *Die Bewaffnung des altägyptischen Heeres*. Leipzig 1926.

WOLF, W. *Kulturgeschichte des Alten Ägyptens*. Stuttgart 1962.

WOLLEY, C.L. 'Excavations at Tell el-Amarna'. *JEA* 8-1922: 48-82.

WRESZINSKI, W. *Atlas zur altägyptischen Kulturgeschichte*. I-III. Leipzig 1923-1938.

WRESZINSKI, W. *Die Medizin der Alten Ägypter*. I-III. Leipzig 1909-1913.

YOYOTTE, J. 'Les os et la semence masculine'. *BIFAO* 61-1962: 139-146.

ŽÁBA, Z. 'Orientation astronomique dans l'ancienne Égypte et la précession de l'axe du monde'. *Archív Orientální, Supplementa II*, Prague 1953.

ŽÁBA, Z. *Les Maximes du Ptahhotep*, Prague 1956.

Index

Map of Ancient Egypt

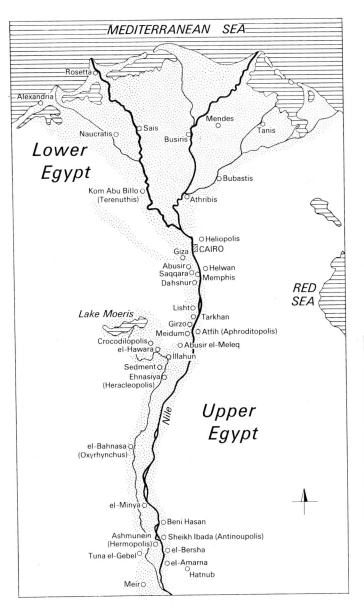

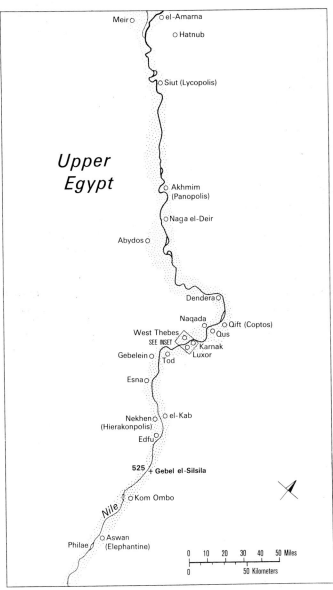